The Angela Y. Davis Reader

BLACKWELL READERS

In a number of disciplines, across a number of decades, and in a number of languages, writers and texts have emerged which require the attention of students and scholars around the world. United only by a concern with radical ideas, Blackwell Readers collect and introduce the works of pre-eminent theorists. Often translating works for the first time (Levinas, Irigaray, Lyotard, Blanchot, Kristeva), or presenting material previously inaccessible (C. L. R. James, Fanon, Elias), each volume in the series introduces and represents work which is now fundamental to study in the humanities and social sciences.

The Lyotard Reader
Edited by Andrew Benjamin

The Irigaray Reader
Edited by Margaret Whitford

The Kristeva Reader
Edited by Toril Moi

The Levinas Reader
Edited by Sean Hand

The C. L. R. James Reader
Edited by Anna Grimshaw

The Wittgenstein Reader
Edited by Anthony Kenny

The Blanchot Reader
Edited by Michael Holland

The Elias Reader
Edited by S. Mennell

The Lukács Reader
Edited by Arpad Kardakay

The Cavell Reader
Edited by Stephen Mulhall

The Guattari Reader
Edited by Garry Genosko

The Bataille Reader
Edited by Fred Botting and Scott Wilson

The Eagleton Reader
Edited by Stephen Regan

The Žižek Reader
Edited by Elizabeth and Edmond Wright

The Castoriadis Reader
Edited by David Ames Curtis

The Goffman Reader
Edited by Charles Lemert and Ann Branaman

The Frege Reader
Edited by Michael Beaney

The Hegel Reader
Edited by Stephen Houlgate

The Virilio Reader
Edited by James Der Derian

The Angela Y. Davis Reader
Edited by Joy James

The Stanley Fish Reader
Edited by H. Aram Veeser

The Angela Y. Davis Reader

Edited by
Joy James

BLACKWELL
Publishers

Copyright © Blackwell Publishers Ltd 1998

Introduction, selection, and arrangement copyright © Joy James 1998
All articles copyright © Angela Y. Davis

First published 1998

2 4 6 8 10 9 7 5 3 1

Blackwell Publishers Inc.
350 Main Street
Malden, Massachusetts 02148
USA

Blackwell Publishers Ltd
108 Cowley Road
Oxford OX4 1JF
UK

Library of Congress Cataloging-in-Publication Data

Davis, Angela Yvonne, 1944–
    The Angela Y. Davis reader / edited by Joy James.
    p. cm. – (Blackwell readers)
    Includes index.
    ISBN 0–631–20360–5 (hbk. : alk. paper). – ISBN 0–631–20361–3
  (pbk. : alk. paper)
    1. Afro-Americans – Social conditions – 1975– .   2. Afro-Americans –
Politics and government. 3. United States – Race relations. 4. Social classes –
United States. 5. Afro-American women – Political activity. 6. Feminism –
United States. I. James, Joy, 1958– . II. Title. III. Series.
E185.86.D3817 1998
305.896′073 – dc21   97-37880
                                                        CIP

British Library Cataloguing in Publication Data

A CIP catalogue record for this book is available from the British Library.

Typeset in 10 on 12 pt Plantin
by Best-set Typesetter Ltd., Hong Kong
Printed in Great Britain by M. P. G. Books, Bodmin, Cornwall

This book is printed on acid-free paper.

Contents

Acknowledgments

In addition to her writings and scholarship, Angela Davis generously contributed of her ideas in discussions about theory and political activism.

This book would not have been possible without the support of a number of individuals. Lewis Gordon assisted in the earliest conceptualization of this work. Aliza Wong and Leviticus Ra-Za'mien helped in the final stages of editing. Kit Kim Holder and Zillah Eisenstein provided insightful perspectives on ideology, gender, and radicalism. The Committees of Correspondence kindly granted access to their papers.

At the University of Colorado at Boulder, Department of Ethnic Studies staff Don Dudrey, Karen Moreira, and Richard Jones lent their skills. Students in my Fall 1996, seminar, "The Political Thought of Angela Davis," added their critical voices to this project. Allison Lehman, Kristi Most, Loretta Wahl, and Janessa Wilson provided technical assistance, supported by the University Research Opportunity Program, and Shana Alfaro and Stacey Clarkson.

This work evolved with a constant concern for what forms and influences liberation praxis. The editorial process was sustained by the support of family and friends, and the desire to maintain ground – or some ease in groundlessness – in the movements for progressive, radical thought and action.

Introduction

I felt an almost unbearable tension – it was as if I were two persons, two faces of a Janus head. One profile stared disconsolately into the past – the fretful, violent, confining past broken only by occasional splotches of meaning. . . . The other gazed with longing and apprehension into the future – a future glowing with challenge, but also harboring the possibility of defeat.

Angela Davis, *Angela Davis: An Autobiography*[1]

The Janus Head

In her memoir, Angela Davis evokes Janus – the Roman god of doors or beginnings. Depicted with two visages facing, like portals, in opposite directions, Janus serves as a metaphor for the past and future directions of Davis's political and intellectual life: the past manifests in the violent repression of blacks in the United States, the future reflects the possibility of an internationalist movement for a socialist, feminist, nonracialist democracy. Janus, like Eleggua, the Yoruba orisha of the crossroads, marks awakenings, polarities, and contradictions. In the autobiography, it references the possibilities of choice and realization within struggles for class, race, and sexual liberation. It also symbolizes simultaneous existence in the seemingly exclusive social worlds of black disenfranchisement and poverty and white privilege and education. Representing a dialectic of theory and resistance in revolutionary struggle in Davis's political and intellectual development, Janus signifies conflictual and transitional stages that foster feelings of alienation from the familiar, yet open new avenues. Life is set by a series of decisions, paths taken and paths avoided. The existential dilemmas described in *Angela Davis: An Autobiography* reflect a tension magnified by the heightened expectations and fears characteristic of revolutionary social and political movements. In the US, during the era of militancy depicted in the memoir, radical choices courted triumphs for liberation, or disasters and the possibility of imprisonment and death. Shaping Davis's future as a black radical, Communist, and international feminist, the past and present profiles of the Janus head denote transformative thought and personal/political struggle. Such thought, scanning both directions to avoid stagnation, considers the past from which movements originate in order to maintain momentum for the future. For activist-intellectuals, such as Davis, who struggled with exclusionary but overlapping worlds shaped by race, class, sex, gender, and violence, Janus in its positive manifestation represents the opportunity to confront the contradictory existence of abrogated freedom within the world's most powerful nation-state. In its negative aspect, it represents hypocrisy and denial, a "two-facedness" manifest when states or political systems claim democratic principles while systematically disenfranchising marginalized peoples or political minorities.

The Formation of an Activist-Intellectual

Angela Yvonne Davis was born in Birmingham, Alabama, in 1944, near the close of the Second World War and the emergence of the United States as heir to British hegemony (a dominance which the US militarily retains, despite its slippage in the global economic and intellectual marketplace). She grew up in the Southern United States under Jim Crow segregation and codified racial discrimination. During the late 1940s, her family moved into a neighborhood that subsequently became known as "Dynamite Hill" because of Ku Klux Klan terrorism against black families being integrated into the previously all-white community. Although the Davis home was never targeted by white arsonists, houses across the street were bombed. Bombings and burnings continued for several years; "miraculously," recalls Davis, no one was killed.[2]

Racial segregation had created an apartheid-like Southern US in which African-American students, regardless of their economic status, usually attended the same (underfunded) schools. As a child, Davis was considered part of an elite among impoverished peers. Because of her family's financial security and the extreme poverty of some classmates, the grade schooler stole from her father, giving money to children to buy their school lunch. Partly to escape the social roles defined by her middle-class standing in the black community and the educational limitations of local schools bound by Jim Crow and inequitable state funding, Davis left the South in 1959, for Manhattan, New York, where, under the auspices of a Quaker educational program, she lived with a progressive white family and attended a private high school, Elizabeth Irwin/Little Red School House. There she studied Karl Marx and Frederick Engels's *The Communist Manifesto*, and at age fifteen became active in a youth organization associated with the Communist Party. Familiarity with the Party was part of her family history. Since her birth, Davis's parents had been close friends with black members of the Communist Party USA (CPUSA). Although neither ever joined the Party, they were black middle-class educators who organized as "communist sympathizers." Her mother, Sallye Bell Davis, was a national officer and leading activist in the Southern Negro Youth Congress, an organization associated with the CPUSA which had campaigned to free the Scottsboro Nine.[3]

During her childhood, anti-Communist repression in the McCarthy era forced the elder Davis's friends – the parents of young Angela's playmates – underground. Despite the prevalence of repressive anti-Communism, Davis was profoundly affected by Marxism, and sought a disciplined, antiracist movement against racialized economic exploitation. Like Janus, Marxism with one profile surveyed economic, political, and social oppression while the other provided a glimpse of a possible future without the inequities of capitalism.

Upon high school graduation and with a scholarship in hand, Davis left New York to attend Brandeis University in Massachusetts; she studied there with philosopher Herbert Marcuse, and took her junior year in France at the Sorbonne. This was the height of the civil rights movement emanating from the 1955 Montgomery, Alabama, bus boycotts that had destabilized US apartheid. The memoir describes the young Davis's dissonance as she embarks for Europe to develop as a formally-trained intellectual yet desires to remain connected to black liberation struggles in the US: "The Janus head was still fixed – one eye full of longing to be in the fray in Birmingham, the other contemplating my own future. It would be a long time before the two profiles came together and I would know the direction to both the past and the future."[4] Janus would continue to haunt Davis politically during the civil rights movement as she furthered her academic studies in France and Germany. Like other influential, progressive writers, particularly the black "public intellectuals," Davis's educational and economic privileges both distanced her from the most marginalized (African Americans) and infused her theories of (black) liberation with an internationalist perspective. Parisian anti-Algerian racism had a strong impact on her understandings of international racism and colonialism and their connections to US antiblack racism (European racism also had a marked influence on another black American intellectual living in Paris during that time, James Baldwin). Torn between the desire to learn from different national cultures and political systems and the need to join "the movement," Davis decided not to pursue a doctorate at Goethe University in Frankfurt, Germany, choosing instead to return to the States to work with Marcuse at the University of California at San Diego.

Terrorist assaults against black activists provided the radicalizing impetus to end her European studies in the late 1960s. In fact, the racist murders of childhood acquaintances in her hometown during her first study abroad, in the early 1960s, profoundly affected her. In both the autobiography and a 1993 essay, "Remembering Carole, Cynthia, Addie Mae and Denise,"[5]

Davis recounts how, while in France, she learned of the September 15, 1963, bombing of Birmingham's Sixteenth Street Baptist Church. In that foray by white extremists, fourteen-year-olds Carole Robertson, Cynthia Wesley, and Addie Mae Collins, and eleven-year-old Denise McNair, died. The bombing occurred soon after the historic 1963 March on Washington, DC, and Martin Luther King Jr's eschatological "I Have a Dream" speech. Davis reminisces that declining the scholarship to the private school in Manhattan would have probably placed her nearby at Fisk University in Nashville, Tennessee, at the time of the bombing. It was during her stay in Europe, far from family ties and a society schooled in surviving and confronting white violence, that Davis learned of, and became deeply disturbed by, the girls' deaths: "If I had not been in France, news would not have been broken to me about the deaths . . . in the 'objective journalism' of the *International Herald Tribune*. . . . I was in Biarritz, living among people so far removed from the civil-rights war unfolding in the South that it made little sense to try to express to them how devastated I felt. I wrestled in solitude with my grief, my fear and my rage."[6] The absence of public mourning in France for the slain youths – an absence put into sharp relief several months later when French nationals collectively mourned the assassination of US President John F. Kennedy – was strongly felt: "I carried around in my head for many years an imagined representation of the bombing's aftermath that was far more terrifying than any cinematic image of violence I have ever encountered: the fixed eyes of Carole's and Cynthia's bloody decapitated heads and their dismembered limbs strewn haphazardly among the dynamited bricks and beams in the front yard of the stately church. My own private imagination of what happened that day was so powerful that years would pass before I felt able to listen to the details of my mother's story."[7]

Three decades later, Davis extensively discussed the tragedy with Sallye Davis. In 1963, upon hearing the explosion from her home, the elder Davis had contacted Alpha Bliss Robertson and driven her to the Sunday School class at the church to find her daughter, Carole; instead, the women found debris and parts of the children's bodies. In the collective remembrance of this tragedy, Davis notes erasure: "The time in the country my mother and I spent remembering that terrible day three decades ago – 'Bloody Sunday', she calls it – was both healing and frustrating. As we spoke about the girls as we had known them, it occurred to me that the way the memory of that episode persists in popular imagination is deeply problematic. What bothers me most is that their names have been virtually erased: They are inevitably referred to as 'the four black girls killed in the Birmingham church bombing.' Another traumatic moment occurred in 1964 when James Chaney, Michael Schwerner and Andrew Goodman were killed in

Mississippi. A decade earlier, Emmett Till was found at the bottom of the Tallahatchie River. These boys, whose lives were also consumed by racist fury, still have names in our historical memory. Carole, Denise, Addie Mae and Cynthia do not."[8] "Bloody Sunday," the term used by many activists to describe the atrocity, became a fixture in American political racial memory. Yet few, Davis observes, remember that the girls were young activists, who at the time of their deaths were preparing to speak about civil rights at the church's annual Youth Day program.[9] For most, the four "function abstractly in popular memory as innocent, nameless black girls' bodies destroyed by racist hate."[10] All four shared political commitments with other youths who in that volatile year had confronted police commissioner Eugene "Bull" Conner's high-powered fire hoses and, according to Davis, "filled the jails in Birmingham in a way that reenergized the Civil Rights Movement like nothing since the Montgomery Boycott."[11]

Missing the courageous confrontations with repressive state laws waged by youths, particularly girls and young women, Davis spent most of her years between 1959 and 1967 outside of the South and therefore distanced from the Southern civil rights movement (as did other African-American women, such as Black Panther leaders Elaine Brown, Kathleen Cleaver, and Assata Shakur). However, Davis periodically "touched base" with the movement. For instance, testing voter disenfranchisement of blacks, in 1965, when she became twenty-one, she attempted to register to vote in Birmingham and was denied that right because of her race. In the early 1980s, during a National Women's Studies Association keynote address, Davis recalled the abrogation of her civil rights to illustrate the political repression of women. Examining the repressive legacy of continuing voter disenfranchisement during the Reagan administration's destabilization of social and political gains from the civil rights and women's movements, she cited the case of Julia Wilder and Maggie Bozeman of the Black Belt of Alabama who were convicted in January 1982, of voter fraud. Both women had "assisted older people and people who, as a result of the racist educational system that is particularly acute in the South, never managed to learn how to read and write well enough to fill out a ballot . . . [consequently] they were tried and convicted by an all-white jury and sentenced to four and five years, respectively, in the state penitentiary."[12]

With the 1964 Voting Rights Act and the de jure right to vote won by the "second reconstruction," the de facto abrogation of rights continued. Paradoxically, as repression continued, the definition of rights for the dispossessed expanded beyond that of civil rights to the more encompassing social and economic rights. This growing demand for justice and equality also sparked calls to militancy.

SNCC and the Black Panther Party

The search for human liberation greater than the US Constitution's promise of electoral powers led Angela Davis to the Student Nonviolent Coordinating Committee (SNCC) and the Black Panther Party (BPP). The Black Panther logo of the Lowndes County, Alabama, Freedom Democratic Party was propelled into the national spotlight in 1966 by television broadcasts of a Greenwood, Mississippi, march. There – with Martin Luther King Jr in attendance – SNCC's Stokely Carmichael, having just been released from jail by local police attempting to destabilize the demonstration, galvanized the black gathering to chant for "Black Power!" The "Panther" captured the political imagination of black youths. Speaking to black political frustrations with the intransigence of an entrenched white power structure, one enforced by police malfeasance and brutality, it echoed Malcolm X's calls for self-defense with the heightened sense of risk and confrontation which followed his 1965 assassination. The Panther – which remains *the* political–cultural symbol for black militancy and resistance in the US – became the contested namesake and symbol for several organizations; interestingly, these organizations emerged on the west coast far from the civil rights struggles of the north- and southeast.

Huey Newton and Bobby Seale's Black Panther Party for Self-Defense emerged in Oakland, California, in 1966, and later expanded into Los Angeles where Davis was a member of the Black Panther Political Party. In 1967, at the demands of Oakland's leadership for exclusive claim to the title and SNCC national leaders Carmichael and James Forman's suggestion, the Black Panther Political Party became "Los Angeles SNCC." It was short-lived as a political group. Los Angeles SNCC women ran the office but men dominated as official spokespersons and media figures, according to Davis, who states that Los Angeles SNCC dissolved because of women's refusal to accept the sexist and masculinist posturing of male leadership. Other factors leading to the demise of the organization were national SNCC's anti-Communism, and attempts by the New York-based national SNCC office (under the leadership of H. Rap Brown, but over the protests of Forman) to dictate policy to chapters; one dictate led to an aborted attempt to merge with Newton's Panthers.

Upon leaving SNCC, Davis joined the Black Panther Party for Self-Defense. She describes her affiliation with the Panther organization as a "permanently ambiguous status" that fluctuated between "'member' and 'fellow-traveler'." Active in community organizing, temporarily in charge of political education in the West Side office (which she worked with Bunchy Carter and John Huggins to open) and formulating political education for the Los Angeles Chapter, Davis remained on the fringes of the Panthers' internal contestations. Years later, she recalls her doubts about the Party's militarist posturing: "I thoroughly respected the BPP's visible defiance and principally supported the right to self-defense. . . . I also found myself using funerals and shootings as the most obvious signposts of the passage of time. However, sensing ways in which this danger and chaos emanated not only from the enemy outside, but from the very core of the Black Panther Party, I preferred to remain uninformed about the organization's inner operations."[13]

Part of the contradictions of internal operations revolved around sexual politics. The Black Panther Party as a masculinist, revolutionary organization operated in ways that promoted both males and females to perceive women "as objects of male sexual desire," according to Davis.[14] No matter how close a woman came to approximating the contributions of the most esteemed male leader, maintains Davis, the respect granted a Panther woman, even those in high-ranking leadership, could be and was "reversed with the language and practice of [male- or female initiated] sexual seduction." Davis's generalizations concerning Panther women (and men) universalize the behavior of elite Oakland leadership (as portrayed by Elaine Brown), suggesting a gender uniformity for the leadership and rank-and-file of chapters and branches across the country.[15] Despite its sexism, complexity marked Panther sexual politics; for example, the BPP newspaper took a stance for gay/lesbian, and women's rights as Davis remarks elsewhere.

Davis notes that although some African-American women in revolutionary organizations "detested the overt sexism of male leaders," they also associated feminism with middle-class white women: "In failing to recognize the profoundly masculinist emphasis of our own struggles, we were all at risk. We often ended up affirming hierarchies in the realm of gender relations that we militantly challenged in the area of race relations."[16] Of her romanticizing of the Panthers, Davis writes: "I cannot deny the attraction that the Panther representations of black militant masculinity held for me at a time when precious few of us had begun thinking about the politics of sexism and compulsory heterosexuality."[17] The construction of the revolutionary, of the militant leader with transformative agency for social justice, was masculine: "Revolutionary practice was conceived as quintessentially masculinist. The Party's imagined power was too often conflated with power over the means of violence, wielded both against the 'enemy' and in the ranks of the Party itself. This power was sexualized so that women's place was always defined as unalterably inferior. It articulated notions of revolutionary democracy with gang-inspired, authoritarian organizational principles. It sexualized politics and politicized sexuality in unconscious and dangerous ways."[18]

The Black Panther Party, as "part of our historical memory," provides a contested terrain, one often navigated with blinders of romanticized or demonized iconography. Romanticization and demonization would also extend to the Communist Party, which by the 1960s was a radical (rather than revolutionary) organization, perceived as less of a political threat than the BPP and so less of a target for violent destabilization on the part of local and federal police agencies. The BPP was in decline by 1969 due to infiltration by police and FBI agents and provocateurs, internal factionalism, gender bias, and the corruption of west-coast elite leadership. The CPUSA, which had been infiltrated decades earlier and crippled by the McCarthy era's persecution, had its own internal contradictions around race and gender.

The Communist Party USA

Davis became a member of the Communist Party USA in 1968, at the same time that she joined the Panthers; however, her ties with the CPUSA proved less problematic than her relationship with the BPP. Her affiliation with the Panthers would last less than two years; with the Communist Party, it would endure for over twenty. Initially Davis joined the CPUSA because of her commitments to internationalist struggle. Like W. E. B. Du Bois, who after the Second World War, began to incorporate Marxist theory into his analyses of oppression, Davis felt that black liberation was unobtainable apart from an international workers' movement against capitalism, imperialism, and racism. Her understanding that a mass liberation struggle needed to be class-based in order to confront the racist foundations of capitalism was strengthened by a 1969 trip to Cuba. (In 1959, Cuba had waged a successful revolution against the US-backed Batista dictatorship, and in 1963, again successfully, defended itself against the US Bay of Pigs invasion.)

In part, joining the Communist Party was Davis's response to the deficiencies she found in the black liberation movement's nationalism. For her, black nationalism inspired African Americans by emphasizing the collective African past and a "black aesthetic," but its dominant culturalist outlook lacked comprehensive economic and political analyses for black equality and human rights. In her view, black nationalist ideology's construction of "race" distilled from economic, gender, ethnic, and class considerations erased the connections between oppressed blacks, other racially marginalized peoples, the exploitation of white workers, and sexism. The limitations of cultural nationalism in the 1960s led Davis (by then a Marxist for over a decade) to ideologies such as those espoused by the Che-Lumumba Club of southern California. One of the CPUSA's few all-black collectives, the Club conducted successful campaigns against police brutality and executions in black neighborhoods. Davis found Che-Lumumba unhampered by the conservative gender and sexual politics undermining radical organizations such as the west-coast Student Nonviolent Coordinating Committee and the west-coast Black Panther Party.

Davis's political work and personal life within organizations such as the Communist Party and the Black Panther Party made her vulnerable to attacks by university administrations. By 1969, the new assistant philosophy professor at the University of California at Los Angeles (UCLA) was recognized in the state as a radical antiracist and a Communist. Although it had no formal punitive measures for ousting antiracists (as did schools in the South which had criminalized membership in the National Association for the Advancement of Colored People), the university administration codified persecution of Communists. In 1949, in the advent of McCarthyism, the University of California Regents had passed a bylaw banning the hiring of Communists. Twenty years later, it terminated Davis's contract under the leadership of then California Governor and later US President Ronald Reagan (when head of the Hollywood Screen Actors Guild, Reagan had provided the names of film artists/artisans suspected of "communist leanings" to the FBI).[19] It would be two decades before Davis, who had trained for years to become an academic, would be permitted a tenured professorship in the University of California.

Despite the professional costs, she openly served for twenty-three years in active leadership on the Party's Central Committee and twice ran for Vice-President on its national ticket. In 1991, on the eve of the CPUSA 25th National Convention, seeking with other long-time Party members to democratize the internal life of the CPUSA, Davis and approximately eight hundred activists and intellectuals formulated, signed, and disseminated an internal document designed to open up avenues of debate, "An Initiative to Unite and Renew the Party." The "Initiative" criticized the CPUSA for elitism and racial and sexual bias. For example, it argues for the need to restore "the principle of black and white leadership,"[20] maintaining that the Party has "gone backward in attention to the struggle for African-American equality."[21] Referring to the struggle for gender equality, the document states: "While the ultra-right has furiously attacked women's rights precisely to divide the people, a kind of simplistic interpretation of a class approach has led us to pay scant attention to the very dynamic women's movement."[22] Advocating a stronger grassroots mandate for the CPUSA, the "Initiative" criticizes past Party practices as non-democratic: "Our participation in mass struggles should be our primary task and yardstick."[23] The "Initiative" makes no mention of sexuality, homophobia, and gay, lesbian, bi- and transsexual rights.

During the national elections that followed, Communist Party leaders who signed the paper were refused placement on the official slate; consequently, none of the "Initiative" signatories were re-elected to office. Later that year, along with most of the eight hundred, including leaders such as Charlene Mitchell, Herbert Aptheker, and James Jackson, Davis left the Communist Party. The following year, at a Berkeley, California, conference, the reformers created the Committees of Correspondence, on whose National Coordinating Committee Davis briefly served.

Political Trials

Active in the Communist Party, Davis became engaged in prisoners' rights activism during the time that she was defending her right to teach at UCLA. Her organizing focused on a mass defense for the Soledad Brothers: George Jackson, Fleeta Drumgo, and John Clutchette. These three incarcerated African-American leaders in the California prisoners' rights movement were falsely charged with killing a prison guard in January 1970. Through the Soledad Brothers' Defense Committee she met prison intellectual and liberation theorist George Jackson. Author of *Blood in My Eye* and *Soledad Brother*,[24] he would eventually become an intimate friend of Davis. At the age of eighteen, Jackson had been sentenced to an indeterminate sentence of from one year to life for driving a car involved in a gas-station robbery which netted seventy dollars. Jackson, who had served ten years at the time Davis met him, maintained that he was unaware of his acquaintance's robbery as he sat in the car. On August 21, 1971, at the age of thirty, this Soledad prison leader and Field Marshall for the Black Panther Party was shot and killed by a guard, in what many activists viewed as a political assassination.

Before meeting Jackson, Davis established friendships with his family – mother Georgia, sisters Penny and Frances, and seventeen-year-old brother Jonathan, who eventually became one of her bodyguards. The activist-academic was daily receiving multiple death threats. Campus police provided some measure of protection as she taught classes and met with students. Friends and co-activists provided off-campus security, often with guns legally purchased by the twenty-six-year-old assistant professor and kept in her apartment. To publicize prison conditions and state abuses against the Soledad Brothers, and out of love for his brother, George, in August 1970, Jonathan Jackson, a member of Davis's security, carried guns into a courtroom in northern California's Marin County. With prisoners James McClain, William Christmas, and Ruchell Magee, he took as hostages the judge, district attorney, and several members of the jury. The high school student and inmates brought the hostages to a van in the parking lot. San Quentin guards fired on the parked vehicle, killing Judge Haley, Jonathan Jackson, and prisoners McClain and Christmas, while seriously wounding the district attorney, several jurors, and prisoner Magee who later became Davis's codefendant.[25] She was not in northern California at the time, but because the guns were registered in her name, Davis was named by police as an accomplice. In that era, at the height of the FBI's counterintelligence program (COINTELPRO) to undermine the civil rights and black liberation movements – police, assisted by federal agents, had killed or assassinated over twenty black revolutionaries in the Black Panther Party.[26] Rather than turn herself in to the authorities, Davis went underground and for two months was on the Federal Bureau of Investigation's "Ten Most Wanted List." Captured in Manhattan on October 13, 1970, she would spend the next sixteen months in prison, most of it in solitary confinement, before her release on bail.

On January 5, 1971, in *The People of the State of California* vs. *Angela Y. Davis*, the state arraigned Angela Davis in a small Marin County Courtroom on charges of murder,[27] kidnapping, and conspiracy. Throughout 1971, various judges denied more than thirty pre-trial motions made by defense counsel. Responding to the defense team's motion for a change of venue – the defense hoped that the trial would be relocated to the more racially mixed Alameda county – the state moved the case to Santa Clara County, ensuring the likelihood of an all-white, conservative jury. Nevertheless, the case was closely monitored by progressive activists and intellectuals who petitioned for a fair trial. In April 1972 the National United Committee to Free Angela Davis published her opening defense statement in a pamphlet entitled *Frame-Up*, which argues that Davis was prosecuted because of her effective leadership in mobilizing African Americans to support political prisoners such as the Soledad Brothers, and to oppose the state's efforts to "eliminate" the Brothers and derail the radical movement.[28] California Assistant Attorney General Albert Harris, who was specially appointed to prosecute Davis, would latter complain about the "international conspiracy to free the defendant" when Santa Clara County jail authorities were flooded with calls, telegrams, and letters from around the world protesting the conditions under which Davis was housed. President Richard Nixon, Attorney General John Mitchell, FBI Director J. Edgar Hoover (architect of the illegal and violent counterrevolutionary COINTELPRO), and Governor Reagan were also deluged with millions of pieces of mail objecting to inadequate conditions hampering Davis's defense team.

The trial took place in a time of severe government repression against radicals and revolutionaries that included the use of state juries to tie up black activists in court on falsified criminal charges or to falsely incarcerate them.[29] Nationwide though, exposés on COINTELPRO, state malfeasance, and flimsy evidence, coupled with educational campaigns and demonstrations to end repressive policing and judiciaries, led juries to throw out cases or rule in favor of activists. In New Haven, New York, New Orleans,

Los Angeles, San Francisco, Denver, and Detroit, juries exonerated defendants such as the Harrisburg 7, Ericka Huggins and Bobby Seale, the New York 21, and others. In fact, at the time of Davis's trial, jurors in a San Rafael court acquitted the Soledad Brothers of all charges (George Jackson did not live to see his exoneration), with some jurors greeting the defendants after the reading of the verdict, according to *Frame-Up*.

In February 1972, after intense and lengthy lobbying by activists to end dehumanizing prison conditions and judicial racism in sentencing, the state Supreme Court abolished the death penalty in California,[30] a decision that would facilitate Davis's release on bail. Organizers had effectively mobilized a massive, (inter)national campaign, inundating the trial judge with demands for immediate bail, including a telegram signed by all thirteen of the African-American US Congressmen, at that time, the entire membership of the Congressional Black Caucus. On February 23, 1972, noting the magnitude of the public demands, the presiding judge granted bail. Given that her release undermined the presumption of guilt, which had been promoted in most media, prosecutors sought, and were denied, a delay in the trial proceedings. The trial, which progressed throughout 1971 and into the following year, ended just as the Soledad Brothers' trial had: Angela Yvonne Davis was acquitted of all charges when the jury rendered its "not guilty" verdict on June 4, 1972.

Prison Writings

Davis's, pioneering works include her "prison writings," and the memoir *If They Come in the Morning: Voices of Resistance*.[31] Women's rights and leadership remain a central theme in her work on liberation politics. Her leadership in the Soledad Brothers' Defense Committee led to correspondence with George Jackson (reprinted in Jackson's *Soledad Brother*), whose letters included critiques of the social function of prisons and a chauvinism antithetical to liberation praxis. According to Davis, "He seemed to have internalized the notions of black women as domineering matriarchs, as castrating females, notions associated with the Moynihan Report. I could detect this in the comments he made in his letters, especially comments about his mother."[32] To challenge Jackson's gender politics, she began to investigate the role of African-American females during slavery and eventually developed the essay "Reflections on the Black Woman's Role in the Community of Slaves."[33] At the time, little had been written on enslaved black women from a feminist perspective. As an inmate, Davis was able to research this article only with extreme difficulty, obtaining books only by stating that they were pertinent to her case: "I informed the jail authorities that I had the right to whatever literature I needed for the preparation of my defense. In a large sense this research really was very helpful for the preparation of my defense because in my trial I focused a great deal on the misogynist character of the prosecution's case. The theoretical work I did on black women actually assisted me to develop a strategy for my own defense."[34] Sexist imagery was a pillar in Prosecutor Harris's March 27, 1971, opening argument in which he depicted Davis as a "student of violence," and, referring to her relationship with George Jackson, a "'woman of uncontrollable passions', the vicious conspirator blinded by love."[35]

Davis's autobiography recounts the conditions under which she was held while awaiting trial, describing the penal environment and key moments of her imprisonment and trial defense. Despite adverse conditions while incarcerated, she served as co-counsel, preparing her defense with movement attorneys. Scholarly literature produced while in jail, such as the above mentioned "Reflections on the Black Woman's Role in the Community of Slaves," reflected her own political experiences of sexism. Davis traces the thesis of black matriarchy (expressed by Jackson) to various theories, including E. Franklin Frazier's in the 1930s, that argue that black women "remained the only real vestige of family life" because slavery had destroyed the black family and consequently created hybrid black women, overwhelming creatures that oppressed or emasculated black males. Senator Daniel Moynihan's 1965 government report, *The Negro Family – A Case for National Action*, promoted this image as it portrayed black mothers as matriarchs who pathologized the black family through their subversion of gender roles. Davis's critique of the "Moynihan Report" addresses labor exploitation of black women and men in the community of slaves. Responding to the pervasive depiction of black women as domineering matriarchs, Davis offers one of the earliest analyses of the intersections of racism, sexism, and capitalism within the slave economy and one of the earliest essays on antiracist feminist theory contextualized in the black experience in the Americas. She also provides a corrective to biased historiography that marginalizes or caricatures the realities of enslaved women. Introducing the concept that equal exploitation or "deformed equality" tended to disrupt gender hierarchies for black women and men, the essay both challenges common misperceptions of black female life under slavery and highlights the manner in which stereotypes shape contemporary perspectives and scholarship. Precisely because it demystified stereotypical images of enslaved black women and emphasized the specificity of historical women in resistance, this influential essay became widely circulated among feminist and black studies readers.

Another prison essay, "Political Prisoners and Black Liberation," first appeared in *If They Come in the Morning: Voices of Resistance*, an anthology edited by Davis, from her cell, and activist-academic Bettina Aptheker, with contributions from US radicals such as Aptheker, and political prisoners or prison intellectuals such as Davis and Newton. "Political Prisoners and Black Liberation" is perhaps the first essay authored by an African-American woman within the genre of contemporary black protest and prison literature, a genre traceable to Martin Luther King Jr's 1955, "Letter from Birmingham Jail." Davis writes in this essay, which was first published in 1971, that "the entire apparatus of the bourgeois democratic state, especially its judicial system and its prisons, is disintegrating. The judicial and prison systems are to be increasingly defined as instruments for unbridled repression, institutions which may be successfully resisted but which are more and more impervious to meaningful reform."[36] While she was incarcerated, her 1969 philosophy lectures on the Hegelian dialectic and the slave-turned-abolitionist Frederick Douglass (for a course she designed, "Recurring Philosophical Themes in Black Literature," as UCLA's first class on black philosophy, and to encourage philosophical reflections on black enslavement and freedom) were collected. The New York-based Committee to Free Angela Davis printed the lecture notes in 1971, as the pamphlet *Lectures on Liberation*. Later edited into "Unfinished Lectures on Liberation – II," Davis's first published theoretical piece appeared in the groundbreaking anthology on African-American philosophy, *Philosophy Born of Struggle*.[37]

Davis's analysis of enslavement and freedom, developed prior to her own incarceration, proves relevant to both the postbellum and postmodern US where law codifies slavery. The Thirteenth Amendment to the US Constitution legalizes "involuntary servitude" within penal institutions, while US politics and racism create a racialist legal system marked by sentencing disparity so that the majority of the nearly two million now incarcerated in prisons or detention centers are African-American, Chicano-Latino, and Native American. The desire for freedom on the part of the enslaved in the nineteenth century reflects the rights – or limitation of rights – of those incarcerated in the twentieth (and twenty-first) century. Her most recent writings return to the consuming interests of three decades ago. Her analysis of contemporary imprisonment in "Race and Criminalization: Black Americans and the Punishment Industry" details the rationalization of racist punishment in connection with militarism and industrialism within prisons. In "From the Prison of Slavery to the Slavery of Prison: Frederick Douglass and the Convict Lease System," Davis discusses how "blackness is ideologically linked to criminality in ways that are more complicated and pernicious than Douglass ever could have imagined." Writing about the racialization of crime in "Racialized Punishment and Prison Abolition," she critically examines Michel Foucault's *Discipline and Punish: The Birth of the Prison*.[38] Arguing for a new "abolitionism," Davis maintains that raising "the possibility of abolishing jails and prisons as the institutionalized and normalized means of addressing social problems in an era of migrating corporations, unemployment and homelessness, and collapsing public services [may] . . . help to interrupt the current law-and-order discourse that has such a grip on the collective imagination, facilitated as it is by deep and hidden influences of racism."[39]

Antiracist Feminist Writings

As mentioned earlier, the most distinctive contribution of Davis's prison writings, in fact her work in general, is the gender analysis in which she radicalizes feminism through a class and antiracist analysis and offers new constructions for black female identity and politics. In the intersectional analyses of Marxism, antiracism, and feminism, exists the body of written work for which Davis is best known. Activist women's contributions to Marxism and Communism are frequently and easily overlooked, according to Davis. Citing women such as Lucy Gonzales Parsons and Claudia Jones, Davis notes that many women who devoted their lives to organizing for a revolutionary, socialist society produced neither theoretical nor autobiographical literature. In the absence of such writings, their intellectual and political agency has often "disappeared" or been dismissed. The reappearance of, and recognition for, the contributions of the intersections of Marxist, antiracist, and feminist praxes and radical female activists characterizes Davis's work.

Her writings examine the contradictions and contributions of contemporary women to radical and feminist politics. Davis asserts that the feminist movement of the 1960s and 1970s held little attraction for black female militants and other progressive Chicana, Puerto Rican, Asian, and Native American women, despite the gender hierarchies within their respective antiracist or nationalist movements (one exception she notes is the black or Third World Women's Alliance which grew out of SNCC chapters on the east coast to focus on a tripartite struggle against racism, sexism, and imperialism). In the nascent movements, the bifurcation of antiracist and antisexist struggles took curious turns: (middle-class) white women struggled with learned passivity and a hyper-femininity; black women were castigated for being too assertive and aggressive, or not feminine (passive) enough. In Davis's evolving feminism, radical black women and antiracist white women altered the nature of feminist theory and feminist practice, expanding praxes and ideologies, and leading to differentiations of feminisms. Feminists seeking "to open the executive suites of the corporations to women, regardless of the fact that these corporations are exploiting people" present an alien gender politics, writes Davis; she maintains that when women "oppressed not only by virtue of their gender but by virtue of their class and their race win victories for themselves, then other women will inevitably reap the benefits of these victories"; asserting the value of Marxism for feminism, she continues, "it is possible to be a Marxist, emphasize the central role of the working class, but at the same time participate in the effort to win liberation for all women."[40] A theory that accepts the overlapping interests of different groups reflects the present range of social and political repression. Drawing on the intersections of racist, sexist, and heterosexist repression, Davis contends that sexism has a "racist component which affects not only women of color but white women as well. Ku-Klux-Klan-instigated violence against black people incites, for example, violence against women who attempt to use the services of abortion clinics. Low wages for women of color establishes a standard which leads to low wages for white women. So that white women are the victims of any upsurge in racism."[41] For Davis, it is "not coincidental that the same forces" attacking "abortion clinics and their personnel have also tried to prevent integrated schools."[42] Likewise, decrying the lack of a *mass* effort to challenge homophobia, and the "ghettoization" of the gay and lesbian political movements, Davis writes that the roots of homophobia are intertwined with the roots of racism, sexism, and economic exploitation. Reactionary intellectuals and activists, including extremists, have promoted violence against gays and lesbians, and a "fraudulent analysis holding homosexuals responsible for the so-called breakdown of the family."[43] Linking the repression of heterosexuals' sexuality and that of their gay, lesbian, bi- and transgender counterparts, Davis maintains that racism has played a central role in creating the prevailing repressive sexual environment.[44]

Describing how African-American women's work in black liberation organizations constituted a form of feminist consciousness-raising, she marks the developing feminisms that presented an alternative to the women's circles in the emerging (white) feminist movement: "Black women and women of color were making important contributions to the effort to elevate people's consciousness about the impact of sexism. While we didn't define ourselves as women's liberationists, we were in fact fighting for our right to make equal contributions to the fight against racism."[45] Making an equal contribution often entailed confronting sexism both within the movement and embedded in literature and academic discourse about black women.

Unique to mainstream feminist thought of the early 1970s (and still somewhat of a novelty in contemporary mainstream feminism) were analyses of the intersections of racist and sexual violence. Addressing the simultaneous and intersectional appearances of sexism and racism, and by extension sexual and racist violence, Davis's early work presented a corrective to feminist theory that erased racist violence, and antiracist theory that masked sexist violence. "Rape, Racism, and the Capitalist Setting,"[46] which first appeared in *The Black Scholar*'s 1978 special issue on "The Black Woman," critiques the role of class in racial–sexual violence. Likewise, "Violence Against Women and the Ongoing Challenge to Racism,"[47] issued as a 1985 pamphlet, investigates the function of racist and sexist violence in a racialized, patriarchal society. Nowhere were the intersections of race and gender so volatile as in the antirape movement within the women's liberation movement, which in the late sixties or early seventies tended to represent rape only as a gender issue of male dominance of females, ignoring the impact of race and class on state prosecution and "protection."[48] As Davis notes, the black community bore the brunt of white women's demands for more police and longer prison sentences. In the early days of the feminist movement, the disparity in perspectives promised few possibilities for coalitions between black and white women. Yet they did coalesce, for instance in antirape/antiracist organizing around the JoAnne Little case. In "JoAnne Little: The Dialectics of Rape,"[49] Davis reflects on the case of the young black woman incarcerated in North Carolina for petty theft who in 1974 killed the white prison guard who was raping her. The Little case highlighted the complicitous role of the state in the intersections of racial–sexual violence. Little's act of self-defense, and subsequent flight, led to charges of murder and a "shoot to kill" edict from authorities. Her extradition from New York and subsequent trial in North Carolina were marked by effective mass mobilization and legal defense which led to her acquittal. After the trial, according to Davis, Little issued a call for women who had supported her to organize around the Florida case of a young black man fraudulently charged with raping a white woman, yet most white feminist groups initially refused (some later changed their position) to assist in a defense committee for an accused rapist. The possibilities for, and obstacles hindering, multiracial women's alliances against violence is a recurring theme in Davis's discourse on freedom.

The issues of women's emancipation are tied not only to countering violence but also to work – labor, reproductive, and political work. "Women and Capitalism: Dialectics of Oppression and Liberation"[50] explores economic exploitation in the workforce. Exploitation in nonwaged labor or reproductive labor for the household is the focus of "The Approaching Obsolescence of Housework: A Working-Class Perspective;"[51] and its critique of the reconstruction of domestic labor is based in part on the Italian feminist movement's "Wages for Housework," which was influential in Europe in the 1970s. Davis presents an economic proposal for the liberation of women from domestic labor exploitation through restructuring domestic work as government-subsidized wage labor, suggesting that the deprivatization of labor coupled with attractive salaries and generous benefits liberates domestic work from its debased status as women's "free" contribution to familial and social units, and national and international economies. She briefly discusses how the select group licensed to perform this labor may remain alienated given that the repetitive, isolated nature of the work is not necessarily altered through higher wages. Biological reproduction is another form of women's unpaid labor addressed by Davis in "Surrogates and Outcast Mothers: Racism and Reproductive Politics in the Nineties,"[52] which reviews the medical ethics, health hazards, and social stigmatism associated with black women's fertility and reproduction in the late twentieth century. "Black Women and the Academy"[53] raises the issues of women's political work, responsibilities, and rights in connection with representation and education for social justice.

Essays on Culture and Political Interviews

Examining representation and commodification in popular and visual culture, Davis explores the impact of African-American music and politics on American (and by extension, world) culture. An early investigation into cultural studies, "Art for the People" appeared in the Communist Party publication *Political Affairs*, focusing on black rap artists, such as Gil Scott-Heron, engaged in cultural oppositional politics against the Reagan era's assaults on progressives. Political messages surfaced in music that predated the rap emerging in the 1980s. Davis's "I Used To Be Your Sweet Mama: Ideology, Sexuality, and Domesticity" examines black female sexuality and feminist identity in the lyrics of blues artists such as Bessie Smith and Ma Rainey.

Regarding the black image, "Photography and Afro-American History" discusses controversial representations and the erasure of people of African descent in visual culture and art, focusing on artist Roy DeCarava and Harlem photography. More recently, Davis has explored photographic representations of contemporary black revolutionary struggles in "Afro Images: Politics, Fashion, and Nostalgia," which also examines the commodification of black resistance through imaging. "Meditations on the Legacy of Malcolm X" reviews the growth of the famed black revolutionary beyond cultural nationalism and religious sectarianism and the contradictions surrounding his current iconographic status. Contesting the reified masculinity surrounding Malcolm X, Davis raises questions about consumers' "passive reception of Malcolm" in apparel and the consumption of his image and voice in ways that "fix male supremacy" within "challenges" to white supremacy. In "Black Nationalism: The Sixties and the Nineties," she reflects on the future, youths, cultural consumerism, and revolutionary politics.

Her interviews, "Coalition Building Among People of Color" (with

Elizabeth Martinez) and "Reflections on Race, Class, and Gender in the USA," discuss political organizing and social theory, liberation praxis and community-building. The oral and collective nature of liberation theory, as well as critiques that counter solipsistic academic theory influenced by masculinist, eurocentric, or nationalist ideologies, are central to these interviews.

Conclusion: Revolutionary Actors and Radical Intellectuals

The books *If They Come in the Morning*; *Women, Race, and Class*; *Women, Culture, and Politics*; and *Blues Legacies and Black Feminism* as well as articles in Communist, women's, ethnic/black studies, and cultural studies publications reflect thirty years of writings. In *The Angela Y. Davis Reader*, selected essays from this body of work are organized into four parts: prisoners' rights; intersectional analyses in Marxism and antiracist feminism; culture; and contemporary interviews. Although she has written extensively for nearly thirty years as a radical intellectual, Davis remains best known as a representational figure of a revolutionary movement in US domestic racial politics.

Consequently, her writings are surpassed in the popular mind by her iconographic status. This raises a number of questions for our consideration as readers and consumers. In an essay contained in this collection, Davis quotes from Marx's *Eleventh Feuerbach*: "Philosophers have interpreted the world in various ways. The point, however, is to change it." If the point is to change the world, one must address what constituted liberation praxis in the radical and revolutionary movements and moments of previous decades; and, what constitutes it today for intellectuals and activists at a time when both the Black Panther Party and the Communist Party are considered by many to be anachronistic or romanticized organizations.

Davis herself grappled with these questions in a 1997 course which she taught at the University of California at Berkeley. Discussing the distinctions between radical and revolutionary politics, and intellectual critique and political engagement, Davis recounted how black militant activists would define "radicals" as bourgeois whites who had political critiques and intellectual commitments to opposing racism and economic exploitation but little experiential confrontation with the state; "revolutionaries," on the other hand, were those whose philosophical ideals about a just society and democratic state were manifested in their risk-taking political acts against oppressive state apparatuses. Today few if any US writers qualify as "revolutionaries" (perhaps a notable exception, the over one hundred political prisoners that Amnesty International documents as being held in the US, raises the issue of the relationship between radical intellectuals and revolutionaries).

Within the context of a past liberation movement, a younger Davis had offered insights into revolutionary liberation praxis in the 1970 *LIFE Magazine* profile published while she was underground. *LIFE*'s cover superimposed the caption "The Making of a Fugitive" over her photograph, while the feature article reprinted the following quote taken from one of Davis's speeches for the Soledad Brothers:

> Liberation is synonymous with revolution. . . . A revolution is not just armed struggle. It's not just the period in which you can take over. A revolution has a very, very long spectrum. . . . Che made the very important point that the society you're going to build is already reflected in the nature of the struggle that you're carrying out. And one of the most important things in relationship to that is the building of a collective spirit, getting away from this individualistic orientation towards personal salvation, personal involvement. . . . One of the most important things that has to be done in the process of carrying out a revolutionary struggle is to merge those two different levels, to merge the personal with the political where they're no longer separate.[54]

Merging the personal with the political, young militants faced the urgent immediacy of struggle in which they attended funerals of slain activists and, with and as survivors, attempted to continue in their commitments for radical social change despite deadly state repression. Although the revolutionary movement of the previous era was derailed, according to Davis, contemporary progressive or Left intellectuals have "achieved a measure of lucidity, based on those experiences." For Davis, "There is much more extensive consciousness of that dialectic between the concrete work that we do, the activist work, and the international context. . . . [The challenge is to make] the transition from consciousness to action, from theory to practice."[55] In contradistinction to the construction of the theorist or philosopher as the disengaged, nonactivist, Davis adds, "while theoretical work, intellectual work, is extremely important, the work of the activist will determine whether or not we will move to a new stage . . . everyone should learn how to become an activist on some level, in some way. Everyone who considers herself or himself a part of this overall progressive movement must establish some kind of organizational ties, and must definitely participate in one or more movements."[56]

Spanning three decades, Davis's work chronicles and contributes to progressive movements in radical philosophy and politics, emphasizing prison intellectualism, Marxism, antiracism, feminism, cultural studies and activism. This collection reveals the range of her writings, which have been published in scholarly journals as well as popular magazines. Some are agitational and others are analytical. Her work mirrors and documents intersectionality in the phenomenal critiques and confrontations (and the countervailing forces of state repression) that flared at the height of revolutionary struggles in the US only to mutate and eventually become muted in progressive academic writings. Transformative American intellectualism and political culture can be marked, and in some ways measured, by Davis's integrative analyses of class, race, sex, and the commodification of (black) political culture. These themes contextualize the social condition as bound by repression and resistance, reflecting the collective desire and demand for freedom. Challenging mainstream analytical and political discourse, to illuminate a doorway in liberation praxis, her work has deeply influenced democratic theory and political struggles.

Readers have varying perspectives on Davis as political-intellectual. Some see her as a revolutionary of the late 1960s and early 1970s; still others, as a former political prisoner who now functions as a radical public intellectual. Whatever one's "read," it is clear that through her writing and political advocacy, Angela Y. Davis has expanded the scope of social thought and political theory. Scanning both directions, one recognizes Janus at the crossroads. In an encounter with her work, one sees the past revolutionary acts and state repressions which radicalized her political consciousness, the progressive intellectualism of contemporary thinkers, and the fluid, dynamic tension which charges the relationships between the two.

NOTES

1 Angela Y. Davis, *Angela Davis: An Autobiography* (New York: Random House, 1974). Davis was given a University of California Presidential Chair, 1994–7.
2 Angela Y. Davis, "Remembering Carole, Cynthia, Addie Mae and Denise," *Essence*, February 1993, 92.
3 The Scottsboro Nine were African Americans falsely accused of raping two white women. Tried and sentenced in Scottsboro, Alabama, the young males were incarcerated for decades before their pardon.
4 Davis, *Angela Davis*, 113.
5 Davis, "Remembering Carole, Cynthia, Addie Mae and Denise," 92.
6 Ibid.
7 Ibid.
8 Ibid., 123.
9 Carole Robertson had contacted Sallye B. Davis days before the bombing to ask for a ride to a "Friendship and Action" meeting, a new organization formed by black and white parents and teachers to develop grassroots antiracist activism amid school desegregation and allow Birmingham School children to meet each other. Davis, "Remembering Carole, Cynthia, Addie Mae and Denise," 123.
10 Davis, "Remembering Carole, Cynthia, Addie Mae and Denise," 123.

11   Ibid., 123.
12   Angela Y. Davis, "Women, Race and Class: An Activist Perspective," *Women's Studies Quarterly*, X: 4 (Winter 1982), 5. This Keynote Address was first delivered at the Fourth National Women's Studies Association Convention at Humboldt State University, in Arcata, California, June 17, 1982, 5.
13   Angela Y. Davis, "The Making of a Revolutionary," Review of Elaine Brown's *A Taste of Power: A Black Woman's Story*, in *Women's Review of Books* (June 1993).
14   Ibid.
15   While a graduate student in philosophy at the University of California at San Diego, Davis's first major political project was a campaign on behalf of a young African-American Navy-enlisted man who faced court-martial charges during the Vietnam war for having circulated a petition accusing President Lyndon Baines Johnson of racist policies. Working in this campaign as a member of the Black Student Alliance, in 1967/68 she met Elaine Brown, who like Davis later joined the Panthers (Brown would serve as Chair of the Black Panther Party, taking over from Huey Newton).
       Kit Kim Holder argues that by the time that Brown became Chair of the Black Panther Party it functioned as a local organization rather than as the central leadership of a unified Party or national movement. See: Kit Kim Holder, "The History of the Black Panther Party, 1966–1972," dissertation, University of Massachusetts at Amherst, School of Education, May 1990.
16   Davis, "The Making of a Revolutionary."
17   Ibid.
18   Ibid.
19   Regents continue to denounce Davis, an influential academic and Professor of History of Consciousness at the University of California at Santa Cruz, as they demonize past liberation movements in order to oppose contemporary progressivism. In his March 18, 1996 correspondence to Davis, University of California Regent Ward Connolly, Chairman of the conservative Civil Rights Initiative which led California's anti-affirmative action legislation, castigated her for campus speeches to defeat the Initiative, writing: "your record as a revolutionary is not merely disturbing but it may impair your effectiveness as a member of the faculty of one of this nation's most highly respected academic institutions." Along with other conservative state officials, Connolly had opposed Davis's 1994 appointment to a University of California Presidential Chair, and her sharing the Chair's research funds with the UC-Santa Cruz "Women of Color Research Cluster" to support graduate and undergraduate research and teaching in multicultural, antiracist feminist studies. (Correspondence, author's papers.)
20   "An Initiative to Unite and Renew the Party".
21   Ibid., 3.
22   Ibid.
23   Ibid., 2.
24   See: George Jackson, *Blood in My Eye* (New York: Random House, 1970) and *Soledad Brother: The Prison Letters of George Jackson* (New York: Coward-McCann, 1970).

25 Ruchell Magee remains imprisoned. The autobiography's record of the trial testimony includes the defense cross-examination of a prison officer concerning official policy on escapes. To defense attorney Leo Branton's question, as to whether standard prison policy requires guards to prevent escapes where prisoners use hostages as shields "even if it means that every hostage is killed?" – San Quentin's Sergeant Murphy answered: "That is correct." Davis, *Angela Davis*, 370.

26 See Joanne Grant, *Black Protest: History, Documents and Analyses 1619 to Present* (New York: Ballantine, 1968); Ward Churchill and Jim Vander Wall, *Agents of Repression: The FBI's War Against AIM and the Black Panther Party* (Boston: South End Press, 1989); Clayborne Carson, *Malcolm X: The FBI File*, ed. David Gallen (New York: Carroll and Graf, 1991). FBI director J. Edgar Hoover designated the Black Panther Party as a pre-eminent threat to national security.

27 Although all deaths were a result of police shootings, under US law the defendants were charged with the killings.

28 *Frame-Up* (author's papers).

29 Geronimo ji Jaga (Pratt) is one such case. After spending twenty-seven years in prison for the murder of Caroline Olson, he was released on a $25,000 bail in June 1997 when a California judge ruled that his incarceration was based on perjured testimony by a felon, FBI and LAPD informer Julio Butler, and that the District Attorney's office had withheld information from the jury concerning Pratt's innocence. Pratt maintains that he was in northern California at the time of the southern California shootings; FBI wire taps that could place him at a BPP meeting in northern California mysteriously disappeared when they were requested by his defense team. See Don Terry, "Los Angeles Confronts Bitter Racial Legacy," *New York Times*, July 20, 1997, A1, A10.

30 The death penalty was reinstated in California in 1977.

31 Angela Y. Davis (ed.), *If They Come in the Morning: Voices of Resistance* (New Jersey: Third World Press, 1971).

32 Ibid., 75.

33 Angela Y. Davis, "Reflections on the Black Woman's Role in the Community of Slaves," *The Black Scholar*, vol. 3, no. 4 (December 1971).

34 Davis, *Angela Davis*.

35 *Frame-Up*, iii (author's papers).

36 Davis (ed.), *If They Come in the Morning*, 3.

37 Leonard Harris (ed.), *Philosophy Born of Struggle* (Dubuque, Iowa: Kendall Hunt, 1981).

38 Michel Foucault, *Discipline and Punish: The Birth of the Prison*, translation by Alan Sheridan (New York: Random House, 1979).

39 Davis notes the hypocrisy of attacking Mexican and Latin American "migrating working class people" while exonerating "migrating transnational corporations . . . immigrant corporations in search of nations providing cheap labor pools" that abandon communities and destabilize their economic base, turning workers "into perfect candidates for welfare and for prison." She states that these corporations simultaneously, and cyclically, "create an economic demand for prisons, which stimulates the economy, provides jobs for people

who have been left without work" (Angela Y. Davis, Keynote Address for Defensa de Mujeres Benefit, Santa Cruz, California, June 9, 1995, author's papers).

40   Angela Y. Davis, "COMPLEXITY, ACTIVISM, OPTIMISM: An Interview with Angela Y. Davis," *Feminist Review*, Fall 1988 (Interview by Kum-Kum Bhavnani, July 1988, Berkeley, California).

41   Ibid., 71.

42   Ibid.

43   Ibid.

44   Coalition-building is a central theme in Davis's writings and political work. Advocating the necessity of a multiracial feminist formation, she states in the 1988 Bhavani interview: "To shed the attitudinal forms of racism and class bias inevitable in any racist society, white middle-class women cannot continue simply to work among themselves. . . . [Antiracist politics] will not happen as a result of white women attending workshops. . . . White women must learn in activist contexts how to take leadership from women of color."

Discussing such leadership in an address, "Women, Race and Class: An Activist Perspective," for the National Women's Studies Association, Davis refers to the 1851 women's conference in Akron, Ohio, and cites the speech "Ain't I a Woman," erroneously attributed to Sojourner Truth (historian Nell Painter's *Sojourner Truth: A Life, A Symbol* [New York: W. W. Norton, 1996] documents this common misperception): "Sojourner Truth spoke from her own experiences as the voice of black women during that era, as a matter of fact she could speak more effectively for all of the [middle-class white] women there than those women could speak for themselves, because of the political experiences that she had accumulated. She had had to fight for her own survival, as a slave: she had had to struggle for her children . . . practically all of her children were sold off to slavery. . . . there were lessons that could have been learned from her that would perhaps have assisted the women's rights movement" to progress more rapidly (Davis, "Women, Race and Class: An Activist Perspective," 7).

45   Davis, "COMPLEXITY, ACTIVISM, OPTIMISM," 69.

46   Angela Y. Davis, "Rape, Racism and the Capitalist Setting," *The Black Scholar*, April 1978, 24–30.

47   Angela Y. Davis, "Violence Against Women and the Ongoing Challenge to Racism," *The Freedom Organizing Pamphlet Series* (Latham, NY: Women of Color Press, 1985).

48   "The Myth of the Black Rapist," in Angela Y. Davis, *Women, Race, and Class* (New York: Vintage, 1981), proved a groundbreaking intervention in feminist critique of white racism and sexual violence.

49   Angela Y. Davis, "JoAnne Little: The Dialectics of Rape," *Ms. Magazine*, June 1975, 74–7, 106–8.

50   Angela Y. Davis, "Women and Capitalism: Dialectics of Oppression and Liberation," in *Marxism, Revolution, and Peace*, Howard Parsons and John Sommerville, eds (Amsterdam: B. R. Grüner, 1977).

51   Angela Y. Davis, "The Approaching Obsolescence of Housework: A Working-Class Perspective," *Women, Race, and Class*.

52 Angela Y. Davis, "Surrogates and Outcast Mothers: Racism and Reproductive Politics in the Nineties," in Annette Dula (ed.), *"It Jus' Ain't Fair": The Ethics of Health Care for African Americans* (Westport, CT: Praeger, 1994).

53 Angela Y. Davis, Keynote Address, January 1994, "Black Women and the Academy," Massachusetts Institute for Technology, Cambridge, MA.

54 *LIFE Magazine*, September 11, 1970, vol. 69, no. 11, 26. The quote, from a speech Davis made for the Soledad Brothers, comes from a June 27, 1970, interview with Maeland Productions, which was doing a documentary on Davis.

55 Ibid.

56 Ibid.

PART I

Prisons, Repression, and Resistance

1

Excerpts from *Angela Davis: An Autobiography*

The entire jail was shrouded in darkness when I finally reached the cell in 4b. It was no more than four and a half feet wide. The only furnishings were an iron cot bolted to the floor and a seatless toilet at the foot of the bed. Some minutes after they had locked me in, the officer in charge of that unit – another young black woman – came to the iron door. She whispered through the grating that she was shoving a piece of candy under the door. She sounded sincere enough, but I couldn't take any chances. I didn't want to be paranoid, but it was better to be too distrustful than not cautious enough. I was familiar with jailhouse "suicides" in California. For all I knew, there might be poison in the candy.

The first night in jail, I had no desire to sleep. I thought about George and his brothers in San Quentin. I thought about Jonathan. I thought about my mother and father and hoped that they would make it through this ordeal. And then I thought about the demonstration outside, about all the people who had dropped everything to fight for my freedom.

I had just been captured; a trial awaited me in California on the charges of murder, kidnapping, and conspiracy. A conviction on any one of these charges could mean death in the gas chamber. One would have thought that this was an enormous defeat. Yet, at that moment, I was feeling better than I had felt in a long time. The struggle would be difficult, but there was already a hint of victory. In the heavy silence of the jail, I discovered that if I concentrated hard enough, I could hear echoes of slogans being chanted on the other side of the walls. "Free Angela Davis." "Free All Political Prisoners."

The key rattling in the cell-gate lock startled me. A guard was opening the gate for a plump young black woman wearing a faded blue prisoner's uniform and holding a big tray in her hands.

Smiling, she said in a very soft voice, "Here's your breakfast. Do you want some coffee?"

Her gentle manner was comforting and made me feel like I was among human beings again. I sat up on the cot, thanked her and told her that I would very much like a cup of coffee.

Looking around, I realized that there was no place to put the food – the bed and the toilet were the only furnishings in the tiny cell. But the sister, obviously having gone through this many times before, had already stooped down to a squatting position and was placing the food on the floor: a small box of cornflakes, a paper cup filled with watery milk, two pieces of plain white bread and a paper cup into which she began to pour the coffee.

"Is there any black coffee?" I asked her, partly because I didn't drink coffee with milk and partly because I wanted an excuse to exchange a few more words with her.

"When they give it to us, it's already like this," she answered, "but I'll see what I can do about getting you some black coffee tomorrow."

The guard told me I had to get ready for my court appearance. Then she slammed the gate on the young woman's exit. While she was unlocking the next cell, the sister whispered through the bars, "Don't worry about a thing. We're all on your side." And she disappeared down the corridor.

I looked down at my breakfast, and saw that a roach had already discovered it. I left it all spread out on the bare floor untouched. After I had gone through the elaborate steps involved in getting dressed for court, a matron led me downstairs. A crowd of white men was milling around the receiving room. Seeing me, they swept toward me like vultures and clamped handcuffs around my wrists, which still ached from the previous day. Outside, shiny tin cars crowded into the cobblestone courtyard. It was still dark when the caravan reached the federal courthouse. A glimpse of the morning paper's bold-lettered headlines, peeping out from under some man's arm, stunned me: ANGELA DAVIS CAPTURED IN NEW YORK. It suddenly struck me that the huge crowd of press people summoned by the FBI the evening before had probably written similar headline stories throughout the country. Knowing that my name was now familiar to millions of people, I felt overwhelmed. Yet I knew that all this publicity was not really aimed at me as an individual. Using me as an example, they wanted to discredit the black liberation movement, the Left in general and obviously also the Communist Party. I was only the occasion for their manipulations.

The holding cell where I spent the next several hours was cleaner than the jail cell I had just left and looked like a giant, unfinished bathroom. It had sparkling white tile walls and a light-colored linoleum floor. A seatless toilet stood in one of the corners. Long metal benches lined the three walls.

One of the federal bureaucrats came into the cell.

"I have nothing to say," I told him, "until I see my lawyer."

"Your father's lawyer is waiting outside," he said.

My father's lawyer? Perhaps it was a friend posing as my "father's lawyer" in order to get permission to see me.

In a large hall filled with rows of desks, John Abt was waiting to see me. Although I had never met him before I knew about the trials in which he had successfully defended members of our Party. With a great feeling of relief, I sat down to talk with him.

"I waited for hours last night at the jail, but they refused to let me in," John said. "I had to get your father to call them before they would let me see you this morning."

He went on to explain that I was about to be arraigned on the federal charge – interstate flight to avoid prosecution. Before he had gotten very far in his discussion of the legal proceedings before us, a group of people pressed through a door at the other end of the room. Without my glasses, which the FBI had not bothered to return, the people's faces were blurred. Noticing a young black woman involved in a heated exchange with the marshals, I squinted in order to see her more clearly.

"That's Margaret!" I shouted.

Margaret Burnham was a very old friend of mine. During my youngest years, her family and mine had lived in the same housing project in Birmingham. When the Burnhams moved to New York, we visited them every summer for four years, then we alternated the visits – sometimes they would come to Birmingham and sometimes we would go to New York. Our families had been so close that I had always considered Margaret, her sisters Claudia and Linda, and her brother Charles more family than friends. I had not seen her for several years. She had been in Mississippi, gotten married and given birth to a child. I knew that she had recently graduated from law school and I assumed she was now practicing in New York.

"Margaret," I called, as loudly as I could, "come on over." Apparently this was enough to settle the argument she was having with the marshal, for he did nothing to prevent her from walking over to the desk where John and I were. It felt so good to embrace her. "Margaret," I said to her, "I'm so glad you came. You don't know how glad I am to see you." As we started talking about personal things, I almost forgot that there was business to be taken care of.

"Can you work on the case?" I asked her finally, desperately hoping she would say yes.

"You know I will, Angela," she answered, "if that's what you think I should do."

It was as if half the battle had already been won.

John Abt went on to explain the legal situation.

Back in August, Marin County had charged me with murder, kidnapping, and conspiracy to commit murder and rescue prisoners. On the basis of an FBI agent's affidavit declaring that I had been seen by "reliable sources" in Birmingham, a federal judge had issued a warrant charging me with "interstate flight to avoid prosecution." It was possible, John said, that I might be "removed" to California, which meant that without further litigation I would simply be transferred from the New York Federal District to the California Federal District. But more than likely, he surmised, I would be "turned over" to the State of New York for extradition to California, and we would be able to challenge California in the New York courts.

As we were winding up this conference, David[1] walked into the room, encircled by guards. I hadn't seen him since our arrest. He looked as if he hadn't slept either.

In a cool, crisp tone, he called out to me, "Remember now, no matter what, we're going to beat this thing."

"No talking between the prisoners," a voice announced. It could have come from any one of the marshals standing around.

"OK, David," I said, ignoring the command. "You be sure to keep strong yourself."

I had never seen a courtroom so small. With its marred walls of blond wood, it had the worn-out elegance of an old mansion. There was just enough room for the bench and a single row of chairs lining the back wall. The smallness of the courtroom exaggerated the height of the judge's bench. The judge himself was little, like his courtroom. He was wearing old-fashioned plastic-rimmed glasses, and his white hair was spread sparsely over his head. I thought about Soledad guard O. G. Miller perched in his gun tower, aiming his carbine at the three brothers he killed in the yard in January.[2]

There were no spectators. The only non-official people were reporters – and there were not very many of them. As I entered, a sister sitting in the seat closest to the door held up a copy of the hardcover edition of George's *Soledad Brother*. This was the first time I had seen the book, which I had read in manuscript.

The arraignment on the federal charges was short and to the point. All the prosecutor was required to do was to prove, for the record, that I was the Angela Davis named in the warrant. The bail figure was a farce. Who could even contemplate raising $250,000 to get me out of jail?

It was still early – late morning or early afternoon – when I returned to the holding cell. The last time I had been in the cell, my thoughts had been monopolized by the problem of finding a lawyer. Now that I had two fine lawyers whom I trusted and loved, I could no longer ward off thoughts of my imprisonment. I was alone with the shiny tile walls and the gray steel bars. Walls and bars, nothing more. I wished I had a book or, if not something to read, at least a pencil and a sheet of paper.

I fought the tendency to individualize my predicament. Pacing from one end of this cell to the other, from a bench along one wall to a bench along the other, I kept telling myself that I didn't have the right to get upset about a few hours of being alone in a holding cell. What about the brother – Charles Jordon was his name – who had spent, not hours, but days and weeks in a pitch-dark strip-cell in Soledad Prison, hardly large enough for him to stretch out on the cold cement, reeking of urine and human excrement because the only available toilet was a hole in the floor which could hardly be seen in the dark.

I thought about the scene George had described in the manuscript of his book – the brother who had painted a night sky on the ceiling of his cell, because it had been years since he had seen the moon and stars. (When it was discovered, the guards painted over it in gray.) And there was Ericka Huggins at Niantic State Farm for Women in Connecticut. Ericka, Bobby, the Soledad Brothers, the Soledad 7, the Tombs Rebels and all the countless others whose identities were hidden behind so much concrete and steel, so many locks and chains. How could I indulge even the faintest inclination toward self-pity? Yet I paced faster across the holding cell. I walked with the determination of someone who has someplace very important to go. At the same time, I was trying not to let the jailers see my agitation.

When someone finally opened the gate, it was late in the evening. Margaret and John were waiting to accompany me to a court appearance in the same courtroom we had appeared in that morning. Aside from us, there were no "civilians" in the courtroom, not even the reporters from the morning session. I wondered what kind of secret appearance this was going to be.

The elderly judge announced that he was rescinding the bail and releasing me on my own recognizance. I was sure I had misheard his words. But already, the Feds were approaching me to unlock the handcuffs. The judge said something else, which I hardly heard, and then suddenly several New York policemen moved in to replace the federal handcuffs with their own manacles.

With the New York handcuffs binding my wrists, there was a trip to a musty police precinct office, where I was officially booked as a prisoner of the State of New York. Forms, fingerprints, mug shots – the same routine. The New York police seemed to be as confused as their surroundings. Amid all the papers haphazardly strewn on desks and counters, they were running around like novices. Their incompetence calmed me. It must have been around ten in the evening when one of them announced that there would be yet another court appearance. (Did Margaret and John know about this third court session?)

The courtroom in the New York County Courthouse was larger than any I had ever seen. Its high ceilings and interminable rows of benches made it look like a church from another era. Most courtrooms are windowless, but this one seemed especially isolated from the outside world. It was so dimly lit, with hardly anyone but policemen sitting randomly on the benches, that I had the impression that what was about to happen was supposed to be hidden from the people outside. Neither Margaret nor John was there. When they told me that I had to be arraigned before a New York judge, I said that I wasn't budging from my seat until they contacted my lawyers. I was prepared to wait the whole night.

When John finally arrived, he said that the police had directed him to the wrong courtroom. He had been running all over New York trying to find me. After hours of waiting, the court appearance lasted all of two minutes.

Back at the jail, I was so physically and emotionally exhausted that I only wanted to sleep. Even the hard cell cot in the "mental" ward felt comfortable. But as soon as I closed my eyes, I was jolted out of my exhaustion by piercing screams in a language which sounded Slavic. They came from a cell at the other end of the corridor. Footsteps approached the cell in the darkness. Voices tried to calm the woman in English but could not assuage her terror. I listened to her all night – until they took her away in the morning. [. . .]

While I was in solitary, I finally began to receive regular evening visits from several friends. An officer would stand just close enough to hear my side of the conversation. (I assumed that they summarized it in the log book.) I was not a stranger to visiting arrangements in jails, for I had visited friends and comrades in prison on many occasions. But this visiting room was by far the worst I had seen. It is not unusual to have to speak to a visitor through a glass pane, but the panes in the House of Detention were less than a square foot in size, and the rust-colored dirt that covered them made it impossible to get a clear look at the person who had come to see you. The prisoners had to stand up during these twenty-minute visits and shout into telephones which inevitably seemed to stop functioning just when the most important part of the conversation had gotten under way.

One evening while I was still in solitary, I received a visit from Kendra Alexander, who had been subpoenaed to New York along with her husband Franklin to testify before the Grand Jury in the case against David Poindexter.[3] She informed me that the demonstration protesting my solitary confinement was about to begin. They knew more or less where my room was located – I had carefully detailed the areas of Greenwich Avenue I could see from my window. The demonstrators were to gather on the corner of Greenwich and West Tenth.

I ran back upstairs. The officer guarding me was one of the friendlier ones, and turned her head and closed her ears while I spread the news. On five or six floors, the women who lived in the corridors with windows looking out on Greenwich Avenue would be able to see and hear the demonstration.

It was an enthusiastic crowd. Their shouts "Free Angela! Free all our sisters!" rang through the night. Looking down from my cell window, I became altogether engrossed in the speeches, sometimes losing the sensation of captivity, feeling myself down there on the street with them. My mind flashed back to past demonstrations – "Free the Soledad Brothers," "Free Bobby and Ericka," "Free Huey," "End the war in Vietnam," "Stop police killings in our community now . . ."

Jose Stevens, a communist leader from Harlem, had wound up his speech. Franklin was addressing his words, full of passion, to all the prisoners locked up in the Women's House of Detention. Then my sister, Fania, took the megaphone. The sound of her voice shocked me back into the reality of my situation, for I momentarily had forgotten that this demonstration was centered around me. I had been so absorbed in the rally that I had actually felt as if I were down there in the streets with them. Reflecting upon the impenetrability of this fortress, on all the things that kept me separated from my comrades barely a few hundred yards away, and reflecting on my solitary confinement – this prison within a prison that kept me separated from my sisters in captivity – I felt the weight of imprisonment perhaps more at that moment than at any time before.

My frustration was immense. But before my thoughts led me further in the direction of self-pity, I brought them to a halt, reminding myself that this was precisely what solitary confinement was supposed to evoke. In such a state the keepers could control their victim. I would not let them conquer me. I transformed my frustration into raging energy for the fight.

Against the background of the chants ringing up from the demonstration below, I took myself to task for having indulged in self-pity. What about George, John and Fleeta, and my co-defendant, Ruchell Magee, who had endured far worse than I could ever expect to grapple with? What about Charles Jordan and his bout with that medieval strip-cell in Soledad Prison? What about those who had given their lives – Jonathan, McClain, and Christmas?

The experience of the demonstration had worked up so much tension in me that I felt none of the debilitating effects of the fast. I did an extra heavy set of exercises to sufficiently lower my energy level so I could lie in bed in relative calm. There was no question of getting a full night's sleep. On this evening, I had to be especially vigilant. All was quiet in the jail, but I was convinced that the demonstration had aroused the jailers, and I had to hold myself in readiness in case they decided to strike sometime during the night. On the tenth day of my hunger strike, at a time when I had persuaded myself that I could continue indefinitely without eating, the Federal Court handed down a ruling enjoining the jail administration from holding me any longer in isolation and under maximum security conditions. They had decided – under pressure, of course – that this unwarranted punishment was meted out to me because of my political beliefs and affiliation. The court was all but saying that Commissioner of Corrections George McGrath and Jessie Behagan, the superintendent of the Women's House of D., were so fearful of letting the women in the jail discover what communism was that they preferred to violate my most basic constitutional rights.

This ruling came as a surprise. I hadn't expected it to be so swift and to the point. It was an important victory, for we had firmly established that those in the Department of Corrections in New York would not have a clear course before them when they attempted to persecute the next political prisoner delivered into their hands. At the same time, however, I did not put it past the jail administration to concoct another situation which might not be solitary confinement, but which would give me an equally bad time. This thought subdued my delight at the news of the injunction.

Next destination: seventh floor, C corridor. When I arrived, there was a big shake-up going on. Women were being moved out, others were coming in. For a moment the thought struck me that they were preparing a special corridor for informers, jailer's confidantes – and me. But as it turned out, the lawsuit had forced the administration to get on its toes – so-called "first offenders" were supposed to be jailed separately from those who had already spent time in the House of Detention. Apparently the necessary shifts were being made.

There was little time to learn my way about before all the cell gates were locked, but some of my neighbors gave me a guided tour of my 8' × 5' cell. Because mine was the corner cell – the one which could be easily spied on from the officer's desk in the main hallway – it was also the smallest one on the corridor; the double bunk made it appear even smaller. The fixtures – the bed, the tiny sink, the toilet – were all arranged in a straight line, leaving no more than a width of two feet of floor at any point in the cell.

The sisters helped me improvise a curtain in front of the toilet and sink so they could not be seen from the corridor. They showed me how to use newspaper wrapped in scrap cloth to make a seat cover so the toilet could be turned into a chair to be used at the iron table that folded down from the wall in front of it. I laughed out loud at the thought of doing all my writing while sitting on the toilet stool.

Lock-in time was approaching; a sister remembered that she had forgotten to warn me about one of the dangers of night-life in the House of D. " 'Mickey' will be trying to get into your cell tonight," she said, and I would have to take precautionary steps to "keep him out."

"Mickey?" Was there some maniac the jailers let loose at night to pester the women?

The sister laughingly told me she was referring to the mice which scampered about in the darkness of the corridors looking for cell doors not securely stuffed with newspapers.

It became a nightly ritual: placing meticulously folded newspapers in the little space between the gate and the floor and halfway up the gate along the wall. Despite the preventive measures we took, Mickey could always chew through the barricade in at least one cell, and we were often awakened by the shouts of a woman calling the officer to get the mouse out. One night Mickey joined me in the top bunk. When I felt him crawling around my neck, I brushed him away thinking that it was roaches. When I finally realized what it was, I called for the broom – our only weapon against him. Apparently mousetraps were too expensive, and they were not going to exterminate.

There was one good thing about Mickey. His presence reassured us that there were no rats in the vicinity. The two never share the same turf.

In a sense our daily struggles with Mickey – with all the various makeshift means devised to get the better of him – were symbolic of a larger struggle with the system. Indulging in a flight of fancy, I would sometimes imagine that all the preparations that were made at night to ward off those creatures were the barricades being erected against that larger enemy. That hundreds of women, all over the jail, politically conscious, politically committed, were acting in revolutionary unison.

That first evening, shortly after the sister had helped me stuff the gate with newspapers, an officer called out, "Lock-in time, girls. Into your cells." As the women slid their heavy iron gates closed, loud metallic crashing noises thundered from all four corridors of the seventh floor. I could hear the same sounds at a distance echoing from throughout the jail. (In 4b, I had never been able to figure out what all this commotion was about. The first time I heard it, I thought a rebellion had been unleashed.)

The officer came around to count each prisoner, and at 9 p.m. all lights in the corridor and cells were turned off by a master switch. In the darkness, a goodnight ritual was acted out. One sister shouted goodnight to another, calling her by name. The latter, catching the identity of the voice, would shout goodnight, also calling the first sister by name. Early on, someone from my corridor called out warmly, "Good night, Angela!" But having learned hardly anyone's name, much less to recognize their voices, I was an outsider to this ritual and could only respond with a lonesome, un-supported, though no less vigorous) "goodnight." My call sparked off goodnight shouts to me, which came not only from my own corridor but from the others as well. I am sure that there had never been such a prolonged "saying of goodnights." The officers did not interrupt, though silence should have prevailed long before.

NOTES

1 Editor's note: David Poindexter traveled with Davis during the two months she was underground. He was acquitted of federal charges of harboring a fugitive.

2 Editor's note: O. G. Miller was the Soledad prison guard who killed three black prisoners (W. L. Nolen, Cleveland Edwards, and Alvin Miller) on January 13, 1970. When the grand jury ruled his action was "justifiable homicide," the prisoners' riot resulted in the killing of a guard who was on duty at the time. The Soledad Brothers were charged with the murder of this guard.

3 Editor's note: Angela Davis first met Kendra and Franklin Alexander through her work with the Black Student Alliance. Franklin Alexander and Davis were active together in the organization, Black Panther Political Party, and it was as a result of Davis's growing political relationship with the Alexanders that she decided to join their organization, the Che-Lumumba Club of the Communist Party, USA. Kendra Alexander died in 1993, Franklin in 1994.

2

Political Prisoners, Prisons, and Black Liberation

Despite a long history of exalted appeals to man's inherent right of resistance, there has seldom been agreement on how to relate *in practice* to unjust, immoral laws and the oppressive social order from which they emanate.* The conservative, who does not dispute the validity of revolutions deeply buried in history, invokes visions of impending anarchy in order to legitimize his demand for absolute obedience. Law and order, with the major emphasis on order, is his watchword. The liberal articulates his sensitivity to certain of society's intolerable details, but will almost never prescribe methods of resistance that exceed the limits of legality – redress through electoral channels is the liberal's panacea.

In the heat of our pursuit of fundamental human rights, black people have been continually cautioned to be patient. We are advised that as long as we remain faithful to the *existing* democratic order, the glorious moment will eventually arrive when we will come into our own as full-fledged human beings.

But having been taught by bitter experience, we know that there is a glaring incongruity between democracy and the capitalist economy which is the source of our ills. Regardless of all rhetoric to the contrary, the people are not the ultimate matrix of the laws and the system which govern them – certainly not black people and other nationally oppressed people, but not even the mass of whites. The people do not exercise decisive control over the determining factors of their lives.

Official assertions that meaningful dissent is always welcome, provided it falls within the boundaries of legality, are frequently a smokescreen obscuring the invitation to acquiesce in oppression. Slavery may have been un-

---

* *Author's note, 1998*: I have opted to leave masculinist formulations in this and other early essays, which I hope will be considered in the context of the historical period in which they were produced.

This essay first appeared in Angela Y. Davis (ed.), *If They Come in the Morning: Voices of Resistance* (New York: Third Press, 1971). Copyright © 1971 by the National United Committee to Free Angela Davis.

righteous, the constitutional provision for the enslavement of blacks may have been unjust, but conditions were not to be considered so unbearable (especially since they were profitable to a small circle) as to justify escape and other acts proscribed by law. This was the import of the fugitive slave laws.

Needless to say, the history of the United States has been marred from its inception by an enormous quantity of unjust laws, far too many expressly bolstering the oppression of black people. Particularized reflections of existing social inequities, these laws have repeatedly borne witness to the exploitative and racist core of the society itself. For blacks, Chicanos, for all nationally oppressed people, the problem of opposing unjust laws and the social conditions which nourish their growth, has always had immediate practical implications. Our very survival has frequently been a direct function of our skill in forging effective channels of resistance. In resisting we have sometimes been compelled to openly violate those laws which directly or indirectly buttress our oppression. But even when containing our resistance within the orbit of legality, we have been labeled criminals and have been methodically persecuted by a racist legal apparatus.

Under the ruthless conditions of slavery, the underground railroad provided the framework for extra-legal anti-slavery activity pursued by vast numbers of people, both black and white. Its functioning was in flagrant violation of the fugitive slave laws; those who were apprehended were subjected to severe penalties. Of the innumerable recorded attempts to rescue fugitive slaves from the clutches of slave-catchers, one of the most striking is the case of Anthony Burns, a slave from Virginia, captured in Boston in 1853. A team of his supporters, in attempting to rescue him by force during the course of his trial, engaged the police in a fierce courtroom battle. During the gun fight, a prominent abolitionist, Thomas Wentworth Higginson, was wounded. Although the rescuers were unsuccessful in their efforts, the impact of this incident ". . . did more to crystallize Northern sentiment against slavery than any other except the exploit of John Brown, 'and this was the last time a fugitive slave was taken from Boston. It took 22 companies of state militia, four platoons of marines, a battalion of United States artillerymen, and the city's police force . . . to ensure the performance of this shameful act, the cost of which, to the Federal government alone, came to forty thousand dollars.' "[1]

Throughout the era of slavery, blacks, as well as progressive whites, repeatedly discovered that their commitment to the anti-slavery cause frequently entailed the overt violation of the laws of the land. Even as slavery faded away into a more subtle yet equally pernicious apparatus to dominate black people, "illegal" resistance was still on the agenda. After the Civil War, the Black Codes, successors to the old Slave Codes, legalized convict labor, prohibited social intercourse between blacks and whites, gave white employers an excessive degree of control over the private lives of black workers, and generally codified racism and terror. Naturally, numerous individual as well as collective acts of resistance prevailed. On many occasions, blacks formed armed teams to protect themselves from white terrorists who were, in turn, protected by law enforcement agencies, if not actually identical with them.

By the second decade of the twentieth century, the mass movement, headed by Marcus Garvey, proclaimed in its Declaration of Rights that black people should not hesitate to disobey all discriminatory laws. Moreover, the Declaration announced, they should utilize all means available to them, legal or illegal, to defend themselves from legalized terror as well as Ku Klux Klan violence. During the era of intense activity around civil rights issues, systematic disobedience of oppressive laws was a primary tactic. The sit-ins were organized transgressions of racist legislation.

All these historical instances involving the overt violation of the laws of the land converge around an unmistakable common denominator. At stake has been the collective welfare and survival of a people. There is a distinct and qualitative difference between one breaking a law for one's own individual self-interest and violating it in the interests of a class or a people whose oppression is expressed either directly or indirectly through that particular law. The former might be called a criminal (though in many instances he is a victim), but the latter, as a reformist or revolutionary, is interested in universal social change. Captured, he or she is a political prisoner.

The political prisoner's words or deeds have in one form or another embodied political protests against the established order and have consequently brought him into acute conflict with the state. In light of the political content of his act, the "crime" (which may or may not have been committed) assumes a minor importance. In this country, however, where the special category of political prisoners is not officially acknowledged, the political prisoner inevitably stands trial for a specific criminal offense, not for a political act. Often the so-called crime does not even have a nominal existence. As in the 1914 murder frame-up of the IWW organizer, Joe Hill, it is a blatant fabrication, a mere excuse for silencing a militant crusader against oppression. In all instances, however, the political prisoner has violated the unwritten law which prohibits disturbances and upheavals in the status quo of exploitation and racism. This unwritten law has been contested by actually and explicitly breaking a law or by utilizing constitutionally protected channels to educate, agitate, and organize the masses to resist.

A deep-seated ambivalence has always characterized the official response to the political prisoner. Charged and tried for a criminal act, his guilt is always political in nature. This ambivalence is perhaps best captured by

Judge Webster Thayer's comment upon sentencing Bartolomeo Vanzetti to fifteen years for an attempted payroll robbery: "This man, although he may not have actually committed the crime attributed to him, is nevertheless morally culpable, because he is the enemy of our existing institutions."[2] (The very same judge incidentally, sentenced Sacco and Vanzetti to death for a robbery and murder of which they were manifestly innocent.) It is not surprising that Nazi Germany's foremost constitutional lawyer, Carl Schmitt, advanced a theory which generalized this *a priori* culpability. A thief, for example, was not necessarily one who has committed an overt act of theft, but rather one whose character renders him a thief (*wer nach seinem wesen ein Dieb ist*). [President Richard] Nixon's and [FBI Director] J. Edgar Hoover's pronouncements lead one to believe that they would readily accept Schmitt's fascist legal theory. Anyone who seeks to overthrow oppressive institutions, whether or not he has engaged in an overt illegal act, is *a priori* a criminal who must be buried away in one of America's dungeons.

Even in all of Martin Luther King's numerous arrests, he was not so much charged with the nominal crimes of trespassing, and disturbance of the peace, as with being an enemy of southern society, an inveterate foe of racism. When Robert Williams was accused of kidnapping, this charge never managed to conceal his real offense – the advocacy of black people's incontestable right to bear arms in their own defense.

The offense of the political prisoner is political boldness, the persistent challenging – legally or extra-legally – of fundamental social wrongs fostered and reinforced by the state. The political prisoner has opposed unjust laws and exploitative, racist social conditions in general, with the ultimate aim of transforming these laws and this society into an order harmonious with the material and spiritual needs and interests of the vast majority of its members.

Nat Turner and John Brown were political prisoners in their time. The acts for which they were charged and subsequently hanged, were the practical extensions of their profound commitment to the abolition of slavery. They fearlessly bore the responsibility for their actions. The significance of their executions and the accompanying widespread repression did not lie so much in the fact that they were being punished for specific crimes, nor even in the effort to use their punishment as an implicit threat to deter others from similar *armed* acts of resistance. These executions, and the surrounding repression of slaves, were intended to terrorize the anti-slavery movement in general; to discourage and diminish both legal and illegal forms of abolitionist activity. As usual, the effect of repression was miscalculated and in both instances, anti-slavery activity was accelerated and intensified as a result.

Nat Turner and John Brown can be viewed as examples of the political prisoner who has actually committed an act which is defined by the state as "criminal." They killed and were consequently tried for murder. But did they commit murder? This raises the question of whether American revolutionaries had *murdered* the British in their struggle for liberation. Nat Turner and his followers killed some sixty-five white people, yet shortly before the revolt had begun, Nat is reputed to have said to the other rebelling slaves: "Remember that ours is not war for robbery nor to satisfy our passions, it is a *struggle for freedom*. Ours must be deeds not words."[3]

The very institutions which condemned Nat Turner and reduced his struggle for freedom to a simple criminal case of murder, owed their existence to the decision, made a half-century earlier, to take up arms against the British oppressor.

The battle for the liquidation of slavery had no legitimate existence in the eyes of the government and therefore the special quality of deeds carried out in the interests of freedom was deliberately ignored. There were no political prisoners, there were only criminals; just as the movement out of which these deeds flowed was largely considered criminal.

Likewise, the significance of activities which are pursued in the interests of liberation today is minimized not so much because officials are unable to *see* the collective surge against oppression, but because they have consciously set out to subvert such movements. In the Spring of 1970, Los Angeles Panthers took up arms to defend themselves from an assault initiated by the local police force on their office and on their persons. They were charged with criminal assault. If one believed the official propaganda, they were bandits and rogues who pathologically found pleasure in attacking policemen. It was not mentioned that their community activities – educational work, services such as free breakfast and free medical programs – which had legitimized them in the black community, were the immediate reason for which the wrath of the police had fallen upon them. In defending themselves from the attack waged by some 600 policemen (there were only eleven Panthers in the office) they were defending not only their lives, but even more important their accomplishments in the black community surrounding them, and in the broader thrust for black liberation. Whenever blacks in struggle have recourse to self-defense, particularly armed self-defense, it is twisted and distorted on official levels and ultimately rendered synonymous with criminal aggression. On the other hand, when policemen are clearly indulging in acts of criminal aggression, officially they are defending themselves through "justifiable assault" or "justifiable homicide."

The ideological acrobatics characteristic of official attempts to explain away the existence of the political prisoner do not end with the equation of the individual political act with the individual criminal act. The political act is defined as criminal in order to discredit radical and revolutionary movements. A political event is reduced to a criminal event in order to affirm the absolute invulnerability of the existing order. In a revealing contradiction, the court resisted the description of the New York Panther 21 trial as "political," yet the prosecutor entered as evidence of criminal intent, literature which represented, so he purported, the political ideology of the Black Panther Party.

The legal apparatus designates the black liberation fighter a criminal, prompting Nixon, [Vice President Spiro] Agnew, [California Governor Ronald] Reagan et al. to proceed to mystify with their demagogy millions of Americans whose senses have been dulled and whose critical powers have been eroded by the continual onslaught of racist ideology.

As the black liberation movement and other progressive struggles increase in magnitude and intensity, the judicial system and its extension, the penal system, consequently become key weapons in the state's fight to preserve the existing conditions of class domination, therefore racism, poverty, and war.

In 1951, W. E. B. Du Bois, as Chairman of the Peace Information Center, was indicted by the federal government for "failure to register as an agent of a foreign principal." In assessing this ordeal, which occurred in the ninth decade of his life, he turned his attention to the inhabitants of the nation's jails and prisons:

> What turns me cold in all this experience is the certainty that thousands of innocent victims are in jail today because they had neither money nor friends to help them. The eyes of the world were on our trial despite the desperate efforts of press and radio to suppress the facts and cloud the real issues; the courage and money of friends and of strangers who dared stand for a principle freed me; but God only knows how many who were as innocent as I and my colleagues are today in hell. They daily stagger out of prison doors embittered, vengeful, hopeless, ruined. And of this army of the wronged, the proportion of Negroes is frightful. We protect and defend sensational cases where Negroes are involved. But the great mass of arrested or accused black folk have no defense. There is desperate need of nationwide organizations to oppose this national racket of railroading to jails and chain gangs the poor, friendless, and black.[4]

Almost two decades passed before the realization attained by Du Bois on the occasion of his own encounter with the judicial system achieved extensive acceptance. A number of factors have combined to transform the penal system into a prominent terrain of struggle, both for the captives inside and the masses outside. The impact of large numbers of political prisoners both on prison populations and on the mass movement has been decisive. The vast majority of political prisoners have not allowed the fact of imprisonment to curtail their educational, agitational, and organizing activities, which they continue behind prison walls. And in the course of developing mass movements around political prisoners, a great deal of attention has inevitably been focused on the institutions in which they are imprisoned. Furthermore the political receptivity of prisoners – especially black and brown captives – has been increased and sharpened by the surge of aggressive political activity rising out of black, Chicano, and other oppressed communities. Finally, a major catalyst for intensified political action in and around prisons has emerged out of the transformation of convicts, originally found guilty of criminal offenses, into exemplary political militants. Their patient educational efforts in the realm of exposing the specific oppressive structures of the penal system in their relation to the larger oppression of the social system have had a profound effect on their fellow captives.

The prison is a key component of the state's coercive apparatus, the overriding function of which is to ensure social control. The etymology of the term "penitentiary" furnishes a clue to the controlling idea behind the "prison system" at its inception. The penitentiary was projected as the locale for doing penitence for an offense against society, the physical and spiritual purging of proclivities to challenge rules and regulations which command total obedience. While cloaking itself with the bourgeois aura of universality – imprisonment was supposed to cut across all class lines, as crimes were to be defined by the act, not the perpetrator – the prison has actually operated as an instrument of class domination, a means of prohibiting the have-nots from encroaching upon the haves.

The occurrence of crime is inevitable in a society in which wealth is unequally distributed, as one of the constant reminders that society's productive forces are being channeled in the wrong direction. The majority of criminal offenses bear a direct relationship to property. Contained in the very concept of property, crimes are profound but suppressed social needs which express themselves in anti-social modes of action. Spontaneously produced by a capitalist organization of society, this type of crime is at once a protest against society and a desire to partake of its exploitative content. It challenges the symptoms of capitalism, but not its essence.

Some Marxists in recent years have tended to banish "criminals" and the lumpenproletariat as a whole from the arena of revolutionary struggle. Apart from the absence of any link binding the criminal to the means of production, underlying this exclusion has been the assumption that individuals who have recourse to anti-social acts are incapable of developing the discipline and collective orientation required by revolutionary struggle.

With the declassed character of lumpenproletarians in mind, Marx had stated that they are as capable of "the most heroic deeds and the most exalted sacrifices, as of the basest banditry and the dirtiest corruption."[5] He emphasized the fact that the provisional government's mobile guards under the Paris Commune – some 24,000 troops – were largely formed out of young lumpenproletarians from fifteen to twenty years of age. Too many Marxists have been inclined to overvalue the second part of Marx's observation – that the lumpenproletariat is capable of the basest banditry and the dirtiest corruption – while minimizing or indeed totally disregarding his first remark, applauding the lumpen for their heroic deeds and exalted sacrifices.

Especially today when so many black, Chicano, and Puerto Rican men and women are jobless as a consequence of the internal dynamic of the capitalist system, the role of the unemployed, which includes the lumpenproletariat in revolutionary struggle, must be given serious thought. Increased unemployment, particularly for the nationally oppressed, will continue to be an inevitable by-product of technological development. At least 30 percent of black youth are presently without jobs. [In 1997, over 30 percent of young black men were in prison, on probation or on parole.] In the context of class exploitation and national oppression it should be clear that numerous individuals are compelled to resort to criminal acts, not as a result of conscious choice – implying other alternatives – but because society has objectively reduced their possibilities of subsistence and survival to this level. This recognition should signal the urgent need to organize the unemployed and lumpenproletariat, as indeed the Black Panther Party as well as activists in prison have already begun to do.

In evaluating the susceptibility of the black and brown unemployed to organizing efforts, the peculiar historical features of the US, specifically racism and national oppression, must be taken into account. There already exists in the black and brown communities, the lumpenproletariat included, a long tradition of collective resistance to national oppression.

Moreover, in assessing the revolutionary potential of prisoners in America as a group, it should be borne in mind that not all prisoners have actually committed crimes. The built-in racism of the judicial system expresses itself, as Du Bois has suggested, in the railroading of countless innocent blacks and other national minorities into the country's coercive institutions.

One must also appreciate the effects of disproportionally long prison terms on black and brown inmates. The typical criminal mentality sees imprisonment as a calculated risk for a particular criminal act. One's prison term is more or less rationally predictable. The function of racism in the judicial-penal complex is to shatter that predictability. The black burglar, anticipating a two- to four-year term, may end up doing ten to fifteen years, while the white burglar leaves after two years.

Within the contained, coercive universe of the prison, the captive is confronted with the realities of racism, not simply as individual acts dictated by attitudinal bias; rather he is compelled to come to grips with racism as an institutional phenomenon collectively experienced by the victims.

The disproportionate representation of the black and brown communities, the manifest racism of parole boards, the intense brutality inherent in the relationship between prison guards and black and brown inmates – all this and more causes the prisoner to be confronted daily, hourly, with the concentrated, systematic existence of racism.

For the innocent prisoner, the process of radicalization should come easy; for the "guilty" victim, the insight into the nature of racism as it manifests itself in the judicial-penal complex can lead to a questioning of his own past criminal activity and a re-evaluation of the methods he has used to survive in a racist and exploitative society. Needless to say, this process is not automatic, it does not occur spontaneously. The persistent educational work carried out by the prison's political activists plays a key role in developing the political potential of captive men and women.

Prisoners – especially blacks, Chicanos, and Puerto Ricans – are increasingly advancing the proposition that they are *political* prisoners. They contend that they are political prisoners in the sense that they are largely the victims of an oppressive politico-economic order, swiftly becoming conscious of the causes underlying their victimization. The *Folsom Prisoners' Manifesto of Demands and Anti-Oppression Platform* attests to a lucid understanding of the structures of oppression within the prison – structures which contradict even the avowed function of the penal institution: "The program we are submitted to, under the ridiculous title of rehabilitation, is relative to the ancient stupidity of pouring water on the drowning man, in as much as we are treated for our hostilities by our program administrators with their hostility as medication." The *Manifesto* also reflects an awareness that the severe social crisis taking place in this country, predicated in part on the ever-increasing mass consciousness of deepening social contradictions, is forcing the political function of the prisons to surface in all its brutality. Their contention that prisons are being transformed into the "fascist concentration camps of modern America," should not be taken lightly, although it would be erroneous as well as defeatist in a practical sense, to maintain that fascism has irremediably established itself.

The point is this, and this is the truth which is apparent in the *Manifesto*: the ruling circles of America are expanding and intensifying repressive measures designed to nip revolutionary movements in the bud as well as to curtail radical-democratic tendencies, such as the movement to end the war in Indochina. The government is not hesitating to utilize an entire network of fascist tactics, including the monitoring of congressmen's telephone calls, a system of "preventive fascism," as Marcuse has termed it, in which the role of the judicial-penal systems looms large. The sharp edge of political repression, cutting through the heightened militancy of the masses, and bringing growing numbers of activists behind prison walls, must necessarily pour over into the contained world of the prison where it understandably acquires far more ruthless forms.

It is a relatively easy matter to persecute the captive whose life is already dominated by a network of authoritarian mechanisms. This is especially facilitated by the indeterminate sentence policies of many states, for politically conscious prisoners will incur inordinately long sentences on their original conviction. According to Louis S. Nelson, warden of San Quentin Prison, "if the prisons of California become known as schools for violent revolution, the Adult Authority would be remiss in their duty not to keep the inmates longer" (*San Francisco Chronicle*, May 2, 1971). Where this is deemed inadequate, authorities have recourse to the whole spectrum of brutal corporal punishment, including out and out murder. At San Quentin, Fred Billingslea was teargassed to death in February 1970. W. L. Nolen, Alvin Miller, and Cleveland Edwards were assassinated by a prison guard in January 1970, at Soledad Prison. Unusual and inexplicable "suicides" have occurred with incredible regularity in jails and prisons throughout the country.

It should be self-evident that the frame-up becomes a powerful weapon within the spectrum of prison repression, particularly because of the availability of informers, the broken prisoners who will do anything for a price. The Soledad Brothers and the Soledad Three are leading examples of frame-up victims. Both cases involve militant activists who have been charged with killing Soledad prison guards. In both cases, widespread support has been kindled within the California prison system. They have served as occasions to link the immediate needs of the black community with a forceful fight to break the fascist stronghold in the prisons and therefore to abolish the prison system in its present form.

Racist oppression invades the lives of black people on an infinite variety of levels. Blacks are imprisoned in a world where our labor and toil hardly allow us to eke out a decent existence, if we are able to find jobs at all. When the economy begins to falter, we are forever the first victims, always the most deeply wounded. When the economy is on its feet, we continue to live in a depressed state. Unemployment is generally twice as high in the ghettos as it is in the country as a whole and even higher among black women and youth. The unemployment rate among black youth has presently skyrocketed to 30 percent. If one-third of America's white youths were without a means of livelihood, we would either be in the thick of revolution or else under the iron rule of fascism. Substandard schools, medical care hardly fit for animals, over-priced, dilapidated housing, a welfare system based on a policy of skimpy concessions, designed to degrade and divide (and even this may soon be canceled) – this is only the beginning of the list of props in the overall scenery of oppression which, for the mass of blacks, is the universe.

In black communities, wherever they are located, there exists an ever-present reminder that our universe must remain stable in its drabness, its poverty, its brutality. From Birmingham to Harlem to Watts, black ghettos are occupied, patrolled and often attacked by massive deployments of police. The police, domestic caretakers of violence, are the oppressor's emissaries, charged with the task of containing us within the boundaries of our oppression.

The announced function of the police, "to protect and serve the people," becomes the grotesque caricature of protecting and preserving the interests of our oppressors and serving us nothing but injustice. They are there to intimidate blacks, to persuade us with their violence that we are powerless to alter the conditions of our lives. Arrests are frequently based on whims. Bullets from their guns murder human beings with little or no pretext, aside from the universal intimidation they are charged with carrying out. Protection for drug-pushers, and Mafia-style exploiters, support for the most reactionary ideological elements of the black community (especially those who cry out for more police), are among the many functions of forces of law and order. They encircle the community with a shield of violence, too often forcing the natural aggression of the black community inwards. Fanon's analysis of the role of colonial police is an appropriate description of the function of the police in America's ghettos.

It goes without saying that the police would be unable to set into motion their racist machinery were they not sanctioned and supported by the judicial system. The courts not only consistently abstain from prosecuting criminal behavior on the part of the police, but they convict, on the basis of biased police testimony, countless black men and women. Court-appointed attorneys, acting in the twisted interests of overcrowded courts, convince 85 percent of the defendants to plead guilty. Even the manifestly innocent are advised to cop a plea so that the lengthy and expensive process of jury trials is avoided. This is the structure of the apparatus which summarily railroads black people into jails and prisons. (During my imprisonment in the New York Women's House of Detention, I encountered numerous cases involving innocent black women who had been advised to plead guilty. One sister had entered her white landlord's apartment for the purpose of paying rent. He attempted to rape her and in the course of the ensuing struggle, a lit candle toppled over, burning a tablecloth. The landlord ordered her arrested for arson. Following the advice of her court-appointed attorney, she entered a guilty plea, having been deceived by the attorney's insistence that the court would be more lenient. The sister was sentenced to three years.)

The vicious circle linking poverty, police courts, and prison is an integral element of ghetto existence. Unlike the mass of whites, the path which leads to jails and prisons is deeply rooted in the imposed patterns of black existence. For this very reason, an almost instinctive affinity binds the mass of black people to the political prisoners. The vast majority of blacks harbor a deep hatred of the police and are not deluded by official proclamations of justice through the courts.

For the black individual, contact with the law-enforcement–judicial-penal network, directly or through relatives and friends, is inevitable because he or she is black. For the activist become political prisoner, the contact has occurred because he has lodged a protest, in one form or another, against the conditions which nail blacks to this orbit of oppression.

Historically, black people as a group have exhibited a greater potential for resistance than any other part of the population. The iron-clad rule over our communities, the institutional practice of genocide, the ideology of racism have performed a strictly political as well as an economic function. The capitalists have not only extracted super profits from the underpaid labor of over 15 percent of the American population with the aid of a superstructure of terror. This terror and more subtle forms of racism have further served to thwart the flowering of a resistance – even a revolution – that would spread to the working class as a whole.

In the interests of the capitalist class, the consent to racism and terror has been demagogically elicited from the white population, workers included, in order to more efficiently stave off resistance. Today, Nixon, [Attorney General John] Mitchell and J. Edgar Hoover are desperately attempting to persuade the population that dissidents, particularly blacks, Chicanos, Puerto Ricans, must be punished for being members of revolutionary organizations; for advocating the overthrow of the government; for agitating and educating in the streets and behind prison walls. The political function of racist domination is surfacing with accelerated intensity. Whites who have professed their solidarity with the black liberation movement and have moved in a distinctly revolutionary direction find themselves targets of the same repression. Even the anti-war movement, rapidly exhibiting an anti-imperialist consciousness, is falling victim to government repression.

Black people are rushing full speed ahead towards an understanding of the circumstances that give rise to exaggerated forms of political repression and thus an overabundance of political prisoners. This understanding is being forged out of the raw material of their own immediate experiences with racism. Hence, the black masses are growing conscious of their responsibility to defend those who are being persecuted for attempting to bring about the alleviation of the most injurious immediate problems facing black communities and ultimately to bring about total liberation through armed revolution, if it must come to this.

The black liberation movement is presently at a critical juncture. Fascist methods of repression threaten to physically decapitate and obliterate the movement. More subtle, yet no less dangerous ideological tendencies from within threaten to isolate the black movement and diminish its revolutionary impact. Both menaces must be counteracted in order to ensure our survival. Revolutionary blacks must spearhead and provide leadership for a broad anti-fascist movement.

Fascism is a process, its growth and development are cancerous in nature. While today, the threat of fascism may be primarily restricted to the use of the law-enforcement–judicial-penal apparatus to arrest the overt and latent revolutionary trends among nationally oppressed people, tomorrow it may attack the working class *en masse* and eventually even moderate democrats. Even in this period, however, the cancer has already commenced to spread. In addition to the prison army of thousands and thousands of nameless Third World victims of political revenge, there are increasing numbers of white political prisoners – draft resisters, anti-war activists such as the Harrisburg Eight, men and women who have involved themselves on all levels of revolutionary activity.

Among the further symptoms of the fascist threat are official efforts to curtail the power of organized labor, such as the attack on the manifestly conservative construction workers and the trends towards reduced welfare aid. Moreover, court decisions and repressive legislation augmenting police powers – such as the Washington no-knock law, permitting police to enter private dwellings without warning, and Nixon's "Crime Bill" in general – can eventually be used against any citizen. Indeed congressmen are already protesting the use of police-state wire-tapping to survey their activities. The fascist content of the ruthless aggression in Indo-China should be self-evident.

One of the fundamental historical lessons to be learned from past failures to prevent the rise of fascism is the decisive and indispensable character of the fight against fascism in its incipient phases. Once allowed to conquer ground, its growth is facilitated in geometric proportion. Although the most unbridled expressions of the fascist menace are still tied to the racist domination of blacks, Chicanos, Puerto Ricans, Indians, it lurks under the surface wherever there is potential resistance to the power of monopoly capital, the parasitic interests which control this society. Potentially it can profoundly worsen the conditions of existence for the average American citizen. Consequently, the masses of people in this country have a real, direct, and material stake in the struggle to free political prisoners, the struggle to abolish the prison system in its present form, the struggle against all dimensions of racism.

No one should fail to take heed of Georgi Dimitrov's warning: "Whoever does not fight the growth of fascism at these preparatory stages is not in a position to prevent the victory of fascism, but, on the contrary, facilitates that victory" (Report to the VIIth Congress of the Communist International, 1935). The only effective guarantee against the victory of fascism is an indivisible mass movement which refuses to conduct business as usual as long as repression rages on. It is only natural that blacks and other Third World peoples must lead this movement, for we are the first and most deeply injured victims of fascism. But it must embrace all potential victims and most important, all working-class people, for the key to the triumph of fascism is its ideological victory over the entire working class. Given the eruption of a severe economic crisis, the door to such an ideological victory can be opened by the active approval or passive toleration of racism. It is essential that white workers become conscious that historically through their acquiescence in the capitalist-inspired oppression of blacks they have only rendered themselves more vulnerable to attack.

The pivotal struggle which must be waged in the ranks of the working class is consequently the open, unreserved battle against entrenched racism. The white worker must become conscious of the threads which bind him to a James Johnson, a black auto worker, member of UAW, and a political prisoner presently facing charges for the killings of two foremen and a job setter.[6] The merciless proliferation of the power of monopoly capital may ultimately push him inexorably down the very same path of desperation. No potential victim [of the fascist terror] should be without the knowledge that the greatest menace to racism and fascism is unity!

MARIN COUNTY JAIL
May, 1971

NOTES

1   William Z. Foster, *The Negro People in American History* (New York: International Publishers, 1954), 169–70 (quoting Herbert Aptheker).
2   Louis Adamic, *Dynamite: The History of Class Violence in America* (Gloucester, MA: Peter Smith, 1963), 312.
3   Herbert Aptheker, *Nat Turner's Slave Rebellion* (New York: Grove Press, 1968), 45. According to Aptheker these are not Nat Turner's exact words.
4   W. E. B. Du Bois, *Autobiography of W. E. B. Du Bois* (New York: International Publishers, 1968), 390.
5   Karl Marx, "The Class Struggle in France," in *Handbook of Marxism* (New York: International Publishers, 1935), 109.
6   See Angela Y. Davis (ed.), *If They Come in the Morning: Voices of Resistance* (New York: Third Press, 1971); see chapter five on political prisoners for the details of James Johnson's case.

3

Unfinished Lecture on Liberation – II

One of the striking paradoxes of the bourgeois ideological tradition resides in an enduring philosophical emphasis on the idea of freedom alongside an equally pervasive failure to acknowledge the denial of freedom to entire categories of real, social human beings. In ancient Greece, whose legacy of democracy inspired some of the great bourgeois thinkers, citizenship in the *polis*, the real exercise of freedom, was not accessible to the majority of people. Women were not allowed to be citizens and slavery was an uncontested institution. While the lofty notions affirming human liberty were being formulated by those who penned the United States Constitution, Afro-Americans lived and labored in chains. Not even the term "slavery" was allowed to mar the sublime concepts articulated in the Constitution, which euphemistically refers to "persons held to service or labor" as those exceptional human beings who did not merit the rights and guarantees otherwise extended to all.

Are human beings free or are they not? Ought they be free or ought they not be free? The history of Afro-American literature furnishes an illuminating account of the nature of freedom, its extent and limits. Moreover, we should discover in black literature an important perspective that is missing in so many of the discourses on the theme of freedom in the history of bourgeois philosophy. Afro-American literature incorporates the consciousness of a people who have been continually denied entrance into the real world of freedom, a people whose struggles and aspirations have exposed the inadequacies not only of the practice of freedom, but also of its very theoretical formulation.

The central issue of this course "Recurring Philosophical Themes in Black Literature" will be the idea of freedom. Commencing with the *Life*

This essay is based on the second lecture of a 1969 UCLA course, "Recurring Philosophical Themes in Black Literature." It was originally published in *Philosophy Born of Struggle: Anthology of Afro-American Philosophy from 1917*, ed. Leonard Harris (Dubuque IA: Kendall Hunt, 1983). Reprinted by permission of the editor and the Kendall Hunt Publishing Company.

and Times of Frederick Douglass, I will explore the slave's experience of bondage as the basis for a transformation of the principle of freedom into a dynamic, active struggle for liberation. I will then examine the ideas of the great twentieth-century Afro-American thinker W. E. B. Du Bois, and will proceed to trace black ideological development in literature up to the contemporary era. In conclusion, this course will compare the writings of a few representative African and Caribbean writers with the works of Afro-Americans. In each instance, the notion of freedom will be the axis around which we will attempt to develop other philosophical concepts such as the meaning of knowledge, the function of morality, and the perception of history peculiar to an oppressed people striving toward the goal of collective liberation.

Before actually approaching the material, we should familiarize ourselves with some of the questions posed in this exploration of the nature of human freedom. First of all, is freedom an essentially subjective experience? Is it essentially objective? Or is it rather a synthesis of both these poles? In other words, should freedom be conceived as an inherent characteristic of the human mind, whose expression is primarily inward? Or is it a goal to be realized through human action in the real, objective world? Freedom of thought? Freedom of action? Freedom as practical realization? Freedom of the individual? Freedom of the collective? Consider, for instance, this aspect of the philosophy of freedom proposed by the French existentialist Jean-Paul Sartre. Because it is in the nature of the human being to be "condemned to freedom," even those who are held in chains remain essentially free, for they are always at liberty to eliminate their condition of slavery, if only because death is an alternative to captivity. Considering the African's real experience of slavery on this continent, would you attempt to argue that the black slave was essentially free since even in bondage, a person retains the freedom to choose between captivity and death? Or rather would you detect a basic incompatibility between this notion and the real prerequisites of liberation? Would you agree, in other words, that when the slave opts for death, the resulting elimination of the predicament of slavery also abolishes the fundamental condition of freedom, that is, the slave's experience of living, human reality. Nat Turner and Denmark Vesey met with death at the conclusion of the slave revolts they so courageously led, but was it death they chose or was it liberation for their people even at the risk of death for themselves as individuals?

The slave who grasps the real significance of freedom understands that it does not ultimately entail the ability to choose death over life as a slave, but rather the ability to strive toward the abolition of the master–slave relationship itself.

The first part of the *Life and Times of Frederick Douglass*, which is entitled "Life of a Slave," traces both a material and philosophical journey from slavery to freedom. The point of departure is occasioned by the following question posed by Frederick Douglass the child: "Why am I a slave? Why are some people slaves and others masters?" Douglass, of course, has rejected the usual religious explanations based on the belief that God's will was responsible for black people being condemned to lives of bondage and for the slave-masters being bearers of white skin. As the question itself implies, Douglass has also challenged the credibility of all other apologetic theories regarding slavery in the history of Western ideas.

The slave is a human being whom another has absolutely denied the right to express his or her freedom. But is not freedom a property that belongs to the very essence of the human being? Either the slave is not a human being or else the very existence of the slave is itself a contradiction. Of course the prevailing racist ideology, which defined people of African descent as subhuman, was simply a distortion within the realm of ideas based on real and systematic efforts to deny black people their rightful status as human beings. In order to perpetuate the institution of slavery, Africans were forcibly compelled to live and labor under conditions hardly fit for animals. The slave-holder class was determined to fashion black people in the image of those subhumans described in the ideology justifying the oppression meted out to slaves. In this sense, it was the slave-holder whose consciousness was a slave to the socio-economic system that relegated to him the role of oppressor. The master's notion of freedom, in fact, involved this capacity to control the lives of others – the master felt himself free at the expense of the freedom of another. As the conscious slave certainly realized, this merely abstract freedom to suppress the lives of others rendered the master a slave of his own misconceptions, his own misdeeds, his own brutality and infliction of oppression.

If the slave-holder was entrapped within a vicious circle, there was a potential exit gate for the slave: the slave could opt for active resistance. These are the reflections Frederick Douglass offers on his childhood experience of observing a slave resist a flogging: "That slave who had the courage to stand up for himself against the overseer, although he might have many hard stripes at first, became while legally a slave virtually a free man. 'You can shoot me', said a slave to Rigby Hopkins, 'but you can't whip me', and the result was he was neither whipped nor shot." In this posture of resistance, the rudiments of freedom were already present. The stance of self-defense signified far more than a simple refusal to submit to a flogging, for it was also an implicit rejection of the entire institution of slavery, its standards, its morality. It was a microcosmic effort toward liberation.

The slave could thus become conscious of the fact that freedom is not a static quality, a given, but rather is the goal of an active process, something to be fought for, something to be gained in and through the process of struggle. The slave-master, on the other hand, experienced what he defined as his freedom as an inalienable fact: he could hardly become aware that he, too, had been enslaved by the system over which he appeared to rule.

To return to a question we posed earlier – is it possible for a human being to be free within the limits of slavery? – we can argue that the path toward freedom can only be envisioned by the slave when the chains, the lash, and the whipping post of slavery are actively challenged. The first phase of liberation must thus involve a rejection of the material conditions and ideological images contrived in the interests of the slave-holder class. The slave must reject his/her existence as a slave. In the words of Frederick Douglass, "nature never intended that men and women should be either slaves or slave-holders, and nothing but rigid training long persisted in, can perfect the character of the one or the other." Slavery is an alienation from the human condition, a violation of humanity that distorts both parties, but that fundamentally alienates the slave from the freedom to which every human being ought to have a right. This alienation can remain unacknowledged and unchallenged, or it can be recognized in such a way as to provide a theoretical impetus for a practical thrust in the direction of freedom.

The most extreme form of human alienation is the reduction of a productive and thinking human being to the status of property: "Personality swallowed up in the sordid idea of property! Manhood lost in chattelhood! . . . Our destiny was to be *fixed for life*, and we had no more voice in the decision of the question than the oxen and cows that stood chewing at the haymow" (Douglass). "The slave was a fixture," Frederick Douglass compellingly argued. "He had no choice, no goal, but was pegged down to one single spot, and must take root there or nowhere." The slave exercised no control whatsoever over the external circumstances of his/her life. On one day, a woman might be living and working among her children, their father, her relatives, and friends. The very next day she might be headed for a destination miles and miles away, journeying far beyond the possibility of ever again encountering those with whom she had enjoyed intimate contacts for years. For the slave, "his going out into the world was like a living man going into the tomb, who, with open eyes, sees himself buried out of sight and hearing of wife, children, and friends of kindred tie." Describing a related experience, Douglass presents a moving account of his grandmother's last days. Having faithfully served her master from his birth to his death, having borne children for him, she is disdainfully dismissed by her original master's grandson. This old woman is banished from the plantation and sent into the woods to die a horrible, solitary death.

Although unwittingly, Douglass's owner reveals a way for the young boy to become cognizant of his alienation as a slave: "If you give a nigger an inch he will take an ell. Learning will spoil the best nigger in the world. If he learns to read the Bible it will forever unfit him to be a slave. He should know nothing but the will of his master and learn to obey it." In other words, as long as the slave accepts the master's will as the absolute authority over his/her life, the alienation is absolute. With no effective will of one's own, with no realizable desires of one's own, the slave must seek the essence of his/her being in the will of the master. What does this mean? In an important sense, it is the slave's consent that permits the master to perpetuate the condition of slavery – not, of course, free consent, but rather consent based on brutality and force.

Having overheard his master's observations on the revolutionary potential of knowledge, Frederick Douglass reflects: "'Very well,' thought I, 'Knowledge unfits a child to be a slave.' I instinctively assented to the proposition, and from that moment I understood the direct pathway from slavery to freedom." Looking closely at these words, we detect once again the theme of resistance. Douglass's first enlightening experience regarding the possibility of a slave asserting his yearning for freedom involved resistance to a flogging. He later discovers resistance in the form of education, resistance of the mind, a refusal to accept the will of the slave-master, a determination to seek an independent means of judging the world around him.

As the slave who challenged his master to whip him and threatened to physically resist his aggressor's violent lashes, Frederick Douglass appropriates his master's insight – that is, learning unfits a person to be a slave – and vows to use it against his oppressor. Resistance, rejection, physical and mental, are fundamental moments of the journey toward freedom. In the beginning, however, it is inevitable that knowledge, as a process leading to a more profound comprehension of the meaning of slavery, results in despair: "When I was about thirteen years old, and had succeeded in learning to read, every increase of knowledge, especially anything respecting the free states, was an additional weight to the most intolerable burden of my thought – '*I am a slave for life.*' To my bondage I could see no end. It was a terrible reality, and I shall never be able to tell how sadly that thought chafed my young spirit."

The child's despair gives way to an emerging consciousness of his alienated existence. He begins to seek freedom as the negation of his concrete condition – in fact, it seems to be present as the negation of the very air he breathes:

> Liberty, as the inestimable birthright of every man, converted every object into an asserter of this right. I heard it in every sound and saw it in every object. It was ever-present to torment me with a sense of my wretchedness, the more horrible and desolate was my condition. I saw nothing without seeing it and I heard nothing without hearing it. I do not exaggerate when I say that it looked at me in every star, smiled in every calm, breathed in every wind and moved in every storm.

Frederick Douglass has arrived at a consciousness of his predicament as a slave. That consciousness at the same time is a rejection of his predicament. But enlightenment does not result in *real* freedom, or even a mental state of pleasure. Referring to his mistress, Douglass says: "She aimed to keep me ignorant, and I resolved to *know*, although knowledge only increased my misery." Moreover, the slave has not simply rejected his individual condition and his misery does not simply result from his consciousness of his alienation as an individual. "It was *slavery* and not its mere *incidents* that I hated." True consciousness involves a rejection of the institution itself and all of the institution's accompaniments.

As he moves down the pathway from slavery to freedom, Douglass experiences religion as a reinforcement and justification of his yearning for liberation. Out of the doctrines of Christianity, he deduces the equality of all human beings before God. If this is true, he infers, then slave-masters are defying God's will and should consequently suffer God's wrath. Freedom, liberation, the abolition of slavery, the elimination of human alienation – all these visions are given a metaphysical foundation. A supernatural being wills the abolition of slavery and Douglass, slave and believer, must execute God's will by striving toward the aim of liberation. Of course, he was not alone in his efforts to forge a theology of liberation on the basis of the Christian doctrine. Nat Turner's rebellion and John Brown's attack were among the innumerable anti-slavery actions directly inspired by Christianity.

Christianity, when it was offered to the masses of slaves, was originally destined to serve precisely the opposite purpose. Religion was to furnish a metaphysical justification not for freedom, but rather for the institution of slavery itself.

One of the most widely quoted, but least understood passages in the writings of Karl Marx concerns religion as the "opium of the people." This is generally assumed to simply mean that the function of religion is to counsel acquiescence toward worldly oppression and to redirect hopes and yearnings of oppressed people into the supernatural realm. A little suffering during a person's lifetime in the real world is entirely insignificant in comparison with an eternity of bliss. But what is the larger context of Marx's assertion, which is contained in the opening paragraphs of his *Introduction to a Critique of Hegel's Philosophy of Right?* Marx writes:

> *Religious* suffering is at the same time an *expression* of real suffering and a *protest* against real suffering. Religion is the sigh of the oppressed creature, the sentiment of a heartless world, and the soul of soulless conditions. It is the *opium* of the people. The abolition of religion as the *illusory* happiness of men, is a demand for their *real* happiness. The call to abandon their illusions about their condition is a *call to abandon a condition which requires illusions.*

In other words, it is true indeed that real wants, real needs, and real desires can be transformed into impotent wish-dreams via the process of religion, especially if things appear to be utterly hopeless in this world. But it is also true that these dreams can revert to their original state – as real wishes, real needs to change the existing social reality. It is possible to redirect these wish-dreams to the here and now. Frederick Douglass attempted to redirect aspirations that were expressed within a religious context and, like Nat Turner and countless others, placed them within the framework of the real world. Religion can play a potentially revolutionary role since – for oppressed people, at least – its very nature is to satisfy urgent needs grounded in the real, social world.

In his work *The Peculiar Institution*, Kenneth Stampp extensively discusses the role of religion as a vehicle of appeasement for black people, as a means of suppressing potential revolt. In the beginning, he observes, Africans were not converted to Christianity, because this might have established for the slaves a solid argument for freedom. However, the slave-holding colonies eventually began to pass legislation to the effect that black Christians were not to become free simply by virtue of their baptism. Stampp formulates the reasons why slaves could be allowed to enter the sacred doors of Christianity:

> Through religious instruction, the bondman learned that slavery had divine sanction, that insolence was as much an offense against God as against the temporal master. They received the Biblical command that servants should obey their masters and they heard of the punishments awaiting the disobedient slave in the hereafter. They heard, too, that eternal salvation would be their reward for faithful service and that on the day of judgment God would deal impartially with the poor and the rich, the black man and the white.

Thus those passages in the Bible emphasizing obedience, humility, pacifism, patience, were presented to the slave as the essence of Christianity. On the other hand, those passages that emphasized equality, freedom, and happiness as attributes of this world as well as the next – those that Frederick Douglass discovered after teaching himself the illegal activity of reading, were eliminated from the official sermons destined to be heard by slaves. Thus a censored version of Christianity was developed especially for the slaves, and one who emulated the slave-master's piety would never strike a white man and would believe that his master was always right even though the oppressor might violate all human standards of morality. Yet there is no lack of evidence that new criteria for religious piety were developed within the slave community: the militant posture of a Frederick Douglass, a Harriet Tubman, a Gabriel Prosser, and a Nat Turner, and the fact that the Christian spirituals created and sung by the masses of slaves were also powerful songs of freedom demonstrate the extent to which Christianity could be rescued from the ideological context forged by the slave-holders and imbued with a revolutionary content of liberation.

Frederick Douglass's response to Nat Turner's revolt is revealing:

The insurrection of Nat Turner had been quelled, but the alarm and terror which it occasioned had not subsided. The cholera was then on its way to this country, and I remember thinking that God was angry with the white people because of their slave-holding wickedness, and therefore his judgments were abroad in the land. Of course it was impossible for me not to hope much for the abolition movement when I saw it supported by the Almighty, and armed with death.

4

Race and Criminalization: Black Americans and the Punishment Industry

In this post-civil-rights era, as racial barriers in high economic and political realms are apparently shattered with predictable regularity, race itself becomes an increasingly proscribed subject. In the dominant political discourse it is no longer acknowledged as a pervasive structural phenomenon, requiring the continuation of such strategies as affirmative action, but rather is represented primarily as a complex of prejudicial attitudes, which carry equal weight across all racial boundaries. Black leadership is thus often discredited and the identification of race as a public, political issue itself called into question through the invocation of, and application of the epithet "black racist" to such figures as Louis Farrakhan and Khalid Abdul Muhammad. Public debates about the role of the state that once focused very sharply and openly on issues of "race" and racism are now expected to unfold in the absence of any direct acknowledgment of the persistence – and indeed further entrenchment – of racially structured power relationships. Because race is ostracized from some of the most impassioned political debates of this period, their racialized character becomes increasingly difficult to identify, especially by those who are unable – or do not want – to decipher the encoded language. This means that hidden racist arguments can be mobilized readily across racial boundaries and political alignments. Political positions once easily defined as conservative, liberal, and sometimes even radical therefore have a tendency to lose their distinctiveness in the face of the seductions of this camouflaged racism.

President Clinton chose the date of the Million Man March, convened by Minister Louis Farrakhan of the Nation of Islam, to issue a call for a "national conversation on race," borrowing ironically the exact words of Lani Guinier (whose nomination for Assistant Attorney General in charge of civil rights he had previously withdrawn because her writings focused too sharply on issues of race).[1] Guinier's ideas had been so easily dismissed because of the prevailing ideological equation of the "end of racism" with the removal of all allusions to race. If conservative positions argue that race consciousness itself impedes the process of solving the problem of race – i.e., achieving race blindness – then Clinton's speech indicated an attempt to reconcile the two, positing race consciousness as a means of moving toward race blindness. "There are too many today, white and black, on the left and the right, on the street corners and radio waves, who seek to sow division for their own purposes. To them I say: 'No more. We must be one.'"

While Clinton did acknowledge "the awful history and stubborn persistence of racism," his remarks foregrounded those reasons for the "racial divide" that "are rooted in the fact that we still haven't learned to talk frankly, to listen carefully and to work together across racial lines." Race, he insisted, is not about government, but about the hearts of people. Of course, it would be absurd to deny the degree to which racism infects in deep and multiple ways the national psyche. However, the relegation of race to matters of the heart tends to render it increasingly difficult to identify the deep structural entrenchment of contemporary racism.

When the structural character of racism is ignored in discussions about crime and the rising population of incarcerated people, the racial imbalance in jails and prisons is treated as a contingency, at best as a product of the "culture of poverty," and at worst as proof of an assumed black monopoly on criminality. The high proportion of black people in the criminal justice system is thus normalized and neither the state nor the general public is required to talk about and act on the meaning of that racial imbalance. Thus Republican and Democratic elected officials alike have successfully called for laws mandating life sentences for three-time "criminals," without having to answer for the racial implications of these laws. By relying on the alleged "race-blindness" of such laws, black people are surreptitiously constructed as racial subjects, thus manipulated, exploited, and abused, while the structural persistence of racism – albeit in changed forms – in social and economic institutions, and in the national culture as a whole, is adamantly denied.

Crime is thus one of the masquerades behind which "race," with all its menacing ideological complexity, mobilizes old public fears and creates new ones. The current anti-crime debate takes place within a reified mathematical realm – a strategy reminiscent of Malthus's notion of the geometrical increase in population and the arithmetical increase in food sources, thus the inevitability of poverty and the means of suppressing it: war, disease, famine, and natural disasters. As a matter of fact, the persisting neo-Malthusian approach to population control, which, instead of seeking to solve those pressing social problems that result in real pain and suffering in people's lives, calls for the elimination of those suffering lives – finds strong resonances in the public discussion about expurgating the "nation" of crime. These discussions include arguments deployed by those who are leading the call for more prisons and employ statistics in the same fetishistic and misleading way as Malthus did more than two centuries ago. Take for example James Wooten's comments in the *Heritage Foundation State Backgrounder*:

> If the 55 percent of the estimated 800,000 current state and federal prisoners who are violent offenders were subject to serving 85 percent of their sentence, and assuming that those violent offenders would have committed 10 violent crimes a year while on the street, then the number of crimes prevented each year by truth in sentencing would be 4,000,000. That would be over $\frac{2}{3}$ of the 6,000,000 violent crimes reported.[2]

In *Reader's Digest*, Senior Editor Eugene H. Methvin writes:

> If we again double the present federal and state prison population – to somewhere between 1 million and 1.5 million and leave our city and county jail population at the present 400,000, we will break the back of America's thirty-year crime wave.[3]

The real human beings – a vastly disproportionate number of whom are black and Latino/a men and women – designated by these numbers in a seemingly race-neutral way are deemed fetishistically exchangeable with the crimes they have already committed or will allegedly commit in the future. The real impact of imprisonment on their lives never need be examined. The inevitable part played by the punishment industry in the reproduction of crime never need be discussed. The dangerous and indeed fascistic trend toward progressively greater numbers of hidden, incarcerated human populations is itself rendered invisible. All that matters is the elimination of crime – and you get rid of crime by getting rid of people who, according to the prevailing racial common sense, are the most likely people to whom criminal acts will be attributed. Never mind that if this strategy is seriously and consistently pursued, the majority of young black men and a fast-growing proportion of young black women will spend a good portion of their lives behind walls and bars in order to serve as a reminder that the state is aggressively confronting its enemy.[4]

While I do not want to locate a response to these arguments on the same level of mathematical abstraction and fetishism I have been problematizing, it is helpful, I think, to consider how many people are presently incarcerated or whose lives are subject to the direct surveillance of the criminal justice system. There are already approximately 1 million people in state and federal prisons in the United States, not counting the 500,000 in city and county jails or the 600,000 on parole or the 3 million people on probation or the 60,000 young people in juvenile facilities. Which is to say that there are presently over 5.1 million people either incarcerated, on parole, or on probation. Many of those presently on probation or parole would be behind bars under the conditions of the recently passed crime bill. According to the Sentencing Project, even before the passage of the crime bill, black people were 7.8 times more likely to be imprisoned than whites.[5] The Sentencing Project's most recent report[6] indicates that 32.2 percent of young black men and 12.3 percent of young Latino men between the ages of twenty and twenty-nine are either in prison, in jail, or on probation or parole. This is in comparison with 6.7 percent of young white men. A total of 827,440 young African-American males are under the supervision of the criminal justice system, at a cost of $6 billion per year. A major strength of the 1995 report, as compared to its predecessor, is its acknowledgment that the racialized impact of the criminal justice system is also gendered and that the relatively smaller number of African-American women drawn into the system should not relieve us of the responsibility of understanding the encounter of gender and race in arrest and incarceration practices. Moreover, the increases in women's contact with the criminal justice system have been even more dramatic than those of men.

> The 78 percent increase in criminal justice control rates for black women was more than double the increase for black men and for white women, and more than nine times the increase for white men. . . . Although research on women of color in the criminal justice system is limited, existing data and research suggest that it is the combination of race and sex effects that is at the root of the trends which appear in our data. For example, while the number of blacks and Hispanics in prison is growing at an alarming rate, the rate of increase for women is even greater. Between 1980 and 1992 the female prison population increased 276 percent, compared to 163 percent for men. Unlike men of color, women of color thus belong to two groups that are experiencing particular dramatic growth in their contact with the criminal justice system.[7]

It has been estimated that by the year 2000 the number of people imprisoned will surpass 2 million, a grossly disproportionate number of whom will be black people, and that the cost will be over $40 billion a year,[8] a figure that is reminiscent of the way the military budget devoured – and continues to devour – the country's resources. This out-of-control punishment industry is an extremely effective criminalization industry, for the racial imbalance in incarcerated populations is not recognized as evidence of structural racism, but rather is invoked as a consequence of the assumed criminality of black people. In other words, the criminalization process works so well precisely because of the hidden logic of racism. Racist logic is deeply entrenched in the nation's material and psychic structures. It is something with which we all are very familiar. The logic, in fact, can persist, even when direct allusions to "race" are removed.

Even those communities that are most deeply injured by this racist logic have learned how to rely upon it, particularly when open allusions to race are not necessary. Thus, in the absence of broad, radical grassroots movements in poor black communities so devastated by new forms of youth-perpetrated violence, the ideological options are extremely sparse. Often there are no other ways to express collective rage and despair but to demand that police sweep the community clean of crack and Uzis, and of the people who use and sell drugs and wield weapons. Ironically, Carol Moseley-Braun, the first black woman senator in our nation's history, was an enthusiastic sponsor of the Senate Anticrime Bill, whose passage in November 1993 paved the way for the August 25, 1994, passage of the bill by the House. Or perhaps there is little irony here. It may be precisely because there is a Carol Moseley-Braun in the Senate and a Clarence Thomas in the Supreme Court – and concomitant class differentiations and other factors responsible for far more heterogeneity in black communities than at any other time in this country's history – that implicit consent to antiblack racist logic (not to speak of racism toward other groups) becomes far more widespread among black people. Wahneema Lubiano's explorations of the complexities of state domination as it operates within and through the subjectivities of those who are the targets of this domination facilitates an understanding of this dilemma.[9]

Borrowing the title of Cornel West's recent work, race *matters*. Moreover, it matters in ways that are far more threatening and simultaneously less discernible than those to which we have grown accustomed. Race matters inform, more than ever, the ideological and material structures of US society. And, as the current discourses on crime, welfare, and immigration reveal, race, gender, and class matter enormously in the continuing elaboration of public policy and its impact on the real lives of human beings.

And how does race matter? Fear has always been an integral component of racism. The ideological reproduction of a fear of black people, whether economically or sexually grounded, is rapidly gravitating toward and being grounded in a fear of crime. A question to be raised in this context is whether and how the increasing fear of crime – this ideologically produced fear of crime – serves to render racism simultaneously more invisible and more virulent. Perhaps one way to approach an answer to this question is to consider how this fear of crime effectively summons black people to imagine black people as the enemy. How many black people present at this conference have successfully extricated ourselves from the ideological power of the figure of the young black male as criminal – or at least seriously confronted it? The lack of a significant black presence in the rather feeble opposition to the "three strikes, you're out" bills, which have been proposed and/or passed in forty states already, evidences the disarming effect of this ideology.

California is one of the states that has passed the "three strikes, you're out" bill. Immediately after the passage of that bill, Governor Pete Wilson began to argue for a "two strikes, you're out" bill. Three, he said, is too many. Soon we will hear calls for "one strike, you're out." Following this mathematical regression, we can imagine that at some point the hardcore anticrime advocates will be arguing that to stop the crime wave, we can't wait until even one crime is committed. Their slogan will be: "Get them before the first strike!" And because certain populations have already been criminalized, there will be those who say, "We know who the real criminals are – let's get them before they have a chance to act out their criminality."

The fear of crime has attained a status that bears a sinister similarity to the fear of communism as it came to restructure social perceptions during the fifties and sixties. The figure of the "criminal" – the racialized figure of the criminal – has come to represent the most menacing enemy of "American society." Virtually anything is acceptable – torture, brutality, vast expenditures of public funds – as long as it is done in the name of public safety. Racism has always found an easy route from its embeddedness in social structures to the psyches of collectives and individuals precisely because it mobilizes deep fears. While explicit, old-style racism may be increasingly socially unacceptable – precisely as a result of antiracist movements over the last forty years – this does not mean that US society has been purged of racism. In fact, racism is more deeply embedded in socio-economic structures, and the vast populations of incarcerated people of color is dramatic evidence of the way racism systematically structures economic relations. At the same time, this structural racism is rarely recognized as "racism." What we have come to recognize as open, explicit racism has in many ways begun to be replaced by a secluded, camouflaged kind of racism, whose influence on people's daily lives is as pervasive and systematic as the explicit forms of racism associated with the era of the struggle for civil rights.

The ideological space for the proliferations of this racialized fear of crime has been opened by the transformations in international politics created by the fall of the European socialist countries. Communism is no longer the quintessential enemy against which the nation imagines its identity. This space is now inhabited by ideological constructions of crime, drugs, immigration, and welfare. Of course, the enemy within is far more dangerous than the enemy without, and a black enemy within is the most dangerous of all.

Because of the tendency to view it as an abstract site into which all manner of undesirables are deposited, the prison is the perfect site for the simultaneous production and concealment of racism. The abstract character of the public perception of prisons militates against an engagement with the real issues afflicting the communities from which prisoners are drawn in such disproportionate numbers. This is the ideological work that the prison performs – it relieves us of the responsibility of seriously engaging with the problems of late capitalism, of transnational capitalism. The naturalization of black people as criminals thus also erects ideological barriers to an understanding of the connections between late twentieth-century structural racism and the globalization of capital.

The vast expansion of the power of capitalist corporations over the lives of people of color and poor people in general has been accompanied by a waning anticapitalist consciousness. As capital moves with ease across national borders, legitimized by recent trade agreements such as NAFTA [North American Free Trade Agreement] and GATT [General Agreement on Tariffs and Trade], corporations are allowed to close shop in the United States and transfer manufacturing operations to nations providing cheap labor pools. In fleeing organized labor in the US to avoid paying higher wages and benefits, they leave entire communities in shambles, consigning huge numbers of people to joblessness, leaving them prey to the drug trade, destroying the economic base of these communities, thus affecting the education system, social welfare – and turning the people who live in those communities into perfect candidates for prison. At the same time, they create an economic demand for prisons, which stimulates the economy, providing jobs in the correctional industry for people who often come from the very populations that are criminalized by this process. It is a horrifying and self-reproducing cycle.

Ironically, prisons themselves are becoming a source of cheap labor that attracts corporate capitalism – as yet on a relatively small scale – in a way that parallels the attraction unorganized labor in Third World countries exerts. A statement by Michael Lamar Powell, a prisoner in Capshaw, Alabama, dramatically reveals this new development:

> I cannot go on strike, nor can I unionize. I am not covered by workers' compensation of the Fair Labor Standards Act. I agree to work late-night and weekend shifts. I do just what I am told, no matter what it is. I am hired and fired at will, and I am not even paid minimum wage: I earn one dollar a month. I cannot even voice grievances or complaints, except at the risk of incurring arbitrary discipline or some covert retaliation.
>
> You need not worry about NAFTA and your jobs going to Mexico and other Third World countries. I will have at least five percent of your jobs by the end of this decade.
>
> I am called prison labor. I am The New American Worker.[10]

This "new American worker" will be drawn from the ranks of a racialized population whose historical superexploitation – from the era of slavery to the present – has been legitimized by racism. At the same time, the expansion of convict labor is accompanied in some states by the old paraphernalia of ankle chains that symbolically links convict labor with slave labor. At least three states – Alabama, Florida, and Arizona – have reinstituted the chain gang. Moreover, as Michael Powell so incisively reveals, there is a new dimension to the racism inherent in this process, which structurally links the superexploitation of prison labor to the globalization of capital.

In California, whose prison system is the largest in the country and one of the largest in the world, the passage of an inmate labor initiative in 1990 has presented businesses seeking cheap labor with opportunities uncannily similar to those in Third World countries. As of June 1994, a range of companies were employing prison labor in nine California prisons. Under the auspices of the Joint Venture Program, work now being performed on prison grounds includes computerized telephone messaging, dental apparatus assembly, computer data entry, plastic parts fabrication, electronic component manufacturing at the Central California Women's facility at Chowchilla, security glass manufacturing, swine production, oak furniture manufacturing, and the production of stainless steel tanks and equipment. In a California Corrections Department brochure designed to promote the program, it is described as "an innovative public–private partnership that makes good business sense."[11] According to the owner of Tower Communications, whom the brochure quotes,

> The operation is cost effective, dependable and trouble free. . . . Tower Communications has successfully operated a message center utilizing inmates on the grounds of a California state prison. If you're a business leader planning expansion, considering relocation because of a deficient labor pool, starting a new enterprise, look into the benefits of using inmate labor.

The employer benefits listed by the brochure include

> federal and state tax incentives; no benefit package (retirement pay, vacation pay, sick leave, medical benefits); long-term lease agreements at far below market value costs; discount rates on Workers Compensation; build a consistent, qualified work force; on call labor pool (no car breakdowns, no babysitting problems); option of hiring job-ready ex-offenders and minimizing costs; becoming a partner in public safety.

There is a major, yet invisible, racial supposition in such claims about the profitability of a convict labor force. The acceptability of the superexploitation of convict labor is largely based on the historical conjuncture of racism and incarceration practices. The already disproportionately black convict labor force will become increasingly black if the racially imbalanced incarceration practices continue.

The complicated yet unacknowledged structural presence of racism in the US punishment industry also includes the fact that the punishment industry which sequesters ever larger sectors of the black population attracts vast amounts of capital. Ideologically, as I have argued, the racialized fear of crime has begun to succeed the fear of communism. This corresponds to a structural tendency for capital that previously flowed toward the military industry to now move toward the punishment industry. The ease with which suggestions are made for prison construction costing in the multibillions of dollars is reminiscent of the military build-up: economic mobilization to defeat communism has turned into economic mobilization to defeat crime. The ideological construction of crime is thus complemented and bolstered by the material construction of jails and prisons. The more jails and prisons are constructed, the greater the fear of crime, and the greater the fear of crime, the stronger the cry for more jails and prisons, ad infinitum. The law enforcement industry bears remarkable parallels to the military industry (just as there are anti-communist resonances in the anti-crime campaign). This connection between the military industry and the punishment industry is revealed in a May 1994 *Wall Street Journal* article entitled "Making Crime Pay: The Cold War of the '90s":

> Parts of the defense establishment are cashing in, too, scenting a logical new line of business to help them offset military cutbacks. Westinghouse Electric Corp., Minnesota Mining and Manufacturing Co., GDE Systems (a division of the old General Dynamics) and Alliant Techsystems Inc., for instance, are pushing crime-fighting equipment and have created special divisions to retool their defense technology for America's streets.

According to the article, a conference sponsored by the National Institute of Justice, the research arm of the Justice Department, was organized around the theme "Law Enforcement Technology in the Twenty-first Century." The Secretary of Defense was a major presenter at this conference, which explored topics like "the role of the defense industry, particularly for dual use and conversion":

> Hot topics: defense – industry technology that could lower the level of violence involved in crime fighting. Sandia National Laboratories, for instance, is experimenting with a dense foam that can be sprayed at suspects, temporarily blinding and deafening them under breathable bubbles. Stinger Corporation is working on "smart guns," which will fire only for the owner, and retractable spiked barrier strips to unfurl in front of fleeing vehicles. Westinghouse is promoting the "smart car," in which minicomputers could

be linked up with big mainframes at the police department, allowing for speedy booking of prisoners, as well as quick exchanges of information.[12]

Again, race provides a silent justification for the technological expansion of law enforcement, which, in turn, intensifies racist arrest and incarceration practices. This skyrocketing punishment industry, whose growth is silently but powerfully sustained by the persistence of racism, creates an economic demand for more jails and prisons and thus for similarly spiraling criminalization practices, which, in turn, fuels the fear of crime.

Most debates addressing the crisis resulting from overcrowding in prisons and jails focus on male institutions. Meanwhile, women's institutions and jail space for women are proportionately proliferating at an even more astounding rate than men's. If race is largely an absent factor in the discussions about crime and punishment, gender seems not even to merit a place carved out by its absence. Historically, the imprisonment of women has served to criminalize women in a way that is more complicated than is the case with men. This female criminalization process has had more to do with the marking of certain groups of women as undomesticated and hypersexual, as women who refuse to embrace the nuclear family as paradigm. The current liberal–conservative discourse around welfare criminalizes black single mothers, who are represented as deficient, manless, drug-using breeders of children, and as reproducers of an attendant culture of poverty. The woman who does drugs is criminalized both because she is a drug user and because, as a consequence, she cannot be a good mother. In some states, pregnant women are being imprisoned for using crack because of possible damage to the fetus.

According to the US Department of Justice, women are far more likely than men to be imprisoned for a drug conviction.[13] However, if women wish to receive treatment for their drug problems, often their only option, if they cannot pay for a drug program, is to be arrested and sentenced to a drug program via the criminal justice system. Yet when US Surgeon General Joycelyn Elders alluded to the importance of opening discussion on the decriminalization of drugs, the Clinton administration immediately disassociated itself from her remarks. Decriminalization of drugs would greatly reduce the numbers of incarcerated women, for the 278 percent increase in the numbers of black women in state and federal prisons (as compared with the 186 percent increase in the numbers of black men) can be largely attributed to the phenomenal rise in drug-related and specifically crack-related imprisonment. According to the Sentencing Project's 1995 report, the increase amounted to 828 percent.[14]

Official refusals to even consider decriminalization of drugs as a possible strategy that might begin to reverse present incarceration practices further bolsters the ideological staying power of the prison. In his well-known study of the history of the prison and its related technologies of discipline, Michel Foucault pointed out that an evolving contradiction is at the very heart of the historical project of imprisonment.

> For a century and a half, the prison has always been offered as its own remedy: . . . the realization of the corrective project as the only method of overcoming the impossibility of implementing it.[15]

As I have attempted to argue, within the US historical context, racism plays a pivotal role in sustaining this contradiction. In fact, Foucault's theory regarding the prison's tendency to serve as its own enduring justification becomes even more compelling if the role of race is also acknowledged. Moreover, moving beyond the parameters of what I consider the double impasse implied by his theory – the discursive impasse his theory discovers and that of the theory itself – I want to conclude by suggesting the possibility of radical race-conscious strategies designed to disrupt the stranglehold of criminalization and incarceration practices.

In the course of a recent collaborative research project with UC Santa Barbara sociologist Kum-Kum Bhavnani, in which we interviewed thirty-five women at the San Francisco County Jail, the complex ways in which race and gender help to produce a punishment industry that reproduces the very problems it purports to solve became dramatically apparent. Our interviews focused on the women's ideas about imprisonment and how they themselves imagine alternatives to incarceration. Their various critiques of the prison system and of the existing "alternatives," all of which are tied to reimprisonment as a last resort, led us to reflect more deeply about the importance of retrieving, retheorizing, and reactivating the radical abolitionist strategy first proposed in connection with the prison reform movements of the sixties and seventies.

We are presently attempting to theorize women's imprisonment in ways that allow us to formulate a radical abolitionist strategy departing from, but not restricted in its conclusions to, women's jails and prisons. Our goal is to formulate alternatives to incarceration that substantively reflect the voices and agency of a variety of imprisoned women. We wish to open up channels for their involvement in the current debates around alternatives to incarceration, while not denying our own role as mediators and interpreters and our own political positioning in these debates. We also want to distinguish our explorations of alternatives from the spate of "alternative punishments" or what are now called "intermediate sanctions" presently being proposed and/or implemented by and through state and local correctional systems.

This is a long-range project that has three dimensions: academic research, public policy, and community organizing. In other words, for this project to be successful, it must build bridges between academic work, legislative and other policy interventions, and grassroots campaigns calling, for example, for the decriminalization of drugs and prostitution – and for the reversal of the present proliferation of jails and prisons.

Raising the possibility of abolishing jails and prisons as the institutionalized and normalized means of addressing social problems in an era of migrating corporations, unemployment and homelessness, and collapsing public services, from health care to education, can hopefully help to interrupt the current law-and-order discourse that has such a grip on the collective imagination, facilitated as it is by deep and hidden influences of racism. This late twentieth-century "abolitionism," with its nineteenth-century resonances, may also lead to a historical recontextualization of the practice of imprisonment. With the passage of the Thirteenth Amendment, slavery was abolished for all except convicts – and in a sense the exclusion from citizenship accomplished by the slave system has persisted within the US prison system. Only three states allow prisoners to vote, and approximately 4 million people are denied the right to vote because of their present or past incarceration. A radical strategy to abolish jails and prisons as the normal way of dealing with the social problems of late capitalism is not a strategy for abstract abolition. It is designed to force a rethinking of the increasingly repressive role of the state during this era of late capitalism and to carve out a space for resistance.

NOTES

1 See corerage by the *Austin-American Statesman*, October 17, 1995.
2 Quoted in Charles S. Clark, "Prison Overcrowding," *Congressional Quarterly Researcher*, 4, no. 5 (February 4, 1994), 97–119.
3 Ibid.
4 Marc Mauer, *Young Black Men and the Criminal Justice System: A Growing National Problem* (Washington, DC: The Sentencing Project, February 1990).
5 Reported in an Alexander Cockburn article, *Philadelphia Inquirer*, August 29, 1994.
6 Marc Mauer and Tracy Huling, *Young Black Americans and the Criminal Justice System: Five Years Later* (Washington, DC: The Sentencing Project, October 1995).
7 Ibid., 18.
8 See Cockburn, *Philadelphia Inquirer*, August 29, 1994.
9 See Wahneema Lubiano, "Black Ladies, Welfare Queens, and State Minstrels: Ideological War by Narrative Means," in *Race-ing Justice, En-gendering Power: Essays on Anita Hill, Clarence Thomas, and the Construction of Social Reality,* ed. Toni Morrison (New York: Pantheon, 1992).
10 Michael Powell, "Modern Slavery American Style," 1995, unpublished essay (author's papers).

11 I wish to acknowledge Julie Brown, who acquired this brochure from the California Department of Correction in the course of researching the role of convict labor.

12 "Making Crime Pay: The Cold War of the '90s," *Wall Street Journal*, May 12, 1994.

13 Lawrence Rence, A. Greenfield, Stephanie Minor-Harper, *Women in Prison* (Washington DC: US Dept. of Justice, Office of Justice Programs, Bureau of Statistics, 1991).

14 Mauer and Huling, *Young Black Americans and the Criminal Justice System: Five Years Later*, 19.

15 Michel Foucault, *Discipline and Punish: The Birth of the Prison*, trans. Alan Sheridan (New York: Vintage, 1979), 395.

5

From the Prison of Slavery to the Slavery of Prison: Frederick Douglass and the Convict Lease System

"Slavery in the United States," wrote Frederick Douglass in 1846, "is the granting of that power by which one man exercises and enforces a right of property in the body and soul of another." Throughout his career as an abolitionist, his writings and speeches probed the contradictions of the legal definition of the slave as "a piece of property – a marketable commodity."[1] He used this definition of the slave as property, for example, as the basis for his analysis of theft by slaves as an everyday practice of resistance to slavery. The slave "can own nothing, possess nothing, acquire nothing, but what must belong to another. To eat the fruit of his own toil, to clothe his person with the work of his own hands, is considered stealing."[2] Because the slave "was born into a society organized to defraud him of the results of his labor . . . he naturally enough thought it no robbery to obtain by stealth – the only way open to him – a part of what was forced from him under the hard conditions of the lash."[3] When Douglass himself escaped from slavery, he also stole property which belonged, in the eyes of the law, to his master. As a fugitive slave, both state and federal law constructed him as a criminal – a thief who absconded with his own body.

Throughout his life, Douglass periodically referred to the criminalization of the black population as a by-product of slavery. In 1877 President Rutherford Hayes appointed him US Marshall in the District of Columbia (over much criticism by both blacks and whites), which he said brought him into direct contact with black individuals stigmatized as criminals.[4] While he invariably contested the prevailing presumption of ex-slaves' natural proclivities toward crime, he nevertheless agreed that "they furnish a larger proportion of petty thieves than any other class,"[5] attributing this "thieving propensity" to holdovers from slavery. A central component in Douglass's philosophy of history was the assumption that over time, as the black population became increasingly removed from the era of slavery, these criminal propensities would recede accordingly.

> It is sad to think of the multitude who only dropped out of slavery to drop into prisons and chain-gangs, for the crimes for which they are punished seldom rise higher than the stealing of a pig or a pair of shoes; but it is consoling to think that the fact is not due to liberty, but to slavery, and that the evil will disappear as these people recede from the system in which they were born.[6]

More than a century after Douglass expressed his confidence that over time the black population would be transformed by material progress and spiritual enlightenment and would thus cease to be treated as a criminalized class, blackness is ideologically linked to criminality in ways that are more complicated and pernicious than Douglass ever could have imagined. The overwhelming numbers and percentages of imprisoned black men and women tend to define the black population as one that is subject *a priori* to incarceration and surveillance. In 1997, 1.8 million people were in the country's jails and prisons, approximately half of whom were black. Almost one-third of all young black males are either incarcerated or directly under criminal justice surveillance.[7] Although women constitute a statistically small percentage of the overall prison population (7.4 percent), the rate of increase in the incarceration of black women surpasses that of their male counterparts.[8] Whereas the prison system established its authority as a major institution of discipline and control for black communities during the last two decades of the nineteenth century, at the close of the twentieth century, carceral regulation of black communities has reached crisis proportions.

Considering the central role race has played in the emergence of a contemporary prison industrial complex and the attendant expansion of incarcerated populations, an examination of Douglass's historical views on the criminalization of black communities and the racialization of crime may yield important insights. In this paper, I am especially interested in Douglass's silence regarding the post-Civil War southern system of convict lease, which transferred symbolically significant numbers of black people from the prison of slavery to the slavery of prison. Through this transference, ideological and institutional carryovers from slavery began to fortify the equation of blackness and criminality in US society.

When the Thirteenth Amendment was passed in 1865, thus legally abolishing the slave economy, it also contained a provision that was universally celebrated as a declaration of the unconstitutionality of peonage. "Neither slavery nor involuntary servitude, *except as a punishment for crime,* whereof the party shall have been duly convicted, shall exist within the United States, or anyplace subject to their jurisdiction" (emphasis added). That exception would render penal servitude constitutional – from 1865 to the present day. That black human beings might continue to be enslaved under the auspices of southern systems of justice (and that this might set a precedent for imprisonment outside the South) seems not to have occurred to Douglass and other abolitionist leaders. It certainly is understandable that this loophole might be overlooked amid the general jubilation with which emancipation initially was greeted. However, the southern states' rapid passage of Black Codes – which criminalized such behavior as vagrancy, breech of job contracts, absence from work, the possession of firearms, and insulting gestures or acts[9] – should have stimulated critical reconsideration of the dangerous potential of the amendment's loophole. Replacing the Slave Codes of the previous era, the Black Codes simultaneously acknowledged and nullified black people's new juridical status as US citizens. The racialization of specific crimes meant that, according to state law, there were crimes for which only black people could be "duly convicted." The Mississippi Black Codes, for example, which were adopted soon after the close of the Civil War, declared vagrant "anyone/who was guilty of theft, had run away [from a job, apparently], was drunk, was wanton in conduct or speech, had neglected job or family, handled money carelessly, and . . . all other idle and disorderly persons."[10] Thus vagrancy was coded as a black crime, one punishable by incarceration and forced labor.

Considering the importance Douglass accorded the institution of slavery as an explanatory factor in relation to the vast numbers of "free" black people who were identified as criminal, it is surprising that he did not directly criticize the expansion of the convict lease system and the related system of peonage. As the premier black public intellectual of his time, he seems to have established a pattern of relative silence vis-à-vis convict leasing, peonage, and the penitentiary system, all of which clearly were institutional descendants of slavery. Douglass's most explicit denunciation of peonage did not occur until 1888, after a trip he made to South Carolina during which, according to Phillip Foner, he "realized how little he had known about the true conditions of his people in the South."[11] In a speech on the occasion of the twenty-sixth anniversary of Emancipation in the District of Columbia, Douglass said that the landlord and tenant laws in the South sounded like "the grating hinges of a slave prison" and kept black people "firmly bound in a strong, remorseless, and deadly grasp, a grasp from which only death can free [them]."[12] However, by the time he made this observation, tenant farming, peonage, and convict leasing had been in place for over two decades in some states. The Hayes–Tilden Compromise of 1877 led to the expansion and strengthening of these systems throughout the South. Precisely at the time Frederick Douglass's voice was most needed to trouble the rise of this new form of slavery – experienced directly by thousands of black people and symbolically by millions – his political loyalties to the Republican Party and his absolute faith in principles of Enlightenment seemed to blind him to the role the federal government was playing in the development of convict leasing and peonage. In fact, just as President Rutherford Hayes decided to withdraw federal troops from the South, he also decided to appoint Frederick Douglass as US Marshall of the District of Columbia.

According to Milfred Fierce, who has authored one of the few extended studies of the convict lease system within the field of African-American Studies, little is known about Douglass's views on convict leasing or those of other black leaders of his era.[13] Later, Booker T. Washington did occasionally speak out against convict leasing, and he integrated into his own project of industrial education some efforts to assist individuals caught up in the system of debt peonage. But he never developed an explicit strategy to abolish convict leasing. W. E. B. Du Bois published an essay in 1901 entitled "The Spawn of Slavery: The Convict Lease System of the South" in a now obscure missionary periodical, and while it proposed a radical analysis, it seems that it was not widely read or discussed.[14] Du Bois argued not only that crime was a "symptom of wrong social conditions," but that the entrenchment of convict leasing "linked crime and slavery indissolubly in [black people's] minds."[15] In 1907, Mary Church Terrell published an essay in *The Nineteenth Century* entitled "Peonage in the United States: The Convict Lease System and the Chain Gangs."[16]

Fierce explains the relative silence on the part of leaders like Frederick Douglass in part as a result of their limited knowledge of the atrocities connected with this system. However, it is difficult to believe that Douglass was unaware of the development of the lease system in the aftermath of Emancipation or of its expansion at the close of Radical Reconstruction. While his speeches and writings suggest that he did not consider this an issue important enough to deserve a place on his agenda for black liberation, recurring references to presumptions of black criminality and evocations, albeit abstract, of chain gangs persuade me that Douglass must have been aware of the atrocities committed in the name of justice. I therefore tend to think that Fierce is more accurate when he contends that

in addition, black leaders fell victim to the notion that "criminals" were getting what they deserved and, despite the cruelty of convict leasing, a crusade on behalf of prisoners was not seen as more important than fighting the lynching bee, opposing voting restrictions, or protesting the acts of racial bigotry that abounded. Those who accepted this analysis failed to fully appreciate how many of the convicts were kidnapped, held beyond their sentences, or actually innocent of the crimes for which they were incarcerated, the total number of which will never be known.[17]

They also failed to recognize that black boys and girls were not exempt from the convict labor system. David Oshinsky, author of *Worse Than Slavery*, refers to a pardon petition for a six-year-old girl named Mary Gay, who was sentenced to thirty days "plus court costs" on charges of stealing a hat.[18]

The general impact of the convict leasing system was even more far-reaching than the horrors it brought to individual black lives. According to Oshinsky:

> From its beginnings in Mississippi in the late 1860s until its abolition in Alabama in the late 1920s, convict leasing would serve to undermine legal equality, harden racial stereotypes, spur industrial development, intimidate free workers, and breed open contempt for the law. It would turn a few men into millionaires and crush thousands of ordinary lives.[19]

By the time the National Committee on Prison Labor convened in 1911, a number of southern states had already abolished convict labor and the abolitionist campaign had been rendered legitimate by the rising influence of the penal reform movement. The General Secretary of the National Committee on Prison Labor entitled his book on the Committee's findings *Penal Servitude* and introduced it with the following observation:

> The State has a property right in the labor of the prisoner. The 13th Amendment of the Constitution of the United States provides that neither slavery nor involuntary servitude shall exist, yet by inference allows its continuance as punishment for crime, after due process of law. This property right the state may lease or retain for its own use, the manner being set forth in state constitutions and acts of legislature.[20]

Although the loophole in the Thirteenth Amendment was apparently missed by most at the time of its passage, in retrospect it is easy to see how the very limitation of "slavery" and "involuntary servitude" to "criminals" could facilitate the further criminalization of former slaves.

Throughout his post-War writings and speeches Frederick Douglass argued that vast numbers of black people discovered that crimes were imputed to them which carried no prison sentence for whites. Had he decided to examine this attribution of criminality to black people more thoroughly, he might have discovered a link between the leasing system and other institutions for the control of black labor. The Thirteenth Amendment putatively freed black labor from the total control to which it was subject during slavery. In actuality, new forms of quasi-total control developed – sharecropping, tenant farming, the scrip system and the most dramatic evidence of the persistence of slavery, the convict lease system. Although Alabama and Louisiana had begun to use the lease system before the Civil War, it was only with the emancipation of the slaves that they and the other southern states began to use convict leasing on a relatively large scale. During the post-Civil War period, the percentages of black convicts in relation to white was often higher than 90 percent. In Alabama, the prison population tripled between 1874 and 1877 – and the increase consisted almost entirely of blacks.[21]

Radical Reconstruction did not abruptly end with the withdrawal of federal troops in 1877. However, as the first black recipient of a federal appointment that required senate confirmation, Douglass failed to use his position to forcefully challenge the Republican Party's complicity with the repressive process of re-establishing control over southern black labor. "It was clear by inauguration day," Phillip Foner contends, "that Hayes' agreement to remove the last remaining federal troops from the South had rendered meaningless his pledge to uphold the rights of the colored people. At this crucial moment Douglass voiced no opposition to Hayes' policy."[22] Instead, Douglass continued to define freedom as access to political rights, thus prioritizing political progress over economic freedom. His argument that "slavery is not abolished until the black man has the ballot"[23] was transformed into intransigent – although not always uncritical – support for the Republican Party, which was combined with an Enlightenment philosophy of history that emphasized inevitable future progress for the former slaves. Throughout his campaign for the Fifteenth Amendment and for the legislation necessary to enforce it, Douglass represented the ballot as the engine of progress for African Americans – even if these political rights were explicitly gendered as male and proscribed by the criminalization process to which all black people were vulnerable. However, after the fall of Radical Reconstruction and the solidification of the move toward disfranchisement, Douglass developed other arguments which revealed the Hegelian character of his unswerving belief in Enlightenment and historical progress.

In an 1879 paper opposing the Exoduster movement, Douglass contended that black people were the only hope for progress in the South. He argued that "whatever prosperity, beauty, and civilization are now possessed by the South" could be attributed to the labor of black slaves. This dependence of the South on black people was no less the case in the aftermath of slavery. "[The Negro] is the arbiter of her destiny."[24]

> The Exodus has revealed to southern men the humiliating fact that the prosperity and civilization of the South are at the mercy of the despised and hated Negro. That it is for him, more than for any other, to say what shall be the future of the late Confederate States; that within their ample borders, he alone can stand between the contending powers of savage and civilized life; that the giving or withholding of his labor will bless or blast their beautiful country.[25]

That Douglass could represent black workers as already having achieved the status accorded white workers – that is they were free to sell or withhold their labor to southern employers – revealed his astounding failure to engage with the actual position of black labor in the South.

> The Negro . . . has labor, the South wants it, and must have it or perish. Since he is free he can now give it, or withhold it; use it where he is, or take it elsewhere, as he pleases. His labor made him a slave, and his labor can, if he will, make him free, comfortable and independent. It is more to him than either fire, sword, ballot-boxes, or bayonet. It touches the heart of the South through its pocket.[26]

Ironically, Douglass's argument here foreshadows in starkly literal terms Booker T. Washington's admonition to "cast down your bucket where you are." If black labor was free at all, it was only in the formal sense that the economic system of slavery had been declared unconstitutional. Tenant farming, sharecropping, peonage, the practice of paying wages in scrip – and, for a vastly disproportionate number of black people, convict labor – militated against any assertion of economic freedom on the part of the masses of former slaves. Although a relatively small number of people were directly affected by the convict labor system, its symbolic importance resided in its demonstration to all black workers that incarceration and penal servitude were their possible fate. Convict leasing was a totalitarian effort to control black labor in the post-Emancipation era and it served as a symbolic reminder to black people that slavery had not been fully disestablished.[27] That black women could be housed, worked and physically and sexually abused by inmates and guards in camps that were largely male constituted a message that there was a fate even worse than slavery awaiting them. D. E. Tobias, one of the few black intellectuals at the turn of the century to prioritize the campaign against convict leasing, referred to the "immorality" abounding in the convict camps because of the co-correctional housing policies and because women were whipped nude in the presence of male convicts.[28] As long as it was possible to arrest and imprison black people (not only on serious charges, but also on petty charges that would never land a white person in jail) and lease out their labor under oppressive conditions that often surpassed those of slavery, black labor could not be said to be free.

In *Black Reconstruction*, W. E. B. Du Bois would later argue that because there was no historical precedent for a black presence in southern prisons and because white convicts were released during the war to join the Confederate armies, the role of southern penitentiary systems was reconceptualized after the outbreak of the Civil War. "The whole criminal system," wrote Du Bois, "came to be used as a method of keeping Negroes at work and intimidating them. Consequently there began to be a demand for jails and penitentiaries beyond the natural demand due to the rise of crime."[29] After the initiation of the convict lease system, one black member of the legislature presented a bill for the abolition of the penitentiary system.[30]

Douglass's argument against the Exoduster movement was thus based on a highly abstract construction of "free labor" that bore no relationship to black economic realities in the South and, in this context, served as a surrogate for the failed notion that the ballot promised full freedom and equality for the former slaves. However, to do Douglass's argument justice, it should be pointed out that he did not deploy it against emigration per se, but rather he focused his opposition on the organized Exoduster movement and its demands for federal financing. In light of the horrendous situation in the South, he suggested that "voluntary, spontaneous, self-sustained emigration on the part of the freedmen may or may not be commendable. It is a matter with which they alone have to do."[31] As long as emigration remained a private and individual matter, Douglass had no objections. However, when it was raised publicly and politically as a strategy for liberation, he strongly opposed it.

In summarizing the arguments in favor of emigration, he refers to Senate testimony by the emigrants themselves. He points to their contention "that for a crime for which a white man goes free, a black man is severely punished" and "that the law is the refuge of crime rather than of innocence; that even the old slave driver's whip has reappeared, and the inhuman and disgusting spectacle of the chain-gang is beginning to be seen."[32] Douglass did not contest the truth of this testimony – in fact, he had relied and would continue to rely on the fact that the criminal justice system had become a sanctuary for racism of the cruelest sort – but he nonetheless chose to respond to it by maintaining that black labor was "free" and held a far greater promise than emigration.

But even though the violent racism that was at the core of restructured criminal justice systems in the South did not, in Douglass's opinion, furnish compelling arguments for a political strategy of exodus from the South, his speeches and writings for the rest of his life powerfully evoked ways in which crime was racialized and race criminalized. In an essay for *North American Review* in 1881, challenging essentialist constructions of race prejudice, he wrote that "the colored man is the Jean Valjean of American society. He has escaped from the galleys, and hence all presumptions are against him."[33] Although Douglass's contentions that the social conditions of slavery and the persistence of racism during the post-slavery era were entirely responsible for the criminalization of black people led him to challenge these presumptions of criminality, they also steered him toward an analytical impasse. If slavery produced criminals, then black people had to be acknowledged as criminals. On the other hand, he argued against the imputation of guilt where none was present.

> If a crime is committed, and the criminal is not positively known, a suspicious-looking colored man is sure to have been seen in the neighborhood. If an unarmed colored man is shot down and dies in his tracks, a jury, under the influence of this spirit, does not hesitate to find the murdered man the real criminal, and the murderer innocent.[34]

As indicated above, Douglass often alluded to the fact that black people were punished for minor offenses as if they were hardened criminals, that "the crimes for which they are punished seldom rise higher than the stealing of a pig or a pair of shoes." In fact, the Mississippi Legislature passed its notorious "Pig Law" in 1876, classifying the theft of any cattle or swine as grand larceny and carrying up to five years in the penitentiary. This law was in part responsible for a vast increase in the penitentiary population in that state.[35] In 1875, the Democratic legislature in Arkansas passed a similar law classifying the theft of property worth two dollars as a felony punishable by one to five years.[36] Several weeks after the Mississippi Pig Law was passed, the legislature legalized the leasing of convict labor to private companies. Prisoners, according to this act, would be permitted to "work outside the penitentiary in building railroads, levees or in any private labor or employment."[37] As David Oshinsky observes, "throughout the South, thousands of ex-slaves were being arrested, tried, and convicted for acts that in the past had been dealt with by the master alone. . . . An offense against [the master] had become an offense against the state."[38] In 1875 Governor John Brown of Tennessee expressed his opinion that to imprison a black man who had stolen a pig with a white murderer was a gross injustice – to the white man.[39]

Because black people were more likely to be imprisoned for minor offenses than white people, in states like Florida, large numbers of black people convicted on charges of stealing were incarcerated alongside white men who had often committed appalling crimes. The author of an account on forced labor in the Florida turpentine camps pointed out that it was possible to send a negro to prison on almost any pretext but difficult to get a white there, unless he committed a very heinous crime."[40]

Douglass was certainly conscious of the degree to which crime itself was racialized, of the South's tendency to "impute crime to color."[41] With his usual eloquence, he said that "justice is often painted with bandaged eyes . . . but a mask of iron, however thick, could never blind American justice, when a black man happens to be on trial."[42] Not only was guilt assigned to black communities, regardless of the race of the perpetrator of a crime; white men, Douglass claimed, sometimes sought to escape punishment by disguising themselves as black.

In certain parts of our country, when any white man wishes to commit a heinous offence, he wisely resorts to burnt cork and blackens his face and goes forth under the similitude of a Negro. When the deed is done, a little soap and water destroys his identity, and he goes unwhipt of justice. Some Negro is at once suspected and brought before the victim of wrong for identification, and there is never much trouble here, for as in the eyes of many white people, all Negroes look alike, and as the man arrested and who sits in the dock in irons is black, he is undoubtedly the criminal.[43]

Douglass made these comments during an 1883 speech in celebration of the twenty-first anniversary of Emancipation in the District of Columbia. Three years later on the same occasion, he referred to his previous remarks and produced a recent example of a white man in Tennessee who had been killed while committing a crime in blackface:

Only a few days ago a Mr J. H. Justice, an eminent citizen of Granger county, Tennessee, attempted under this disguise to commit a cunningly devised robbery and have his offense fixed upon a Negro. All worked well till a bullet brought him to the ground and a little soap and water was applied to his face, when he was found to be no Negro at all, but a very respectable white citizen.[44]

Cheryl Harris argues that a property interest in whiteness emerged from the conditions of slavery and that "owning white identity as property affirmed the self-identity and liberty of whites and, conversely, denied the self-identity of blacks."[45] Douglass's comments indicate how this property interest in whiteness was easily reversed in schemes to deny black people their rights to due process. Interestingly, cases similar to the ones Douglass discussed have emerged during the 1990s – the case of Charles Stuart, who killed his wife in Boston and attempted to place the blame on an anonymous black murderer, and Susan Smith who killed her children in Union, South Carolina, and claimed they had been abducted by a black carjacker.

The last period of Frederick Douglass's life coincided with the consolidation of Jim Crow segregation in the South. Within the penitentiaries and convict labor camps, the criminality imputed to blackness gave rise to ideologies of separation that, in comparison to those of the "free" world, were magnified and exaggerated. In the "free" world, school systems, transportation systems, hospitals and neighborhoods were being subjected to strict laws of segregation. In some states there was the practice of incarcerating white convicts in penitentiaries and sending black convicts to labor camps.[46] While the prisons and labor camps were establishing lines of racial demarcation, black convicts who were incarcerated on charges of petty larceny were often treated as a danger to white convicts, even those in prison for murder. During the 1880s meetings of the National Prison Association (NPA) were replete with racist defenses of convict leasing, including arguments that the camps were a notch above black people's living conditions in freedom and that prison simply denied them "liberty, liquor and lust." White convicts, on the other hand, endured a much more trying ordeal, largely because they were compelled to live among black people.[47] It was claimed that the law "lays on the Caucasian a dreadful grief, which the African does not feel. . . . The fact remains, and will remain, that there is a psychological repulsion between races, horrible to one but not the other."[48] Southerners speaking before the NPA meetings called up such exaggerated comparisons as that between incarcerated whites with blacks and "the 'ancient torture' of tying up murderers with 'decaying corpses,' resulting in death to the living murderer."[49]

In light of Frederick Douglass's reticence regarding penal servitude, an analysis of his response to the prevailing discourses on race – which rendered criminality an obligatory ideological companion of blackness – might yield insights into the relative silence regarding penal servitude in black intellectual circles today. Douglass was quite outspoken on the issue of lynching and, in his many speeches and essays devoted to this subject, he was certainly required to address the criminalizing ideology of racism. But why speak out against lynching and remain silent on leasing? Lynching was outside the pale of the law. It could be opposed on the basis of its un-lawfulness, of its seemingly chaotic and aberrant quality. The issue, as Douglass formulated it, was not so much the guilt or innocence of lynch victims, but rather that they were divested of their right to confront their accusers in an arena structured by law. To take on convict leasing would have required Douglass to relinquish some of his major Enlightenment principles – and his vision of black liberation was too solidly anchored in the promise of legislated justice to permit him to ponder the possibility of the profound complicity of legal institutions in the continuation of this micro-cosmic slave system.

Consider this description of lynching from his well-known essay, "Why is the Negro Lynched?":

It [mob-law] laughs at legal processes, courts and juries, and its red-handed murderers range abroad unchecked and unchallenged by law or by public opinion. If the mob is in pursuit of Negroes who happen to be accused of crime, innocent or guilty, prison walls and iron bars afford no protection. Jail doors are battered down in the presence of unresisting jailors, and the accused, awaiting trial in the courts of law, are dragged out and hanged, shot, stabbed or burned to death, as the blind and irresponsible mob may elect.[50]

What Douglass fails to recognize is that the very iron bars that he looked to for security were as much a weapon of terror as the mob itself. "In a perverse way," according to Oshinsky, "emancipation had made the black population more vulnerable than before. It now faced threats from two directions: white mobs and white courts. Like the Ku Klux Klan, the criminal justice system would become a dragnet for the Negro."[51]

Perhaps Douglass's confidence in the law blinded him to ways in which black people were constructed, precisely through law, as only fit for slavery. This was the symbolic meaning of the convict lease system. By 1911, the National Prison Association openly acknowledged the links between the prison system and slavery:

> The *status of the convict* is that of one in *penal servitude* – the last surviving vestige of the old slave system. With its sanction in the common law, its regulation in the acts of legislatures, and its implied recognition in the Constitution of the United States, it continues unchallenged and without question, as a basic institution, supposedly necessary to the continued stability of our social structure.[52]

When Douglass wrote in 1894 about "the determination of slavery to perpetuate itself, if not under one form, then under another,"[53] he referred to the landlord tenant system as well as the practice of paying black laborers with store orders (instead of with money) as ways of perpetuating slavery. "The landowners of the South want the labor of the Negro on the hardest terms possible. They once had it for nothing. They now want it for next to nothing."[54] Interestingly, he suggests that landowners employ three strategies, yet he only mentions two (tenant farming and payment in scrip). Perhaps he originally meant to include convict leasing and/or peonage, but, on second thought, decided to remove references to these systems because they involved direct intervention or implicit sanction by the state.

Convict leasing and the accompanying laws permitting the criminal prosecution of people who did not fulfill their job contract were even more closely linked to slavery than the systems explicitly mentioned by Douglass. At the same time, all these legal and economic systems – leasing, peonage, tenant farming, sharecropping, and payment in scrip – mutually informed each other, all overdetermined by slavery in their techniques of controlling black labor. With respect to the fact that most people subject to these systems were black, Milfred Fierce points out that "for them, the distinction between antebellum de jure slavery and postbellum de facto slavery was close to being much ado about nothing:"[55]

> Southern blacks were trapped in [a] penal quagmire in excessive numbers and percentages of the total prison population of each southern state. For the victims, many of whom were ex-slaves, this predicament represented nothing

short of a revisit to slavery. Those blacks who were former slaves, and became victims of the convict lease system – especially those convicted and incarcerated on trumped up charges, or otherwise innocent of crimes for which they were imprisoned – must have imagined themselves in a time warp.[56]

Fierce argues – as indicated by the title of his study, *Slavery Revisited* – that the lease system established conditions that were tantamount to slavery, permitting plantation owners and industrialists to rent crews of mostly black convicts, using the same methods of coercion to guarantee their labor that had been practiced during slavery.

While Douglass may not have addressed the convict lease system because of its legal status and its affiliation with the criminal justice system, had he examined this system more closely, he might have discovered that the authority of the state was not directly exercised through the lease system. Rather the state served to mediate the privatization of convict labor. Alabama had already set a precedent for the privatization of convict labor before the abolition of slavery, which further affirms the historical link between slavery and leasing. The first penitentiary was constructed in Alabama in 1840 and by 1845 it was so much in debt that the entire prison was leased for a period of six years to a J. G. Graham. Graham simply became warden and took the profits from the convicts' labor.[57]

When all the southern states established the system of convict leasing, it made overwhelmingly black convict labor forces available to planters and capitalists under conditions modeled along the lines of slavery, conditions that, in many ways, proved worse than the slave system. Matthew Mancini, author of *One Dies, Get Another*, proposes an analysis of the lease system that complicates the obvious connection with slavery. He persuasively argues that given the indisputable similarities and continuities, it is the differences and discontinuities that provide the most interesting perspective on convict leasing. He points out that the rate of economic exploitation – defined in Marxian terms as the value of unpaid labor (and thus also the rate of profit) – was actually greater with the lease system than with slavery. Slaveholders were not only responsible for the maintenance of the laboring subjects, but were expected to guarantee the maintenance of the entire slave community – including children and elders who were not able to work.[58] Lessees, on the other hand, were only responsible for individual convicts, each of which represented a labor unit. Moreover, lessees purchased the labor of entire crews of convicts, not of individuals. According to Mancini:

The individual convict as such did not represent a significant investment, and his death or release, therefore, not a loss. When considered as a source of labor, then, slaves received a "wage" best thought of as aggregated, convicts one that was individual; as a form of capital, by contrast, slaves were individually significant, convicts collectively so. This does turn out to be a relevant distinction rather than a metaphysical exercise, for the consequence was an economic incentive to abuse prisoners. These two economic factors – the subsistence or lower-than-subsistence "wage" the convicts received and their status as aggregated capital – served to reinforce one another and to make leasing, from the point of view of the economic definition, "worse" than slavery.[59]

A small but significant number of black men and women were con-demned to live out the worst nightmares of what slavery might have been had the cost of purchasing slaves been low enough to justify conditions of genocide, i.e. no man, woman or child unable to work would be supported by the slave owners. Under these conditions (which were not entirely unheard of during slavery), it also would have been profitable to literally work slaves to death, because the cost of purchasing new ones would not have interfered with profits. Precisely because of this, Mancini decided to entitle his study of convict leasing *One Dies, Get Another*. We can only speculate as to how Frederick Douglass might have responded to the convict lease system had he extricated himself from his faith in formal legalities and examined more closely this symbolic and malignant reincarceration of slavery. We can also only speculate about the impact his engagement with the lease system might have had on future agendas for black liberation and on the future relationship between black intellectuals and social movements against the US prison system.

Although Frederick Douglass did not enlist his communicative powers in an examination of convict leasing, three of his intellectual descendants did see fit to write about this issue.[60] D. E. Tobias, a self-taught researcher and organic intellectual in the Gramscian sense, published an essay in 1899, a significant portion of which was devoted to leasing. In 1901, W. E. B. Du Bois published a relatively obscure article on convict leasing, and in 1907, Mary Church Terrell wrote about the subject in the same journal that had published Tobias's piece.

In his article "A Negro on the Position of the Negro in America," D. E. Tobias described himself as a twenty-nine-year-old black man, son of slaves, who was studying the prison system in the US.[61] Unfortunately, this seems to be Tobias's only published writing. Interestingly, he positioned the campaign against convict leasing at the very top of his agenda for black liberation. In this sense, he directly contested the philosophical tradition initiated by Frederick Douglass – and later taken up by Du Bois in his debate with Washington – according to which black political rights were the sine qua non of black liberation. Tobias did not deny the importance of the ballot. But he argued, in effect, that as long as convict leasing continued to exist, black people could never fully enjoy the franchise. Moreover, he suggested that the imprisonment of such large numbers of black people was tantamount to robbing them forever of their rights as citizens. "Once a Negro voter is sent to prison, he is forever thereafter disfranchised, and for this reason alone the whites have made thousands of negro convicts for the purpose of depriving them of their votes."[62] The use of incarceration as an explicit scheme to erode the potential political power of the black population reflected, in Tobias's view, what Frederick Douglass had referred to as "the determination of slavery to perpetuate itself." "The sole purpose of the South in going to war with the Nation," Tobias wrote,

> was to keep the black race as chattels, and having been defeated in that, ex-slaveholders were determined that the negroes should be held in bondage to serve them. Accordingly the remarkable ingenious scheme of making the negroes prisoners was soon devised, and at once scores and thousands of ex-slaves were arrested and convicted on any sort of flimsy charges, and farmed out to the highest bidders for human flesh. By reason of this new form of slavery, hundreds and thousands of black men and women have never known that they were emancipated.[63]

Tobias points out that southern authorities justified the institution of the convict lease system by evoking the Civil War destruction of most of the South's prison structures and thus by representing the lease plan as a "makeshift and an experiment until other means of caring for the large negro criminal population could be found."[64] However, after more than three decades, the lease system had become a critical component of southern criminal justice.

W. E. B. Du Bois's 1901 article "The Spawn of Slavery: The Convict-Lease System in the South" examines the lease system as a structural inheritance of slavery wherein black people accused of committing crimes were disciplined by the private imposition of labor, using "the slave theory of punishment – pain and intimidation."[65] He defined this system as "the slavery in private hands of persons convicted of crimes and misdemeanors in the courts."[66] This method of controlling black labor, Du Bois argued, emerged alongside a juridical construction of black criminality in the chaos that followed Emancipation when punishment was no longer the private purview of slavemasters, when black slaves were no longer legally recognized as the property of their masters. "Consequently, so far as the state was concerned, there was no crime of any consequence among Negroes. The system of criminal jurisprudence had to do, therefore, with whites almost exclusively. . . ."[67] Although the Freedman's Bureau attempted to create innovative methods of mediating legal relationships, these new strategies failed and the state courts re-established their authority.

As the regular state courts gradually regained power, it was necessary for them to fix by their decisions the new status of the freedmen. It was perhaps as natural as it was unfortunate that amid this chaos the courts sought to do by judicial decisions what the legislatures had formerly sought to do by specific law – namely, reduce the freedmen to serfdom. As a result, the small peccadillos of a careless, untrained class were made the excuse for severe sentences. The courts and jails became filled with the careless and ignorant, with those who sought to emphasize their new-found freedom, and too often with innocent victims of oppression. The testimony of a Negro counted for little or nothing in court, while the accusation of white witnesses was usually decisive. The result of this was a sudden large increase in the apparent criminal population of the Southern states – an increase so large that there was no way for the state to house it or watch it even had the state wished to. And the state did not wish to. Throughout the South laws were immediately passed authorizing public officials to lease the labor of convicts to the highest bidder. The lessee then took charge of the convicts – worked them as he wished under the nominal control of the state. Thus a new slavery and slave-trade was established.[68]

I quote this long passage because it is such an insightful summary of the way the convict lease system served as a decisive lever for the transition from a bifurcated system of criminal justice – privatized punishment for blacks and public punishment for whites – to a system in which the state concentrated on the punishment of blacks and functioned as a mediator for punishment through privatized labor. In other words, "the state became a dealer in crime, profited by it so as to derive a net annual income for her prisoners."[69] Du Bois would later write in *Black Reconstruction* that "[i]n no part of the modern world has there been so open and conscious a traffic in crime for deliberate social degradation and private profit as in the South since slavery."[70]

Du Bois's analysis of the convict lease system implicitly contested Douglass's construction of black labor as "free." Du Bois made the astute observation that so-called "free" black labor was, in a very concrete sense, chained to black convict labor, for in many industries in which black people sought employment – such as brick-making, mining, roadbuilding – wages were severely depressed by the fact that convicts could be leased from the state at costs as low as $3 a month.[71] Moreover, Du Bois pointed out that the very theory of work embodied in convict leasing would have to be radically transformed in order to establish a criminal justice system free of racial bias. Instead of convict labor serving as a scheme for both private and state profit, it would have to be reconstructed as a means of correction and reformation of the convict him/herself. With the abolition of the profit motive, Du Bois seemed to imply, a powerful incentive for the racism at the core of the system would cease to exist.

Unfortunately, this insightful and radical analysis of the convict lease system was not taken up by Du Bois's contemporaries. The relative obscurity to which it was relegated may be attributed to the fact that the essay appeared in a Protestant periodical devoted to writings on missionary projects, *The Missionary Review of the World*. As a result, its audience probably consisted largely of theologians and missionaries. Today, it is probably only read by students of religious studies and scholars researching convict leasing. However, Du Bois did refer to convict leasing and peonage in his monumental study *Black Reconstruction*.

Twelve years after Douglass's death, Mary Church Terrell remarked that "it is surprising how few there are among even intelligent people in this country who seem to have anything but a hazy idea of what the convict lease system means."[72] Her essay on convict leasing was published in the prestigious review *The Nineteenth Century*, and although it is difficult to document how the essay was received, Milfred Fierce asserts that it "influenced many others, both black and White."[73] Terrell, like Douglass in the preceding generation, was one of the major figures in the anti-lynching crusade. However, she wrote as passionately against the convict lease system as she had against lynching, meticulously documenting her allegations of untold cruelty with references to comments by southern legal authorities and official reports. "It is no exaggeration," Terrell wrote,

> to say that in some respects the convict lease system, as it is operated in certain southern States, is less humane than was the bondage endured by slaves fifty years ago. For, under the old *régime*, it was to the master's interest to clothe and shelter and feed his slaves properly, even if he were not moved to do so by considerations of mercy and humanity, because the death of a slave meant an actual loss in dollars and cents, whereas the death of a convict to-day involves no loss whatsoever either to the lessee or to the State.[74]

There are several references in the article to the way women were integrated into the convict lease system with little regard to their gender – they worked and were housed together with men. Focusing her examination on the state of Georgia, she quotes extensively from a report issued several years before by Colonel Alton Byrd, who had been appointed a special investigator into the conditions of Georgia's convict camps. In one passage he described a young black woman,

> . . . Lizzie Boatwright, a nineteen-year-old negress sent up from Thomas, Georgia, for larceny. She was clad in women's clothing, was working side by side with male convicts under a guard, cutting a ditch through a meadow. This girl was small of stature and pleasant of address, and her life in this camp must have been one of long drawn out agony, horror, and suffering. She told me she had been whipped twice, each time by the brutal white guard who had

beaten McRay (an elderly black convict at the camp) to death, and who prostituted his legal rights to whip into a most revolting and disgusting outrage. This girl and another woman were stripped and beaten unmercifully in plain view of the men convicts, because they stopped on the side of the road to bind a rag about their sore feet.[75]

It is probably the case that Terrell devoted her most extensive discussion of women in the labor camps to white women because she assumed that the brutal treatment of white women would provoke more widespread expressions of outrage than would that of black women. Although she did not indicate the source of her information, she wrote that in the preceding year, news was released about "one thousand white girls . . . [who] wear men's clothing and work side by side with coloured men who are held in slavery as well as the girls. . . . In the black depths of [Florida] pinewoods, living in huts never seen by civilised white men other than the bosses of the turpentine camps, girls are said to have grown old in servitude."[76] Terrell concluded this section with the observation that "not only does peonage still rage violently in the Southern states and in a variety of forms, but that while it formerly affected only coloured people, it now attacks white men and women as well."[77] In this sense Terrell was probably influenced by the discourse of prison reform, which tended to equate the cruelty of peonage and convict leasing with its allegedly increasing impact on white people. For example, Richard Barry's 1907 article in *Cosmopolitan Magazine* emphasized the fact that employers in Florida had come under investigation because of the "monumental error" they made "in going beyond the black man with their slavery. Had they stuck to the racial division they might have escaped castigation, as they have for a decade. But, insatiate, and not finding enough blacks to satisfy their ambitious wants, they reached out and took in white men."[78]

Consequently, the movement to abolish convict leasing tended to reinforce notions of black criminality even as it emphasized the brutality of the leasing system. This abolitionist movement coincided with the increasing influence of discourses on eugenics and scientific racism. Although black leaders attempted to refute essentialist theories of innate criminality by emphasizing the historical conditions under which black criminality emerged, they did not openly examine the structural role of the expanding network of penitentiaries and convict labor camps in constructing and affirming these ideologies. Philosophically, this represented an engagement with the presumption of criminality, but not with the institutions that concretely structured this ideology of criminality.

If Douglass was consistently silent on the issue of convict leasing, then Terrell did not integrate her insights on leasing into her anti-lynching work and thus could not effectively challenge a criminal justice system that perpetuated notions of black criminality that still persist during the contemporary era. The same observation may be made of Du Bois. This is particularly important in light of the popular historical memory of lynching that remains a critical component of African-American identity. If convict leasing and the accompanying disproportionality with which black people were made to inhabit jails and prisons during the post-Emancipation period had been taken up with the same intensity and seriousness as – and in connection with – the campaign against lynching, then the contemporary radical call for prison abolition might not sound so implausible today.

Of course it is not fair to blame Douglass for over a century of failure to take on the pivotal role of the prison system in constructing and preserving ideological equations of blackness and criminality. And it certainly is not fair to hold him responsible for the "common sense" acceptance of the inevitability of prisons. However – and this is the conclusion of my examination of Douglass's silence vis-à-vis the convict lease system – scholars who rightfully criticize Douglass for the tenacity with which he embraced Enlightenment principles and a philosophy of history that accorded the bourgeois state a foundational role in guaranteeing racial progress, also should acknowledge how this philosophy militated against an understanding of the prison system, and its specific role in preserving and deepening structures of racism. Moreover, by understanding Douglass's reluctance to directly oppose the penitentiary system of his era, we may acquire much needed insight into the difficulties activists encounter today in organizing movements against the contemporary prison industrial complex.

NOTES

1   Frederick Douglass, "An Appeal to the British People," reception speech at Finsbury Chapel, Moorfields, England, May 12, 1846, in Phillip Foner, *The Life and Writings of Frederick Douglass*, vol. 1 (New York: International Publishers, 1950), 155.
2   "Frederick Douglass Discusses Slavery," in Herbert Aptheker, *Documentary History of the Negro People* (New York: Citadel Press, 1969), 310.
3   Frederick Douglass, "The Condition of the Freedman," *Harper's Weekly*, Dec. 8, 1883, in Phillip Foner, *The Life and Writings of Frederick Douglass*, vol. 4 (New York: International Publishers, 1955), 406.
4   In his speech on the occasion of the Twenty-Fourth Anniversary of Emancipation in the District of Columbia, he said: "Look at these black criminals, as they are brought into your police courts; view and study their faces, their forms, and their features, as I have done for years as Marshal of this District, and you will see that their antecedents are written all over them." Foner, *Life and Writings*, vol. 4, 435.
5   Ibid., 434.

6   Foner, *Life and Writings*, vol. 4, 406.

7   Marc Mauer and Tracy Huling, *Young Black Americans and the Criminal Justice System: Five Years Later* (Washington, DC: The Sentencing Project, 1995).

8   Ibid.

9   E. Franklin Frazier, *From Slavery to Freedom* (New York: Vintage, 1969), 303.

10 Milfred Fierce, *Slavery Revisited: Blacks and the Southern Convict Lease System, 1865–1933* (New York: Brooklyn College, CUNY, Africana Studies Research Center, 1994), 85–6.

11 Foner, *Life and Writings*, vol. 4, 109.

12 Ibid., 110.

13 Fierce, *Slavery Revisited*, 230.

14 W. E. B. Du Bois, "The Spawn of Slavery: The Convict Lease System of the South," *Missionary Review of the World*, October 1901.

15 Fierce, *Slavery Revisited*, 240.

16 Mary Church Terrell, "Peonage in the United States: The Convict Lease System and the Chain Gangs," *The Nineteenth Century and After*, vol. 42 (August 1907).

17 Fierce, *Slavery Revisited*, 229.

18 David Oshinsky, *"Worse than Slavery": Parchman Farm and the Ordeal of Jim Crow Justice* (New York: Free Press, 1996), 47.

19 Ibid., 56.

20 E. Stagg Whitin, *Penal Servitude* (New York: National Committee on Prison Labor, 1912), i.

21 Fierce, *Slavery Revisited*, 88.

22 Foner, *Life and Writings*, vol. 4, 101.

23 Douglass, "The Need for Continuing Anti-Slavery Work," speech at 32nd Annual Meeting of the American Anti-Slavery Society. May 9, 1865, in Foner, *Life and Writings*, vol. 4, 166.

24 Douglass was invited to present this paper along with Richard T. Greener, the first black graduate of Harvard. Because he did not wish to engage in open debate around this controversial issue, he decided not to appear in person at the meeting but to send his paper to be read by someone else. Greener, who had taught at the University of South Carolina during Reconstruction, now taught at Howard and was a prominent organizer of support for the emigrants. See William S. McFeely, *Frederick Douglass* (New York: W. W. Norton, 1991), 301; Douglass, "The Negro Exodus from the Gulf States," address before Convention of the American Social Science Association, Saratoga Springs, September 12, 1879, published in *Journal of Social Science*, vol. XI (May 1880), 1–21, reprinted in Foner, *Life and Writings*, vol. 4, 327.

25 Ibid., 325.

26 Ibid., 327.

27 "Certainly the control of black labor was a leading motivation behind every significant effort to establish and maintain convict leasing for fifty years. Just as plain is the similarity between the brutal hardships of convict life and the oppression of slavery times. Finally, the racial character of convict leasing reinforced connections with the slavery regime." Matthew J. Mancini, *One*

Dies, Get Another: Convict Leasing in the American South, 1866–1928 (Columbia, SC: University of South Carolina Press, 1996), 20.

28   D. E. Tobias, "A Negro on the Position of the Negro in America," in *The Nineteenth Century*, no. 274 (Dec. 1899), 960–1.

29   W. E. B. Du Bois, *Black Reconstruction* (New York: Russell and Russell, 1963), 506.

30   Ibid.

31   Foner, *Life and Writings*, vol. 4, 332.

32   Ibid., 330.

33   Frederick Douglass, "The Color Line," *North American Review*, vol. CXXXII (June 1881), reprinted in Foner, *Life and Writings*, vol. 4, 344.

34   Ibid., 345.

35   Fierce, *Slavery Revisited*, 128–9, n. 16. Matthew Mancini argues that while the "Pig Law" may have been in part responsible for an immediate increase in the number of convicts, in 1877, the penitentiary population began to drop – and in fact began to soar immediately after the repeal of this law in 1888. Mancini, *One Dies, Get Another*, 135–6.

36   Mancini, *One Dies, Get Another*, 120.

37   Mississippi Laws, 1876, c. 110, sec. 1.3, 194–5. Quoted by Oshinsky, *Worse than Slavery*, 41.

38   Oshinsky, *Worse than Slavery*, 28.

39   Fierce, *Slavery Revisited*, 89.

40   "Captain" J. C. Powell's *American Siberia* is quoted by Oshinsky, *Worse than Slavery*, 71.

41   Frederick Douglass, "Address to the People of the United States," delivered at a Convention of Colored Men, Louisville, Kentucky, September 24, 1883, in Foner, *Life and Writings*, vol. 4, 379.

42   Frederick Douglass, "The United States Cannot Remain Half-Slave and Half-Free," speech on the occasion of the Twenty-First Anniversary of Emancipation in the District of Columbia, April 1883, in Foner, *Life and Writings*, vol. 4, 357. Several months later at a Convention of Colored Men, he said, "Taking advantage of the general disposition in this country to impute crime to color, white men *color* their faces to commit crime and wash off the hated color to escape punishment," "Address to the People of the United States," Louisville, Kentucky, September 24, 1883, 379.

43   Ibid., 359.

44   "Southern Barbarism," speech on the occasion of the Twenty-Fourth Anniversary of Emancipation in the District of Columbia, Washington, DC, 1886, in Foner, *Life and Writings*, vol. 4, 434.

45   Cheryl Harris, "Whiteness as Property," in Kimberle Crenshaw et al. (eds), *Critical Race Theory: The Key Writings that Formed the Movement* (New York: New Press, 1995), 285.

46   Oshinsky, *Worse than Slavery*, 41.

47   Mancini, *One Dies, Get Another*, 92.

48   Ibid., 93. Mancini quotes the 1886 NPA proceedings.

49   Fierce, *Slavery Revisited*, 89.

50   "Why is the Negro Lynched," in Foner, *Life and Writings*, vol. 4, 492.

51   Oshinsky, *Worse than Slavery*, 29.
52   Whitin, *Penal Servitude*, 1–2.
53   Douglass, "Why is the Negro Lynched," in Foner, *Life and Writings*, vol. 4, 516.
54   Ibid.
55   Fierce, *Slavery Revisited*, 43.
56   Ibid., 78.
57   Mancini, *One Dies, Get Another*, 99–100.
58   Ibid., 22.
59   Ibid., 23.
60   I obtained references for these three essays from Milfred Fierce's *Slavery Revisited*.
61   Fierce indicates that "[n]ot much is known about Tobias except that his parents were illiterate former slaves and that he was born in South Carolina around 1870. He described himself as 'a member of the effete African race' and indicated that he was educated in the South and North, an education he financed by working with his hands," *Slavery Revisited*, 243.
62   D. E. Tobias, "A Negro on the Position of the Negro in America," *The Nineteenth Century and After*, 960.
63   Ibid., 959.
64   Ibid., 960.
65   W. E. B. Du Bois, "The Spawn of Slavery: The Convict-Lease System in the South," *The Missionary Review of the World*, vol. XXIV, no. 10 (New Series, vol. XIV, no. 10) (October 1901), 743.
66   Ibid., 738.
67   Ibid.
68   Ibid., 740.
69   Ibid., 741.
70   Du Bois, *Black Reconstruction*, 698.
71   Ibid., 744–5.
72   Terrell, "Peonage in the United States."
73   Fierce, *Slavery Revisited*, 231.
74   Terrell, "Peonage in the United States," 306.
75   Ibid., 317.
76   Ibid., 311.
77   Ibid., 313.
78   Richard Barry, "Slavery in the South To-Day," *Cosmopolitan Magazine*, March 1907, reproduced in Donald P. DeNevi and Doris A. Holmes (eds), *Racism at the Turn of the Century: Documentary Perspectives, 1870–1910* (San Rafael, CA: Leswing Press, 1973), 131.

6

Racialized Punishment and Prison Abolition

Michel Foucault's *Discipline and Punish* is arguably the most influential text in contemporary studies of the prison system. Although its subtitle is *The Birth of the Prison System*, Foucault was not so much interested in the prison *per se* as in the disciplinary technologies perfected within this institution. He attempts to explain the production of manipulable bodies within the context of a panoptic carceral network that reaches far beyond the prison. While the category of class plays a pivotal role in his analysis – though his reconceptualization of power leads to critical revisions of class as a Marxist category – gender and race are virtually absent. Feminist critiques of Foucault have led to a proliferating body of Foucauldian literature on gender discipline, including an extended study on women in prison by Dobash, Dobash and Gutteridge.[1] However, few scholars have seriously examined the racial implications of Foucault's theory of power and his history of the prison. Joy James's assertion that "Foucault's elision of racial bias in historical lynching and contemporary policing predicts his silence on the racialization of prisons"[2] points to the need to move beyond a strictly Foucauldian genealogy in examining histories of punishment.

Foucault revises the penal historiography that privileges the development of the penitentiary in the United States, arguing that the oldest model of imprisonment as punishment rather than detention is the Rasphuis of Amsterdam, which opened in 1596 and originally "was intended for beggars or young malefactors."[3] The eighteenth-century *maison de force* in Ghent, in which idlers were imprisoned and subjected to "a universal pedagogy of work,"[4] and the penitentiary built in Gloucester to implement Blackstone and Howard's principles of imprisonment, served as the models for the Walnut Street Jail in Philadelphia, which opened its doors in 1790.[5]

As interesting as it may be, however, to examine the influences of the earlier European models on the emergent US prison system, what may help us to understand the way in which this system would eventually incorporate, sustain and transform structures and ideologies of racism is an examination of the impact of the institution of slavery on US systems of punishment. Beyond slavery, which is the focus of this paper, a more expansive analysis of US historical specificities might serve as the basis for a genealogy of imprisonment that would differ significantly from Foucault's. Such a genealogy would accentuate the links between confinement, punishment and race. At least four great systems of incarceration could be identified: the reservation system, slavery, the mission system, and the internment camps of World War II. Within the US, incarceration has thus played a pivotal role in the histories of Native Americans and people of African, Mexican, and Asian descent. In all of these cases, people were involuntarily confined and punished for no reason other than their race or ethnicity.

As Foucault points out, soon after the establishment of imprisonment as the dominant mode of punishment, prison acquired a "self-evident character." "[O]ne cannot 'see' how to replace it. It is the detestable solution, which one seems unable to do without."

> This "self-evident" character of the prison, which we find so difficult to abandon, is based first of all on the simple form of "deprivation of liberty." How could prison not be the penalty *par excellence* in a society in which liberty is a good that belongs to all in the same way and to which each individually is attached, as Duport put it, by a "universal and constant" feeling? Its loss has therefore the same value for all; unlike the fine, it is an "egalitarian" punishment. The prison is the clearest, simplest, most equitable of penalties. Moreover, it makes possible to quantify the penalty exactly according to the variable of time. There is a wages-form of imprisonment that constitutes, in industrial societies, its economic "self-evidence" – and enables it to appear as a reparation.[6]

The modes of punishment associated with the two dominant models of imprisonment developed at the beginning of the nineteenth century in the US – the Philadelphia and Auburn models – were based on a construction of the individual that did not apply to people excluded from citizenship by virtue of their race and thus from a recognition of their communities as composed of individuals possessing rights and liberties. These prisons were thus largely designed to punish and reform white wage-earning individuals, who violated the social contract of the new industrial capitalist order by allegedly committing crimes. The gendering of these institutions as male reflected the marginalization of women within a domestic, rather than public, economy. In fact the history and specific architecture of women's prisons reveal a quite different penal function: that of restoring white women to their place as wives and mothers, rather than as rights-bearing public individuals.

Within the US – and increasingly in postcolonial Europe – the disproportionate presence of people of color among incarcerated populations has
also acquired a "self-evident" character. But this reification is not based on
the reasoning proposed by Foucault in *Discipline and Punish*. In an analysis
that predates the publication of *Discipline and Punish*, Foucault allows for
the possibility that the prison's purpose is not so much to transform, but to
concentrate and eliminate politically dissident and racialized populations.
After an April 1972 visit to Attica – the very first visit Foucault made to a
prison, which occurred just eight months after the Attica uprising and
massacre – he commented in an interview:

> At the time of the creation of Auburn and the Philadelphia prison, which
> served as models (with very little change until now) for the great machines of
> incarceration, it was believed that something indeed was produced: "virtu-
> ous" men. Now we know, and the administration is perfectly aware, that no
> such thing is produced. That nothing at all is produced. That it is a question
> simply of a great sleight of hand, a curious mechanism of circular elimination:
> society eliminates by sending to prison people whom prison breaks up,
> crushes, physically eliminates; the prison eliminates them by "freeing" them
> and sending them back to society; . . . the state in which they come out
> insures that society will eliminate them once again, sending them to prison.
> . . . Attica is a machine for elimination, a form of prodigious stomach,
> a kidney that consumes, destroys, breaks up and then rejects, and that
> consumes in order to eliminate what it has already eliminated.[7]

Foucault was especially struck by the disproportionately large population of
black men and commented that "in the United States, there must be one
out of 30 or 40 black men in prison: it is here that one can see the function
of massive elimination in the American prison."[8] One wonders how Foucault might have responded in the 1990s to the fact that one out of three
young black men is presently incarcerated or under the direct control of the
criminal justice system.[9]

Historically, people of African descent consigned to slavery in the US
were certainly not treated as rights-bearing individuals and therefore were
not considered worthy of the moral re-education that was the announced
philosophical goal of the penitentiary. Indeed, the slave system had its own
forms of punishment, which remained primarily corporal and of the sort
that predated the emergence of incarceration as punishment. In her slave
narrative, Harriet Jacobs described a neighboring planter whose plantation
included six hundred slaves, a jail and a whipping post. The jail, however,
did not serve as a means of depriving the slave of his/her time and rights,
but rather as a means of torture, for "[i]f a slave stole from him even a
pound of meat or a peck of corn, if detection followed, he was put in chains

and imprisoned, and so kept till his form was attenuated by hunger and suffering." One of the planter's favorite punishments "was to tie a rope round a man's body, and suspend him from the ground. A fire was kindled over him, from which was suspended a piece of fat pork. As this cooked, the scalding drops of fat continually fell on the bare flesh."[10]

If, as Foucault insists, the locus of the new European mode of punishment shifted from the body to the soul, black slaves in the US were largely perceived as lacking the soul that might be shaped and transformed by punishment. Within the institution of slavery, itself a form of incarceration, racialized forms of punishment developed alongside the emergence of the prison system within and as a negative affirmation of the "free world," from which slavery was twice removed. Thus the deprivation of white freedom tended to affirm the whiteness of democratic rights and liberties. As white men acquired the privilege to be punished in ways that acknowledged their equality and the racialized universality of liberty, the punishment of black slaves was corporal, concrete and particular.

It is also instructive to consider the role labor played in these different systems of incarceration. In the philosophical conception of the penitentiary, labor was a reforming activity. It was supposed to assist the imprisoned individual in his (and on occasion her) putative quest for religious penitence and moral re-education. Labor was a means toward a moral end. In the case of slavery, labor was the only thing that mattered: the individual slaves were constructed essentially as labor units. Thus punishment was designed to maximize labor. And in a larger sense, labor was punishment attached not to crime, but to race.

Even if the forms of punishment inherent in and associated with slavery had been entirely revoked with the abolition of slavery, the persistent second-class citizenship status to which former slaves were relegated would have had an implicit impact on punishment practices. However, an explicit linkage between slavery and punishment was written into the constitution precisely at the moment of the abolition of slavery. In fact, there was no reference to imprisonment in the US Constitution until the passage of the Thirteenth Amendment declared chattel slavery unconstitutional: "Neither slavery nor involuntary servitude, except as a punishment for crime whereof the party shall have been duly convicted, shall exist within the United States, or any place subject to their jurisdiction."

The abolition of slavery thus corresponded to the authorization of slavery as punishment. In actual practice, both Emancipation and the authorization of penal servitude combined to create an immense black presence within southern prisons and to transform the character of punishment into a means of managing former slaves as opposed to addressing problems of serious crime.

The incarceration of former slaves served not so much to affirm the rights and liberties of the freedmen and women (i.e. as rights and liberties of which they could be deprived), nor to discipline a potential labor force; rather it symbolically emphasized that black people's social status continued to be that of slaves, even though the institution of slavery had been disestablished. In constructing prisoners as human beings who deserved subjection to slavery, the Constitution allowed for a further, more elusive linkage of prison and slavery, namely the criminalization of former slaves. This criminalization process became evident in the rapid transformation of prison populations in the southern states, where the majority of black Americans resided. Prior to Emancipation, prisoners were primarily white, but "[d]uring the post Civil War period, the percentages of black convicts in relation to white was often higher than 90%. In Alabama, the prison population tripled between 1874 and 1877 – and the increase consisted almost entirely of blacks."[11] According to Matthew Mancini,

> for a half-century after the Civil War, the southern states had no prisons to speak of and those they did have played a peripheral role in those states' criminal justice systems. Instead, persons convicted of criminal offenses were sent to sugar and cotton plantations, as well as to coal mines, turpentine farms, phosphate beds, brickyards [and] sawmills.[12]

The swift racial transformation of imprisoned southern populations was largely due to the passage of Black Codes, which criminalized such behavior as vagrancy, breech of job contracts, absence from work, the possession of firearms, insulting gestures or acts.[13] The Mississippi Black Codes, for example, defined a vagrant "as anyone/who was guilty of theft, had run away [from a job, apparently], was drunk, was wanton in conduct or speech, had neglected job or family, handled money carelessly, and . . . all other idle and disorderly persons."[14] In other words, white behavior that was commended and thus went unnoticed by the criminal justice system could lead to the conviction of black individuals and to the ideological criminalization of black communities. "Arguing or even questioning a white man could result in a criminal charge."[15] Moreover, as many slave narratives confirm, many of these acts – for example theft and escape – had been considered effective forms of resistance to slavery. Now they were defined as crimes and what during slavery had been the particular repressive power of the master, became the far more devastating universal power of the state.

"Free" black people entered into a relationship with the state unmediated by a master, they were divested of their status as slaves in order to be accorded a new status as criminals. "Throughout the South, thousands of ex-slaves were being arrested, and convicted for acts that in the past had been dealt with by the master alone. . . . An offense against [the master] had become an offense against the state."[16] Thus, the criminal justice system played a significant role in constructing the new social status of former slaves as human beings whose citizenship status was acknowledged precisely in order to be denied.

Southern prison populations not only became predominantly black in the aftermath of slavery, penitentiaries were either replaced by convict leasing or they were restricted to white convicts. This racialization of punishment practices determined that black people were to be socially defined in large part by re-created conditions of slavery. In fact, as historian David Oshinsky has documented, convict leasing in institutions like Mississippi's Parchman Farm created conditions "worse than slavery."[17] When Arkansas governor George Donaghey called for the abolition of convict leasing in 1912, he argued that leasing was "a form of legalized murder that sentenced thousands of faceless victims to a 'death by oppression' for often trivial acts. Under no other system, he believed, did the punishment so poorly fit the crime."[18] His list of abuses included:

Instance No. 1. In Phillips County . . . two negroes jointly forged nine orders for one quart of whiskey each. For this offense one of them was convicted for eighteen years and the other for thirty-six years. . . .

Instance No. 10. In Miller County a negro convicted in a justice of the peace court was . . . sentenced [to] over three years for stealing a few articles of clothing off a clothes-line.[19]

During the last three decades of the nineteenth century, southern criminal justice systems were profoundly transformed by their role as a totalitarian means of controlling black labor in the post-Emancipation era. Because so many of the particular crimes with which black people were charged served more as pretexts than as causal factors for arrest, these punishment strategies were explicitly directed at black communities, rather than at black individuals, and they eventually informed the history of imprisonment outside the South as well. In the process, white prisoners, along with the black people this system specifically targeted, were affected by its cruelty as well.

The widespread use of torture in connection with convict leasing consolidated forms of punishment that Foucault periodizes as pre-capitalist and thus pre-dating incarceration, inextricably linking them with incarceration itself. As Mancini has pointed out, Foucault's assumption that torture had become historically obsolete in the industrial capitalist countries "misses a fundamental aspect of convict leasing – namely the license it gave for the display not of a sovereign's but of a petty camp boss's power. Leasing allowed the accumulated reservoirs of human cruelty to overflow in the isolated camps and stockades."[20] As flogging was the primary mode of punishment during slavery, "the lash, along with the chain, became the very emblem of servitude for slaves and prisoners."[21] Mancini points out that as late as 1941, the state of Texas still relied principally on the whip.

I have devoted a considerable portion of this article to an exploration of some of the ways slavery's underlying philosophy of punishment insinuated itself into the history of imprisonment. In this concluding section, I want to argue that the tendency to treat racism as a contingent element of the criminal justice system in research, advocacy, and activism associated with the prison abolition movement results in part from its marginalization in histories and theories of punishment. If the category of race rarely appears in Foucault's analyses, so it is also generally absent in the leading contemporary abolitionist texts. Although racism has often been evoked in activist campaigns, the absence of race as an analytical category in the diverse literature associated with prison abolitionism points to problems of the same order as those Joy James detects in Foucault.

Like Foucault, the major theorists of prison abolition have worked within European contexts, and in a large measure in those European countries that can claim historically less repressive penal systems – the Scandinavian countries and the Netherlands. Academics in Norway and the Netherlands began to produce abolitionist theories during the 1960s.[22] Thomas Mathieson, author of *The Politics of Abolition*,[23] grounded his analysis in the work of the Norwegian prisoners' movement, KROM, in which he actively participated during the sixties and seventies. Mathieson's formal approach calls for abolitionist activism that attempts strategically to avoid demands for reform that might further strengthen the prison system, as prison reform has historically tended to do. The local and tactical emphasis of his analysis, first published in 1974, militates against a substantive engagement with issues of race. While Dutch criminologist Willem de Haan, author of a recent work entitled *The Politics of Redress: Crime, Punishment and Penal Abolition*, explores the implications of prison reform in North America and Cuba as well as in Western Europe, his interests do not include an analysis of the close links between punishment practices and structures of racism. It should be pointed out, however, that as postcolonial immigration has radically transformed the racial composition of European populations in general, the prison population in the Netherlands approaches the US in its disproportionate numbers of people of color.

Since an extensive review of the literature on abolitionism is beyond the scope of this article, I will simply point out that while the works of other leading European criminologists and philosophers associated with the international movement for penal abolition – such as René van Swaaningen, Herman Bianchi, Nils Christie, Stanley Cohen, Louk Hulsman, and Rolf de Folter – contain many important insights, there is no sustained analysis of the part antiracism might play in the theory and practice of abolitionism.

In the US, abolitionists can discover a historical relationship of prison activism and antiracism. During the late eighteenth and early nineteenth centuries, Quaker reformers played a pivotal role in developing the US penitentiary. Indeed, the penitentiary system emerged from an abolitionist movement of sorts – a campaign to abolish medieval corporal punishment. The campaign to replace corporal punishment with the penitentiary and the abolitionist movement against slavery invoked similar philosophical arguments based on the Enlightenment belief in a universal humanity and in the moral perfectibility of every human being. If the inherent humanity of African slaves required their release from bondage, then the humanity of "criminals" demanded that they be given the opportunity to repent and perfect their characters.

It is therefore understandable that in North America, the dominant abolitionist trend in scholarship and activism is peacemaking. Harold Pepinsky has observed that as he organized the Fifth International Conference on Penal Abolition,

> I discovered that by far the strongest contingent among the hundreds of correspondents are workers and activists with religious affiliations, notably the peace churches and ecumenical peace groups. Religiously self-identified people cross all eight intellectual traditions which have emerged: academicians and theorists, activists and reformers, feminists, lawmakers, mediators, native traditionalists, peoples of color, and prisoners.[24]

Nevertheless, it seems that no sustained contemporary analysis has emerged of the role antiracism might play in effective abolitionist theories and practices.

One of the major critiques proposed by abolitionists in Europe and North America is directed at social-scientific and popular discourses that assume a necessary conjunction between crime and punishment. Likewise, in the philosophical literature on imprisonment, the prevailing assumption is that individuals are punished because of the crimes they commit. The literature in the field of philosophy of punishment rarely goes further than exploring what Adrian Howe refers to as "relentless repetitions of the unholy trinity of retribution, deterrence and reform."[25] The problems these literatures address largely have to do with the justification and function of punishment. Thus a major theoretical and practical challenge of penal abolitionism is to disarticulate crime and punishment. In fact, many abolitionists deploy statistics that demonstrate how relatively few people who have broken a law are actually called upon by criminal justice systems to answer for their crimes. Sociologists Jim Thomas and Sharon Boehlefeld, for example, who are both critics and advocates of abolitionism, use US Bureau of Justice statistics to demonstrate that "only three persons are incarcerated (in prisons or jails) for every 100 crimes committed."[26]

The Institute for Social Research published Rusche and Kirchheimer's ground-breaking study, *Punishment and Social Structure*, in 1939, which would later have a significant influence on the critical sociology of punishment. Kirchheimer wrote in the introduction that it was

> necessary to strip from the social institution of punishment its ideological veils and juristic appearance and to describe it in its real relationships. The bond, transparent or not, that is supposed to exist between crime and punishment prevents any insight into the independent significance of the history of penal systems. It must be broken. Punishment is neither a simple consequence of crime, nor the reverse side of crime, nor a mere means which is determined by the end to be achieved. Punishment must be understood as a social phenomenon freed from both its juristic concept and its social ends. We do not deny that punishment has specific ends, but we do deny that it can be understood from its ends alone.[27]

Rusche and Kirchheimer, as well as others influenced by their attempt to develop a political economy of punishment, examine the influence of the capitalist market and bourgeois ideology in shaping punishment practices. According to legal scholar Adrian Howe,

> Ruschean-inspired studies . . . made a crucial break with the analytically restricting "legal syllogism" – the common-sense idea that punishment is simply the consequence of crime and that, if there is a need for sociological explanation, "social structure explains crime and crime explains punishment."[28]

However, they, too, do not explore the extent to which the penitentiary system and its attendant forms of labor were heavily influenced by the prevailing ideologies and economic structures of racism, nor, as Howe points out, do they give serious consideration to gender. Nevertheless, their insistence on disarticulating punishment from crime can be seen as opening the way for a consideration of the relationship between race and punishment, a much-needed dimension in the scholarship and activism associated with the abolitionist movement today.

In the contemporary era, the tendency toward more prisons and harsher punishment leads to gross violations of prisoners' human rights and, within the US context, it summons up new perils of racism. The rising numbers of imprisoned black and Latino men and women tell a compelling story of an increasingly intimate link between race and criminalization. While academic and popular discourses assume a necessary conjunction between crime and punishment, it is the conjunction of race, class, and punishment that is most consistent.

In 1926, the first year in which there was a national recording, 21 percent of prison admissions were black. By 1970, black people constituted 39 percent of admissions and in 1992, 54 percent.[29] In 1995, almost one-third of young black men were either in prison or directly under the control of a correctional system. If we consider that "[m]ost people have been involved in delinquent behavior at some point of their lives, and only a small fraction of overall criminal activities are touched by the criminal justice system,"[30] against the backdrop of the increasing proportion of black people entering the ranks of the imprisoned, we are faced with a startling implication. One has a greater chance of going to jail or prison if one is a young black man than if one is actually a law-breaker. While most imprisoned young black men may have broken a law, it is the fact that they are young black men rather than the fact that they are law-breakers which brings them into contact with the criminal justice system.

In this paper, I am specifically concerned with the way the prison system in the US took up and was bolstered by historical forms of racism and how it continues to play a critical role in the racialization of punishment. An effective abolitionist campaign will have to directly address the role of race in the criminalization process. I emphasize the need to disarticulate notions of punishment from crime because I want to argue for a serious consideration of abolitionist strategies to dismantle the prison system in its present role as an institution which preserves existing structures of racism as well as creates more complicated modes of racism in US society. This strategy, I argue, is no more outlandish than is the fact that race and economic status play more prominent roles in shaping the practices of social punishment than does crime, which is always assumed to be the basis for punishment in this society.

NOTES

1 Russel P. Dobash, R. Emerson Dobash, and Sue Gutteridge, *The Imprisonment of Women* (London: Basil Blackwell, 1986).
2 Joy James, *Resisting State Violence: Radicalism, Gender and Race in US Culture* (Minneapolis: University of Minnesota Press, 1996).
3 Michel Foucault, *Discipline and Punish: The Birth of the Prison* (New York: Vintage, 1979), 120–1.
4 Ibid., 121.
5 Ibid., 122.
6 Ibid., 232.
7 John K. Simon, "Michel Foucault on Attica: An Interview," *Social Justice*, 18 (3) (Fall 1991), 27.

8   Ibid., 29.
9   Marc Mauer and Tracy Huling, *Young Black Americans and the Criminal Justice System: Five Years Later* (Washington, DC: The Sentencing Project, 1995).
10 Harriet A. Jacobs, *Incidents in the Life of a Slave Girl* (Cambridge: Harvard University Press, 1987), 46.
11 Milfred C. Fierce, *Slavery Revisited: Blacks and the Southern Convict Lease System, 1865–1933* (New York: Africana Studies Research Center, Brooklyn College, CUNY, 1994), 88.
12 Matthew Mancini, *One Dies, Get Another: Convict Leasing in the American South, 1866–1928* (Columbia, South Carolina: University of South Carolina Press, 1996), 1.
13 E. Franklin Frazier, *From Slavery to Freedom* (New York: Random House), 303.
14 Fierce, *Slavery Revisited*, 85–6.
15 Mancini, *One Dies, Get Another*, 41–2.
16 David Oshinsky, *"Worse than Slavery": Parchman Farm and the Ordeal of Jim Crow Justice* (New York: The Free Press, 1996), 28.
17 As indicated in the above note, Oshinsky chose to entitle his study of Parchman Prison *Worse than Slavery*. According to Matthew Mancini, "[o]f all the factors that distinguish convict leasing from slavery, however, none was more economically important than the fact that the lessee had only a minimal capital investment in any individual convict. This reality combined with a relative – to be sure, also variable – abundance of supply to produce a level of oppression that, taking convict leasing as a whole, can be said to have been 'worse' than slavery during the period of the convict's sentence" (37).
18 Ibid., 67.
19 Ibid., 69.
20 Mancini, *One Dies, Get Another*, 75.
21 Ibid.
22 Criminologist René van Swaaningen refers to Nils Christie and Thomas Mathiesen in Norway and Herman Bianchi and Louk Hulsman in the Netherlands. "What is Abolitionism: An Introduction," in *Abolitionism: Toward a Non-Repressive Approach to Crime*. Proceedings of the Second International Conference on Prison Abolition, Amsterdam, 1985. Edited by Herman Bianchi and René van Swaaningen (Amsterdam: Free University Press, 1986), 9.
23 Thomas Mathiesen, *The Politics of Abolition* (published under the auspices of the Scandinavian Research Council for Criminology, *Scandinavian Studies in Criminology Law in Society* Series) (New York: John Wiley and Sons, 1974).
24 Harold Pepinsky and Richard Quinney (eds), *Criminology as Peacemaking* (Bloomington and Indianapolis: Indiana University Press, 1991), 300.
25 Adrian Howe, *Punish and Critique: Toward a Feminist Analysis of Penality* (New York: Routledge, 1994), 3.
26 Jim Thomas and Sharon Boehlefeld, "Rethinking Abolitionism: 'What Do We Do With Henry?'" *Social Justice*, 18 (Fall 1991), quoted from http://www.soci.nie.edu/-citerim/dp/dppapers/henry, p. 7. "Less than 40 percent of victimization offenses are reported to police (*Bureau of Justice Statistics Bulletin*,

1988: 2), and only about 20 percent of known crimes are cleared by arrest (*CJS Sourcebook*, 1989: 449). The *CJS Sourcebook* shows that of those arrested, about 80 percent are prosecuted, three-quarters of those prosecuted are convicted, and about 70 percent of all felony convictions result in a prison or jail sentence."

27 George Rusche and Otto Kirchheimer, *Punishment and Social Structure* (New York: Morningside Heights, Columbia University Press, 1939), 5.

28 Adrian Howe, *Punish and Critique*, 37. She quotes Dario Melossi, the biographer and leading interpreter of Rusche's work. "An Introduction: Fifty Years Later, Punishment and Social Structure in Comparative Analysis," *Contemporary Crises*, 13 (4), 311.

29 John Irwin and James Austin, *It's About Time: America's Imprisonment Binge* (Belmont, California: Wadsworth, 1997), 7.

30 Edgardo Rotman, *Beyond Punishment: A New View on the Rehabilitation of Criminal Offenders* (New York: Greenwood Press, 1990), 115.

PART II

Marxism, Anti-Racism, and Feminism

7

Reflections on the Black Woman's Role in the Community of Slaves

*The paucity of literature [in 1971] on the black woman, is outrageous on its face. But we must also contend with the fact that too many of these rare studies must claim as their signal achievement the reinforcement of fictitious clichés. They have given credence to grossly distorted categories through which the black woman continues to be perceived. In the words of Nathan and Julia Hare, "she has been labeled 'aggressive' or 'matriarchal' by white scholars and 'castrating female' by [some] blacks" (*Transaction, November–December, 1970*). Many have recently sought to remedy this situation. But for the time being, at least, we are still confronted with these reified images of ourselves. And for now, we must still assume the responsibility of shattering them.*

Initially, I did not envision this paper as strictly confined to the era of slavery. Yet, as I began to think through the issue of the black matriarch, I came to the conclusion that it had to be refuted at its presumed historical inception.

The chief problem I encountered stemmed from the conditions of my incarceration: opportunities for researching the issue I wanted to explore were extremely limited. I chose, therefore, to entitle this piece "Reflections . . ." It does not pretend to be more than a collection of ideas which would constitute a starting point – a framework within which to conduct a rigorous reinvestigation of the black woman as she interacted with her people and with her oppressive environment during slavery.

I would like to dedicate these reflections to one of the most admirable black leaders to emerge from the ranks of our liberation movement – to George Jackson, whom I loved and respected in every way. As I came to know and love him, I saw him developing an acute sensitivity to the real problems facing black women and thus refining his ability to distinguish these from their mythical transpositions. George was uniquely aware of the need to extricate himself and other black men

"Reflections on the Black Woman's Role in the Community of Slaves" was written when Angela Davis was in jail and was first published in *The Black Scholar*, vol. 3, no. 4 (December 1971). Reprinted by permission of *The Black Scholar* journal.

from the remnants of divisive and destructive myths purporting to represent the black woman. If his life had not been so precipitously and savagely extinguished, he would have surely accomplished a task he had already outlined some time ago: a systematic critique of his past misconceptions about black women and of their roots in the ideology of the established order. He wanted to appeal to other black men, still similarly disoriented, to likewise correct themselves through self-criticism. George viewed this obligation as a revolutionary duty, but also, and equally important, as an expression of his boundless love for all black women.

The matriarchal black woman has been repeatedly invoked as one of the fatal by-products of slavery. When the Moynihan Report consecrated this myth with Washington's stamp of approval, its spurious content and propagandistic mission should have become apparent. Yet even outside the established ideological apparatus, and also among black people, unfortunate references to the matriarchate can still be encountered. Occasionally, there is even acknowledgment of the "tangle of pathology" it supposedly engendered. (This black matriarchate, according to Moynihan et al. defines the roots of our oppression as a people.) An accurate portrait of the African woman in bondage must debunk the myth of the matriarchate. Such a portrait must simultaneously attempt to illuminate the historical matrix of her oppression and must evoke her varied, often heroic, responses to the slave-holder's domination.

Lingering beneath the notion of the black matriarch is an unspoken indictment of our female forebears as having actively assented to slavery. The notorious cliché, the "emasculating female," has its roots in the fallacious inference that in playing a central part in the slave "family," the black woman related to the slave-holding class as collaborator. Nothing could be further from the truth. In the most fundamental sense, the slave system did not – and could not – engender and recognize a matriarchal family structure. Inherent in the very concept of the matriarchy is "power." It would have been exceedingly risky for the slave-holding class to openly acknowledge symbols of authority – female symbols no less than male. Such legitimized concentrations of authority might eventually unleash their "power" against the slave system itself.

The American brand of slavery strove toward a rigidified disorganization in family life, just as it had to proscribe all potential social structures within which black people might forge a collective and conscious existence.[1] Mothers and fathers were brutally separated; children, when they became of age, were branded and frequently severed from their mothers. That the mother was "the only legitimate parent of her child" did not therefore mean that she was even permitted to guide it to maturity.

Those who lived under a common roof were often unrelated through blood. Frederick Douglass, for instance, had no recollection of his father. He only vaguely recalled having seen his mother – and then on extremely rare occasions. Moreover, at the age of seven, he was forced to abandon the dwelling of his grandmother, of whom he would later say: "She was to me a mother and a father."[2] The strong personal bonds between immediate family members which oftentimes persisted despite coerced separation bore witness to the remarkable capacity of black people for resisting the disorder so violently imposed on their lives.

Where families were allowed to thrive, they were, for the most part, external fabrications serving the designs of an avaricious, profit-seeking slave-holder.

> The strong hand of the slave-owner dominated the Negro family, which existed at his mercy and often at his own personal instigation. An ex-slave has told of getting married on one plantation: "When you married, you had to jump over a broom three times."[3]

This slave went on to describe the various ways in which his master forcibly coupled men and women with the aim of producing the maximum number of healthy child-slaves. In the words of John Henrik Clarke,

> The family as a functional entity was outlawed and permitted to exist only when it benefited the slave-master. Maintenance of the slave family as a family unit benefited the slave-owners only when, and to the extent that such unions created new slaves who could be exploited.[4]

The designation of the black woman as a matriarch is a cruel misnomer. It is a misnomer because it implies stable kinship structures within which the mother exercises decisive authority. It is cruel because it ignores the profound traumas the black woman must have experienced when she had to surrender her child-bearing to alien and predatory economic interests.

Even the broadest construction of the matriarch concept would not render it applicable to the black slave woman. But it should not be inferred that she therefore played no significant role in the community of slaves. Her indispensable efforts to ensure the survival of her people can hardly be contested. Even if she had done no more, her deeds would still be laudable. But her concern and struggles for physical survival, while clearly important, did not constitute her most outstanding contributions. It will be submitted that by virtue of the brutal force of circumstances, the black woman was assigned the mission of promoting the consciousness and practice of resistance. A great deal has been said about the black *man* and resistance, but very little about the unique relationship black women bore to the resistance struggles during slavery. To understand the part she played in developing and sharpening the thrust towards freedom, the broader meaning of slavery and of American slavery in particular must be explored. Slavery is an ancient human institution. Of slave labor in its traditional form and of serfdom as well, Karl Marx stated:

The slave stands in absolutely no relation to the objective conditions of his labor; it is rather the *labor* itself, in the form of the slave as of the serf, which is placed in the category of *inorganic condition* of production alongside the other natural beings, e.g. cattle, or regarded as an appendage of the earth.[5]

The bondsman's existence as a natural condition of production is complemented and reinforced, according to Marx, by his membership in a social grouping which he perceives to be an extension of nature. Enmeshed in what appears to be a natural state of affairs, the attitude of the slave, to a greater or lesser degree, would be an acquiescence in his subjugation. Friedrich Engels points out that in Athens, the state could depend on a police force consisting entirely of slaves.[6]

The fabric of American slavery differed significantly from ancient slavery and feudalism. True, black people were forced to act as if they were inorganic conditions of production. For slavery was "personality swallowed up in the sordid idea of property – manhood lost in chattelhood."[7] But there were no pre-existent social structures or cultural dictates which might induce reconciliation to the circumstances of their bondage. On the contrary, Africans had been uprooted from their natural environment, their social relations, their culture. No legitimate socio-cultural surroundings would be permitted to develop and flourish, for, in all likelihood, they would be utterly incompatible with the demands of slavery.

Yet another fact would militate against harmony and equilibrium in the slave's relation to his bondage: slavery was enclosed in a society otherwise characterized by "free" wage-labor. Black men and women could always contrast their chains with the nominally free status of white working people. This was quite literally true in such cases where, like Frederick Douglass, they were contracted out as wage-laborers. Unlike the "free" white men alongside whom they worked, they had no right to the meager wages they earned. Such were some of the many contradictions unloosed by the effort to forcibly inject slavery into the early stages of American capitalism.

The combination of a historically superseded slave-labor system based almost exclusively on race and the drive to strip black people of all their social and cultural bonds would create a fateful rupture at the heart of the slave system itself. The slaves would not readily adopt fatalistic attitudes towards the conditions surrounding and ensnaring their lives. They were a people who had been violently thrust into a patently "unnatural" subjugation. If the slave-holders had not maintained an absolute monopoly of violence, if they had not been able to rely on large numbers of their fellow white men – indeed the entire ruling class as well as misled working people – to assist them in their terrorist machinations, slavery would have been far less feasible than it actually proved to be.

The magnitude and effects of the black people's defiant rejection of slavery has not yet been fully documented and illuminated. But there is more than ample evidence that they consistently refused to succumb to the all-encompassing dehumanization objectively demanded by the slave system. Comparatively recent studies have demonstrated that the few slave uprisings – too spectacular to be relegated to oblivion by the racism of ruling-class historians – were not isolated occurrences, as the latter would have had us believe. The reality, we know now, was that these open rebellions erupted with such a frequency that they were as much a part of the texture of slavery as the conditions of servitude themselves. And these revolts were only the tip of an iceberg: resistance expressed itself in other grand modes and also in the seemingly trivial forms of feigned illness and studied indolence.

If resistance was an organic ingredient of slave life, it had to be directly nurtured by the social organization which the slaves themselves improvised. The consciousness of their oppression, the conscious thrust towards its abolition could not have been sustained without impetus from the community they pulled together through the sheer force of their own strength. Of necessity, this community would revolve around the realm which was furthermost removed from the immediate arena of domination. It could only be located in and around the living quarters, the area where the basic needs of physical life were met.

In the area of production, the slaves – pressed into the mold of beasts of burden – were forcibly deprived of their humanity. (And a human being thoroughly dehumanized has no desire for freedom.) But the community gravitating around the domestic quarters might possibly permit a retrieval of the man and the woman in their fundamental humanity. We can assume that in a very real material sense, it was only in domestic life – away from the eyes and whip of the overseer – that the slaves could attempt to assert the modicum of freedom they still retained, it was only there that they might be inspired to project techniques of expanding it further by leveling what few weapons they had against the slave-holding class whose unmitigated drive for profit was the source of their misery.

Via this path, we return to the African slave woman: in the living quarters, the major responsibilities "naturally" fell to her. It was the woman who was charged with keeping the "home in order." This role was dictated by the male supremacist ideology of white society in America; it was also woven into the patriarchal traditions of Africa. As her biological destiny, the woman bore the fruits of procreation; as her social destiny, she cooked, sewed, washed, cleaned house, raised the children. Traditionally the labor of females, domestic work is supposed to complement and confirm their inferiority.

But with the black slave woman, there is a strange twist of affairs: in the infinite anguish of ministering to the needs of the men and children around her (who were not necessarily members of her immediate family), she was performing the *only* labor of the slave community which could not be directly and immediately claimed by the oppressor. There was no compensation for work in the fields; it served no useful purpose for the slaves. Domestic labor was the only meaningful labor for the slave community as a whole (discounting as negligible the exceptional situations where slaves received some pay for their work).

Precisely through performing the drudgery which has long been a central expression of the socially conditioned inferiority of women, the black woman in chains could help to lay the foundation for some degree of autonomy, both for herself and her men. Even as she was suffering under her unique oppression as female, she was thrust by the force of circumstances into the center of the slave community. She was, therefore, essential to the *survival* of the community. Not all people have survived enslavement; hence her survival-oriented activities were themselves a form of resistance. Survival, moreover, was the prerequisite of all higher levels of struggle.

But much more remains to be said of the black woman during slavery. The dialectics of her oppression will become far more complex. It is true that she was a victim of the myth that only the woman, with her diminished capacity for mental and physical labor, should do degrading household work. Yet, the alleged benefits of the ideology of femininity did not accrue to her. She was not sheltered or protected; she would not remain oblivious to the desperate struggle for existence unfolding outside the "home." She was also there in the fields, alongside the man, toiling under the lash from sun-up to sun-down.

This was one of the supreme ironies of slavery: in order to approach its strategic goal – to extract the greatest possible surplus from the labor of the slaves – the black woman had to be released from the chains of the myth of femininity. In the words of W. E. B. Du Bois, "our women in black had freedom contemptuously thrust upon them."[8] In order to function as slave, the black woman had to be annulled as woman, that is, as woman in her historical stance of wardship under the entire male hierarchy. The sheer force of things rendered her equal to her man.

Excepting the woman's role as caretaker of the household, male supremacist structures could not become deeply embedded in the internal workings of the slave system. Though the ruling class was male and rabidly chauvinistic, the slave system could not confer upon the black man the appearance of a privileged position vis-à-vis the black woman. The man-slave could not be the unquestioned superior within the "family" or community, for there was no such thing as the "family provider" among the slaves. The attainment of slavery's intrinsic goals was contingent upon the fullest and most brutal utilization of the productive capacities of every man, woman, and child. They all had to "provide" for the master. The black woman was therefore wholly integrated into the productive force: "The bell rings at four o'clock in the morning and they have half an hour to get ready. Men and women start together, and the women must work as steadily as the men and perform the same tasks as the men."[9]

Even in the posture of motherhood – otherwise the occasion for hypocritical adoration – the black woman was treated with no greater compassion and with no less severity than her man. As one slave related in a narrative of his life: "women who had sucking children suffered much from their breasts becoming full of milk, the infants being left at home; they therefore could not keep up with the other hands: I have seen the overseer beat them with raw hide so that the blood and the milk flew mingled from their breasts."[10]

Moses Grandy, ex-slave, continues his description with an account of a typical form of field punishment reserved for the black woman with child: "She is compelled to lie down over a hole made to receive her corpulency, and is flogged with the whip, or beat with a paddle, which has holes in it; at every stroke comes a blister."[11]

The unbridled cruelty of this leveling process whereby the black woman was forced into equality with the black man requires no further explanation. She shared in the deformed equality of equal oppression.

But out of this deformed equality was forged quite undeliberately, yet inexorably, a state of affairs which could harness an immense potential in the black woman. Expending indispensable labor for the enrichment of her oppressor, she could attain a practical awareness of the oppressor's utter dependence on her – for the master needs the slave far more than the slave needs the master. At the same time she could realize that while her productive activity was wholly subordinated to the will of the master, it was nevertheless proof of her ability to transform things. For "labor is the living, shaping fire; it represents the impermanence of things, their temporality."[12]

The black woman's consciousness of the oppression suffered by her people was honed in the bestial realities of daily experience. It would not be the stunted awareness of a woman confined to the home. She would be prepared to ascend to the same levels of resistance which were accessible to her men. Even as she performed her housework, the black woman's role in the slave community could not be identical to the historically evolved female role. Stripped of the palliative feminine veneer which might have encouraged a passive performance of domestic tasks, she was now uniquely capable of weaving into the warp and woof of domestic life a profound consciousness of resistance.

With the contributions of strong black women, the slave community as a whole could achieve heights unscaleable within the families of the white oppressed or even within the patriarchal kinship groups of Africa. Latently or actively it was always a community of resistance. It frequently erupted in insurgency, but was daily animated by the minor acts of sabotage which harassed the slave-master to no end. Had the black woman failed to rise to the occasion, the community of slaves could not have fully developed in this direction. The slave system would have to deal with the black woman as the custodian of a house of resistance.

The oppression of black women during the era of slavery, therefore, had to be buttressed by a level of overt ruling-class repression. Her routine oppression had to assume an unconcealed dimension of outright counter-insurgency.

To say that the oppression of black slave women necessarily incorporated open forms of counter-insurgency is not as extravagant as it might initially appear. The penetration of counter-insurgency into the day-to-day routine of the slave-master's domination will be considered towards the end of this paper. First, the participation of black women in the overt and explosive upheavals which constantly rocked the slave system must be confirmed. This will be an indication of the magnitude of her role as caretaker of a household of resistance – of the degree to which she could concretely encourage those around her to keep their eyes on freedom. It will also confirm the objective circumstances to which the slave-master's counter-insurgency was a response.

With the sole exceptions of Harriet Tubman and Sojourner Truth, black women of the slave era remain more or less enshrouded in unrevealed history. And, as Earl Conrad has demonstrated, even "General Tubman's" role has been consistently and grossly minimized. She was a far greater warrior against slavery than is suggested by the prevalent misconception that her only outstanding contribution was to make nineteen trips into the South, bringing over 300 slaves to their freedom.

> [She] was head of the Intelligence Service in the Department of the South throughout the Civil War; she is the only American woman to lead troops black and white on the field of battle, as she did in the Department of the South. . . . She was a compelling and stirring orator in the councils of the abolitionists and the anti-slavers, a favorite of the anti-slavery conferences. She was the fellow planner with Douglass, Martin Delany, Wendell Phillips, Gerrit Smith and other leaders of the anti-slavery movement.[13]

No extensive and systematic study of the role of black women in resisting slavery has come to my attention. It has been noted that large numbers of freed black women worked towards the purchase of their relatives' and friends' freedom. About the participation of women in both the well-known and the more obscure slave revolts, only casual remarks have been made. It has been observed, for instance, that Gabriel's wife was active in planning the rebellion spearheaded by her husband, but little else has been said about her.

The sketch which follows is based in its entirety on the works of Herbert Aptheker, the only resources available to me at the time of this writing.[14] These facts, gleaned from Aptheker's works on slave revolts and other forms of resistance, should signal the urgency to undertake a thorough study of the black woman as anti-slavery rebel.

Aptheker's research has disclosed the widespread existence of communities of blacks who were neither free nor in bondage. Throughout the South (in South and North Carolina, Virginia, Louisiana, Florida, Georgia, Mississippi and Alabama), maroon communities consisting of fugitive slaves and their descendants were "an ever present feature" – from 1642 to 1864 – of slavery. They provided "havens for fugitives, served as bases for marauding expeditions against nearby plantations and, at times, supplied leadership to planned uprisings."[15]

Every detail of these communities was invariably determined by and steeped in resistance, for their raison d'être emanated from their perpetual assault on slavery. Only in a fighting stance could the maroons hope to secure their constantly imperiled freedom. As a matter of necessity, the women of those communities were compelled to define themselves – no less than the men – through their many acts of resistance. Hence, throughout this brief survey the counter-attacks and heroic efforts at defense assisted by maroon women will be a recurring motif.

As it will be seen, black women often poisoned the food and set fire to the houses of their masters. For those who were also employed as domestics these particular overt forms of resistance were especially available.

The vast majority of the incidents to be related involve either tactically unsuccessful assaults or eventually thwarted attempts at defense. In all likelihood, numerous successes were achieved, even against the formidable obstacles posed by the slave system. Many of these were probably unpublicized even at the time of their occurrence, lest they provide encouragement to the rebellious proclivities of other slaves and, for other slaveholders, an occasion for fear and despair.

During the early years of the slave era (1708) a rebellion broke out in New York. Among its participants were surely many women, for one, along with three men, was executed in retaliation for the killing of seven whites. It may not be entirely insignificant that while the men were hanged, she was heinously burned alive.[16] In the same colony, women played an active role in a 1712 uprising in the course of which slaves, with their guns, clubs, and knives, killed members of the slave-holding class and managed to wound others. While some of the insurgents – among them a pregnant woman – were captured, others – including a woman – committed suicide rather than surrender.[17]

"In New Orleans one day in 1730 a woman slave received 'a violent blow from a French soldier for refusing to obey him' and in her anger shouted 'that the French should not long insult Negroes.'"[18] As it was later disclosed, she and undoubtedly many other women, had joined in a vast plan to destroy slave-holders. Along with eight men, this dauntless woman was executed. Two years later, Louisiana pronounced a woman and four men leaders of a planned rebellion. They were all executed and, in a typically savage gesture, their heads publicly displayed on poles.[19]

Charleston, South Carolina condemned a black woman to die in 1740 for arson,[20] a form of sabotage, as earlier noted, frequently carried out by women. In Maryland, for instance, a slave woman was executed in 1776 for having destroyed by fire her master's house, his outhouses and tobacco house.[21]

In the thick of the colonials' war with England, a group of defiant slave women and men were arrested in Saint Andrew's Parish, Georgia in 1774. But before they were captured, they had already brought a number of slave owners to their death.[22]

The maroon communities have been briefly described; from 1782 to 1784, Louisiana was a constant target of maroon attacks. When twenty-five of this community's members were finally taken prisoner, men and women alike were all severely punished.[23]

As can be inferred from previous examples, the North did not escape the tremendous impact of fighting black women. In Albany, New York, two women were among three slaves executed for anti-slavery activities in 1794.[24] The respect and admiration accorded the black woman fighter by her people is strikingly illustrated by an incident which transpired in York, Pennsylvania: when, during the early months of 1803, Margaret Bradley was convicted of attempting to poison two white people, the black inhabitants of the area revolted *en masse*.

> They made several attempts to destroy the town by fire and succeeded, within a period of three weeks, in burning eleven buildings. Patrols were established, strong guards set up, the militia dispatched to the scene of the unrest . . . and a reward of three hundred dollars offered for the capture of the insurrectionists.[25]

A successful elimination by poisoning of several "of our respectable men" (said a letter to the governor of North Carolina) was met by the execution of four or five slaves. One was a woman who was burned alive.[26] In 1810, two women and a man were accused of arson in Virginia.[27]

In 1811 North Carolina was the scene of a confrontation between a maroon community and a slave-catching posse. Local newspapers reported that its members "had bid defiance to any force whatever and were resolved to stand their ground." Of the entire community, two were killed, one wounded and two – both women – were captured.[28]

Aptheker's *Documentary History of the Negro People in the United States* contains a portion of the transcript of an 1812 confession of a slave rebel in Virginia. The latter divulged the information that a black woman brought him into a plan to kill their master and that yet another black woman had been charged with concealing him after the killing occurred.[29]

In 1816 it was discovered that a community of three hundred escaped slaves – men, women, children – had occupied a fort in Florida. After the US Army was dispatched with instructions to destroy the community, a ten-day siege terminated with all but forty of the three hundred dead. All the slaves fought to the very end.[30] In the course of a similar, though smaller confrontation between maroons and a militia group (in South Carolina, 1826), a woman and a child were killed.[31] Still another maroon community was attacked in Mobile, Alabama in 1837. Its inhabitants, men and women alike, resisted fiercely – according to local newspapers, "fighting like Spartans."[32]

Convicted of having been among those who, in 1829, had been the cause of a devastating fire in Augusta, Georgia, a black woman was "executed, dissected, and exposed" (according to an English visitor). Moreover, the execution of yet another woman, about to give birth, was imminent.[33] During the same year, a group of slaves, being led from Maryland to be sold in the South, had apparently planned to kill the traders and make their way to freedom. One of the traders was successfully done away with, but eventually a posse captured all the slaves. Of the six leaders sentenced to death, one was a woman. She was first permitted, for reasons of economy, to give birth to her child.[34] Afterwards, she was publicly hanged.

The slave class in Louisiana, as noted earlier, was not unaware of the formidable threat posed by the black woman who chose to fight. It responded accordingly: in 1846 a posse of slave-owners ambushed a community of maroons, killing one woman and wounding two others. A black man was also assassinated.[35] Neither could the border states escape the recognition that slave women were eager to battle for their freedom. In 1850 in the state of Missouri, "about thirty slaves, men and women, of four different owners, had armed themselves with knives, clubs and three guns and set out for a free state." Their pursuers, who could unleash a far more powerful violence than they, eventually thwarted their plans.[36]

This factual survey of but a few of the open acts of resistance in which black women played major roles will close with two further events. When a maroon camp in Mississippi was destroyed in 1857, four of its members did not manage to elude capture, one of whom was a fugitive slave woman.[37] All of them, women as well as men, must have waged a valiant fight. Finally, there occurred in October 1862, a skirmish between maroons and a scouting party of Confederate soldiers in the state of Virginia.[38] This time, however, the maroons were the victors and it may well have been that some of the many women helped to put the soldiers to death.

The oppression of slave women had to assume dimensions of open counter-insurgency. Against the background of the facts presented above, it would be difficult indeed to refute this contention. As for those who engaged in open battle, they were no less ruthlessly punished than slave men. It would even appear that in many cases they may have suffered penalties which were more excessive than those meted out to the men. On occasion, when men were hanged, the women were burned alive. If such practices were widespread, their logic would be clear. They would be terrorist methods designed to dissuade other black women from following the examples of their fighting sisters. If all black women rose up alongside their men, the institution of slavery would be in difficult straits.

It is against the backdrop of her role as fighter that the routine oppression of the slave woman must be explored once more. If she was burned, hanged, broken on the wheel, her head paraded on poles before her oppressed brothers and sisters, she must have also felt the edge of this counter-insurgency as a fact of her daily existence. The slave system would not only have to make conscious efforts to stifle the tendencies towards acts of the kind described above; it would be no less necessary to stave off escape attempts (escapes to maroon country!) and all the various forms of sabotage within the system. Feigning illness was also resistance, as were work slow-downs and actions destructive to the crops. The more extensive these acts, the more the slave-holder's profits would tend to diminish.

While a detailed study of the myriad modes in which this counter-insurgency was manifested can and should be conducted, the following reflections will focus on a single aspect of the slave woman's oppression particularly prominent in its brutality.

Much has been said about the sexual abuses to which the black woman was forced to submit. They are generally explained as an outgrowth of the male supremacy of Southern culture: the purity of white womanhood could not be violated by the aggressive sexual activity desired by the white male. His instinctual urges would find expression in his relationships with his property – the black slave woman, who would have to become his unwilling concubine. No doubt there is an element of truth in these statements, but it is equally important to unearth the meaning of these sexual abuses from the vantage point of the woman who was assaulted.

In keeping with the theme of these reflections, it will be submitted that the slave-master's sexual domination of the black woman contained an unveiled element of counter-insurgency. To understand the basis for this assertion, the dialectical moments of the slave woman's oppression must be restated and their movement recaptured. The prime factor, it has been said, was the total and violent expropriation of her labor with no compensation save the pittance necessary for bare existence.

Secondly, as female, she was the housekeeper of the living quarters. In this sense, she was already doubly oppressed. However, having been wrested from passive, "feminine" existence by the sheer force of things – literally by forced labor – confining domestic tasks were incommensurable with what she had become. That is to say, by virtue of her participation in production, she would not act the part of the passive female, but could experience the same need as her men to challenge the conditions of her subjugation. As the center of domestic life, the only life at all removed from the arena of exploitation, and thus as an important source of survival, the black woman could play a pivotal role in nurturing the thrust towards freedom.

The slave-master would attempt to thwart this process. He knew that as female, this slave woman could be particularly vulnerable in her sexual existence. Although he would not pet her and deck her out in frills, the white master could endeavor to re-establish her femaleness by reducing her to the level of her *biological* being. Aspiring with his sexual assaults to establish her as a female *animal*, he would be striving to destroy her proclivities towards resistance. Of the sexual relations of animals, taken at their abstract biological level (and not in terms of their quite different social potential for human beings), Simone de Beauvoir says the following:

> It is unquestionably the male who *takes* the female – she is *taken*. Often the word applies literally, for whether by means of special organs or through superior strength, the male seizes her and holds her in place; he performs the copulatory movements; and, among insects, birds, and mammals, he penetrates. . . . Her body becomes a resistance to be broken through. . . .[39]

The act of copulation, reduced by the white man to an animal-like act, would be symbolic of the effort to conquer the resistance the black woman could unloose.

In confronting the black woman as adversary in a sexual contest, the master would be subjecting her to the most elemental form of terrorism distinctively suited for the female: rape. Given the already terroristic texture of plantation life, it would be as potential victim of rape that the slave woman would be most unguarded. Further, she might be most conveniently manipulable if the master contrived a ransom system of sorts, forcing her to pay with her body for food, diminished severity in treatment, the safety of her children, etc.

The integration of rape into the sparsely furnished legitimate social life of the slaves harks back to the feudal "right of the first night," the *jus primae noctis.* The feudal lord manifested and reinforced his domination over the serfs by asserting his authority to have sexual intercourse with all the females. The right itself referred specifically to all freshly married women. But while the right to the first night eventually evolved into the institution-alized "virgin tax,"[40] the American slave-holder's sexual domination never lost its openly terroristic character.

As a direct attack on the black female as potential insurgent, this sexual repression finds its parallels in virtually every historical situation where the woman actively challenges oppression. Thus, Frantz Fanon could say of the Algerian woman, "A woman led away by soldiers who comes back a week later – it is not necessary to question her to understand that she has been violated dozens of times."[41]

In its political contours, the rape of the black woman was not exclusively an attack upon her. Indirectly, its target was also the slave community as a whole. In launching the sexual war on the woman, the master would not only assert his sovereignty over a critically important figure of the slave community, he would also be aiming a blow against the black man. The latter's instinct to protect his female relations and comrades (now stripped of its male supremacist implications) would be frustrated and violated to the extreme. Placing the white male's sexual barbarity in bold relief, Du Bois cries out in a rhetorical vein: "I shall forgive the South much in its final judgment day: I shall forgive its slavery, for slavery is a world-old habit; I shall forgive its fighting for a well-lost cause, and for remembering that struggle with tender tears; I shall forgive its so-called 'pride of race,' the passion of its hot blood, and even its dear, old, laughable strutting and posing; but one thing I shall never forgive, neither in this world nor the world to come: its wanton and continued and persistent insulting of the black womanhood which it sought and seeks to prostitute to its lust."[42]

The retaliatory import of the rape for the black man would be entrap-ment in an untenable situation. Clearly the master hoped that once the black man was struck by his manifest inability to rescue his women from sexual assaults of the master, he would begin to experience deep-seated doubts about his ability to resist at all.

Certainly the wholesale rape of slave women must have had a profound impact on the slave community. Yet it could not succeed in its intrinsic aim of stifling the impetus towards struggle. Countless black women did not passively submit to these abuses, as the slaves in general refused to passively accept their bondage. The struggles of the slave woman in the sexual realm were a continuation of the resistance interlaced in the slave's daily exist-ence. As such, this was yet another form of insurgency, a response to a politically tinged sexual repression.

Even E. Franklin Frazier (who goes out of his way to defend the thesis that "the master in his mansion and his colored mistress in her special house nearby represented the final triumph of social ritual in the presence of the deepest feelings of human solidarity"[43]) could not entirely ignore the black woman who fought back. He notes: "That physical compulsion was necessary at times to secure submission on the part of black women . . . is supported by historical evidence and has been preserved in the tradition of Negro families."[44]

The sexual contest was one of many arenas in which the black woman had to prove herself as a warrior against oppression. What Frazier unwillingly concedes would mean that countless children brutally fathered by whites were conceived in the thick of battle. Frazier himself cites the story of a black woman whose great grandmother, a former slave, would describe with great zest the battles behind all her numerous scars – that is, all save one. In response to questions concerning the unexplained scar, she had always simply said: "White men are as low as dogs, child, stay away from them." The mystery was not unveiled until after the death of this brave woman: "She received that scar at the hands of her master's youngest son, a boy of about eighteen years at the time she conceived their child, my grandmother Ellen."[45]

An intricate and savage web of oppression intruded at every moment into the black woman's life during slavery. Yet a single theme appears at every juncture: the woman transcending, refusing, fighting back, asserting herself over and against terrifying obstacles. It was not her comrade brother against whom her incredible strength was directed. She fought alongside her man, accepting or providing guidance according to her talents and the nature of their tasks. She was in no sense an authoritarian figure; neither her domestic role nor her acts of resistance could relegate the man to the shadows. On the contrary, she herself had just been forced to leave behind the shadowy realm of female passivity in order to assume her rightful place beside the insurgent male.

This portrait cannot, of course, presume to represent every individual slave woman. It is rather a portrait of the potentials and possibilities inherent in the situation to which slave women were anchored. Invariably there were those who did not realize this potential. There were those who were indifferent and a few who were outright traitors. But certainly they were not the vast majority. The image of black women enchaining their men, cultivating relationships with the oppressor, is a cruel fabrication which must be called by its right name. It is a dastardly ideological weapon designed to impair our capacity for resistance today by foisting upon us the ideal of male supremacy.

According to a time-honored principle, advanced by Marx, Lenin, Fanon, and numerous other theorists, the status of women in any given society is a barometer measuring the overall level of social development. As Fanon has masterfully shown, the strength and efficacy of social struggles –

and especially revolutionary movements – bear an immediate relationship to the range and quality of female participation.

The meaning of this principle is strikingly illustrated by the role of the black woman during slavery. Attendant to the indiscriminate, brutal pursuit of profit, the slave woman attained a correspondingly brutal status of equality. But in practice, she could work up a fresh content for this deformed equality by inspiring and participating in acts of resistance of every form and color. She could turn the weapon of equality in struggle against the avaricious slave system which had engendered the mere caricature of equality in oppression. The black woman's activities increased the total incidence of anti-slavery assaults. But most important, without consciously rebellious black women, the theme of resistance could not have become so thoroughly intertwined in the fabric of daily existence. The status of black women within the community of slaves was definitely a barometer indicating the overall potential for resistance.

This process did not end with the formal dissolution of slavery. Under the impact of racism, the black woman has been continually constrained to inject herself into the desperate struggle for existence. She – like her man – has been compelled to work for wages, providing for her family as she was previously forced to provide for the slave-holding class. The infinitely onerous nature of this equality should never be overlooked. For the black woman has always also remained harnessed to the chores of the household. Yet, she could never be exhaustively defined by her uniquely "female" responsibilities.

As a result, black women have made significant contributions to struggles against the racism and the dehumanizing exploitation of a wrongly organized society. In fact, it would appear that the intense levels of resistance historically maintained by black people and thus the historical function of the black liberation struggle as harbinger of change throughout the society are due in part to the greater *objective* equality between the black man and the black woman. Du Bois put it this way: "In the great rank and file of our five million women, we have the up-working of new revolutionary ideals, which must in time have vast influence on the thought and action of this land."[46]

Official and unofficial attempts to blunt the effects of the egalitarian tendencies as between the black man and woman should come as no surprise. The matriarch concept, embracing the clichéd "female castrator," is, in the last instance, an open weapon of ideological warfare. Black men and women alike remain its potential victims – men unconsciously lunging at the woman, equating her with the myth, women sinking back into the shadows, lest an aggressive posture resurrect the myth in themselves.

The myth must be consciously repudiated as myth and the black woman in her true historical contours must be resurrected. We, the black women of today, must accept the full weight of a legacy wrought in blood by our mothers in chains. Our fight, while identical in spirit, reflects different conditions and thus implies different paths of struggle. But as heirs to a tradition of supreme perseverance and heroic resistance, we must hasten to take our place wherever our people are forging on towards freedom.

NOTES

1 It is interesting to note a parallel in Nazi Germany: with all its ranting and raving about motherhood and the family, Hitler's regime made a conscious attempt to strip the family of virtually all its social functions. The thrust of their unspoken program for the family was to reduce it to a biological unit and to force its members to relate in an unmediated fashion to the fascist bureaucracy. Clearly the Nazis endeavored to crush the family in order to ensure that it could not become a center from which oppositional activity might originate.

2 Herbert Aptheker, ed., *A Documentary History of the Negro People in the United States* (New York: Citadel Press, 1969), 207.

3 Douglass quoted in Andrew Billingsley, *Black Families in White America* (Englewood, NJ: Prentice-Hall Inc., 1968), 61.

4 John Henrik Clarke, "The Black Woman: A Figure in World History," Part III, *Essence* (July 1971).

5 Karl Marx, *Grundrisse der Kritik der Politischen Oekonomie* (Berlin: Dietz Verlag, 1953), 389.

6 Friedrich Engels, *Origin of the Family, Private Property and the State* (New York: International Publishers, 1942), 107.

7 Frederick Douglass, *Life and Times of Frederick Douglass* (New York: Collier Books, 1962), 96.

8 W. E. B. Du Bois, *Darkwater, Voices from Within the Veil* (New York: AMS Press, 1969), 185.

9 Lewis Clarke, *Narrative of the Sufferings of Lewis and Milton Clarke, Sons of a Soldier of the Revolution* (Boston, 1846), 127 [quoted by E. Franklin Frazier, *The Negro Family in the United States*, Chicago: University of Chicago Press, 1966].

10 Moses Grandy, *Narrative of the Life of Moses Grandy; Late a Slave in the United States of America* (Boston, 1844), 18 [quoted by E. Franklin Frazier, *The Negro Family in the United States*, Chicago: University of Chicago Press, 1966].

11 Ibid.

12 Marx, *Grundrisse*, 266.

13 Earl Conrad, "I Bring You General Tubman," *The Black Scholar*, vol. 1, no. 3–4, January–February 1970, 4.

14 In February 1949, Herbert Aptheker published an essay in *Masses and Mainstream* entitled "The Negro Woman."

15 Herbert Aptheker, "Slave Guerrilla Warfare," in *To Be Free, Studies in American Negro History* (New York: International Publishers, 1969 [1st edn, 1948]), 11.

16　Herbert Aptheker, *American Negro Slave Revolts* (New York: International Publishers, 1970 [1st edn, 1943]), 169.
17　Ibid., 173.
18　Ibid., 181.
19　Ibid., 182.
20　Ibid., 190.
21　Ibid., 145.
22　Ibid., 201.
23　Ibid., 207.
24　Ibid., 215.
25　Ibid., 239.
26　Ibid., 241–2.
27　Ibid., 247.
28　Ibid., 251.
29　Aptheker, *Documentary History*, 55–7.
30　Aptheker, *Slave Revolts*, 259.
31　Ibid., 277.
32　Ibid., 259.
33　Ibid., 281.
34　Ibid., 487.
35　Aptheker, "Guerrilla Warfare," 27.
36　Aptheker, *Slave Revolts*, 342.
37　Aptheker, "Guerrilla Warfare," 28.
38　Ibid., 29.
39　Simone de Beauvoir, *The Second Sex* (New York: Bantam Books, 1961), 18–19.
40　August Bebel, *Women and Socialism* (New York: Socialist Literature Co., 1910), 66–9.
41　Frantz Fanon, *A Dying Colonialism* (New York: Grove Press, 1967), 119.
42　Du Bois, *Darkwater*, 172.
43　E. Franklin Frazier, *The Negro Family in the United States* (Chicago: University of Chicago Press, 1966 [1st edn, 1939]), 69.
44　Ibid., 53.
45　Ibid., 53–4.
46　Du Bois, *Darkwater*, 185.

8

Rape, Racism, and the Capitalist Setting

Some of the most flagrant symptoms of social deterioration are acknowledged as serious problems only when they have assumed such epidemic proportions that they appear to defy solution. Rape is a case in point. After ages of silence, suffering, and misplaced guilt, sexual violence is emerging as a serious problem plaguing present-day capitalist society.

There is nothing new about rape itself; what is new is its pervasiveness and seeming uncontrollability in capitalist countries today. Although it is shocking enough to learn that in the United States, for example, rape is now the fastest growing violent crime,[1] the profoundly pathological nature of this epidemic cannot be genuinely understood unless the high incidence of sexual violence in the capitalist countries is contracted with its virtual absence in the socialist world.*

The infrequent occurrence of rape in socialist countries boldly contradicts a widespread assumption in the anti-rape movement: that the roots of the urge to rape lie in the instinctual make-up of men. What appears, instead, to be confirmed is the connection between the rising number of rapes and the social relations of capitalism. It is in this context that serious questions must be raised about anti-rape measures which rely in the first place on the repressive powers of the criminal justice system.

It is true, of course, that if men rape because they are men – as Susan Brownmiller and other theorists have argued – women will always be forced to regard the police, courts, and prisons as their only glimmer of hope. If, on the other hand, the incentives for rape are not a natural product of male

*Author's note, 1998: Information regarding rape in the then socialist countries was not readily available at the time this essay was written. Today I would argue for a relationship between sexual violence and capitalist economies that is far more complex than this analysis acknowledges.

This essay first appeared in The Black Scholar, vol. 9, no. 7 (April 1978). An extended version, entitled "Rape, Racism, and the Myth of the Black Rapist," appeared in Women, Race, and Class by Angela Y. Davis (New York: Random House, 1981). Reprinted by permission of The Black Scholar journal.

anatomy or psychology, but are rather social in nature, the prospects for eradicating sexual violence will depend on changes of an entirely different order.

In the US and other capitalist countries, rape laws were originally framed for the protection of men of the upper classes, whose women ran the risk of being assaulted. What happens to working-class women has always been of little concern to the courts. As a result, appallingly few rapists have been prosecuted – appallingly few, that is, if black men are exempted from consideration. While rapists of working-class women have so rarely been brought to justice, rape charges have been aimed indiscriminately at black men, guilty and innocent alike. Thus, of the 455 men executed between 1930 and 1967 for rape convictions, 405 of them were black.[2]

In the history of the United States, the fraudulent rape charge is one of the most formidable artifices invented by racism. The myth of the black rapist has been methodically conjured up when recurrent waves of violence and terror against the black community required a convincing explanation. If black women are conspicuously absent from the ranks of the anti-rape movement today, it is, in large part, their way of protesting the movement's posture of indifference toward the frame-up rape charge as an incitement to racist aggression. Too many innocents have been sacrificed to gas chambers and lifer's cells for black women to seek aid from police and judges. Moreover, as rape victims themselves, they have found little if any sympathy from these men in uniforms and robes. And stories about police assaults on black rape victims are heard too frequently to be dismissed as aberrations.

That black women have not joined the anti-rape movement *en masse* does not mean that they oppose anti-rape measures in general. It was black women, after all, who conducted many decades ago the very first organized protest against sexual abuse. Their eighty-year-old tradition of organized struggle against rape is a reflection of the fact that for black women, the threat of sexual abuse has always loomed large. Indeed, one of the salient historical features of racism has been the assumption that white men – primarily those who are economically powerful – possess an incontestable right of access to black women's bodies.

Slavery relied as much on routine sexual abuse as on the whip and the lash. Excessive sex urges, whether they existed among individual white men or not, had nothing to do with this institutionalized rape. Sexual coercion was an essential dimension of the social relations between slave-master and slave. In other words, the right claimed by slave-owners and their agents over the bodies of female slaves was a direct expression of their presumed property rights over black people in general. The license to rape derived from and facilitated the ruthless economic domination that was the gruesome hallmark of slavery.

This pattern of institutionalized sexual abuse was so strongly established that it survived the abolition of slavery. The group rapes committed by the Ku Klux Klan and other terrorist organizations of the post-Civil War period were thinly disguised political weapons – attempts to thwart the drive for black equality. Meanwhile, the daily drama of racism continued to unfold in the countless anonymous confrontations between black women and those white men who were convinced that rape was only natural. These assaults were ideologically sanctioned by politicians, historians, novelists and other public figures who systematically represented black women as promiscuous and immoral. Not even writers like Gertrude Stein could resist: one of her black women characters "had the simple, promiscuous unmorality of the black people."[3] The imposition of this attitude on white men of the working class was a key element in the development of racist ideology.

Racism has always bolstered sexual coercion. While black women and their sisters of color have been the main targets, white women have suffered as well. For, once white men were persuaded that they could commit sexual assaults on women of color with impunity, their conduct toward women of their own race could not have remained unscarred. To what extent has racism served as a provocation to rape? To what extent have white women become victims of the ricochet fire of racist-inspired sexual abuse? These are questions which deserve far more attention than they have received within the anti-rape movement.

If there has ever been any doubt about the importance of these questions, the Vietnam experience certainly should have dispelled it. Because it was drummed into the heads of US soldiers that they were confronting an inferior race, they could be made to believe that raping Vietnamese women was a necessary soldierly duty. They could even be instructed to "search" the women with their penises. It was the unwritten policy of the US Military Command to systematically encourage rape, for it was an extremely effective weapon of mass terrorism.[4]

Where are the thousands upon thousands of Vietnam veterans who witnessed and participated in these horrors? How did that experience condition their attitudes toward women in general? While it would be quite erroneous to single out Vietnam veterans as the main perpetrators of sexual crimes, there can be little doubt that the horrendous echoes of Vietnam are still being heard by women of all colors in the United States today.

It is a painful irony that the very anti-rape theorists who fail to explore the part played by racism in instigating rape single out men of color as those most likely to assault women. In her widely read study of rape, Susan Brownmiller claims that the historical oppression of black men has deprived them of many of the "legitimate" modes of expressing their male supremacist proclivities. They resort, therefore, to acts of sexual violence.

Describing "ghetto inhabitants," Brownmiller contends that corporate executive dining rooms and climbs up Mount Everest are not usually accessible to those who form the subculture of violence. Access to a female body – through force – is within their ken.[5]

Brownmiller is not alone among contemporary theorists in arguing that black men are disproportionately inclined to become rapists. This passage from Jean MacKellar's *Rape: The Bait and the Trap* is a sample of the ideas to be found in the current literature on rape. "Blacks raised in the hard life of the ghetto learn that they can get what they want only by seizing it. Violence is the rule in the game for survival. Women are fair prey: to obtain a woman one subdues her."[6]

MacKellar has been so completely mesmerized by the myth of the black rapist that she makes the unabashed claim that 90 percent of all reported rapes in the US are committed by black men. Inasmuch as the FBI's corresponding figure is 47 percent, it is difficult to believe that MacKellar's statement is not an intentional provocation.

All recent studies on rape in the United States have acknowledged the disparity between the actual incidence of sexual assaults and those that are reported to the police. According to Brownmiller, for example, reported rapes range anywhere from one in five to one in twenty.[7] The discrepancy may be even greater: a study published by the New York Radical Feminists concludes that reported rapes may run as low as 5 percent.[8] There is, nevertheless, a tendency to equate the "police blotter rapist" with the "typical rapist" in much of the literature against rape. If this tendency persists, it will be impossible to uncover the real causes of rape.

Diana Russell's *The Politics of Rape* reinforces the current notion that the typical rapist is a man of color or, if he is white, a poor or working-class man. Her book is based on a series of interviews conducted with rape victims in the San Francisco Bay Area. Of the twenty-two cases she describes, twelve, i.e. more than half, involve women who have been raped by black, Chicano, or Native American men. It is revealing that of the original 95 interviews she recorded during the preparation of her book, only 26 percent involved men of color. If this dubious process of selection is not enough to evoke deep suspicions of racism, consider the advice she offers to white women: "If some black men see rape of white women as an act of revenge or as a justifiable expression of hostility toward whites, I think it is equally realistic for white women to be less trusting of black men than many of them are."[9]

Brownmiller, MacKellar, and Russell succumb to the old racist sophistry of blaming the victim. Whether innocently or consciously, their pronouncements have facilitated the resurrection of the timeworn myth of the black rapist. Their historical myopia further prevents them from comprehending the way in which the portrayal of black men as rapists reinforces racism's open invitation to white men to sexually avail themselves of black women's bodies.

The fictional image of the black man as rapist has always strengthened its inseparable companion; the image of the black woman as chronically promiscuous; for once the notion is accepted that black men harbor irresistible, animal-like sexual urges, the entire race is invested with bestiality If black men are ravishers of white women, black women must welcome the sexual attentions of white men. "Loose" women and whores, their claims of rape will always lack legitimacy.

The spectre of the black rapist could come alive only with its terrible powers of persuasion within the irrational world of racist ideology. But it is not enough to relegate the black rapist to the cast of fictional characters peopling racist mythology. However irrational the myth may be, it was not a spontaneous aberration. It was, on the contrary, a distinctly political invention. Unless its historical genesis is understood, the myth of the black rapist can never be torn down.

When black men were slaves, they were not labeled unrestrained rapists; as astounding as it may sound, there was not a single publicized accusation of rape against black males during the entire Civil War. It was Frederick Douglass who pointed out that this alleged rape instinct would certainly have been activated at a time when white women were unprotected by their male guardians, who had left *en masse* for the front.[10]

In the immediate aftermath of the Civil War, the specter of the black rapist had not yet appeared on the historical scene. But lynchings, reserved during slavery for white abolitionists, were proving to be valuable political weapons. Before lynching could be consolidated as a popularly accepted institution, however, its savagery had to be justified convincingly. These were the circumstances which spawned the myth of the black rapist, for the rape charge turned out to be the most powerful of several attempts to justify the institution of lynching. Lynching, in turn, complemented by the systematic rape of black women, became an essential ingredient of a strategy of terror that guaranteed the over-exploitation of black labor and, after the dismantling of gains made during the reconstruction, the political domination of black people as a whole.

The northern capitalist takeover of the post-war southern economy gave lynching its most vigorous impulse. If black people could remain the most intensively exploited group within the swelling ranks of the working class, a twofold advantage could be enjoyed by the capitalists; extra profits would result from over-exploitation, and white workers' hostilities toward their employers could be defused. The second advantage was critical, for the white worker who assumed a racist posture toward the black worker would consequently feel a racial affinity – or even solidarity – with the bosses he should have been challenging.

Had black people accepted this stamp of economic and political inferiority passively, the necessity for lynching would not have arisen. But lynchings did occur – more than ten thousand during the three decades following the war[11] – because vast numbers of ex-slaves would not willingly discard their dreams of progress. Anyone challenging the racial hierarchy became a potential victim of the mob. The endless roster of dead came to include every sort of insurgent, from the owners of successful black businesses and workers pressing for higher wages to those who refused to be called "boy" and the defiant women who resisted white men's sexual attentions.

The number of lynch victims actually accused of rape is signally unimpressive. Yet public opinion had been captured by the myth of the black rapist, who was denounced in legislatures and pulpits alike. It was simply taken for granted that lynching was a just response to barbarous sexual crimes against white womanhood. That the majority of lynchings did not even involve an alleged rape was entirely hidden by the blinding power of the myth. And the question remained unasked: what about the numerous black women who were lynched and especially those who were raped before they were murdered?

Given the central role played by the fictional black rapist in the shaping of post-slavery racism, it is, at best, irresponsible theorizing to represent black men today as the most frequent perpetrators of sexual violence. At worst, it is an aggression against black people, for the mythical rapist implies the mythical whore – and a race of rapists and whores deserves punishment. But beyond irresponsibility and racist provocations, the failure to expose the ideological illusion behind the persisting belief that black men are incorrigible rapists will lead to devastating distortions in any theory of rape.

If this myth is not still insidiously at work, how can we account for the failure of those anti-rape theorists to examine the enormous disparity between reported rapes and those which remain anonymous? As long as the analysis focuses on accused rapists who are arrested, black men – and other men of color – will inevitably bear a disproportionate responsibility for the current epidemic of sexual violence. And thus the myth is confirmed. The anonymity characterizing the vast majority of rapes is consequently treated as an incidental detail with purely statistical implications or as a mystery whose meaning is inaccessible.

Is this anonymity really so incidental or mysterious? Or is it not rather a privilege enjoyed by men whose status protects them from prosecution? Although men who are employers, executives, politicians, doctors, and professors are known for their tendency to "take advantage of" women they consider socially inferior to them, it is seldom the case that their deeds come to light in court. Is it not, then, quite probable that these men of the

capitalist and middle classes account for a significant proportion of unreported rapes?

Many of these unreported rapes undoubtedly involve black women as
victims. The historical experience of black women proves nothing about
sexual abuse at all if not that racist ideology implies an open invitation to
rape. But if the hidden basis of this implied invitation is economic power,
then it must be the class structure of capitalist society that harbors the
incentive to rape. It seems, in fact, that men of the capitalist class and their
middle-class partners are immune to prosecution because they commit
sexual assaults with the same unchallenged authority that legitimizes their
daily assaults on the labor and dignity of working people.

The widespread sexual coercion that occurs on the job has never been
much of a secret. Indeed, it is precisely on the job that women are most
vulnerable. Having already established their domination over their female
subordinates, employers, managers, and foremen may well be convinced
that they can assert this authority in sexual terms. That working-class
women are even more intensely exploited than their men increases their
vulnerability to rape, while sexual coercion reinforces their vulnerability on
the job.

Working-class men, whatever their color, can be motivated to rape by
the belief that their maleness has accorded them the privilege of dominating
women. Yet since they have no guarantee of immunity from prosecution –
unless it is a white man who rapes a woman of color – the incentive is not
nearly as powerful as it is for the men of the capitalist class. When working-
class men accept the invitation to rape extended through the ideology of
male supremacy, they are accepting a bribe, an illusory compensation for
powerlessness.

It would appear, therefore, that those men who wield power in the
economic and political realm are encouraged by the class structure of
capitalism to become agents of sexual exploitation. Their authority guards
them against punishment in all circles except one: they may not violate a
woman of their own standing. Or, in less euphemistic terms, they possess
no rights over the property of their equals, wives and daughters included.
With this single exception, the man of authority can rape as he will, for he
is merely exercising his authority.

The only absolute privilege to rape enjoyed by working-class men is
reserved for white men alone and can only be invoked when a woman of
color is victimized. While these men may be motivated by the sexist illusion
of power to rape women of their own race, the likelihood that actual assaults
will occur is increased by patterns of conduct toward women that arise from
a racialized assumption of the right to rape. But for the white man who rapes
within his own race (as for other intra-racial rapes) there is always some risk
of prosecution. Where working-class people are involved, the rapist always

has greater odds than his victim (unless, of course, a black-on-white rape is at issue). Yet he can never overcome the vulnerability of his class position, which, in the final analysis, leaves him at the mercy of the courts.*

The current increase in sexual assaults appears to confirm the part played by capitalist class relations in providing an incentive for rape. It is no mere coincidence that the present rape epidemic is occurring at a time when the capitalist class is furiously reasserting its authority in the face of global and internal challenges. Central to its domestic strategy, both racism and sexism are receiving unprecedented encouragement.

It would be difficult to argue that the eroding position of women workers bears no relationship to the rising incidence of rape. So severe are women's economic losses that their wages in relationship to men are lower than they were a decade ago. The proliferation of sexual violence is the brutal face of a general intensification of sexism which necessarily accompanies the economic assault.

Following a pattern established by racism, the attack on women mirrors the worsening situation of workers of color, the mounting evidence of racism in the judicial system and educational institutions, as well as the government's posture of studied neglect toward black people and other people of color. The most dramatic sign of the rising level of racism is the rapid expansion of such vigilante groups as the Ku Klux Klan and the resulting epidemic of violent assaults on blacks, Chicanos, Puerto Ricans, and Native American Indians. As the most dramatic sign of the excessive influence of sexism, the present rape epidemic bears an extraordinary likeness to the violence kindled by racism.

Given the complexity of the social context of rape today, any attempt to treat it as an isolated phenomenon is bound to founder. For the same reason, an effective strategy against rape must aim for much more than the eradication of the act alone. It must even aim for more than the elimination of sexism alone. Recognizing the part played by racism in abetting sexual violence, the anti-rape movement must not only defend women of color, it must also defend growing numbers of victims of false rape charges.

As important as it may be to defend victims of all colors, a strategy of defense alone will hardly succeed in arresting the rape epidemic. The causes of this phenomenon must be attacked. For instance, offensive measures which can force an improvement in the status of women workers – especially women of color – can reduce the overall vulnerability of women to rape.

The crisis dimensions of sexual violence constitute one of the facets of a deep-going crisis of capitalism. Even if this crisis subsides, however, the

---

Author's note: This analysis does not pay sufficient attention to the relative invisibility of black-on-black rape.

problem of rape will remain. As the violent face of sexism, the threat of rape will exist as long as capitalist society survives. If the anti-rape movement is to avoid the dilemma of Sisyphus, its current activities – ranging from emotional and legal aid to defense methods and educational campaigns – must be complemented by larger offensive measures and situated in a strategic context which envisages the ultimate defeat of monopoly capitalism.

NOTES

1 Nancy Gager and Cathleen Schurr, *Sexual Assault Confronting Rape in America* (New York: Grosset and Dunlap, 1976), 1.
2 Michael Meltsner, *Cruel and Unusual: The Supreme Court and Capital Punishment* (New York: Random House, 1973), 75.
3 Gertrude Stein, *Three Lives* (Norfolk, CT: The Modern Library, Inc., 1933 [first published 1909]), 86.
4 Arlene Eisen-Bergman, *Women of Vietnam* (San Francisco: People's Press, 1974), 61.
5 Susan Brownmiller, *Against Our Will: Men, Women and Rape* (New York: Simon and Schuster, 1975), 194.
6 Jean MacKellar, *Rape: The Bait and the Trap* (New York: Crown Publishers, 1975), 72.
7 Brownmiller, *Against Our Will*, 175.
8 Noreen Connell and Cassandra Wilson (eds), *Rape: The First Sourcebook for Women by New York Radical Feminists* (New York: New American Library, 1974).
9 Diana Russell, *The Politics of Rape* (New York: Stein and Day, 1975), 168.
10 Frederick Douglass, "Why Is the Negro Lynched" (1894), in Philip Foner (ed.), *The Life and Writings of Frederick Douglass*, vol. 4 (New York: International Publishers, 1955).
11 Ida Wells-Barnett, *On Lynchings* (New York: Arno Press and the *New York Times*, 1969), 8.

9

Violence Against Women and the Ongoing Challenge to Racism

Even tonight and I need to take a walk and clear
my head about this poem about why I can't
go out without changing my clothes my shoes
my body posture my gender identity my age
my status as a woman alone in the evening/
alone on the streets/alone not being the point/
the point being that I can't do what I want
to do with my own body because I am the wrong
sex the wrong age the wrong skin and
suppose it was not here in the city but down on the
beach/
or far into the woods and I wanted to go
there by myself thinking about God/or thinking
about children or thinking about the world/all of it
disclosed by the stars and the silence:
I could not go and I could not think and I could not
stay there
alone
as I need to be
alone because I can't do what I want to do with my own
body and
who in the hell set things up
like this
and in France they say if the guy penetrates
but does not ejaculate then he did not rape me
and if after stabbing him if after screams if
after begging the bastard and if even after smashing
a hammer to his head if even after that if he

This essay, which is based on a talk delivered at Florida State University, Tallahassee, Florida, October 16, 1985, was published the same year by Kitchen Table: Women of Color Press, as a pamphlet in the Freedom Organizing Series. Copyright © 1985 by Angela Y. Davis. The excerpt from June Jordan's "Poem About My Rights" is used by kind permission of the author.

and his buddies fuck me after that
then I consented and there was
no rape because finally you understand finally
they fucked me over because I was wrong I was
wrong again to be me being me where I was/wrong
to be who I am
which is exactly like South Africa
penetrating into Namibia penetrating into
Angola and does that mean I mean how do you know if
Pretoria ejaculates what will the evidence look like the
proof of the monster jackboot ejaculation on Blackland
and if
after Namibia and if after Angola and if after Zimbabwe
and if after all of my kinsmen and women resist even to
self-immolation of the villages and if after that
we lose nevertheless what will the big boys say will they
claim my consent:
Do You Follow Me: We are the wrong people of
the wrong skin on the wrong continent and what
in the hell is everybody being reasonable about . . .

June Jordan, "Poem About My Rights"[1]

June Jordan's poem draws some striking parallels between sexual violence against individual women and neo-colonial violence against peoples and nations. I share her words with you this evening in order to suggest that we cannot grasp the true nature of sexual assault unless we consider its larger social and political context. During this week of anti-rape activities and consciousness-raising, you will be specifically focusing on sexual violence as it affects women as individuals. At the same time, you must attempt to develop an awareness of its relationship to the violence suffered, for example, by the people of Nicaragua, the people of South Africa, and indeed Afro-American people and other racially oppressed people here in the United States.

Rape, sexual extortion, battering, spousal rape, child sexual abuse and incest are among the many forms of overt sexual violence suffered by millions of women in this country. We also experience violence aimed at our reproductive choices and sexuality when we are denied access to abortion rights because federal subsidies for abortion have been withdrawn and because abortion clinics are increasingly becoming targets of terrorist bombings. Here in Tallahassee, numerous bomb threats have been made against the Feminist Women's Health Clinic and when anti-abortion demonstrators attacked the niece of one of the clinic's coordinators, it was she and others associated with the clinic who were arrested.

Poor women, and specifically women of color, continue to be targets of sterilization abuse. Innumerable women injure their bodies with the Dalkon shield and other potentially fatal methods of birth control, while differently abled women are assumed to be non-sexual and to therefore have no special birth control needs. Reproductive rights, however, involve more than access to abortions and safe birth control methods. They encompass, for example, the right of lesbians to reproduce outside of the confines of heterosexual relationships.

These particular manifestations of violence against women are situated on a larger continuum of systematic and equally violent assaults on women's economic and political rights, especially the rights of women of color and their white working-class sisters. The dreadful rape epidemic of our times, which has become so widespread that one out of every three women in this country can expect to be raped at some point during her life, directly reflects the deteriorating economic and social status of women today. Moreover, this rising violence against women is related to domestic racial violence as well as to global imperialist aggression. In fact, the conduct of the Reagan administration over the last four and a half years makes clear the fact that it is not only the most sexist government – the only one, for example, to actively oppose the Equal Rights Amendment at the same time that it supports the sexist and homophobic Family Life Amendment; it is not only the most racist government, persistently attempting to dismantle thirty years of gains by the civil rights movement; but it is also by far the most fiercely warmongering government of this century. Indeed for the first time in the history of humankind, we face the very real threat of global nuclear omnicide.

But let us focus more sharply on the issue of sexual assaults against women and our challenge to this misogynist violence. The contemporary anti-rape movement began to take shape during the early 1970s, shortly after the emergence of the women's liberation movement. Along with the campaign to decriminalize abortion, the anti-rape movement proved to be the most dramatic activist mass movement associated with the fight for women's freedom. In January of 1971, the New York Radical Feminists organized a Rape Speak-Out which, for the first time in history, provided large numbers for women with a forum in which to publicly relate their often terrifying individual experiences of rape.[2] Also in 1971, women in Berkeley responded to the painfully discriminatory treatment received by rape survivors in police departments, hospitals, and the courts by organizing a community-based 24-hour crisis line known as Bay Area Women Against Rape. This Crisis Center was the model for countless other similar institutions which arose throughout the country during the 1970s. It is still operating today, almost fifteen years later.

In 1971, Susan Griffin published an historic article in *Ramparts* magazine entitled "Rape: The All American Crime."[3] Her article opened with these words:

I have never been free of the fear of rape. From a very early age I, like most women, have thought of rape as part of my natural environment – something to be feared and prayed against like fire or lightning. I never asked why men raped; I simply thought it one of the many mysteries of human nature.

At the age of eight . . . my grandmother took me to the back of the house where the men wouldn't hear, and told me that strange men wanted to do harm to little girls. I learned not to walk on dark streets, not to talk to strangers or get into strange cars, to lock doors, and to be modest. She never explained why a man would want to harm a little girl, and I never asked.

If I thought for a while that my grandmother's fears were imaginary, the illusion was brief. That year, on the way home from school, a schoolmate a few years older than I tried to rape me. Later in an obscure aisle of the local library (while I was reading *Freddy the Pig*) I turned to discover a man exposing himself. Then, the friendly man around the corner was arrested for child molesting.

Virtually all of us have had one or another of these childhood experiences. I recall when I was an elementary school student – I must have been about ten years old – a girlfriend of mine who lived around the corner suddenly disappeared for a week or so. During her absence from school, there were embarrassed whispers that she had been raped. When she returned, she never mentioned the reason for her absence and no one dared attempt to break through her shroud of silence. I remember distinctly that all of the hushed conversations behind her back assumed that my friend had done something terribly wrong, and she walked around with a mysterious aura of immorality surrounding her for the rest of the time we spent in elementary school. More than any of the other girls, she was the target of the boys' sexual jeers. Assuming that she had transgressed against the moral standards of our community, no one ventured to argue that she was the tragic victim of a crime, which should never have gone uninvestigated and unpunished.

The anti-rape movement of the early seventies challenged many of the prevalent myths regarding rape. For example, women militantly refuted the myth that the rape victim is morally responsible for the crime committed against her – a myth which is based upon the notion that women have control over whether or not their bodies are violated during the act of rape. Defense attorneys sometimes attempted to demonstrate the supposed impossibility of rape by asking witnesses to insert a phallic object into a receptacle which was being rapidly moved from one point to another. Oleta Abrams, one of the co-founders of Bay Area Women Against Rape, has related an anecdote which clearly reveals the most probable power relations in an actual rape incident. When a policeman asked a woman to insert his billy club into a cup which he continually maneuvered around, the woman simply took the club and struck him on the shoulder causing him to drop the cup, into which she easily inserted the billy club.[4]

Another widespread myth is that if a woman does not resist, she is implicitly inviting the violation of her body. Compare this assumption with those concerning the criminal violation of property. Is a businessman asked to resist the encroachment of a robber in order to guarantee that his property rights will be protected by the courts? Even today, the persisting mystification of rape causes it to be perceived as a victim-precipitated crime, as illustrated by the 1977 ruling of a Wisconsin judge who found a fifteen-year-old male's rape of a teenager, who was wearing a loose shirt, Levi's and tennis shoes, to be a "normal" reaction to the "provocative" dress of the young woman.

Although there is a pervasive fear among most women of being raped, at the same time, many women feel that it cannot really happen to them. Yet *one* out of *three* women will be sexually assaulted in her lifetime, and *one* out of *four* girls will be raped before the age of eighteen. Despite these startling statistics, there is only a 4 percent conviction rate of rapists – and these convictions only reflect the minute percentage of rapes that are actually reported.

Rape happens anytime, anywhere, to females of all ages – from infants of four months to women over ninety years old, although the single largest group of rape survivors is composed of adolescent girls between the ages of sixteen and eighteen. Rape happens to women of all races and all classes, regardless of their sexual orientation.

Although most of us tend to visualize rape episodes as sudden, unanticipated attacks by total strangers, most victims actually know their rapists and, in fact, more than half of all rapes occur in the home of either the survivor or the offender. Furthermore, it is often assumed that rape is an act of lust and that, consequently, rapists are men who cannot control their sexual desire. The truth, though, is that most rapists do not impulsively rape in order to satisfy an uncontrollable sexual passion. Instead, men's motives for rape often arise from their socially imposed need to exercise power and control over women through the use of violence. Most rapists indeed are not psychopaths, as we are led to believe by typical media portrayals of men who commit crimes of sexual violence. To the contrary, the overwhelming majority of rapists would be considered "normal" according to prevailing social standards of male normality.

Certainly, the most insidious myth about rape is that it is most likely to be committed by a black man. As a direct consequence of rampant racism, white women are socialized to harbor far more fear that they will be raped by a black man than by a white man. In actuality, however, as a direct result of the fact that white men compose a larger proportion of the population, many more rapes are committed by white men than by black men. But as a consequence of this country's history of ubiquitous racism in law enforcement, there is a disproportionately large number of black men in prison on the basis of rape convictions. The myth of the black rapist renders people oblivious to the realities of rape and to the fact, for example, that over 90 percent of all rapes are intra-racial rather than inter-racial. Moreover, as pointed out in studies on sexual assault – and as was indeed the case during the era of slavery – proportionately more white men rape black women than black men rape white women. Nonetheless, the average white woman in this country maintains a far greater suspicion of black men than of white men as potential rapists. These distorted social attitudes, which are shaped by prevailing racist ideas, constitute an enormous obstacle to the development of a movement which can win victories in the struggle against rape.

If we examine some of the reasons why it has been such an arduous process to lay the foundation for an effective multiracial anti-rape movement, the influence of the myth of the black rapist plays a pivotal role. During the early seventies, when the anti-rape campaign was in its infancy, the presence of Afro-American women in that movement was a rarity. This no doubt was in part attributable to the relatively low level of awareness regarding the interconnectedness of racism and sexism in general among the white women who initiated the women's liberation movement. At the same time, anti-rape activists failed to develop an understanding of the degree to which rape and the racist use of the fraudulent rape charge are historically inseparable. If, throughout our history in this country, the rape of black women by white men has constituted a political weapon of terror, then the flip side of the coin has been the frame-up rape charge directed at black men. Thousands of terroristic lynchings have been justified by conjuring up the myth of the black rapist.

Since much of the early activism against rape was focused on delivering rapists into the hands of the judicial system, Afro-American women were understandably reluctant to become involved with a movement which might well lead to further repressive assaults on their families and their communities. Yet, at the same time, black women were and continue to be sorely in need of an anti-rape movement, since we comprise a disproportionately large number of rape survivors. It is all the more ironic that black women were absent from the contemporary anti-rape movement during its early days, since anti-rape activism actually has a long history in the black community. Probably the first movement to launch a frontal challenge to sexual violence was the Black Women's Club Movement, which originated in the late 1890s as an outgrowth of the anti-lynching activities of women like Ida B. Wells.[5] Today, organizations such as the National Black Women's Health Project in Atlanta are conducting organizing and educational campaigns around such issues as rape and sterilization abuse.

Numerous women of color have been active in organizing against domestic violence on both the local and national level and have provided essential movement leadership, especially in the National Coalition Against Domestic Violence and its member coalitions. Increasingly, women of color are involved in working on sexual assault, often in projects based in Third World communities.

Certainly any woman can understand the intense emotional anger which characterized the first phase of the anti-rape campaign. Throughout all of history, the judicial system and society in general had not even acknowledged women as legitimate victims of a crime if the crime committed against them was rape. Much of women's cumulative rage about rape was understandably aimed at men. When a feminist theoretical foundation for the campaign began to develop, however, the theories tended to simply bolster and legitimize anti-male anger by defining rape as an inevitable product of masculine nature. Masculinity was understood not so much as it has come to be, as socially defined, especially under conditions of capitalism, but rather as an immutable, biologically and psychologically determined product of men's inherent nature.

These theories most often did not take into account the class and racial components of many rapes suffered by working-class women and women of color. In fact, the failure of the anti-rape movement of the early seventies to develop an analysis of rape which acknowledged the social conditions that foster sexual violence as well as the centrality of racism in determining those social conditions, resulted in the initial reluctance of black, Latina, Native American, and Asian-American women to associate themselves with that movement. Throughout Afro-American women's economic history in this country, for example, sexual abuse has been perceived as an occupational hazard. In slavery, black women's bodies were considered to be accessible at all times to the slave-master as well as to his surrogates. In "freedom," the job most frequently open to black women was domestic work, and it was the case until the late 1950s that the majority of black women working outside the home were domestic workers. It has been amply documented that as maids and washerwomen, black women were repeatedly the victims of sexual assault committed by the white men in the families for which they worked.

Sexual harassment and sexual extortion are still occupational hazards for working women of *all* racial backgrounds. In a survey conducted by *Redbook* in 1976, 90 percent of the 9,000 respondents reported that they had encountered sexual harassment on the job.[6] According to Julia and Herman Schwendinger's book *Rape and Inequality*, one congresswoman discovered that a certain congressman was asking prospective women employees whether they engaged in oral sex, as if this were a requirement for the job.[7]

If we assume that rape is simply a by-product of maleness, a result of men's anatomical construction or of an immutable male psychological constitution, then how do we explain that the countries which are now experiencing an epidemic of rape are precisely those advanced capitalist countries which face severe economic and social crises and are saturated with violence on all levels? Do men rape because they are men, or are they socialized by their own economic, social, and political oppression – as well as by the overall level of social violence in the country in question – to inflict sexual violence on women?

Sexual violence often flows directly from official policy. In Vietnam, as Arlene Eisen has pointed out in her book *Women in Vietnam*, US soldiers often received instructions for their search and destroy missions which involved "searching" Vietnamese women's vaginas with their penises.[8] The following observation has been made about sexual violence under the conditions of fascist dictatorship in Chile:

> The tortures of women included the agony of scorching their nipples and genitals, the blind terror of applying shock treatments to all parts of their bodies, and, of course gang rape. An unknown number of women have been raped; some of them pregnant after rape have been refused abortions. Women have had insects forced up their vaginas; pregnant women have been beaten with rifle butts until they have aborted.[9]

Indeed, rape is frequently a component of torture inflicted on women political prisoners by fascist governments and counter-revolutionary forces. In the history of our own country, the Ku Klux Klan and other racist groups have used rape as a weapon of political terror.

I want to suggest to you that rape bears a direct relationship to all of the existing power structures in a given society. This relationship is not a simple mechanical one, but rather involves complex structures reflecting the complex interconnectedness of race, gender, and class oppression which characterize that society. If we do not attempt to understand the nature of sexual violence as it relates to racial, class, and governmental violence and power, we cannot even begin to develop strategies which will allow us to eventually purge our society of the oppressiveness of rape.

In our attempt to understand rape, it would be a grievous mistake for us to stop at the level of analyzing individual cases or even at the level of male psychology. The only logical strategies for the elimination of rape which could follow from this type of analysis would involve the reliance on repression to punish rapists. But as the use of the repressive paraphernalia of the state has generally demonstrated, crimes are seldom deterred as a result of the punishment received by those who are caught committing them. Thus for each punished rapist, how many more would be lurking in our neighborhoods, indeed in our workplaces and even in our homes? This is not to argue that those men who commit rape should go unpunished, but rather that punishment alone will not stem the tide of the omnipresent sexual violence in our country.

As I mentioned earlier, the experience of the seventies demonstrates that anti-rape strategies that depend primarily on law enforcement agencies will continue to alienate many women of color. Indeed the experience of black women has been that the very same white policeman who would supposedly protect them from rape, will sometimes go so far as to rape black women in their custody. Ann Braden, a veteran civil rights organizer, has referred to such conduct by southern white policemen who arrested black women activists during the civil rights struggle and subsequently raped them. I recall an experience I had as a graduate student in San Diego when a friend and I found a young black woman, beaten and bloody, on the shoulder of the freeway. The story she told us was horrifying. She had been raped by several white men and dropped by the side of the road. When the police found her, they too raped her and left her on the freeway barely conscious. Because such experiences are by no means exceptional, black women have found it difficult to accept policemen as the enforcers of anti-rape measures.

Moreover, police forces often utilize tactics ostensibly designed to capture rapists which will simultaneously augment their arsenal of racist repression. During the 1970s, a rapist was terrorizing the Berkeley community. He initially attacked black women – scores and scores of them. Hundreds of rapes in the area were attributed to "Stinky," as he was called. However, it was not until he began to rape white women, and specifically when he raped a well-known black woman television newscaster, that the police began to turn their attention to the case. They released a description of him so general that it fit at least a third of the black men in the area, and countless black men who obviously had nothing to do with the Stinky rapes were arrested simply because they were black. Moreover, Berkeley police proposed to the city council a strategy to capture Stinky which involved hiring more police, acquiring helicopters and other aircraft, and using tracking and attack dogs. The police department had been attempting to get approval for the use of dogs since the student movement of the sixties, but had failed because of community opposition. They seized a situation which had caused so many women to be terror stricken, in order to implement their repressive, racist agenda. Unfortunately, the anti-rape movement, which at that time was almost exclusively white, did not perceive the hidden agenda of the police force and agreed to cooperate with the proposed strategy. Thus, they unwittingly became collaborators in a plan which would inevitably bring increased racist assaults on Berkeley's black community.

The anti-rape movement today must not ignore these looming pitfalls. Nor can it focus exclusively on strategies such as rape crisis centers which, as important as they might be, treat only the effects and leave the cause of the crime untouched. The very same social conditions which spawn racist violence – the same social conditions which encourage attacks on workers, and the political posture which justifies US intervention in Central America and aid to the apartheid government in South Africa – are the same forces which encourage sexual violence. Thus, sexual violence can never be completely eradicated until we have succeeded in effecting a whole range of radical social transformations in our country.

In conclusion, I want to direct your attention to the connections we must establish between our efforts to ensure the safety of women and our concern for the safety of this planet. It is no coincidence that the explosion of sexual violence in this country takes place at a time when the United States government has developed the means with which to annihilate human life itself. It is no accident that a government which will be spending one billion dollars a day on weapons next year, forty-one million dollars a minute on the most devastating instruments of violence human history has ever known, also encourages the proliferation of violence on all levels of society, including sexual attacks on women. Moreover, consider that $200 million, just five hours of military spending, could provide annual support for 1,600 rape crisis centers and battered women's shelters.

Let us now move forward in our battle to eliminate the horrendous violence done to women in our society by realizing that we will never get past the first step if we do not recognize the issue of rape within its context, as one element in a complex web of women's oppression. And the systematic oppression of women in our society cannot be accurately evaluated except as it is connected to racism and class exploitation at home and imperialist aggression and the potential nuclear holocaust which menace the entire globe.

The anti-rape movement should attempt to establish closer ties not only to the campaigns for women's economic and political rights, but also to labor struggles wherever they unfold. At this moment, Chicana and Mexicana women and men are out on strike against the canneries in Watsonville, California. Anti-rape and other feminist activists should hasten to join them on the picket line.

If we are militant activists challenging violence against women, we must also see ourselves as fearless fighters against police violence, and in passionate solidarity with the racially and nationally oppressed people who are its main targets. We must defend, for example, the memory of Eleanor Bumpurs, the sixty-seven-year-old black woman from the Bronx who was murdered in 1984 by New York Housing Authority policemen because she dared resist an attempted eviction.

The banners and voices we raise against rape must also be raised against racist and anti-Semitic Ku Klux Klan violence. And they must be raised in defense of political prisoners like Leonard Peltier, the American Indian leader, and Johnny Imani Harris, the black prison activist who presently faces the death penalty in Alabama.

If we aspire to eventually eradicate sexual violence, we must also call for the immediate freedom of all political prisoners. Our sisters and brothers in Nicaragua and El Salvador need our solidarity, as do our Palestinian friends who are fighting for their land and dignity. And certainly, we cannot forget our Iranian sisters who are attempting to complete the democratic revolution which has been violently stifled by Khomeini's Islamic Republic.

To recognize the larger socio-political context of the contemporary epidemic of sexist violence does not, however, require that we ignore the specific and concrete necessity for the ongoing campaign against rape. Those of you whose political activism is primarily channeled into this movement are involved in a cause which has urgent implications for all women. This battle must be waged quite concretely on all of its myriad fronts. As you further shape the theoretical foundation of this movement and as you implement practical tasks, remind yourselves as often as possible that even as individual victories are claimed, the ultimate elimination of sexist violence will depend on our ability to build a new and revolutionary global order, in which every form of oppression and violence against humankind is obliterated.

NOTES

1 June Jordan, *Passion: New Poems, 1977–1980* (Boston: Beacon Press, 1980).
2 Noreen Connell and Cassandra Wilson, eds, *Rape: The First Sourcebook for Women by New York Radical Feminists* (New York: New American Library, 1974).
3 Jo Freeman (ed.), *Women: A Feminist Perspective* (1st edition) (Palo Alto: Mayfield Publishing Co., 1975).
4 Julia and Herman Schwendinger, *Rape and Inequality* (Beverly Hills: Sage Library of Social Research, 1983), 23.
5 Cf. Paula Giddings, *When and Where I Enter* (New York: Morrow, 1984), chapter 6.
6 Schwendinger and Schwendinger, *Rape and Inequality*, 50.
7 Ibid.
8 Arlene Eisen, *Women in Vietnam* (San Francisco: People's Press, 1975), 62.
9 Schwendinger and Schwendinger, *Rape and Inequality*, 203.

10

JoAnne Little: The Dialectics of Rape

Rape, Lynch Negro Mother
Columbus, Miss., Dec. 17 – Thursday a week ago Cordella Stevenson was found early in the morning hanging to the limb of a tree, without any clothing, dead. . . . The body was found about fifty yards north of the Mobile & Ohio R.R., and the thousands and thousands of passengers that came in and out of this city last Thursday morning were horrified at the sight. She was hung there from the night before by a bloodthirsty mob who had gone to her home, snatched her from slumber, and dragged her through the streets without any resistance. They carried her to a far-off spot, did their dirt and then strung her up.
Chicago *Defender*, December 18, 1915

No one – not even the men in the mob – had bothered to accuse Cordella Stevenson of committing a crime. She was black and that was reason enough. She was black and a woman, trapped in a society pervaded with myths of white superiority and male supremacy. She could be raped and murdered with absolute impunity. The white mob simply claimed that, a few months earlier, Cordella Stevenson's son had burned down a white man's barn.

It was sixty years ago when this black woman was raped and strung up on a tree. There are many who believe that incidents such as these belong to an era of racist terror now forever buried under the historical progress of the intervening years. But history itself allows only the naive to honestly claim these last sixty years as a time of unequivocal progress – especially when the elimination of racism and male supremacy is used as the yardstick.

Today, black women continue to be sexually attacked – and, in some cases, even murdered – by white men who know that, in all likelihood, they will never have to face the consequences of their crimes.

Twenty-year-old JoAnne Little, one of the most recent victims in this racist and sexist tradition, is the cultural grandchild of Cordella Stevenson.

This essay first appeared in *Ms. Magazine*, June 1975. Reprinted by permission of *Ms. Magazine*, © 1975.

She says that she resisted when she was sexually assaulted, but as a result she is currently being tried on charges of first degree murder. In the event of a conviction, she will automatically get a death sentence and will be placed on North Carolina's death row – the result of a "legal" process, but still too close to the lynch law of the past.

The story begins last August 27, [1974] when a guard at the jail in Beaufort County, North Carolina, was found dead in the cell of a missing prisoner. He had been stabbed multiple times with an ice pick, the same ice pick that he had kept in his own desk drawer. The jailer, Clarence Alligood, was white. The missing prisoner was black, and the only woman in the entire jail. Because of a conviction on charges of breaking and entering, larceny, and receiving stolen property, JoAnne Little was serving a sentence of seven to ten years and had already been kept in the Beaufort County jail for three months at the time of her disappearance.

When the autopsy report was released, it contained this evidence of recent sexual activity on the part of Alligood:

> His shoes were in the corridor, his socks on his feet. He was otherwise naked from the waist down. . . . The left arm was under the body and clutching his pants. . . . His right hand contained an icepick. There was blood on the sheet, cell floor, corridor. Beneath his buttocks was a decorated, partially torn woman's kerchief. On the floor was a night gown and on the cell door was a brassiere and night jacket. . . . Extending from his penis to his thigh skin was a stream of what appeared to be seminal fluid. . . . The urethral fluid was loaded with spermatozoa.

After a week of evading police – who conducted their search with riot weapons and helicopters – JoAnne Little turned herself in, stating nothing publicly about the case except that she did what she had to do in self-defense. At her own insistence, Jerry Paul, the lawyer she contacted, received assurances that she would be incarcerated in the women's prison in Raleigh – not in the jail where the incident took place, and where she feared that she would be subjected to further sexual assault and perhaps even that her life would be in danger.

Shortly thereafter, JoAnne Little was charged with murder in the first degree.

The circumstances surrounding this case deserve careful attention, for they raise fundamental questions about the bringing of murder charges against her. Moreover, they expose conditions and situations many women prisoners must confront, especially in the small-town jails of this country.

1　JoAnne Little was being detained in a jail in which she was the only woman – among prisoners and guards alike. Since the Beaufort County Jail had served as a detention center for other women prisoners in the past, why were all the jailers assigned to it men? (Three months later – according to Karen Galloway, one of JoAnne's lawyers – the prison authorities began to claim that there had been a matron on duty during the daytime.)

2   Like any other prisoner, Sister JoAnne was being held under lock and key. Only her jailer, Clarence Alligood, had access to the key to her cell that night. Therefore, how could he have been present there against his will? As part of an escape attempt on the part of JoAnne Little, as the authorities then charged?

3   Alligood was apparently killed by stab wounds inflicted by the same ice pick which he was known to keep in his desk. What was a jail guard doing with an ice pick in the first place? And for what legitimate purpose could he have taken it into a prisoner's cell?

4   Alligood was discovered naked from the waist down. According to Karen Galloway and Jerry Paul, JoAnne Little's attorneys, the authorities maintained for a full three weeks that Alligood's pants were nowhere to be found. Were they afraid that the public would discover that, although he had been stabbed in the legs, there were no such holes in his pants? Were they afraid people would therefore realize that Alligood had removed his pants before the struggle began? In any case, how could such crucial evidence be allowed to disappear?

In fact, the reality of Little's life as a prisoner, even before the rape, may have been one of sexual exploitation; a fate she consistently resisted. Jerry Paul has said, "One possibility is that she was being kept in Beaufort County Jail for openly sexual purposes." She should have been moved to the women's prison in Raleigh shortly after her original conviction, for instance, but she was never transferred. According to Paul, a TV camera was focused on her cell at all times, leaving her no privacy whatever even when she changed clothes or took a shower. When she used her sheets to block the view, they were taken from her. Little's lawyers have said that on one occasion a highway patrolman visiting the jail on business unrelated to JoAnne, went into her cell and urinated on the floor.

If one wonders why JoAnne Little fled, even though circumstances on their face tended to be greatly exculpatory, consider that, when she left, Alligood was still alive. From the appearance of the jail cell, a tremendous struggle must have taken place. She then fled, distraught, out of fear for her life. Alligood, according to the autopsy report, was found still clutching the ice pick. Sister JoAnne may well have felt that, if she hadn't left the jail when she did, she would have become just another number in the statistics surrounding prison deaths.

Essential to a clear perspective on the JoAnne Little case is an analysis of what might have happened if the situation had been reversed. What if

Alligood had overpowered her? What if *he* had stabbed *her* with the ice pick – as he may have intended to do if she could not otherwise be raped? What if the sexually violated body of JoAnne Little had been discovered in that cell on the night of August 27?

There has never, to my knowledge, been a conviction – perhaps not even an indictment – of a white jailer for the murder of a black or any other minority prisoner. We can look to the 1970 case of W. L. Nolen, Alvin Miller, and Cleveland Edwards, for instance, who were shot down, unarmed and in cold blood, in the Soledad recreation yard by a guard perched in a gun tower: killings which the Grand Jury ruled justifiable homicides. There are also the thirty-one prisoners killed during the Attica Rebellion. No one denies that they were victims of gunfire, yet not a single one of the guards or policemen has been charged with a crime. Or consider Tito Perez, a prisoner recently discovered in a New York jail cell, hanged with a belt that did not belong to him. People who knew him insisted it had to be murder, yet police called it suicide. As one of the policemen then added, "It happens all the time."

There can be little speculation about the turn events would have taken had Little been killed by Alligood. A verdict of "justifiable homicide" would have probably closed the books on such a case.

But she had the courage to fend off her assailant. The price of her resistance was a new threat of death, this time issuing from the government of North Carolina.

And so she is being tried – by the same state whose Supreme Court decided, in the nineteenth century, that no white man could be convicted of fornication with a slave woman. By the same state whose judicial apparatus in 1972 permitted Marie Hill to be sentenced to death at the age of twenty-one: convicted by an all-white jury of murder of a white man on the basis of a confession which she insisted had been made under threat of death.

Little stands accused by a court system which, proportionate to its population, has sentenced more political activists to prison than any other state in the country. (Reverend Ben Chavis and the Wilmington Ten, for instance, as well as the Charlotte Three, the Ayden Eleven, and many Tuscarora Indians.) The number of state prison units in North Carolina is staggering: more than five times greater than in California, the most populous state in the country. In fact, North Carolina, along with Georgia, can claim more prisoners per capita than any other state – and they include, of course, an enormously disproportionate number of black men and women.

As this article is being written, there are seventy-one prisoners on death row in North Carolina, making that state number one in the nation in condemning people to legal death. In the event of a conviction, the state's present sentencing policy could make Little the third woman in the country to be sentenced to death since the Supreme Court ruled in 1972 that the death penalty imposed at the discretion of judges and juries was cruel and unusual punishment. North Carolina subsequently mandated that a conviction on a first degree murder charge automatically carried the death penalty. This procedure was appealed to the Supreme Court in late April. The other two women presently on death row are also in North Carolina: a black and a Native American respectively.

Even during the short time JoAnne Little hid from the police, the Sheriff was planning to ask that the courts initiate the procedure of declaring her an outlaw. The result of this declaration would have been, in effect, a call to all state citizens to arrest her on sight and to shoot if she resisted. North Carolina is the only state in the country where this law is still on the books.

Little's attorneys relate numerous possibilities of judicial bias against her. In Beaufort County, for instance, where families are generations old, virtually everyone knows everyone else. Living in the area are numerous Alligoods. One of these Alligoods sat on the Grand Jury which returned the indictment against JoAnne Little.

Without exception, every pre-trial motion filed, as of this writing, has been flatly denied. Despite inflammatory publicity about JoAnne Little – including unfounded and malicious charges that she was a prostitute – and in spite of the unconcealed public sympathy for Alligood, the courts have refused to grant a change of venue for the trial.

Although Little is indigent, her motion to have the court assume the costs of expert witnesses has been denied. It was denied even though the court does not have to pay her attorneys' fees, since the lawyers are donating their services.

Efforts to gain access to the evidence, in the form of discovery motions, have also been thwarted. The sheriff first refused to release a list of female prisoners previously incarcerated in the jail, leading to a belief that authorities feared the exposure of other sexual assaults by Alligood and his colleagues. Later, after the State Bureau of Investigation had questioned sixty-five former prisoners, their names were released to Little's lawyers – but even this SBI report stated that some of these inmates claimed Alligood and other jailers made sexual advances toward them.

After the difficulty in locating Alligood's pants, the defense attempted to have all the evidence assembled and placed in protective custody. This was denied.

Although Little seemed clearly eligible to be released on bail, District Attorney William Griffin employed every trick of his trade to prevent her release. When the defense attorneys attempted to post bail, for instance, Griffin, relying on a technicality, ordered the clerk not to accept the bond. Finally, as a result of a nationwide outcry, she was released in February on bail of $115,000: an amount that is itself clearly exorbitant. Through the case of Little, the courts of North Carolina seem to have decided to extend their long record of racist injustices and betrayal of the rights of poor people. How can these same courts be trusted to fairly determine the fate of the defendant herself?

If justice is to prevail, there must be a struggle. And the only force powerful enough to reverse the normal, oppressive course of events is the organized might of great numbers of people.

Protests have already erupted. Mass actions have been organized in North Carolina – both by black community groups and by women's organizations. The North Carolina Alliance Against Racist and Political Repression has spoken of the case as one of its major concentrations, and Southern Poverty Law Center, directed by Julian Bond, is vigorously supporting her.

These beginnings must be utilized as the foundation of a movement which can ignite massive and militant protests on a national – and even international – scale. Only a movement of this magnitude can rescue JoAnne Little from the gas chamber.

Over the last few years, widespread concern about the increasing incidence of sexual assaults on women has crystallized into a militant campaign against rape. In the JoAnne Little case, as well as in all other instances of sexual assault, it is essential to place the specific incident in its socio-historical context. For rape is not one-dimensional and homogeneous – but one feature that does remain constant is the overt and flagrant treatment of women, through rape, as property. Particular rape cases will then express different modes in which women are handled as property.

Thus when a white man rapes a black woman, the underlying meaning of this crime remains inaccessible if one is blind to the historical dimensions of the act. One must consider, for example, that a little more than a hundred years ago, there were few black women who did not have to endure humiliating and violent sexual attacks as an integral feature of their daily lives. Rape was the rule: immunity from rape the exception. On the one hand the slave-master made use of his tyrannical possession of slave women as chattel in order to violate their bodies with impunity. On the other hand, rape itself was an essential weapon utilized by the white master to reinforce the authority of his ownership of black women.

Although the immediate victim of rape was the black woman – and it was she who endured its pain and anguish – rape served not only to further her oppression, but also as a means of terrorizing the entire black community. It placed brutal emphasis on the fact that black slaves were indeed the property of the white master. Whenever black women or men resisted white men's sexual encroachments on the women of the community, they did so at the risk of injury or death.[1] "Assaults," as Gerda Lerner wrote in *Black Women in White America: A Documentary History* (New York: Pantheon,

1972), were therefore "part of the reinforcing structure upholding a system of racial and economic exploitation."

In conjunction with the sexual exploitation of black women, the social attitude has been encouraged that – and here Lerner quotes a 1902 newspaper reporter – "a colored woman, however respectable, is lower than the white prostitute." This stereotypical image of the black woman branded her as a creature motivated by base, animal-like sexual instincts. It was therefore no sin to rape her. This bestial notion of the black woman, incidentally, played and continues to play a significant role in justifying the overexploitation of her labor. For such a woman would hardly be distinguishable from a beast of burden. Again, she is openly defined as property.

If rape was, in effect, institutionalized during slavery, essentially the same institutionalized form of rape is present today in such vestiges of slavery as domestic work. How many black women working in the homes of white people have not had to confront the "man of the house" as an actual or potential rapist?

The rape of the black woman and its ideological justification are integrally linked to the portrayal of the black man as a bestial rapist of white women – and, of course, the castration and lynching of black men on the basis of such accusations. As Bettina Aptheker explains in an article, "W. E. B. Du Bois and the Struggle for Women's Rights," written for *San Jose Studies*: "The central rationale used to justify the sexual abuse of the black woman was her alleged promiscuity. In this way the racist image of the black woman as whore was correlated to the racist image of the black man as rapist." That is to say, as Lerner puts it, "the myth of the black rapist of white women is the twin myth of the bad black woman – both designed to apologize for and facilitate the continued exploitation of black men and women."

Historically, the connection between the two myths has been very clear. Struggle against the sexual abuse of black women demanded at the same time struggle against the cruel manipulation of sexual accusations against black men. Black women, therefore, have played a vanguard role, not only in the fight against rape, but also in the movement to end lynching.

For black women, rape perpetrated by white men, like the social stereotype of black men as rapists, must be classed among the brutal paraphernalia of racism. It is a weapon employed to further the oppression of our people. Divorced from its definition as a weapon in the arsenal of racism, the rape of black women cannot be successfully challenged. If it is ripped out of its context, if its social function is not understood, it is not possible to eradicate it.

Whenever a campaign is erected around a black woman who has been raped by a white man, therefore, the content of the campaign must be explicitly antiracist. And, as incorrect as it would be to fail to attack racism, it would be equally incorrect to make light of the antisexist content of the movement. Racism and male supremacy have to be projected in their dialectical unity. In the case of the raped black woman, they are mutually reinforcive.

If, for example, the rape and lynching of Cordella Stevenson were lifted out of the context in which they occurred, they would become absolutely incomprehensible. One must not only be cognizant of the fact that she was black and her rapists and murderers were white, but one must also understand that such incidents erupted repeatedly: part of the systematic attack on black women and black people in general. Because they were socially sanctioned, a white man could hardly even be accused of criminal activity when he raped a black woman.

Today, convictions in cases involving white rapists and black victims remain rare: in 1965 when a white man received a life sentence in Mississippi for raping a fifteen-year-old black girl – the case made national headlines.[2]

Little's assailant had probably been exposed to all the racist myths about black women, and was aware of the lack of redress available to victims of white rapists. In the aftermath of the incident, in fact, vicious "accusations were hurled at JoAnne Little: she was called a prostitute and it was claimed that she engaged in sexual activities with jailers."

Of course, the conviction rate for rape is the lowest of all violent crimes – regardless of the victim's ethnic group. Only in those instances where the accused rapist is black and the alleged victim is white can a long prison term or death penalty be anticipated. And history has proved that, in too many of these cases, the black man is not, in reality, a rapist, but rather a victim himself of the myths and social taboos of racism. Ruchell Magee, who was charged along with me, for one, can attest to the inhuman treatment accorded black men accused of rape. He spent eight years of his life in one of the most infamous penitentiaries in the country, all because police charged him, at age sixteen, with the "attempted rape" of a young white woman whom Ruchell knew.[3] The body of fourteen-year-old Emmett Till was found at the bottom of the Tallahatchie River because he smiled at a white woman. The story of the Scottsboro Nine is well known, and there is also Thomas Wansley who, thirteen years after his conviction on a fraudulent rape charge, is still serving a life sentence in a Virginia state prison.

As noted earlier, from 1930 to 1967, 455 men were executed as a result of rape convictions: 405 of them were black: 48 of them were white, and two were of other ethnic groups. This means that almost 90 percent of all rape executions during this period involved black men.

Diana Russell's *The Politics of Rape* advances the extremely questionable theory that "In the North today reverse racism sometimes operates, usually at the expense of a white woman, not a white man." She attempts to argue that a black man is much more likely today to get off or receive lenient treatment on a rape charge because courts and other institutions fear being labeled racist, and describes a case in which a California district attorney appealed a "lenient" sentence of a black man convicted of raping a white woman. On retrial, however, this same defendant received two consecutive three-years-to-life terms; an argument for the presence of traditional prejudice, not the reverse.

In any case, it would be blatant racism to rejoice over such an incident, for white men remain relatively immune from such long terms for the rape of black and white women alike. This sentence was an expression, not of sincere concern for the woman, but rather of racist social and discriminatory judicial policies myths.

This insensitivity to the rape–racism nexus seems to emanate in part from the mistaken conception that, in the fight against rape, men, in the first place, are the enemy. In fact, this society institutionally condones and abets rape in various ways. There are the cultural myths that insist that women who are raped desire it either consciously or unconsciously. As Susan Griffin wrote in a 1971 *Ramparts* article, "The Politics of Rape, an Inquiry": "This same culture which expects aggression from the male expects passivity from the female. Conveniently, the companion myth about the nature of female sexuality is that all women secretly want to be raped."

If a woman really resists, according to these myths, she cannot be raped. Yet if she does resist – and if, like Little, she is black, and if her attacker is white – she stands to be doubly victimized: first by the rapist and then by the courts.

A juror who voted for the conviction of Inez Garcia on second degree murder charges, was asked by reporter Nan Blitman after the trial had concluded, "Could a woman ever get off on the grounds of self-defense if she killed the man during the attack?" As was reported in "The Trial of Inez Garcia" by Nan Blitman and Robin Green in *Ms. Magazine*, May 1975, he answered: "No, because the guy's not trying to kill her. He's just trying to give her a good time. To get off, the guy will have to do her bodily harm, and giving a girl a screw isn't doing her bodily harm." During the deliberation, he added, the juror told the women on the jury that "when I leave here, I'll have less fear of raping a woman now than I did before. At least I known that if I get shot, she won't get away."

Courts have established the pattern of either acquitting or not trying the majority of white men who are charged with rape. In New York, for instance, in 1967, 30 percent of all felony indictments ended in convictions, but in only 13 percent of all rape indictments were there convictions.

There must be a reason behind this social and judicial encouragement given to rape. This reason, in turn, must be related to the social and political function of male supremacy in general. The oppression of women is a vital and integral component of a larger network of oppression which claims as its foremost victims black people, Chicanos, Puerto Ricans, Asians, Indians, and all poor and working-class people. Just as class exploitation, racism, and imperialist subjugation of peoples abroad serve to nourish this larger system and keep it functioning, so male supremacy is likewise essential to its smooth operation. The larger system, of course, is monopoly capitalism and its overall driving motive is profit.

The scope of this article does not permit a detailed discussion of the variety of levels on which male supremacy functions to secure the authority of the ruling class. However, it should be recognized that, while this ruling class is definitely white and is definitely male, only a tiny minority of white males possesses the material qualifications for membership in it.

It is in the interests of that ruling class to cultivate the archaic patriarchal domination of women – based on male ownership of females as property – that flourished during the feudal era. As long as women are oppressed, enormous benefits accrue to the ruling class. Female labor can be even more flagrantly exploited than male labor. (White women's median wages are even lower than black men's [in 1997 they were greater than that of black men] and, of course, women of color receive the lowest wages of all workers.) The social definition of women as housewives provides, as Alva Buxennebaum states in her *Political Affairs* article, "The Status of Women Workers," the most effective "rationale for failing to make housework and child care a social responsibility."

The social incentive given to rape is woven into the logic of the institutions of this society. It is an extremely efficient means of keeping women in a state of fear of rape or of the possibility of it. It is, as Susan Griffin wrote, "a form of mass terrorism." This, in turn, buttresses the general sense of powerlessness and passivity socially inflicted upon women, thus rendering them more easily exploitable. Yet, just as working-class and poor white people who exhibit racist attitudes toward people of color are unconscious agents of a higher power, so rapists (though they may be individually unaware of this) are performing deeds that give sustenance, not to them, but to the existing system.

Historically as well as today, sexist cultural patterns define rape not as a crime against the woman, but rather as a crime against the men who dominate her – her husband, father, or brother. "The laws against rape exist to protect the rights of the male as possessor of the female body," reports Griffin, "and not the right of the female over her body." Women are therefore victimized on two counts. First, they are raped, and second, it is not even considered a serious crime unless they have powerful men behind them. Rape is an assault against the man who "owns" the woman, not the woman herself.

It therefore stands to reason that social wrath about rape is most vehemently invoked when the rapist (or alleged rapist) comes from the lower economic strata of society and the victim comes from the ruling class. And it is true that convictions are at their peak when a black man – the poorest of the working class – is the accused rapist and a white bourgeois woman is the alleged victim.

The white male associated with the capitalist class will protect "his" woman just as he protects "his" property. A real or assumed assault on "his" wife by a working-class white or black man is tantamount to an insurrectionary assault on his property – and, needless to say, under capitalism, property rights are deemed more sacred than the right to life itself. Thus, when there is a conviction in such a case, the law seeks to avenge not the woman who has been raped but the husband (or father) whose property has been defiled.

As for the white woman of working-class background, this dynamic is reduplicated: chances of conviction are high only if her accused assailant is black or a man of color. Racism, as it relates to black people, retains strong ties with its historical origins as an ideology justifying the treatment of black slaves as less than human: as chattel. Therefore *any* sexual approach by a black man – real or imagined – toward a white woman is treated as an attack by a beast. This bestiality woven into the racist image of the black man makes him highly vulnerable to fabricated accusations of rape.

When a white man of the bourgeoisie assaults a white woman of the working class, the rape is just as acceptable as his exploitation of the labor of the men (and women) of her class. The bourgeois sees neither as criminal. In the same way that he believes he has the *right* to manipulate a man's (or woman's) labor-power for the purposes of gaining profits for himself, he believes he has the *right* to sexually manipulate the wife or daughter of the propertyless man. This is the feudal lord's *right to the first night* in its modern, capitalist setting.

When it is a question of a white worker assaulting a white woman of his class, it is as if the rape did not exist at all. Being propertyless in the capitalist sense of having no ownership stake in the means of production, one worker has no real recognizable rights over another worker. And if rape is legally considered to be a crime of one man against another man's property, a working-class white woman has little value in the eyes of the ruling class. Convictions in such instances, therefore, are rare.

Finally, if the victim and rapist alike are people of color, the process becomes less predictable. The rapist may be convicted by dint of judicial racism alone. He may, on the other hand, be acquitted as a result of the racist myths invoked against the woman of color. In the case of Inez Garcia, whose alleged rapist was also Latino, not only was he not tried for the alleged crime, but the victim herself was convicted for having spontaneously vented her rage against the alleged rapist's accomplice.

Should we not then conclude that "the politics of rape are inextricably wedded to the basic institutions of the society?" The meaning of rape and the social attitude toward it must be gleaned from the politics of racism. Griffin articulates it this way in the same *Ramparts* article: "Rape is not an isolated act that can be rooted out from patriarchy without ending patriarchy itself. The same men and power structure who victimized women are engaged in the act of raping Vietnam, raping black people and the very earth we live upon. . . . No simple reforms can eliminate rape."

Little has not only been the victim of a rape attempt by a white racist jailer: she has truly been raped and wronged many times over by the exploitation and discriminatory institutions of this society. All people who see themselves as members of the existing community of struggle for justice, equality, and progress have a responsibility to fulfill toward JoAnne Little. Those of us – women and men – who are black or people of color must understand the connection between racism and sexism that is so strikingly manifested in her case. Those of us who are white and women must grasp the issue of male supremacy in relationship to the racism and class bias which complicate and exacerbate it.

As we struggle for JoAnne Little's right to just legal treatment, we must simultaneously hurl into the faces of the government and the courts – through militant demonstrations, rallies, petitions, protest letters, and cultural shows – a thunderous demand for her full, unconditional freedom.

Finally, let us be sure that the leitmotif running through every aspect of the campaign is unity. Our ability to achieve unity may mean the difference between life and death for Sister JoAnne. Let us then forge among ourselves and our movements an indivisible strength and with it, let us halt and then crush the conspiracy against JoAnne Little's life.

NOTES

1   See "Angela Davis on Black Women," *Ms. Magazine* (August 1972).
2   This case became the exception that proved the rule, as Robert Staples noted in *The Black Woman in America* (Wadsworth, 1973).
3   Ruchell Magee was still in prison at the time of publication, September 1998.

11

Women and Capitalism: Dialectics of Oppression and Liberation

I

Women's liberation recently has been placed on the social agenda in America with a forcefulness and extensiveness that has few historical precedents. The new content and contours of the women's movement are doubtlessly attributable in part to its emergence within, and often in unavoidable opposition to, other social struggles. The expulsion of the proponents of a resolution on women from an SDS [Students for a Democratic Society] convention of the late sixties foreshadowed what would later become a self-imposed isolation. This isolation was at once organizational, theoretical, and developmental. Part of the movement's force and effectiveness has certainly been a function of its intensive focus on sexual oppression. Moreover, the origanization of autonomy was an indispensable prerequisite for a clear formulation of the myriad problems surrounding male supremacy in general. At the same time, however, this isolation fostered a tendency to proclaim the socio-historical primacy of women's oppression over class, national, and racial oppression; and in the process this isolation itself was exaggerated.

In its conceptions and goals, the women's liberation movement is not homogeneous. Its decentralized organizational forms, while genuinely anti-authoritarian in intent, simultaneously reflect pronounced, even irreconcilable, theoretical differences within. Yet, in the midst of this diversity, the predominant tendency of the more militant sector is probably represented by Robin Morgan when she invokes "the profoundly radical analysis beginning to emerge from revolutionary feminism: that capitalism, imperialism,

This essay, written in jail for a symposium of the Society for the Philosophical Study of Dialectical Materialism, first appeared in *Marxism, Revolution, and Peace*, eds Howard Parsons and John Sommerville (Amsterdam: B. R. Grüner, 1977), copyright © 1977 Howard Parsons and John Sommerville. Reprinted by kind permission.

and racism are *symptoms* of male supremacy – sexism."[1] Therefore, Morgan continues, "more and more, I begin to think of a worldwide Women's Revolution as the only hope for life on the planet."[2] The potential impact of widespread female involvement and leadership in oppositional, even revolutionary, political practice should not be underestimated. Yet, the point of departure for this practice, typified by Morgan's words, has not promoted harmonious relations with other important struggles. It is against the backdrop of the unresolved tension between black liberation and women's liberation that the latter's failure to attract more than a negligible number of black women needs to be analyzed.[3]

The women's movement, as consensus has it, found its most enthusiastic adherents among young, "middle-class" white women. Intrusions of male supremacy, as they were gradually brought to light, furnished, for the vast majority, the only conscious experience of the immediacy of social oppression. This may have exacerbated a theoretical inability to discover the threads connecting female oppression to the other visible social antagonisms. It hardly needs to be said that the view which accounts for class exploitation, colonial expansion, national and racial domination as symptoms of male authority has not tackled, but rather has dodged the problem.

Such a weakness – and from a Marxist viewpoint, it *is* considered a weakness – attests to an inadequate theoretical basis. But it may well have a deeper, more fundamental origin. For the identical problem of uncovering the mutual interpenetration of ostensibly unrelated modes of oppression can be detected within almost every radical movement of the contemporary era. A prototypical instance is the difficult question, yet unresolved in practice, of the relation between racism and national oppression on the one hand and exploitation at the point of production on the other.

The acute disjunction of social struggles among themselves has tended to reduplicate a larger process. This is to say, it reflects the increasingly pointed and omnipresent fragmentation of capitalist social relations in an era of advanced technology.

The following reflections, however, will not include an extensive discussion of the composition of the present women's movement nor of the larger societal influences to which it is subject. Rather, they will concentrate on a less sweeping and more narrowly theoretical problem. I will seek to inferentially discover in the works of Karl Marx, after establishing his early sensitivity to the problem, the broad outlines of women's oppression and its socio-historical development. Within the framework of Marx's theoretical reconstruction of history, I will attempt to specify the ways in which the subjugation of women and their ideological relegation to the sphere of nature were indissolubly wedded to the consolidation of capitalism.

The historical development of women's oppression is a highly interesting problem. However, I chose this approach for other reasons as well – reasons related to current theoretical controversies within the women's liberation movement itself. The exponents of the theory that sexual conflict is the matrix of all other social antagonisms frequently rely on historical arguments. Kate Millett, among others, has generous recourse to the notion that the male's enslavement of the female produced the first critical cleavage of human society. According to her method, all subsequent modes of domination are direct outgrowths of this primordial conflict.[4]

Human history is far more complex than this. Unlike the sphere of nature, from which it definitively differentiates itself during its capitalist phase, history evinces few simple causal relationships. Marx made, in fact, his most significant contribution when he ferreted out the deeper meaning of history and laid the basis for theoretical categories whose abstraction would not violate the profound complexities of human development.

Alongside awesome but increasingly irrational technological achievements, women filter through the prevailing ideology as anachronisms. Men (i.e., males) have severed the umbilical cord between themselves and nature. They have deciphered its mysteries, subdued its forces, and have forged their self-definition in contradistinction to the nature they have conquered. But women are projected as embodiments of nature's unrelenting powers. In their alienated portrait, women are still primarily undifferentiated beings – sexual, childbearing, natural. Thus Erik Erikson evokes female self-realization as a function of the "somatic design [which] harbors an 'inner space' destined to bear the offspring of chosen men, and with it, a biological, psychological, and ethical commitment to take care of human infancy."[5]

As instinct is opposed to reflection, as receptivity and gratification are opposed to activity and domination, so the "female principle" is presumptuously (although sometimes in a utopian vein) counterposed to the "male principle." In the epoch of bourgeois rule, a recurring ideological motif proclaims women to be firmly anchored in nature's domain.

Such a characterization of women cannot escape the general ambivalence inherent in the bourgeois perception of nature. Nature is posited as hostility, mysterious inexorability, a resistance to be broken. In the Hobbesian model, human beings, left in the state of nature, are locked in a *bellum omnium contra omnes*. External nature and human nature alike must be conquered by science, industry, the state – and yet other social forces. Because the domination of nature by man has involved also, and above all, the domination of human being by human being, this vision of nature has been persistently accompanied by its own contradiction.

Nature is also portrayed as the realm of original innocence, the never-to-be-retrieved paradise of play, happiness, and peace. In its utopian dimensions, nature has come forth as an implicit – albeit too frequently impotent – denunciation of social repression and the interminable antagonisms of capitalist society.

The ideology of femininity is likewise fraught with contradictions. It is an indictment of the capitalist performance principle[6] and simultaneously one of its targets. As nature, women must be at once dominated and exalted. So, for instance, the toiling black women who populate the novels of William Faulkner are worshipped by virtue of their innocent and unfathomable communion with nature. Here, however, the utopian projection of women as nature loses its progressive content. Under the impact of racism, it emerges as a thinly veiled endorsement of oppression. The authentic but naive utopian implications of a great many portraits of women are not to be ignored. But generally even these are objectively and ultimately based in ideology, although as art they may be a critique and indictment of society. The non-ideological, perhaps revolutionary function of the female as antithesis to the performance principle remains a problem to be explored.

The hypostasized notion that woman, as contrasted with man, is only a creature of nature, is blatantly false and a camouflage for the social subjugation women daily experience. But even in its falsity, there is also a hidden truth: the real oppression of women today is inextricably bound up with the capitalist mode of appropriating and mastering nature.

The definition of women as nature is ideology; it was engendered by and is a response to real conditions of oppression. As illusory consciousness, it is a distorted and obscuring representation of reality. It distorts the oppression of women by making it appear innocuous. It is at once a hint of what human relations might eventually become and a mockery of those relations. Finally, it obscures the whole history of a painful struggle between human beings and nature, the peculiar effect of this struggle on women – and specifically, on the women of the laboring classes.

In a critical, non-ideological sense, women are indeed natural beings; men, however, are equally natural. When Marx states that human beings are natural beings, this fact assumes a very precise dialectical meaning. For, armed with their biological powers and drives, living as they do in and through nature, human beings can only survive by *acting upon* and *transforming* the material of nature. Thus, "labor is a natural condition of human existence, a condition of material interchange between men and nature quite independent of the form of society."[7] In the course of collectively modifying nature – and labor is always social – human beings create and transform their own human nature.

Marx's *Economic and Philosophic Manuscripts* (1844) describes the "essence" of human beings as consisting in their active, creative relationship to nature through labor. In a correctly organized society, the young

Marx contends, social labor would creatively appropriate external nature as the "inorganic body of man [and woman]." External nature would be humanized and the vast potential of human nature could simultaneously unfurl.

The relationships of human beings among themselves are caught up in the process which defines the human posture toward nature. Uniquely crystallized in the female-male bond is the distance human beings have traveled in this process and specifically how far they have gone in awakening the slumbering powers within themselves.

> The immediate, natural, necessary relationship of human being to human being is the *relationship* of *man* to *woman*. In this *natural* species-relationship man's relationship to nature is immediately his relationship to man, as his relationship to man is immediately his relationship to nature, to his own *natural* condition. In this relationship the extent to which the human essence has become nature for man or nature has become the human essence of man is *sensuously manifested*, reduced to a perceptible fact. From this relationship one can thus judge the entire level of mankind's development. From the character of this relationship follows the extent to which *man* has comprehended himself as a *generic* being, as *man*; the relationship of man to woman is the *most natural* relationship of human being to human being. It thus indicates the extent to which man's *natural* behavior has become *human* or the extent to which his human *essence* has become a *natural* essence for him. In this relationship is also apparent the extent to which man's *need* has become *human*, thus the extent to which the *other* human being, as human being, has become a need for him, the extent to which he in his most individual existence is at the same time a social being.[8]

This passage may not be immediately transparent. It presupposes a knowledge of the categories Marx used in developing the anthropology of the 1844 *Manuscripts* – and this is not the place to elaborate on them in any detail.[9] The reproduction of this passage is nevertheless essential; it reveals that the young Marx construed the male–female bond to be a central ingredient of the social complex which must be overturned and remolded by the revolutionary process.

The *most natural* (in this sense, biologically necessary) relationship of human beings among themselves is that between woman and man. But human beings are not inexorably yoked to their biological constitution. Sexual activity, among other activities, can acquire a wealth of social meaning entirely lacking in its abstract, purely biological form. The woman–man union, in all its dimensions, is very much mutable and always subject to social transformation. But as long as social production takes place within the fetters of capitalist relations – as long as the appropriation of nature means the exploitation of human beings – this union between the sexes remains stunted and misshapen.

The worker's alienation has immediate consequences for the relationship between the sexes and, most significantly, for the woman herself. The products of labor are lost to the worker, who has brought them into being. He cannot creatively affirm himself as he works. He thus "feels that he is acting freely only in his animal functions – eating, drinking and procreating. . . . while in his human functions he feels only like an animal."[10]

> To be sure, eating, drinking and procreation are genuine human functions. In abstraction, however, and separated from the remaining sphere of human activities and turned into final and sole ends, they are animal functions.[11]

The implications for the woman who shares in these activities and ministers to her man's needs are formidable. Compelled to make only minimal contributions, or none whatsoever, to social production – not even in and through the alienated patterns of work – she is effectively reduced to the status of a mere *biological* need of man.

An unmistakable inference of Marx's early theory of alienation may be formulated: a critical and *explicit* mission of communism must be to shatter and recast sexual and marital relations, as production itself is transformed. It is essential, of course, that a new, more human, more creative posture toward external nature be adopted. But the man–woman union will always be disfigured unless the woman has liberated herself *as woman*. It will only be radically remolded when she is no longer defined as if she were a natural prolongation of man. The woman must first break out of the female–male union. Only then can she and man come together on a new basis, both experiencing an equal and authentically human need for one another.

This brief discussion of the 1844 *Manuscripts* has served to establish that Marx directly addressed himself – albeit not systematically – to certain dimensions of women's oppression. The bulk of this paper will be concerned with Marx's historical approach to nature and its implications for women's oppression and future liberation. A few preparatory remarks about the transition from the early to the later thought are in order.

The early writings develop the idea that the capitalist ordering of social production has erected an insurmountable hurdle between the worker on the one hand and the material and products of labor on the other. This is equivalent to saying that the human being has been severed from nature and thus, for the young Marx, from his own "inorganic body." The creative interaction with nature is the keystone of human nature. Capitalism disrupts this unity, giving rise to a non-identity between man and his essence. Communism would be the return of man to his essence, "the genuine [definitive] resolution of the antagonism between man and nature, and between man and man."[12]

The mature Marx is far more conscious of the complexity of the human being/nature relationship and its thorough-going historical character. The notion of nature – the material and fruits of labor – as the inorganic body of the human being is discovered to be a peculiar characteristic of pre-capitalist modes of production. This relationship is historically localized as the *naive unity* which binds the pre-capitalist producer to the earth and to other natural conditions of production.[13]

As general background for the remarks which follow, it should be borne in mind that in the later writings, communism is not projected as definitively eradicating the tension between the human being and nature. Social antagonisms rising out of class society are abolished. But labor, insofar as it is *necessary* labor, will always contain an element of restraint and unfreedom.[14] The vestiges of non-identity between humans and nature can never be dissolved unless technology creates a radical metamorphosis at the heart of production itself. In any event, unless and until all work is creative and unrestrained, human beings will have to seek their self-realization, in large part, outside the realm of social production. It is precisely the communist reorganization of production that permits them to do this. In anticipation, it may therefore be proposed that the *full* emancipation of women must ultimately also transcend the goal of her full and equal participation in a new and reorganized system of production.

II

Labor, in the Marxian conception, is a "natural condition of human existence."[15] In exploring the character of women's oppression during the phase of history preceding bourgeois ascendancy, the pre-capitalist function of labor should be revealing. The economic formation in question may be communal landed property, free petty land ownership, slavery, or serfdom; in all these cases, labor is geared by and large toward the production of *use-value*.

> The purpose of this labour is not the *creation of value*. . . . Its purpose is the maintenance of the owner and his family as well as the communal body as a whole. The establishment of the individual as a *worker*, stripped of all qualities except this one, is itself a product of *history*.[16]

Or, in slightly different words, "the object of production itself is to reproduce the producer in and together with [the] objective conditions of his existence."[17] (The slave and serf are treated as "inorganic conditions of production," as animals or as appendages of the land; yet, even as they are dominated, they and their communities are in possession of the means of their subsistence and enter into corresponding social relations among themselves.)[18]

Labor is stimulated by need; its product travels a more or less uninterrupted path towards consumption. Labor functions, therefore, as a natural mediator between external nature and the human community.[19] Considering the character of their labor, pre-capitalist epochs, even the most advanced, retain certain structural features reminiscent of subhuman natural "societies." (It is, of course, capitalism which is always the measuring rod.) Thus when Marx characterizes the earth during those phases as a "natural laboratory," the community as a "natural community," the family as a "natural family," he is by no means romanticizing pre-capitalist history.

Through production, the needs of the community are projected onto nature; external nature is the "inorganic body" of the community.[20] The community, in turn, always bears the stamp of nature, for it is subject, in a fundamental way, to naturally imposed limitations. In appearance, the community and family are natural phenomena – eternal and indifferent to the designs of human beings. Women and men confront collective life, family life, not as human products, but rather as unchangeable preconditions of human existence. Such is the meaning of Marx's contention that whenever labor is bound, in the last instance, to agriculture, social production will always be locked in a natural unity with state, community, and family relations. This holds true with equal force where cities and city labor are ultimately dependent on agriculture.

Against this backdrop, the "natural" roles and the "natural" oppression of the women of these periods take on a significance which transcends the mere fact of their biological constitution. It is certainly conceivable that childbearing and other physiological factors might be the immediate basis for certain social roles carrying the mark of inferiority. But it is not entirely inconceivable that under different conditions these factors could be more or less unrelated to social inferiority. Moreover, even if women's oppression bore no clear relation to biological considerations, it would not, for this reason, be lacking in "natural" dimensions.

Evidence does indicate, however, that during pre-capitalist periods, women, as a rule, were socially tied to their reproductive role. A cluster of child-centered activities attached themselves to the biological fact of maternity. The woman's attachment to the child tended to confine her to the domestic sphere. This allowed, in turn, for the evolution of a whole host of uniquely female household tasks. But even here, her roles were not determined by biological causation. Other and different *social* modes of coping with then insurmountable biological constants were not necessarily excluded from the realm of possibility. Had they arisen, they too, would have been both bound to and independent of natural determination.

Although not rigidly and biologically predetermined, a *sexual* division of labor asserted itself throughout capitalism's pre-history. In those primitive formations where, for example, hunting was necessary, this was generally outside the woman's domain. Likewise her roles were usually limited in those communities maintaining themselves through the military defense of their land.[21] War is here, in Marx's words, "the great communal labor."[22] Perhaps because of what Juliet Mitchell has termed the woman's lesser capacity for violence,[23] military activity was largely performed by the community's male members. Even when the division of labor reached levels of a far greater complexity, women's labor still remained sharply distinguished from the men's.

There are two important points to be made about the pre-capitalist character of women's labor and their related social status. First, the sexual division of labor does not militate against a greater unity – a unity which asserts itself in and through this separation. Because labor is bound up with the community's and family's *needs*, the differences between female and male labor are not *qualitative* in character. The woman's labor in and around the domestic quarters was equally essential and equally constitutive of social production. Recognizing that she experienced intense and drastic forms of oppression, it still remains that she was not exiled from *social production in general*. Rather she was barred from certain *concrete* forms of labor.[24]

Secondly, insofar as the woman was anchored to a relation of servitude, she was unable to attain a critical posture from which to perceive the real meaning of this relation. Her status and attendant oppression was coated with a nature-like inexorability. And what is most important, such an attitude had its objective complement in the prevailing mode of existence. Part of her oppression consisted in her inability to contest her inferior role. The antagonisms inherent in the male–female union tended to remain dormant, lacking the *social* level which would permit their penetration into consciousness.

In a rigorous sense, the peculiar status and oppression of women during pre-capitalist history functioned not so much as a *result* of the prevailing modes of production, but rather as a concrete *precondition* of production. This does not vitiate the material origin of the status of women; the relation is formulated in this way in order to capture the blurred unity between production and the oppression of women. As Marx notes: "Where landed property and agriculture form the basis of the economic order . . . , the economic object is the production of use-values, i.e., the *reproduction of the individual* in certain definite relationships to this community, of which it forms the basis" (Marx's emphasis).[25]

In respect to women in particular, the economy was colored by and tended to support the existing structure of woman's oppression in an equally great or even greater degree than her oppression was determined by the particular mode of production.

In the earliest primitive communities, so Marx infers, the division of labor required for production must have been synonymous with "the division of labour in the sexual act."[26] Marx goes on to say (in *The German Ideology*) that during history's most primitive epochs, the social relations of production in general were the same as the social relations incorporated in the family. Certainly as more advanced economic formations evolve, natural relations are socially modified; yet Marx insisted that before the dawn of the explosive forces rushing in the direction of capitalism, natural limitations decisively conditioned men and women's entire social life.

There prevailed a natural interpenetration of individual, family, community, and even the state on the one hand, and social production on the other. Marx observes, for example, that in a rural patriarchal form of manufacture, "when spinner and weaver lived under the same roof – the women of the family spinning and the men weaving, say, for the requirements of the family – the product of labor bore the specific imprint of the family relation with its naturally evolved division of labour."[27]

In all pre-capitalist formations, according to George Lukács, "natural relations – both in the case of the 'metabolic changes' between man and nature and also in the relations between men – retained the upper hand and dominated man's social being."[28] Alfred Schmidt maintains:

> Pre-bourgeois development had a peculiarly unhistorical character because in it the material prerequisites of labour – the instrument as well as the material – were not themselves the *product* of labour, but were found already to hand in the land, in nature, from which the active subject as well as the community to which it belonged did not essentially differentiate themselves. Under capitalism, however, these subjective and objective conditions of production became something created by the participants in history. Relationships were no longer determined by nature but *set up* by society.[29]

During the pre-capitalist phase of history, women's oppression, strictly construed, was heavily enshrouded in a natural determination not yet superseded or transformed by socio-historical forces. It experienced a corresponding transformation when capitalist society broke onto the scene of history. Then, it, like capitalist social relations in general, would also be *set up* by society.

III

While the pre-capitalist subjugation of women is related to socially insurmountable natural imitations, these limitations are articulated through socially prescribed roles. Highly interesting, in this connection, is the brutally unique situation into which black women were thrust during American slavery.[30] With the rise of capitalism and the subordination of slavery to an incipient commodity economy, black men and women were treated ruthlessly and literally as "inorganic conditions of production" (to use the term with which Marx describes the economic function of slaves). Other forms of slavery merely stamped with the mark of inferiority the social relations of slaves among themselves. But the American system demanded the almost total prohibition of an endemic social life within the community of slaves.

American slavery was not a natural economy based primarily on consumption; its goal was rather the production of commodities. The slave-holding class expressed its drive for profit by seeking the maximum extraction of surplus labor in utter disregard to the age or sex of the slave. Even very real biological limitations were frequently little more than occasions for flogging. As reported in slave narratives, special forms of punishment were meted out to pregnant women who were unable to meet the prescribed work pace. In some instances, a hole was carved in the ground permitting a pregnant woman to lie in a prone position while she was flogged by the overseer.

The family was either nonexistent or its sole and unmediated purpose was to produce future forgers of profit. It is true that the black woman was responsible for the domestic chores of the slave quarters. Yet, this role was not integrated into an overall structure articulating her dependence vis-à-vis the black man. External economic compulsions brought her into an equal partnership in oppression with the man. As a result, the black woman was not systematically molded into an inferior being insofar as the internal workings of the slave community – the relations of the slaves among themselves – were concerned.

This did not prevent the slave system from aspiring to foist upon her the putative inferiority of the woman. The use of her body as a breeding instrument and its sexual violation by the slave-holder were institutional assertions of the lower rank of the female slave. But this oppression was not part of a naturally conditioned order and was thus significantly different in structure from its pre-capitalist counterpart. As overt social coercion, the oppression of black women in slavery could not conceal its contingent social character.

IV

The American slave system was a notable exception in the world historical rise of capitalism. In its peculiar subordination to a commodity economy, it could only have arisen where incipient conditions of capitalism already prevailed. In the broadest sense, as Marx points out, it is the impact of economic exchange on a progressively large scale which overturns old structures and paves the way for the "free" wage laborer – the *sine qua non* of capitalism.

The ingression of exchange, when it occurs, begins to undermine fundamentally and drastically the entire texture of human life. As the central prerequisite for the genesis of capital, labor-power itself, like the products of labor, was eventually reduced to a universally exchangeable commodity. But first the producer had to be decisively severed from the land, from his implements of production, as well as from his control over the means of subsistence.[31] And the natural bonds tying producer to producer, family structures included, had to be deprived of their seemingly objective and necessary mode of existence. Their relationship to production had to take on a contingent appearance. This is to say, the reproduction of the community of producers, and of the family as its unit, could no longer be presumed to be the real goal of production. Use-value had to be supplanted by exchange-value and the aim of production had to become the reproduction of capital.

The family and community ceased to appear as extensions of nature (which has both positive and negative implications) in order to make way for a society composed of fragmented individuals, lacking any organic or human connection. Such a society, infinitely more advanced in its mode of production, is mediated by the abstract principle of exchange.

Marx never fails to accentuate the eminently progressive content of this development. There is progress in the very midst of its ruthlessness. Capitalism marked the release of productive forces which, for the first time in history, could systematically appropriate and transform the fruits of nature.[32] From the vantage point of the producer, it was also an important advance, even as it merely modified the structure of his oppression. The worker was freed from the overt domination by another human being, from the alien and unqualified control over his body and movement. He attained freedom over his body and the liberty to dispose of his labor. The new owners of the means of production would have to bargain with him for the purchase of his labor-power. His wages would not be determined by the capitalist's whim, but rather by socially necessary labor time. As a person, he would be superfluous to production; only his abstract ability to work would be pertinent. Yet, even in this contingency, he could also discover beneficial features, for, with the notable exception of racism, caste-like distinctions should not interfere when he sold his labor-power on the market. The capitalist commodity is totally indifferent to the origin of the labor which produces it; labor becomes "abstract labor-power," and each worker of similar skills should always be equal to the next.

The immanent logic of capitalist production demands the universal equivalence of labor-power. If, for the purposes of analysis, this factor is

isolated from other forces at work, it latently contains profound consequences for the social status of women. In face of the dissolution of the
natural rigidity of the family, and especially as mechanization progresses,
women of the working class should have undergone the same process of
equalization as men. In earlier periods, specific forms of labor belonged
exclusively to women. Part of the quality of their products consisted precisely in the fact that they were products of *female* labor. But when the
product of labor became an exchangeable commodity, all such distinctions
began to vanish. An unprecedented potential thus works its way into
history: *The capitalist mode of production unleashes the condition for the historical supersession of the sexually based division of labor.* The universal equivalence of labor-power conceptually implies the release of the woman from
her naturally infused roles in labor.

This potentiality, needless to say, could not become more than an
abstract promise of equal exploitation. Capitalism could not even proclaim
for women this rudimentary egalitarianism. Instead it transmuted a more or
less naturally conditioned oppression into an oppression whose content
became thoroughly *socio-historical*. It was only then that women were effectively exiled from the sphere of social production – or permitted, at most,
a tangential role. Their containment within the family became, not a
natural necessity, but rather a peculiarly societal phenomenon. It is therefore only in bourgeois society that the oppression of women assumes a
decisive *social* dimension and function.

The capitalist mode of production outstrips all previous modes in transcending virtually all extra-economic determinants. The unique status of
women is not immediately implied in the capitalist organization of labor, as
one of its preconditions. According to Marx: "For capital, the worker does
not constitute a condition of production, but only labor. If this can be
performed by machinery, or even by water or air, so much the better. And
what capital appropriates is not the laborer, but his labor – and not directly,
but by means of exchange."[33]

If it does not matter who does the work – only that it be done – then
certainly women can be non-discriminately employed in production.
Through the eyes of the commodity, in fact, women are indistinguishable
from men. But, as it will be subsequently shown, their oppression is indeed
a *result* of critical social forces in whose absence the mode of production
could not effectively be sustained. A distinctive and indeed defining inno-
vation of capitalist production lies in its *projection of female oppression onto a
socio-historical continuum*. Once this occurs, women's liberation, like the
emancipation of the producers themselves, becomes a *real* historical possibility. The concrete promise of female liberation is bound up inextricably
with the overturning of the social forces fundamentally nourished by her
oppression.

V

The unfettering of the historical ingredients which ushered in the capitalist form of labor in its abstract, universal equivalence, has been examined from a very specific perspective. A closer glimpse at this development, emphasizing its impact on the worker's family as it was dispossessed of its natural foundation, reveals the special basis for women's oppression under capitalism. Engels was essentially correct to link the inferior status of the female to the hierarchical make-up of the family. For the numerous material and cultural manifestations of female inferiority are predicated on the woman's dependent rank within the family unit. This derives in turn, and certainly in the final instance, from the exigencies of capitalism's productive apparatus.

Within Marxist theory, most of the discussion about the insular bourgeois family has concentrated on its mode of existence among the bourgeoisie alone. The private, individual proprietor, it is asserted, needs his own miniature "society" over which he wields unrestricted authority. His wife – and children of undisputed fatherhood – must be his uncontested possessions. The private character of his remaining property must transcend his own mortal existence: his wife, through her child-bearing, must therefore protect it from future alienation and dissolution.

While all this is true and critically important to the functioning of capitalism, the special meaning of the insular family for the worker should not go unacknowledged. Engels insisted that the worker who has nothing to sell but his ability to work cannot be overly concerned about bequeathing this meager property to his undisputed heirs. But this does not mean that the bourgeois family structure was thus *externally* foisted upon the producers, serving no *real* objective purpose. On the contrary, the hierarchical family structure, as it exists among workers, possesses a unique and necessary relationship to the capitalist mode of production. As it will later be maintained, this family also responds to certain irrepressible needs of working human beings themselves.

The central prerequisite for the constitution of capital – and thus for the ascendancy of the bourgeoisie and its family – is the historical appearance of the *private individual* worker. (The emergence of the worker as individual is simultaneously the emergence of the producing individual defined vis-à-vis production only in his capacity as worker.)[34]

> The further back we trace the course of history, the more does the individual, and accordingly also the producing individual, appear to be dependent and belong to a larger whole. At first the individual, in a still quite natural manner is part of the family and of the tribe which evolves from the family. Later he is a part of a community.[35]

And, prior to capitalism, the producer's relation "to the natural prerequisites of his production as *his own* is mediated by his natural membership in a community" (or a state).[36] Even the slave and the serf, it should be recalled, are in direct possession of the means of their subsistence.

As capital makes its ingression into history, the worker is transfigured into an isolated private individual – isolated from the means of production (hence also from the means of subsistence) and equally isolated from the community of producers. To a hitherto unprecedented degree, workers are fragmented among themselves to the point of perceiving their own social relations as the nexus of exchange binding commodity to commodity. The fragmentation of the community of producers thus complements the fetishistic appearance of the commodity, the veiled crystallization of social relations under capitalism.

When the serf or free peasant is ejected from the land; when the artisan is divested of the implements of his labor; when they are cut off from their peers as individual units of labor-power; it is actually they and their miniature societies which are severed from nature and the human community. The worker is sealed off in the false privacy of the insular family.

The utter disintegration of the community of producers relegates, therefore, not the individual, but rather the family unit to a distant realm which bears no organic connection to the activity of social production. Although Marx does not explicitly discuss the process of individuation undergone by the worker as it is related to the fate of the family, a direct connection between these two processes seems to be apparent nevertheless. Marx's observations seem to raise the question of whether the individual worker – carrier of abstract labor-power – demanded by production, would not have to express somewhere the authority of his individuality, an authority without which individuality would not obtain. Assuming an affirmative answer, this authority could very well express itself in the family – but within a family whose dynamic relation to production has been annulled. If this were so, it would be clear why the woman is not permitted to experience the ruthless – although in some respects beneficial – equalizing tendencies of capitalist production. She remains inseparably anchored to the fabric necessary for the maintenance of the worker as individual.

The woman not only remains tied to the family, but must bear the major responsibility for the internal labor guaranteeing its preservation. These *private* domestic duties preclude more than marginal participation in *social* production. Moreover, she is enclosed within a family whose unity with social production has severely eroded; her labor within the household therefore takes on an entirely new character. In pre-bourgeois history, such work, essential to the maintenance of the family and of the larger community as well, was necessarily an important component of social production itself. With capitalism, household labor, generating only the value of utility, is no longer related to the productive apparatus. Production itself has undergone a profound metamorphosis; its fundamental aim is the creation of exchange-value. Thus, with respect to production, women experience a double inferiority. They are first prohibited, by virtue of their family standing, from consistently and equally reaching the point of production. Secondly, the labor they continue to monopolize does not measure up to the characteristic labor of capitalist society.

Kinship, marital, and procreative relations are no longer balanced with the relations of production. The family itself ceases to incorporate the social – although for pre-capitalist history, natural – relations of production. But the *natural* functions of women are abstractly articulated in the family. These functions are rendered abstract exactly to the degree that they are stripped of their *immediate social character*. Through a dialectical inversion, it is the radical separation of the producer from nature that lays the basis for the *social* creation of women as eternally natural beings. This is to say, women are socially imprisoned within natural roles that are no longer naturally necessary.

Hence there occurs under capitalism a necessary dialectic between the potential equality of women, inherent in the apparatus of production, and the inevitable domination of women implied in (but not confined to) the family. This dialectic largely defines the structure of women's oppression (simultaneously signaling the negative conditions for its abolition) and confers upon this structure its overtly societal, therefore transmutable character. New relations of production render such factors as sex superfluous. But the intrinsic social necessity of these relations – the need to buttress the abstract, individual and fragmented nature of labor-power – re-establishes sexual differences in the social edifice resting on the base of production.

These social differences go so far as to apportion to women a *qualitatively* different form of labor – the labor of utility as opposed to that of exchange. Margaret Benston observes that: "The appearance of commodity production has indeed transformed the way that *men* labor. . . . Most household labor in capitalist society remains in the pre-market stage. This is the work which is reserved for women and it is in this fact that we can find the basis for a definition of women."[37]

Yet Benston's position implies that women are *objective* (and not just ideological) anachronisms. This dilemma can only be surmounted if their use-value producing labor is studied against the background of the objectively possible equalization of women by the commodity-producing apparatus.

As it will be subsequently shown, the equalization–repression dialectic has yet another moment, realized with the actual admission of women into capitalist social production. Female labor-power (not concrete labor), even as it is called upon for tasks identical to those performed by men, will be laden with cultural determination. This is not to mention the plethora of "female" occupations. Labor performed by women, even when it produces exchange-value, will not be "abstract labor-power in general" but rather a specific and socially inferior female ability to work.

VI

Reduced to its biological preconditions, the insular structure of the producer's family announces and fortifies the rupture of the human community of producers. In this sense, the family is essential for the ideological reproduction of capitalist society as a whole. Yet, in the course of reinforcing the alienated relations crystallized in the commodity, the family – and more specifically, the woman – must also respond to *real human needs*. "Bourgeois civilization has reduced social relations to the cash nexus. They have become emptied of affection."[38] With due consideration of the factor of sublimation, the human need for affective bonds cannot be eliminated beyond an absolute minimum. If these relations were divested of all immediate expression, human beings could hardly survive the desperate struggle for existence. Love and interpersonal emotions in general are needs which cease to demand at least minimal fulfillment only when human beings have long since ceased to be human. In capitalist society, the woman has the special mission of being both reservoir and receptacle for a whole range of human emotions otherwise banished from society. This mission is directly related to her confinement, in labor, to the production of use-values.

Forbidden to flourish in society at large, and especially at the point of production, personal relations unfolding within the family inevitably are affected adversely. Indeed, from the very outset, the "legitimate" woman–man union already bears the inexorable stamp of exchange. Its legitimacy is a contrivance of the marriage *contract*; like the labor contract, this is also an "unjust exchange." Here, of course, the woman is always victim. All this considered, it must be recognized nonetheless that in the absence of even this far from ideal occasion for interpersonal bonds, capitalist society probably would be much more grotesque than it has actually proved to be. A case in point is Nazi Germany. The unarticulated purpose behind its irrational cult of the family and motherhood was to manipulate family-based emotions into an unmediated fusion with extreme national and racial chauvinism. In this respect, Nazi propaganda was designed, at bottom, to vitiate the family itself as a locus of personal emotions.[39]

In its "bourgeois-democratic" form, capitalism requires the family as a realm within which the natural and instinctive yearning for non-reified human relations may be expressed. Herbert Marcuse discusses their relations:

> Human relations are class relations, and their typical form is the free labor contract. This contractual character of human relationships has spread from the sphere of production to all of social life. Relationships function only in their reified form, mediated through the class distribution of the material output of the contractual partners. If this functional de-personalization were ever breached, not merely by that backslapping familiarity which only under-scores the reciprocal functional distance separating men but rather by mutual concern and solidarity, it would be impossible for men to return to their normal social functions and positions. The contractual structure upon which this society is based would be broken.[40]

Contrasted with prevailing social relations, the family and its web of personal relations add a qualitatively different dimension to social life. On precisely this basis, in fact, the woman is presented in the utopian fringes of bourgeois ideology as an antithesis to the capitalist performance principle. This positive (although still distorted) aspect of the ideology of femininity has been frequently suppressed by the women's liberation movement. In efforts to debunk the myth of the woman as an exclusively emotional being, an equally abstract position has been too often assumed. The abstract negation of "femininity" is embraced; attempts are made to demonstrate that women can be as non-emotional, reality-affirming and dominating as men are alleged to be. The model, however, is usually a concealed "masculine" one.

The most extreme case – extreme to the point of absurdity – of proposing as a solution to male supremacy the abstract negation of "femininity" is furnished by Valerie Solanas and her *SCUM Manifesto* (Society for Cutting Up Men). Her definition of sexuality is exceedingly revealing:

> Sex is not part of a relationship, on the contrary, it is a solitary experience, non-creative, a gross waste of time. The female can easily – far more easily than she may think – condition away her sex drive, leaving her completely cool and cerebral, and free to pursue truly worthy relationships and activities [sic!]. . . . When the female transcends her body, rises above animalism, the male . . . will disappear.[41]

One thing is clear in this drastic formulation of the attack against male supremacy: such a position, in the final analysis, must be a duplication – conscious or unconscious – of the reified relations which have demanded the oppression of women in the first place. This position reinstates the same relations that have engendered a situation where women are exhaustively defined as "affective" – "affective" in a way that men cannot be – and where women's emotionality is presumed to exclude rationality. In order to shatter the ideology of femininity insofar as it implies reified affection, women must also combat the ideology of reified insensibility. If, as Marx has said, liberation is to ultimately also mean "the complete *emancipation* of all the human qualities and senses,"[42] which include "not only the five senses, but the so-called spiritual senses, the practical senses (desiring, loving),"[43] then the positive qualities of femininity must be released from their sexual exclusiveness, from their distorted and distorting forms. They must be *aufgehoben* in a new and liberating socialist society.

Christopher Caudwell draws attention to the fact that within the interstices of capitalism, non-reified modes of behavior continue to exist. He describes these as vestiges of pre-capitalist history:

> Even today, in those few economic forms which still survive in a pre-bourgeois form, we can see tenderness as the essence of the relation. The commodity fetishism which sees in a relation between *men* only a relation between things has not yet dried it up. The economic relation of the mother to her foetus, of the child to the parent [primarily the mother] and vice versa retains its primitive form to show this clearly.[44]

Caudwell envisions "love" as capable of proposing a fierce indictment of bourgeois society. This is undoubtedly utopian idealism, unless, that is, a socio-political mediation can draw love and tenderness into the revolutionary continuum. Love alone is impotent, yet without it, no revolutionary process could ever be truly authentic. From this vantage point, a critical kernel of truth emerges out of Caudwell's vision:

> Today it is as if love and economic relations have gathered at two opposite poles. All the unused tenderness of man's instincts gather at one pole and at the other are economic relations, reduced to bare coercive rights to commodities. This polar segregation is a source of terrific tension and will give rise to a vast transformation of bourgeois society.[45]

It cannot be too strongly emphasized that in seeking to discover the precise role of such categories as Caudwell proposes in developing a revolutionary theory, and particularly as these pertain to women, much caution is necessary. In advancing the most radical construction of the revolutionary function of utopian categories in general (a function possible only with advanced capitalism), Marcuse is always careful to avoid Icarus's dilemma.[46] He reveals the threads which lead directly from utopia to science and back to utopia again.

Germaine Greer soars high with her utopian dreams of women's potential capabilities. But finally she can discover no real solutions and must turn to abstract ethical imperatives. In the last chapter of her book – the chapter entitled "Revolution" – she says, significantly:

> It would be genuine revolution if women would suddenly stop loving the victors in violent encounters ... If soldiers were certainly faced with the withdrawal of all female favors, as Lysistrata observed so long ago, there would suddenly be less glamour in fighting.[47]

Presumably, this is a way of reaching the new society, a society thereby free of "masculine" (she does not say "imperialist") war.

The personal relations which cluster around women contain in germ, albeit in a web of oppression and thus distortedly, the premise of the abolition of alienation, the dissolution of a compulsive performance principle, thus, ultimately, the destruction of the whole nexus of commodity exchange. But yet this utopian content is only a promise and nothing more. Its radical implications remain impotent unless they are integrated into a practical revolutionary process.

In *capitalist* society, although these personal relations are a contrast to the normal flow of social life, they are, in their present form, woven into the warp and woof of capitalist relations as a whole. Even as a negation of these relations, they actually presuppose them and foster their continuance. It is a non-subverting negation. Marcuse characterizes social relations under capitalism as creating a "reciprocal functional distance separating men." It has already been shown that the break-up of pre-capitalist economic and social life gave rise to a historically unprecedented separation of human beings among themselves – in order to separate them from the means of production. The family, it was maintained, is the direct target of these divisive forces which establish a foundation for the most advanced phase of human development by instituting the most systematic method of human exploitation. This "reciprocal functional distance separating men" both requires, and issues out of, the new family structure, closed in upon itself especially for the woman.

A progressively increasing fragmentation among human beings has accompanied an ever more developed capitalism. In the era of advanced capitalism, the insularity is virtually complete. A salient example can be seen in the recently escalated flight toward the suburbs. Workers, especially white workers, have also joined in this exodus. The closed-in cubicle-like housing is a material extension of the ever increasing distance which dissevers them from their fellow producers. (The situation of the woman worker will be discussed later in the paper.) The plight of the woman in the suburbs is especially painful, for solidarity with other human beings is hardly attainable in this isolated environment. When it occurs, it is the artificial, back-slapping type. Her shopping center is in the suburb as is the school for her children (she is often opposed to "busing"), her beauty parlor, her "entertainment." She drives virtually everywhere; nothing is in walking distance from her home. There is no public transportation to speak of. If there is only one car in the family she is often confined to the house until her husband comes home from work. The husband returns each day, forgetting in this plastic environment exactly how toilsome his work has been. His comrade producers are but numbers and bodies to him – at most beer-drinking partners. The worker must thus surmount many insurmountable barriers before he can become aware that he and all other producers are the wellspring of the society. The achievement of solidarity, thus of a revolutionary class consciousness, has never been so difficult as during the present era. This particular phenomenon further attests to the inseparable unity of women's oppression and the exploitation of workers. The role society has given to women reinforces the mechanisms which guarantee the continued domination of the producers.

Perhaps the most concrete instance of the family providing an objective contrast to capitalist social relations as a whole can be sought in the oppressed communities of America. Among black people, for one, the potential for a different, more human quality of relations prevails – relations which often escape the false, "back-slapping" familiarity which is the distorted form of personal association. Families are frequently "extended" rather than "nuclear," embracing more than two generations, as well as cousins and other relatives. The increasing use of "sister" and "brother," which is by no means confined to the politically sophisticated, is an over protest against the compartmentalization of existence. Though the use of those terms has a long tradition encompassing many and diverse associations, the fact that they now transcend political or religious affiliations and are widespread in the community as a whole, points to the yearning for human solidarity in the midst of a situation where solidarity has almost become obsolete.

As it normally functions, the family is a windowless monad of illusory satisfaction. It strengthens the distance between human beings in society. But like Leibniz's monad, it is also a reflection of a larger totality; its duplication of society is strikingly illustrated by its function in respect to the children it conceives. As the human, *natural* sphere par excellence, the family introjects society into the "human nature" of the child. Within the perimeters of the family, a psychological make-up harmonious, or at least compatible, with an exploitative and repressive environment must be reproduced. In this sense, the family's older place and role in the community has remained more or less intact. In pre-capitalist formations it was the family, the kinship group or earlier, the tribe, which regulated and perpetuated a specific metabolism between its members and nature. When "nature" is superseded by the commodity form, and human beings relate to their environment and to one another through the nexus of exchange, the family initially forges a pre-established harmony between individual and capitalist society.

The family has been divested of many of its functions as an instrument of socialization. The educational system and the media – television in particular – surpass the family's importance in the socialization process. Nevertheless, the very earliest formative months and years of the individual are still subject to the family's – and especially the mother's – guidance. As psychoanalysis has verified, the first months of childhood are critically important for the psychological constitution of the mature adult. It is not necessary to invoke the special categories of Freudian psychology to realize, for instance, that it is the mother who introduces the child to language and who first assists it to develop the powers of perception through which it will eventually "receive" the world.

The drudgery of full-time child rearing acquires, in this manner, a more profound and infinitely devastating meaning. Society assigns to women the mission of unknowingly creating human beings who will "feel at home" in a reified world.

VII

In *Capital*, Marx confidently asserted that: "modern industry, by assigning as it does an important part in the process of production, outside the domestic sphere, to women, to young persons, and to children of both sexes, creates a new economical foundation for a higher form of the family and of the relations between the sexes."[48] But, in actuality, female participation in production has remained a mere foundation whose edifice was not – and could not – be erected. It has not greatly upset the structure of the family, nor has it significantly ameliorated the social status of women. While work outside the home has furnished some women with important advantages, most have had to accept its reaffirming and amplifying effect on their oppression. In Clara Colon's words:

> The woman, pivot of home and family life, can only set one foot into the world of opportunity as industrial worker. The other foot is still stuck to the household doorstep. If she tries to combine home and work, she is restricted to performing half-way in each. The working mother finds employment outside the home is a tough and tedious chore, hardly a step toward equality.[49]

As a dependent being, as someone else's "inorganic extension," the price of women's entry into production was surplus exploitation (grossly inferior wages) and jobs which, on the whole, were far less fulfilling than even the stultifying labor assigned to men. Marx pointed out that: "In England women are still occasionally used instead of horses for hauling canal boats, because the labor required to produce horses and machines is an accurately known quantity, while that required to maintain the women of the surplus population is below all calculation."[50]

In America, one-third of all married women currently work outside the home – slightly more than one-half of all working women. But considering that the median earnings of women are about half that of men (and for black women even less), it is clear that female oppression has only sunk deeper into the apparatus. For if and when women's participation in social production becomes viable and necessary, the capitalist contracts the purchase, not of "abstract labor-power in general" but rather of an already socially stigmatized female labor-power.

The family-based structure of oppression – engendered in the final instance by the capitalist mode of production – is reduplicated and exacerbated by her entry into the labor force. For as long as the woman's "natural" place is proclaimed to be the home – in concrete terms: as long as she remains chained to a man and to a private domestic economy – her servile status is inevitable. No matter how excruciating, her overly exploitative job always remains a subsidiary activity. Combined with her multitudinous domestic duties, it shrinks her realm of leisure (strictly speaking, her only freedom beyond the necessity of labor) to practically naught.

It is not to be inferred, however, that women should refrain from seeking further penetration into social production. On the contrary, the demand for job equality – equal jobs and equal pay for the same jobs – is one of the indispensable prerequisites for an effective women's liberation strategy. Such a demand, it need not be said, loses much of its meaning and can fall back into the orbit of oppression unless it is accompanied by the fight for childcare centers, maternity leaves, free abortions and the entire complex of solutions to uniquely female needs. Without such special and only apparently unequal treatment, "equality" tends towards its own negation.

The ultimate meaning of the fight for the equality of women at the point of production should transcend its immediate aim. These efforts must be seen as an essential ingredient of a broader thrust: the assault on the institutional structures which perpetuate the socially enforced inferiority of women. In the warped sexual equality foisted upon the black woman by slavery and subsequent national oppression, there is a revealing hint of the latent but radical potential of the attack on the productive apparatus. The singular status of black people from slavery to the present, has forced the woman to work outside the home – at first as provider of profit for the slave-master, but later as provider for her own family. Certainly, as female, she has been objectively exploited to an even greater degree than the black man. It would therefore be cruel and extravagant to claim that the black woman has been released from the social stigma attached to women in general and particularly to the women of the laboring classes. The black woman's relative independence, emanating from her open participation in the struggle for existence, has always been but another dimension of her oppression. It has thus rendered her household and internal family responsibilities all the more onerous. From these, she had never been objectively freed. The important point, however, is the fact that she has not been – and could not be – exclusively defined by her special, "female" duties. As a result, far more meaningful social roles within the black community – oppressed from without – have been available to black women. Most importantly, black women have made critical contributions to the fight against racism and national oppression – from slavery to the present day.

What has been prompted in the black woman by the utter necessity of trying to survive in face of ruthless and sustained national oppression, should be elevated by the women's movement to the status of a strategic goal. This is especially important as this movement gathers impetus within the existing social framework. Efforts to bring women into production – and always on an equal basis with men – need to be placed on the continuum of revolution. While immediate needs should be pacified, such efforts must assist in bringing to fruition among women a vast and hitherto untapped potential for anti-capitalist consciousness. As one mode of the women's struggle, the assault on sexism which permeates the productive apparatus – conjoined with agitation for all the special female needs – can help women to rid themselves of the "muck of ages," of their self-image as natural extensions of maleness. This is indispensable preparation for revolutionary consciousness and practice.

VIII

Broader strategic questions about the character and direction of women's liberation may now be posed. What ought not to be the strategy of female liberation can be clearly stated. It ought not to be reduced and confined to the abstract and isolated attempt to shift the balance of "sexual politics." In conferring absolute primacy on the sexual dimensions of woman's oppression, the narrow bourgeois feminist approach distorts its social character and function within existing social conditions. This approach has correctly discerned the oppression of women to be a thread linking even the most disparate eras of history. It is true that even the socialist countries have not achieved the emancipation of women. But to conclude that therefore the structures of sexual oppression are primary is to ignore the changing character of women's oppression as history itself has advanced. The narrow feminist approach fails to acknowledge the specificity of the social subjugation of the women who live outside the privileged class under capitalism. It is qualitatively different from the comparatively *natural* oppression which was the lot of women in previous historical periods. And to the extent that some women continue to play subordinate roles in existing socialist societies, their oppression assumes yet another, but far less dangerous character.

Within the existing class relations of capitalism, women in their vast majority are kept in a state of familial servitude and social inferiority not by men in general, but rather by the ruling class. Their oppression serves to maximize the efficacy of domination. The objective oppression of black women in America has a class, and also a national origin. Because the structures of female oppression are inextricably tethered to capitalism, female emancipation must be simultaneously and explicitly the pursuit of black liberation and of the freedom of other nationally oppressed peoples.

An effective women's liberation movement must be cognizant of the primacy of the larger social revolution: the capitalist mode of production must be overturned, like the political and legal structures that sustain it. Conversely, the larger social revolution must be cognizant of the vital place and role of the thrust towards women's emancipation.

The socialist movement must never forget that while the economic struggle is indispensable, it is by no means the sole terrain of significant anti-capitalist activity. Thus, the unique features of the women's struggle cannot be restricted to economic agitation alone.

A socialist revolution will more or less reflect the struggles which led it to its triumphant phase. In this respect, the entire revolutionary continuum must be animated by the consciousness that the real goal of socialism is to shatter the automatism of the economic base. This, indeed, is the requisite condition for preparing the way for a sphere of freedom outside, and undetermined by, the process of production. Perhaps eventually, even work can become an expression of freedom, but this would be far in the distant future. However, even this total transfiguration of the nature of work would presuppose that the economy had long since ceased to be the center of society.

The edifice of the new society cannot spring *sui generis* from the economic and political reconstitution of its fabric. It is therefore misleading to represent women's liberation under socialism as equivalent to the achievement of full and equal female participation in production. Certainly women should perform a proportional part of social labor, but only as their necessary duties in a society oriented towards the satisfaction of its members' material and spiritual needs. Further, job discrimination under socialism attests to and fortifies the continued oppression of women.

Beyond this, women must be liberated from toilsome and time-consuming household duties; the private domestic economy must be dissolved. They must be permitted a maximum range of control over their bodies – exactly to the degree that this is objectively possible through science.

These are but a few of the negative preconditions for an affirmative release of women's human potentialities. That this release will demand an entirely new organization of the family is obvious. Most Marxists have been loath to speculate about new forms the family can assume under socialism. But, as Marcuse has emphasized on numerous occasions, utopian projections at the present phase of technological development must not necessarily lack a scientific and historical foundation. New theoretical approaches to the family – at once scientific and imaginative – can be of immense assistance to the women's movement in the formulation of its long-range goals.

Within the present fabric of domination, the women's movement is confronted with urgent oppositional tasks. For if the material and ideological supports of female inferiority are not to be carried over intact into the socialist order,[51] they must be relentlessly attacked throughout the course of building the revolutionary movement. Not only must there be agitation around the economic situation of women, but equally important, the entire superstructural nexus of women's oppression must be met with constant criticism and organized assaults. While moving towards the overthrow of capitalism, the ideology of female inferiority must be so thoroughly subverted that once the revolution is achieved, it will be impossible to refer with impunity to "my better half" or to be the "natural" place of the woman as in the home.

Perhaps the most significant message for the existing women's movement is this: the ultimate face of women's oppression is revealed precisely there where it is most drastic. In American society, the black woman is most severely encumbered by the male supremacist structures of the larger society. (This does not contradict the fact that a greater sexual equality might prevail inside the oppressed black community.) Its combination with the most devastating forms of class exploitation and national oppression clearly unmasks the socio-historical function of the subjugation of women.

Even as black women have acquired a greater equality as women within certain institutions of the black community, they have always suffered in a far greater proportion and intensity the effects of institutionalized male supremacy. "In partial compensation for [a] narrowed destiny the white world has lavished its politeness on its womankind. . . . From black women of America, however, this gauze has been withheld and without semblance of such apology they have been frankly trodden under the feet of [white] men."[52]

If the quest for black women's liberation is woven as a priority into the larger bid for female emancipation; if the women's movement begins to incorporate a socialist consciousness and forges its practice accordingly; then it can undoubtedly become a radical and subversive force of yet untold proportions. In this way the women's liberation movement may assume its well-earned and unique place among the current gravediggers of capitalism.

NOTES

1   Robin Morgan (ed.), *Sisterhood is Powerful* (New York: Vintage Books, 1970), xxxiv (her emphasis).

2   Ibid., xxxv.

3   Numerous critiques of the "white" women's liberation movement have been proposed by blacks – and specifically by black women. Linda La Rue, for example, cautions against an alliance with the women's movement, which she concludes would be inherently unwise (Linda La Rue, "The Black Movement and Women's Liberation," *The Black Scholar*, May 1970). Toni Morrison contends that there is something intrinsic in the experience and corresponding *Weltanschauung* of black women which renders women's liberation irrelevant and superfluous. (Toni Morrison, "What the Black Woman Thinks about Women's Lib," *The New York Times Magazine*, August 22, 1971). At the other end of the spectrum, there is, for instance, the Third World Women's Alliance, which stresses the critical importance of women's liberation for women of color, while maintaining that their organizational structure and theoretical basis must be separate from and autonomous vis-à-vis the women's movement among whites. (See their manifesto *Triple Jeopardy*, reprinted in *Triple Jeopardy*, vol. 1, no. 1, Sept.–Oct. 1971.)

4   The one classical Marxist text on the oppression of women – Friedrich Engels's *Origin of the Family, Private Property and the State* – has ironically been invoked by many who seek to demonstrate the socio-historical primacy of women's subjugation. Indeed, one of the flaws of this work is that Engels's entire analysis is predicated on a hypothetical pre-historical ascendancy of the woman. What he calls "the world-historical defeat of the female sex" is proposed as the first instance of human beings dominating their own kind. This is the crucial moment of his analysis and thus, in his opinion, the key to an understanding of women's oppression. While it is clearly necessary to recognize the infinitely long history of women's subjugation, the impact of capitalism on women is critical for an understanding of women's present status and oppression. Engels minimizes the qualitatively new form of socially enforced female inferiority which inserts itself into history with the advent of capitalism.

5   Erik Erikson, "Inner Space and Outer Space," *Daedalus*, no. 93, 1964, 580–606.

6   Marcuse says in *Eros and Civilization*, "We designate [the specific reality principle that has governed the origins and the growth of this civilization] as *performance principle* in order to emphasize that under its rule society is stratified according to the competitive economic performance of its members. . . . The performance principle, which is that of an acquisitive and antagonistic society in the process of constant expansion, presupposes a long development during which domination has been increasingly rationalized." (Herbert Marcuse, *Eros and Civilization* [London: Sphere Books Ltd, 1969], 50.)

7   Karl Marx, *A Contribution to a Critique of Political Economy* (New York: International Publishers, 1970), 36.

8   Karl Marx, *Economic and Philosophic Manuscripts* (1844), "Private Property and Communism," in Lloyd D. Easton and Kurt H. Guddat, trans. and ed., *Writings of the Young Marx on Philosophy and Society* (New York: Doubleday and Co., Inc., Anchor Books, 1967), 303. Some mention should be made of the semantic problem posed, at least in the English language, by the unavoidable use of the same term to designate both the male of the species and the species itself. As has been repeatedly noted, the language itself exposes how deeply male supremacy is embedded in the fabric of society. It should be clear that in this passage, Marx is certainly not referring only to the male's relation to the natural human condition and neither does he equate this with his relationship to the female. The same principle is equally applicable to women, their inferior status under capitalism notwithstanding.

9   The notion of man [-woman] as a species-being is a key element of Marx's early anthropology. Although the biological connotation of species is contained within this term, this is not its essential meaning. The deeper meaning Marx attributes to "species-being" emerges from a philosophical tradition which sought to develop a philosophy of man [-woman], proposing various ideal definitions of the human species. "Species-being," as a result, also has ethical implications. Human beings, social "by nature," strive toward the realization of their social potential (which is a creative potential) by transforming nature and thereby making their surroundings more human. For the early Marx, thus, labor itself acquires an ethical, even eudaemonistic mission.

10 Marx, *Economic and Philosophic Manuscripts* (1844), "Alienated Labor," in Easton and Guddat, 292.

11 Ibid.

12 Marx, "Private Property and Communism," 304.

13 In analyzing pre-capitalist formations, Marx asserts that for the spontaneously evolved community, "the earth is the great laboratory, the arsenal which provides both the means and materials of labor, and also the location, the *basis* is the community. Men's relation to it is naive: they regard themselves as its *communal proprietors*, and as those of the community which produces and reproduces itself by living labor" (Karl Marx, *Pre-Capitalist Economic Formations*, New York: International Publishers, 1965, 69).

14 Marx writes, "the realm of freedom actually begins only where labor which is determined by necessity and mundane considerations ceases; thus in the very nature of things it lies beyond the sphere of actual material production. Just as the savage must wrestle with nature to satisfy his wants, to maintain and reproduce life, so must civilized man, and he must do so in all social formations and under all possible modes of production. With his development this realm of physical necessity expands as a result of his wants; but, at the same time, the forces of production which satisfy these wants also increase. Freedom in this field can only consist in socialized man, the associated producers, rationally regulating their interrelations with nature, bringing it under their common control, instead of being ruled by it as by the blind forces of nature; and achieving this with the least expenditure of energy and under conditions most favorable to, and worthy of, their human nature. But it nonetheless still remains a realm of necessity. Beyond it begins that development of human

energy which is an end in itself, the true realm of freedom, which, however, can blossom forth only with this realm of necessity as its basis. The shortening of the working-day is its basic prerequisite" (Karl Marx, *Capital*, New York: International Publishers, 1968, vol. 3, 820).

15 Marx, *A Contribution to a Critique of Political Economy*, 36.

16 Marx, *Pre-Capitalist Economic Formations*, 68.

17 Ibid., 95.

18 "There is a third *possible form* [of property] which is to act as proprietor neither of the land nor of the instrument (i.e., nor of labor itself), but only of the means of subsistence, which are then found as the natural condition of the laboring subject. This is at bottom the formula of slavery and serfdom" (Marx, *Pre-Capitalist Economic Formations*, 101).

19 In describing the transition from various pre-bourgeois formations to capitalism, Marx contends that "closer analysis will show that what is dissolved in all these processes of dissolution are relations of productions in which use-value predominates; production for *immediate* use" (my emphasis) (ibid., 105).

20 Marx proposes this generalization about pre-capitalist epochs as a whole: "They all evince a unity of living and active human beings with the natural, inorganic conditions of their metabolism with nature, and therefore their appropriation of nature" (ibid., 86). Moreover, in describing "the *pre-bourgeois* relationship of the individual to the objective conditions of labor, and in the first instance to the *natural* objective conditions of labor," Marx says: "just as the working subject is a natural individual, a natural being, so the first objective condition of his labor appears as nature, earth, as an inorganic body. He himself is not only the organic body, but also inorganic nature as a subject. The condition is not something he has produced, but something he finds to hand; something existing in nature and which he presupposes" (ibid., 85).

21 There are obviously exceptions to this rule. A salient example is provided by John Henrik Clarke when he discusses the critical role of African women in resisting the encroachments of the slave trade: "In the resistance to the slave trade and the colonial system that followed the death of the Queen [Nzingha of Angola], African women, along with their men helped to mount offensives all over Africa. Among the most outstanding were: Madame Tinubo of Nigeria; Nandi, the mother of the great Zulu warrior Chaka; Kaipkire of the Herero people of South West Africa; and the female army that followed the great Dahomian King, Behanzin Howell" (John Henrik Clarke, "The Black Woman: A Figure in World History," Part I, *Essence Magazine*, May 1971).

22 Marx, *Pre-Capitalist Economic Formations*, 71.

23 Juliet Mitchell, *Women: The Longest Revolution* (pamphlet reprinted from November–December 1966 issue of *New Left Review*, Boston: New England Press), 8.

24 Engels fails to emphasize this pre-capitalist structural necessity, a necessity which is invalidated only by capitalism. Consequently, women's oppression during both pre-capitalist and capitalist history appears, in his analysis, to be essentially homogeneous.

25 Marx, *Pre-Capitalist Economic Formations*, 81.

26 Marx, *The German Ideology* (New York: International Publishers, 1963).

27 Marx, *A Contribution to a Critique of Political Economy*, 33.

28 George Lukács, *History and Class Consciousness* (London: Merlin Press, 1971), 233.

29 Alfred Schmidt, *The Concept of Nature in Marx* (London: New Left Books, 1971), 178.

30 What follows in highly condensed form is a section of a recent essay: Angela Y. Davis, "Reflections on the Black Woman's Role in the Community of Slaves," *The Black Scholar*, vol. 3, no. 4 (December 1971).

31 See note 18. Also consider this paragraph: "Such historic processes of dissolution are the following: the dissolution of the servile relationship which binds the laborer to the soil, but in fact assumes his property in the means of subsistence (which amounts in truth to his separation from the soil); the dissolution of relations of property which constitute a laborer as yeoman, or free, working, petty landowner or tenant (colonus), or free peasant; the dissolution of guild relations which presuppose the laborer's property in the instrument of production and labor itself, as a certain form of craft skill not merely as the source of property but as property itself; also the dissolution of the relations of clientship in its different types, in which *non-proprietors* appear as co-consumers of the surplus produce in the retinue of their lord, and in return wear his livery, take part in his feuds, perform real or imaginary acts of personal service, etc. Closer analysis will show that what is dissolved in all these processes of dissolution are relations of production in which use-value predominates; production of immediate use. Exchange-value and its production presuppose the dominance of the other form" (Marx, *Pre-Capitalist Economic Formations*, 104–5).

32 Consider, for example, the following passage from *Pre-Capitalist Economic Formations:* "the ancient conception, in which man always appears (in however narrowly national, religious or political a definition) as the aim of production, seems very much more exalted than the modern world, in which production is the aim of man and wealth the aim of production. In fact, however, when the narrow bourgeois form has been peeled away, what is wealth, if not the universality of needs, capacities, enjoyments, productive powers, etc., of individuals, produced in universal exchange? What, if not the full development of human control over the forces of nature – those of his own nature as well as those of so-called 'nature'? What, if not the absolute elaboration of his creative dispositions, without any preconditions other than antecedent historical evolution which makes the totality of this evolution – i.e., the evolution of all human powers as such, unmeasured by *any previously established* yardstick – an end in itself? What is this, if not a situation where man does not reproduce himself in any determined form, but produces his totality? Where he does not seek to remain something formed by the past, but is in the absolute movement of becoming? In bourgeois political economy – and in the epoch of production to which it corresponds – this complete alienation, and the destruction of all fixed, one-sided purposes, is the sacrifice of the end in itself to a wholly external compulsion. Hence in one way the childlike world of the ancients appears to be superior; and this is so, in so far as we seek for closed shape, form and established limitation. The ancients provide a narrow satisfaction, whereas the

modern world leaves us unsatisfied, or, where it appears to be satisfied with itself, is *vulgar* and *mean*" (84–5).

33 Ibid., 99.

34 "The establishment of the individual as a worker, stripped of all qualities except this one, is itself a product of history" (ibid., 68).

35 Marx, *A Contribution to a Critique of Political Economy*, 189. Engels comments, in a footnote to this passage, that actually the process is just the reverse. That is to say, the tribe is primary and the smaller family eventually evolves from it.

36 Marx, *Pre-Capitalist Economic Formations*, 88–9.

37 Margaret Benston, "The Political Economy of Women's Liberation," *Monthly Review*, vol. 21, no. 4 (September 1969), 15. She goes on to say: "This assignment of household work, as the function of a special category, 'women,' means that this group *does* stand in a different relation to production than the group, 'men.' We will tentatively define women, then, as that group of people who are responsible for the production of simple use-values in those activities within the home and family" (15–16).

38 Christopher Caudwell, *Studies in a Dying Culture* (New York: Dodd Mead and Co., 1949), 148.

39 According to one student of Nazi culture, the Nazis regarded the family as the original social unit, the "germ cell of the people, an *aid to the state rather than a rival unit of social organization.* The ideal family is a firmly knit group rooted in the soil, contributing numerous racially pure offspring, each child reared to unswerving *love* for the nazi State" (my emphasis). Clifford Fitzpatrick, *Nazi Germany: Its Women and Family Life* (New York: Bobbs Merrill, 1938), 101.

40 Herbert Marcuse, "On Hedonism," *Negations* (Boston: Beacon Press, 1968), 164.

41 Valerie Solanas, *SCUM Manifesto*, quoted in *The Female State, A Journal of Female Liberation* (Somerville, Massachusetts), issue 4 (April 1970), 57.

42 Karl Marx, *Economic and Philosophic Manuscripts* ["Private Property and Communism."] The translation is Bottomore's (T. B. Bottomore, trans. and ed., Karl Marx, *Early Writings*, New York: McGraw-Hill, 1963, 160). Easton and Guddat translate *Eigenschaften* as "aptitudes" instead of "qualities" (308).

43 Ibid., Bottomore, 161. Easton and Guddat use "moral" instead of "practical" (309).

44 Caudwell, *Studies in a Dying Culture*, 148–9.

45 Ibid., 157.

46 "The dynamic of their productivity [i.e., the productivity of contemporary societies] deprives 'utopia' of its traditional unreal content: what is denounced as 'utopian' is no longer that which has 'no place' and cannot have any place in the historical universe, but rather that which is blocked from coming about by the power of the established societies. 'Utopian' possibilities are inherent in the technical and technological forces of advanced capitalism and socialism: the rational utilization of these forces on a global scale would terminate poverty and scarcity within a very foreseeable future" (Herbert Marcuse, *An Essay on Liberation*, Boston: Beacon Press, 1969, 4–5). The unleashing of long repressed emotional potentials is objectively possible exactly to the degree that

the abolition of scarcity is possible. For the latter is indeed predicated on a relaxing of the rigidity of the performance principle.

47   Germaine Greer, *The Female Eunuch* (London: Paladin, 1971), 317.
48   Karl Marx, *Capital*, vol. 1, 495–6.
49   Clara Colon, *Enter Fighting: Today's Woman. A Marxist-Leninist View* (New York: Outlook Publishers, 1970), 8.
50   Karl Marx, *Capital*, vol. 1, 391.
51   A socialist scholar has alluded to the family as an "instance of an alienated social institution that has been taken over lock, stock, and barrel by socialism from the capitalist system." He says that "the traditional form of the family has not only survived, but also it defies any reasonable forecasts about its further development." Adam Schaff, *Marxism and the Human Individual* (New York: McGraw-Hill, 1970), 136.
52   W. E. B. Du Bois, *Darkwater, Voices from Within the Veil* (New York: AMS Press, 1969 [original edition, 1920]), 182.

12

The Approaching Obsolescence of Housework: A Working-Class Perspective

The countless chores collectively known as "housework" – cooking, washing dishes, doing laundry, making beds, sweeping, shopping – apparently consume some three to four thousand hours of the average housewife's year.[1] As startling as this statistic may be, it does not even account for the constant and unquantifiable attention mothers must give to their children. Just as a woman's maternal duties are always taken for granted, her never-ending toil as a housewife rarely occasions expressions of appreciation within her family. Housework, after all, is virtually invisible: "No one notices it until it isn't done – we notice the unmade bed, not the scrubbed and polished floor."[2] Invisible, repetitive, exhausting, unproductive, uncreative – these are the adjectives which most perfectly capture the nature of housework.[3]

The new consciousness associated with the contemporary women's movement has encouraged increasing numbers of women to demand that their men provide some relief from this drudgery. Already, more men have begun to assist their partners around the house, some of them even devoting equal time to household chores. But how many of these men have liberated themselves from the assumption that housework is "women's work"? How many of them would not characterize their house-cleaning activities as "helping" their women partners?

If it were at all possible simultaneously to liquidate the idea that housework is women's work and to redistribute it equally to men and women alike, would this constitute a satisfactory solution? Freed from its exclusive affiliation with the female sex, would housework thereby cease to be oppressive? While most women would joyously hail the advent of the "househusband," the de-sexualization of domestic labor would not really alter the oppressive nature of the work itself. In the final analysis, neither women nor men should waste precious hours of their lives on work that is neither stimulating, creative, nor productive.

One of the most closely guarded secrets of advanced capitalist societies involves the possibility – the real possibility – of radically transforming the nature of housework. A substantial portion of the housewife's domestic tasks can actually be incorporated into the industrial economy. In other words, housework need no longer be considered necessarily and unalterably private in character. Teams of trained and well-paid workers, moving from dwelling to dwelling, engineering technologically advanced cleaning machinery, could swiftly and efficiently accomplish what the present-day housewife does so arduously and primitively. Why the shroud of silence surrounding this potential of radically redefining the nature of domestic labor? Because the capitalist economy is structurally hostile to the industrialization of housework. Socialized housework implies large government subsidies in order to guarantee accessibility to the working-class families whose need for such services is most obvious. Since little in the way of profits would result, industrialized housework – like all unprofitable enterprises – is anathema to the capitalist economy. Nonetheless, the rapid expansion of the female labor force means that more and more women are finding it increasingly difficult to excel as housewives according to the traditional standards. In other words, the industrialization of housework, along with the socialization of housework, is becoming an objective social need. Housework as individual women's private responsibility and as female labor performed under primitive technical conditions, may finally be approaching historical obsolescence.

Although housework as we know it today may eventually become a bygone relic of history, prevailing social attitudes continue to associate the eternal female condition with images of brooms and dustpans, mops and pails, aprons and stoves, pots and pans. And it is true that women's work, from one historical era to another, has been associated in general with the homestead. Yet female domestic labor has not always been what it is today, for like all social phenomena, housework is a fluid product of human history. As economic systems have arisen and faded away, the scope and quality of housework have undergone radical transformations.

As Friedrich Engels argued in his classic work *Origin of the Family, Private Property and the State,*[4] sexual inequality as we know it today did not exist before the advent of private property. During early eras of human history the sexual division of labor within the system of economic production was complementary as opposed to hierarchical. In societies where men may have been responsible for hunting wild animals and women, in turn, for gathering wild vegetables and fruits, both sexes performed economic tasks that were equally essential to their community's survival. Because the community, during those eras, was essentially an extended family, women's central role in domestic affairs meant that they were accordingly valued and respected as productive members of the community.

The centrality of women's domestic tasks in pre-capitalist cultures was dramatized by a personal experience during a jeep trip I took in 1973 across the Masai Plains. On an isolated dirt road in Tanzania, I noticed six Masai women enigmatically balancing an enormous board on their heads. As my Tanzanian friends explained, these women were probably transporting a house roof to a new village which they were in the process of constructing. Among the Masai, as I learned, women are responsible for all domestic activities, thus also for the construction of their nomadic people's frequently relocated houses. Housework, as far as Masai women are concerned, entails not only cooking, cleaning, child rearing, sewing, etc., but house building as well.

Within the pre-capitalist, nomadic economy of the Masai, women's domestic labor is as essential to the economy as the cattle-raising jobs performed by their men. As producers, they enjoy a correspondingly important social status. In advanced capitalist societies, on the other hand, the service-oriented domestic labor of housewives, who can seldom produce tangible evidence of their work, diminishes the social status of women in general. When all is said and done, the housewife, according to bourgeois ideology, is, quite simply, her husband's lifelong servant.

The source of the bourgeois notion of woman as man's eternal servant is itself a revealing story. Within the relatively short history of the United States, the "housewife" as a finished historical product is just a little more than a century old. Housework, during the colonial era, was entirely different from the daily work routine of the housewife in the United States today.

> A woman's work began at sunup and continued by firelight as long as she could hold her eyes open. For two centuries, almost everything that the family used or ate was produced at home under her direction. She spun and dyed the yarn that she wove into cloth and cut and hand-stitched into garments. She grew much of the food her family ate, and preserved enough to last the winter months. She made butter, cheese, bread, candles, and soap and knitted her family's stockings.[5]

In the agrarian economy of pre-industrial North America, a woman performing her household chores was thus a spinner, weaver and seamstress as well as a baker, butter-churner, candle-maker and soap-maker. Et cetera, et cetera, et cetera. As a matter of fact,

> The pressures of home production left very little time for the tasks that we would recognize today as housework. By all accounts, pre-industrial

revolution women were sloppy housekeepers by today's standards. Instead of the daily cleaning or the weekly cleaning, there was the spring cleaning. Meals were simple and repetitive; clothes were changed infrequently; and the household wash was allowed to accumulate, and the washing done once a month, or in some households once in three months. And, of course, since each wash required the carting and heating of many buckets of water, higher standards of cleanliness were easily discouraged.[6]

Colonial women were not "house-cleaners" or "housekeepers" but rather full-fledged and accomplished workers within the home-based economy. Not only did they manufacture most of the products required by their families, they were also the guardians of their families' and their communities' health. "It was [the colonial woman's] responsibility to gather and dry wild herbs used . . . as medicines; she also served as doctor, nurse, and midwife within her own family and in the community."[7] Included in the *United States Practical Recipe Book* – a popular colonial recipe book – are recipes for foods as well as for household chemicals and medicines. To cure ringworm, for example, "obtain some blood-root . . . slice it in vinegar, and afterwards wash the place affected with the liquid."[8]

The economic importance of women's domestic functions in colonial America was complemented by their visible roles in economic activity outside the home. It was entirely acceptable, for example, for a woman to become a tavern keeper.

> Women also ran sawmills and gristmills, caned chairs and built furniture, operated slaughterhouses, printed cotton and other cloth, made lace, and owned and ran dry-goods and clothing stores. They worked in tobacco shops, drug shops (where they sold concoctions they made themselves), and general stores that sold everything from pins to meat scales. Women ground eyeglasses, made netting and rope, cut and stitched leather goods, made cards for wool carding, and even were housepainters. Often they were the town undertakers.[9]

The post-revolutionary surge of industrialization resulted in a proliferation of factories in the northeastern section of the new country. New England's textile mills were the factory system's successful pioneers. Since spinning and weaving were traditional female domestic occupations, women were the first workers recruited by the mill-owners to operate the new power looms. Considering the subsequent exclusion of women from industrial production in general, it is one of the great ironies of this country's economic history that the first industrial workers were women.

As industrialization advanced, shifting economic production from the home to the factory, the importance of women's domestic work suffered a systematic erosion. Women were the losers in a double sense: as their traditional jobs were usurped by the burgeoning factories, the entire economy moved away from the home, leaving many women largely bereft of significant economic roles. By the middle of the nineteenth century the factory provided textiles, candles and soap. Even butter, bread and other food products began to be mass-produced.

> By the end of the century, hardly anyone made their own starch or boiled their laundry in a kettle. In the cities, women bought their bread and at least their underwear ready-made, sent their children out to school and probably some clothes out to be laundered, and were debating the merits of canned foods. . . . The flow of industry had passed on and had left idle the loom in the attic and the soap kettle in the shed.[10]

As industrial capitalism approached consolidation, the cleavage between the new economic sphere and the old home economy became ever more rigorous. The physical relocation of economic production caused by the spread of the factory system was undoubtedly a drastic transformation. But even more radical was the generalized revaluation of production necessitated by the new economic system. While home-manufactured goods were valuable primarily because they fulfilled basic family needs, the importance of factory-produced commodities resided overwhelmingly in their exchange value – in their ability to fulfill employers' demands for profit. This revaluation of economic production revealed – beyond the physical separation of home and factory – a fundamental structural separation between the domestic home economy and the profit-oriented economy of capitalism. Since housework does not generate profit, domestic labor was naturally defined as an inferior form of work as compared with capitalist wage-labor.

An important ideological by-product of this radical economic transformation was the birth of the "housewife." Women began to be ideologically redefined as the guardians of a devalued domestic life. As ideology, however, this redefinition of women's place was boldly contradicted by the vast numbers of immigrant women flooding the ranks of the working class in the Northeast. These white immigrant women were wage earners first and only secondarily housewives. And there were other women – millions of women – who toiled away from home as the unwilling producers of the slave economy in the South. The reality of women's place in nineteenth-century US society involved white women, whose days were spent operating factory machines for wages that were a pittance, as surely as it involved black women, who labored under the coercion of slavery. The "housewife" reflected a partial reality, for she was really a symbol of the economic prosperity enjoyed by the emerging middle classes.

Although the "housewife" was rooted in the social conditions of the bourgeoisie and the middle classes, nineteenth-century ideology established the housewife and the mother as universal models of womanhood. Since popular propaganda represented the vocation of all women as a function of their roles in the home, women compelled to work for wages came to be treated as alien visitors within the masculine world of the public economy. Having stepped outside their "natural" sphere, women were not to be treated as full-fledged wage workers. The price they paid involved long hours, substandard working conditions, and grossly inadequate wages. Their exploitation was even more intense than the exploitation suffered by their male counterparts. Needless to say, sexism emerged as a source of outrageous super-profits for the capitalists.

The structural separation of the public economy of capitalism and the private economy of the home has been continually reinforced by the obstinate primitiveness of household labor. Despite the proliferation of gadgets for the home, domestic work has remained qualitatively unaffected by the technological advances brought on by industrial capitalism. Housework still consumes thousands of hours of the average housewife's year. In 1903 Charlotte Perkins Gilman proposed a definition of domestic labor which reflected the upheavals which had changed the structure and content of housework in the United States: "The phrase 'domestic work' does not apply to a special kind of work, but to a certain grade of work, a state of development through which all kinds pass. All industries were once 'domestic,' that is, were performed at home and in the interests of the family. All industries have since that remote period risen to higher stages, except one or two which have never left their primal stage."[11] "The home," Gilman maintains, "has not developed in proportion to our other institutions." The home economy reveals "the maintenance of primitive industries in a modern industrial community and the confinement of women to these industries and their limited area of expression."[12] Housework, Gilman insists, vitiates women's humanity: "She is feminine, more than enough, as man is masculine, more than enough; but she is not human as he is human. The house-life does not bring out our humanness, for all the distinctive lines of human progress lie outside."[13]

The truth of Gilman's statement is corroborated by the historical experience of black women in the United States. Throughout this country's history, the majority of black women have worked outside their homes. During slavery, women toiled alongside their men in the cotton and tobacco fields, and when industry moved into the South, they could be seen in tobacco factories, sugar refineries, and even in lumber mills and on crews pounding steel for the railroads. In labor, slave women were the equals of their men. Because they suffered a grueling sexual equality at work, they enjoyed a greater sexual equality at home in the slave quarters than did their white sisters who were "housewifes."

As a direct consequence of their outside work – as "free" women no less than as slaves – housework has never been the central focus of black women's lives. They have largely escaped the psychological damage industrial capitalism inflicted on white middle-class housewives, whose alleged virtues were feminine weakness and wifely submissiveness. Black women could hardly strive for weakness; they had to become strong, for their families and their communities needed their strength to survive. Evidence of the accumulated strengths black women have forged through work, work, and more work can be discovered in the contributions of the many outstanding female leaders who have emerged within the black community. Harriet Tubman, Sojourner Truth, Ida Wells and Rosa Parks are not exceptional black women as much as they are epitomes of black womanhood.

Black women, however, have paid a heavy price for the strengths they have acquired and the relative independence they have enjoyed. While they have seldom been "just housewives," they have always done their housework. They have thus carried the double burden of wage labor and housework – a double burden which always demands that working women possess the persevering powers of Sisyphus. As W. E. B. Du Bois observed in 1920: "Some few women are born free, and some amid insult and scarlet letters achieve freedom; but our women in black had freedom thrust contemptuously upon them. With that freedom they are buying an untrammeled independence and dear as is the price they pay for it, it will in the end be worth every taunt and groan."[14]

Like their men, black women have worked until they could work no more. Like their men, they have assumed the responsibilities of family providers. The unorthodox feminine qualities of assertiveness and self-reliance – for which black women have been frequently praised but more often rebuked – are reflections of their labor and their struggles outside the home. But like their white sisters called "housewives," they have cooked and cleaned and have nurtured and reared untold numbers of children. But unlike the white housewives, who learned to lean on their husbands for economic security, black wives and mothers, usually workers as well, have rarely been offered the time and energy to become experts at domesticity. Like their white working-class sisters, who also carry the double burden of working for a living and servicing husbands and children, black women have needed relief from this oppressive predicament for a long, long time.

For black women today and for all their working-class sisters, the notion that the burden of housework and childcare can be shifted from their shoulders to the society contains one of the radical secrets of women's liberation. Childcare should be socialized, meal preparation should be socialized, housework should be industrialized – and all these services should be readily accessible to working-class people.

The shortage, if not absence, of public discussion about the feasibility of transforming housework into a social possibility bears witness to the blinding powers of bourgeois ideology. It is not even the case that women's domestic role has received no attention at all. On the contrary, the contemporary women's movement has represented housework as an essential ingredient of women's oppression. There is even, in a number of capitalist countries, a movement whose main concern is the plight of the housewife. Having reached the conclusion that housework is degrading and oppressive primarily because it is unpaid labor, this movement has raised the demand for wages. A weekly government pay check, its activists argue, is the key to improving the housewife's status and the social position of women in general.

The Wages for Housework Movement originated in Italy, where its first public demonstration took place in March 1974. Addressing the crowd assembled in the city of Mestre, one of the speakers proclaimed: "Half the world's population is unpaid – this is the biggest class contradiction of all! And this is our struggle for wages for housework. It is the strategic demand; at this moment it is the most revolutionary demand for the whole working class. If we win, the class wins, if we lose, the class loses."[15] According to this movement's strategy, wages are the key to the emancipation of housewives, and the demand itself is represented as the central focus of the campaign for women's liberation in general. Moreover, the housewife's struggle for wages is projected as the pivotal issue of the entire working-class movement.

The theoretical origins of the Wages for Housework Movement can be found in an essay by Mariarosa Dalla Costa entitled "Women and the Subversion of the Community."[16] Here, she argues for a redefinition of housework based on her thesis that the private character of household services is actually an illusion. The housewife, she insists, only appears to be ministering to the private needs of her husband and children, for the real beneficiaries of her services are her husband's present employer and the future employers of her children. "[The woman] has been isolated in the home, forced to carry out work that is considered unskilled, the work of giving birth to, raising, disciplining, and servicing the worker for production. Her role in the cycle of production remained invisible because only the product of her labor, the laborer, was visible."[17]

The demand that housewives be paid is based on the assumption that they produce a commodity as important and as valuable as the commodities their husbands produce on the job. Adopting Dalla Costa's logic, the Wages for Housework Movement defines housewives as creators of the labor-power sold by their family members as commodities on the capitalist market.

Dalla Costa was not the first theorist to propose such an analysis of women's oppression. Both Mary Inman's *In Woman's Defense* (1940)[18] and Margaret Benston's "The Political Economy of Women's Liberation" (1969)[19] define housework in such a way as to establish women as a special class of workers exploited by capitalism, called "housewives." That women's procreative, child-rearing and housekeeping roles make it possible for their family members to work – to exchange their labor-power for wages – can hardly be denied. But does it automatically follow that women in general, regardless of their class and race, can be fundamentally defined by their domestic functions? Does it automatically follow that the housewife is actually a secret worker inside the capitalist production process?

If the industrial revolution resulted in the structural separation of the home economy from the public economy, then housework cannot be defined as an integral component of capitalist production. It is, rather, related to production as a precondition. The employer is not concerned in the least about the way labor-power is produced and sustained, he is only concerned about its availability and its ability to generate profit. In other words, the capitalist production process presupposes the existence of a body of exploitable workers. "The replenishment of (workers') labor-power is not a part of the process of social production but a prerequisite to it. It occurs outside of the labor process. Its function is the maintenance of human existence which is the ultimate purpose of production in all societies."[20]

In South African society, where racism has led economic exploitation to its most brutal limits, the capitalist economy betrays its structural separation from domestic life in a characteristically violent fashion. The social architects of apartheid have simply determined that black labor yields higher profits when domestic life is all but entirely discarded. Black men are viewed as labor units whose productive potential renders them valuable to the capitalist class. But their wives and children are "superfluous appendages – non-productive, the women being nothing more than adjuncts to the procreative capacity of the black male labor unit."[21] This characterization of African women as "superfluous appendages" is hardly a metaphor. In accordance with [apartheid] South African law, unemployed black women [were] are banned from the white areas (87 percent of the country!), even, in most cases, from the cities where their husbands live and work.

Black domestic life in South Africa's industrial centers is viewed by apartheid supporters as superfluous and unprofitable. But it is also seen as a threat. "Government officials recognize the homemaking role of the women and fear their presence in the cities will lead to the establishment of a stable black population."[22] The consolidation of African families in the industrialized cities is perceived as a menace because domestic life might become a base for a heightened level of resistance to Apartheid. This is undoubtedly the reason why large numbers of women holding residence permits for white areas are assigned to live in sex-segregated hostels. Married as well as single women end up living in these projects. In such hostels, family life is rigorously prohibited – husbands and wives are unable to visit one another and neither mother nor father can receive visits from their children.[23]

This intense assault on black women in South Africa has already taken its toll, for only 28.2 percent are currently opting for marriage.[24] For reasons of economic expediency and political security, Apartheid was eroding – with the apparent goal of destroying – the very fabric of black domestic life. South African capitalism then blatantly demonstrated the extent to which the capitalist economy is utterly dependent on domestic labor.

The deliberate dissolution of family life in South Africa could not have been undertaken by the government if it were truly the case that the services performed by women in the home are an essential constituent of wage-labor under capitalism. That domestic life can be dispensed with by the South African version of capitalism is a consequence of the separation of the private home economy and the public production process which characterizes capitalist society in general. It seems futile to argue that on the basis of capitalism's internal logic, women ought to be paid wages for housework.

Assuming that the theory underlying the demand for wages is hopelessly flawed, might it not be nonetheless politically desirable to insist that housewives be paid. Couldn't one invoke a moral imperative for women's right to be paid for the hours they devote to housework? The idea of a pay check for housewives would probably sound quite attractive to many women. But the attraction would probably be short-lived. For how many of those women would actually be willing to reconcile themselves to deadening, never-ending household tasks, all for the sake of a wage? Would a wage alter the fact, as Lenin said, that "petty housework crushes, strangles, stultifies and degrades (the woman), chains her to the kitchen and to the nursery, and wastes her labor on barbarously unproductive, petty, nerve-racking, stultifying and crushing drudgery."[25] It would seem that government pay checks for housewives would further legitimize this domestic slavery.

Is it not an implicit critique of the Wages for Housework Movement that women on welfare have rarely demanded compensation for keeping house. Not "wages for housework" but rather "a guaranteed annual income for all" is the slogan articulating the immediate alternative they have most frequently proposed to the dehumanizing welfare system. What they want in the long run, however, is jobs and affordable public childcare. The guaranteed annual income functions, therefore, as unemployment insurance pending the creation of more jobs with adequate wages along with a subsidized system of childcare.

The experiences of yet another group of women reveal the problematic nature of the "wages for housework" strategy. Cleaning women, domestic workers, maids – these are the women who know better than anyone else what it means to receive wages for housework. Their tragic predicament is brilliantly captured in the film by Ousmane Sembene entitled *La Noire de* . . .[26] The main character is a young Senegalese woman who, after a search for work, becomes a governess for a French family living in Dakar. When the family returns to France, she enthusiastically accompanies them. Once in France, however, she discovers she is responsible not only for the children, but for cooking, cleaning, washing and all the other household chores. It is not long before her initial enthusiasm gives way to depression – a depression so profound that she refuses the pay offered her by her employers. Wages cannot compensate for her slavelike situation. Lacking the means to return to Senegal, she is so overwhelmed by her despair that she chooses suicide over an indefinite destiny of cooking, sweeping, dusting, scrubbing. . . .

In the United States, women of color – and especially black women – have been receiving wages for housework for untold decades. In 1910, when over half of all black females were working outside their homes, one-third of them were employed as paid domestic workers. By 1920 over one-half were domestic servants, and in 1930 the proportion had risen to three out of five.[27] One of the consequences of the enormous female employment shifts during World War II was a much-welcomed decline in the number of black domestic workers. Yet in 1960 one-third of all black women holding jobs were still confined to their traditional occupations.[28] It was not until clerical jobs became more accessible to black women that the proportion of black women domestics headed in a definitely downward direction. Today the figure hovers around 13 percent.[29]

The enervating domestic obligations of women in general provide flagrant evidence of the power of sexism. Because of the added intrusion of racism, vast numbers of black women have had to do their own housekeeping and other women's home chores as well. And frequently, the demands of the job in a white woman's home have forced the domestic worker to neglect her own home and even her own children. As paid housekeepers, they have been called upon to be surrogate wives and mothers in millions of white homes.

During their more than fifty years of organizing efforts, domestic workers have tried to redefine their work by rejecting the role of the surrogate housewife. The housewife's chores are unending and undefined. Household workers have demanded in the first place a clear delineation of the jobs they are expected to perform. The name itself of one of the houseworkers' major unions today – Household Technicians of America – emphasizes their refusal to function as surrogate housewives whose job is "just housework." As long as household workers stand in the shadow of the housewife, they will continue to receive wages which are more closely related to a housewife's "allowance" than to a worker's pay check. According to the National Committee on Household Employment, the average, full-time household technician earned only $2,732 in 1976, two-thirds of them earning under $2,000.[30] Although for household workers the protection of the minimum wage law had been extended several years previously, in 1976 an astounding 40 percent still received grossly substandard wages. The Wages for Housework Movement assumes that if women were paid for being housewives, they would accordingly enjoy a higher social status. Quite a different story is told by the age-old struggles of the paid household worker, whose condition is more miserable than that of any other group of workers under capitalism.

Over 50 percent of all US women work for a living today, and they constitute 41 percent of the country's labor force. Yet countless numbers of women are currently unable to find decent jobs. Like racism, sexism is one of the great justifications for high female unemployment rates. Many women are "just housewives" because in reality they are unemployed workers. Cannot, therefore, the "just housewife" role be most effectively challenged by demanding jobs for women on a level of equality with men and by pressing for the social services (childcare, for example) and job benefits (maternity leave, etc.) which will allow more women to work outside the home?

The Wages for Housework Movement discourages women from seeking outside jobs, arguing that "slavery to an assembly line is not liberation from slavery to the kitchen sink."[31] The campaign's spokeswomen insist, nonetheless, that they don't advocate the continued imprisonment of women within the isolated environment of their homes. They claim that while they refuse to work on the capitalist market per se, they do not wish to assign to women the permanent responsibility for housework. As a US representative of this movement says:

> . . . we are not interested in making our work more efficient or more productive for capital. We are interested in reducing our work, and ultimately refusing it altogether. But as long as we work in the home for nothing, no one really cares how long or how hard we work. For capital only introduces advanced technology to cut the costs of production after wage gains by the working class. Only if we make our work cost (i.e., only if we make it uneconomical) will capital "discover" the technology to reduce it. At present, we often have to go out for a second shift of work to afford the dishwasher that should cut down our housework.[32]

Once women have achieved the right to be paid for their work, they can raise demands for higher wages, thus compelling the capitalists to undertake the industrialization of housework. Is this a concrete strategy for women's liberation or is it an unrealizable dream?

How are women supposed to conduct the initial struggle for wages? Dalla Costa advocates the housewives' strike: "We must reject the home, because we want to unite with other women, to struggle against all situations which presume that women will stay at home.... To abandon the home is already a form of struggle, since the social services we perform there would then cease to be carried out in those conditions."[33]

But if women are to leave the home, where are they to go? How will they unite with other women? Will they really leave their homes motivated by no other desire than to protest their housework? Is it not much more realistic to call upon women to "leave home" in search of outside jobs – or at least to participate in a massive campaign for decent jobs for women? Granted, work under the conditions of capitalism is brutalizing work. Granted, it is uncreative and alienating. Yet with all this, the fact remains that on the job, women can unite with their sisters – and indeed with their brothers – in order to challenge the capitalists at the point of production. As workers, as militant activists in the labor movement, women can generate the real power to fight the mainstay and beneficiary of sexism which is the monopoly capitalist system.

If the wages-for-housework strategy does little in the way of providing a long-range solution to the problem of women's oppression, neither does it substantively address the profound discontent of contemporary housewives. Recent sociological studies have revealed that housewives today are more frustrated by their lives than ever before. When Ann Oakley conducted interviews for her book *The Sociology of Housework*,[34] she discovered that even the housewives who initially seemed unbothered by their housework eventually expressed a very deep dissatisfaction. These comments came from a woman who held an outside factory job:

(Do you like housework?) I don't mind it.... I suppose I don't mind housework because I'm not at it all day. I go to work and I'm only on housework half a day. If I did it all day I wouldn't like it – woman's work is never done, she's on the go all the time – even before you go to bed, you've still got something to do – emptying ashtrays, wash a few cups up. You're still working. It's the same thing every day; you can't sort of say you're not going to do it, because you've got to do it – like preparing a meal: it's got to be done because if you don't do it, the children wouldn't eat.... I suppose you get used to it, you just do it automatically.... I'm happier at work than I am at home.

(What would you say are the worst things about being a housewife?) I suppose you get days when you feel you get up and you've got to do the same old things – you get bored, you're stuck in the same routine. I think if you ask any housewife, if they're honest, they'll turn around and say they feel like a drudge half the time – everybody thinks when they get up in the morning "Oh no, I've got the same old things to do today, till I go to bed tonight." It's doing the same things – boredom.[35]

Would wages diminish this boredom? This woman would certainly say no. A full-time housewife told Oakley about the compulsive nature of housework:

The worst thing is I suppose that you've got to do the work because you are at home. Even though I've got the option of not doing it, I don't really feel I could not do it because I feel I ought to do it.[36]

In all likelihood, receiving wages for doing this work would aggravate this woman's obsession.

Oakley reached the conclusion that housework – particularly when it is a full-time job – so thoroughly invades the female personality that the housewife becomes indistinguishable from her job: "The housewife, in an important sense, is her job: separation between subjective and objective elements in the situation is therefore intrinsically more difficult."[37] The psychological consequence is frequently a tragically stunted personality haunted by feelings of inferiority. Psychological liberation can hardly be achieved simply by paying the housewife a wage.

Other sociological studies have confirmed the acute disillusionment suffered by contemporary housewives. When Myra Ferree interviewed over a hundred women in a working community near Boston, "almost twice as many housewives as employed wives said they were dissatisfied with their lives."[38] Needless to say, most of the working women did not have inherently fulfilling jobs: they were waitresses, factory workers, typists, supermarket and department store clerks, etc. Yet their ability to leave the isolation of their homes, "getting out and seeing other people," was as important to them as their earnings. Would the housewives who felt they were "going crazy staying at home" welcome the idea of being paid for driving themselves crazy? One woman complained that "staying at home all day is like being in jail" – would wages tear down the walls of her jail? The only realistic escape path from this jail is the search for work outside the home.

Each one of the more than 50 percent of all US women who work today is a powerful argument for the alleviation of the burden of housework. As a matter of fact, enterprising capitalists have already begun to exploit women's new historical need to emancipate themselves from their roles as housewives. Endless profit-making fast-food chains like McDonald's and Kentucky Fried Chicken bear witness to the fact that more women at work means fewer daily meals prepared at home. However unsavory and unnutritious the food, however exploitative of their workers, these fast-food operations call attention to the approaching obsolescence of the housewife. What is needed, of course, is new social institutions to assume a good portion of the housewife's old duties. This is the challenge emanating from the swelling ranks of women in the working class. The demand for universal and subsidized childcare is a direct consequence of the rising number of working mothers. And as more women organize around the demand for more jobs – for jobs on the basis of full equality with men – serious questions will increasingly be raised about the future viability of women's housewife duties. It may well be true that "slavery to an assembly line" is not in itself "liberation from the kitchen sink," but the assembly line is doubtlessly the most powerful incentive for women to press for the elimination of their age-old domestic slavery.

The abolition of housework as the private responsibility of individual women is clearly a strategic goal of women's liberation. But the socialization of housework – including meal preparation and childcare – presupposes an end to the profit-motive's reign over the economy. The only significant steps toward ending domestic slavery have in fact been taken in the existing socialist countries. Working women, therefore, have a special and vital interest in the struggle for socialism. Moreover, under capitalism, campaigns for jobs on an equal basis with men, combined with movements for institutions such as subsidized public childcare, contain an explosive revolutionary potential. This strategy calls into question the validity of monopoly capitalism and must ultimately point in the direction of socialism.

NOTES

1   Ann Oakley, *The Sociology of Housework* (New York: Pantheon Books, 1974), 6.
2   Barbara Ehrenreich and Deidre English, "The Manufacture of Housework," in *Socialist Revolution*, vol. 5, no. 4 (October–December 1975), 6.
3   Barbara Wertheimer, *We Were There: The Story of Working Women in America* (New York: Pantheon Books, 1977), 12.
4   Friedrich Engels, *Origin of the Family, Private Property and the State*, edited, with an introduction, by Eleanor Burke Leacock (New York: International Publishers, 1973), see chapter 2. Leacock's introduction to this edition contains numerous enlightening observations on Engels's theory of the historical emergence of male supremacy.

5   Ehrenreich and English, "The Manufacture of Housework," 9.

6   Wertheimer, *We Were There: The Story of Working Women in America*, 12.

7   Quoted in Rosalyn Baxandall et al. (eds), *America's Working Women: A Documentary History – 1600 to the Present* (New York: Random House, 1976), 17.

8   Wertheimer, *We Were There: The Story of Working Women in America*, 13.

9   Ehrenreich and English, "The Manufacture of Housework," 10.

10 Charlotte Perkins Gilman, *The Home: Its Work and Influence* (Urbana: University of Illinois Press, 1972; reprint of the 1903 edition), 30–1.

11 Ibid., 10.

12 Ibid., 217.

13 Ibid.

14 W. E. B. Du Bois, *Darkwater, Voices from Within the Veil* (New York: AMS, 1969), 185.

15 Speech by Polga Fortunata. Quoted in Wendy Edmond and Suzie Fleming (eds), *All Work and No Pay: Women, Housework and the Wages Due!* (Bristol, England: Falling Wall Press, 1975), 18.

16 Mariarosa Dalla Costa and Selma James, *The Power of Women and the Subversion of the Community* (Bristol, England: Falling Wall Press, 1973).

17 Ibid., 28.

18 Mary Inman, *In Woman's Defense* (Los Angeles: Committee to Organize the Advancement of Women, 1940). See also Inman, *The Two Forms of Production Under Capitalism* (Long Beach, CA: Published by the Author, 1964).

19 Margaret Benston, "The Political Economy of Women's Liberation," *Monthly Review*, vol. 21, no. 4 (September 1969).

20 "On the Economic Stature of the Housewife," Editorial Comment in *Political Affairs*, vol. 53, no. 3 (March 1974), 4.

21 Hilda Bernstein, *For Their Triumphs and For Their Tears: Women in Apartheid South Africa* (London: International Defence and Aid Fund, 1975), 13.

22 Elizabeth Landis, "Apartheid and the Disabilities of Black Women in South Africa," *Objective: Justice*, vol. 7, no. 1 (January–March 1975), 6. Excerpts from this were published in *Freedomways*, vol. 15, no. 4 (1975).

23 Bernstein, *For Their Triumphs and For Their Tears: Women in Apartheid South Africa*, 33.

24 Landis, "Apartheid and the Disabilities of Black Women in South Africa," 6.

25 V. I. Lenin, "A Great Beginning," pamphlet published in July 1919. Quoted in *Collected Works*, vol. 29 (Moscow: Progress Publishers, 1966), 429.

26 Released in the United States under the title *Black Girl*.

27 Jacqulyne Johnson Jackson, "Black Women in a Racist Society," in Charles Willie et al. (eds), *Racism and Mental Health* (Pittsburgh: University of Pittsburg Press, 1973), 236–7.

28 Victor Perlo, *Economics of Racism, USA, Roots of Black Inequality* (New York: International Publishers, 1975), 24.

29 Robert Staples, *The Black Woman in America* (Wadsworth, 1973), 27.

30 *Daily World*, July 26, 1977, 9.

31 Dalla Costa and James, *The Power of Women and the Subversion of the Community*, 40.

32   Pat Sweeny, "Wages for Housework: The Strategy for Women's Liberation," *Heresies*, January, 1977, 104.

33   Dalla Costa and James, *The Power of Women and the Subversion of the Community*, 41.

34   Oakley, *The Sociology of Housework.*

35   Ibid., 65.

36   Ibid., 44.

37   Ibid., 53.

38   *Psychology Today*, vol. 10, no. 4 (September 1976), 76.

13

Surrogates and Outcast Mothers: Racism and Reproductive Politics in the Nineties

The historical construction of women's reproductive role, which is largely synonymous with the historical failure to acknowledge the possibility of reproductive self-determination, has been informed by a peculiar constellation of racist and misogynist assumptions. These assumptions have undergone mutations even as they remain tethered to their historical origins. To explore the politics of reproduction in a contemporary context is to recognize the growing intervention of technology into the most intimate spaces of human life: from computerized bombings in the Persian Gulf that have taken life from thousands of children and adults as if they were nothing more than the abstract statistics of a video game, to the complex technologies awaiting women who wish to transcend biological or socially induced infertility. I do not mean to suggest that technology is inherently oppressive. Rather, the socio-economic conditions within which reproductive technologies are being developed, applied, and rendered accessible or inaccessible maneuver them in directions that most often maintain or deepen misogynist, anti-working-class, and racist marginalization.

To the extent that fatherhood is denied as a socially significant moment in the process of biological reproduction, the politics of reproduction hinge on the social construction of motherhood. The new developments in reproductive technology have encouraged the contemporary emergence of popular attitudes – at least among the middle classes – that bear a remarkable resemblance to the nineteenth-century cult of motherhood, including the moral, legal, and political taboos it developed against abortion. While the rise of industrial capitalism led to the historical obsolescence of the domes-

This essay originally appeared in *It Just Ain't Fair: The Ethics of Health Care for African Americans*, eds Annette Dula and Sara Goering (Westport CT: Praeger, 1994), copyright © 1994 by Annette Dula and Sara Goering. Reprinted by kind permission.

tic economy and the ideological imprisonment of (white and middle-class) women within a privatized home sphere, the late twentieth-century breakthroughs in reproductive technology are resuscitating that ideology in bizarre and contradictory ways. Women who can afford to take advantage of the new technology – who are often career women for whom motherhood is no longer a primary or exclusive vocation – now encounter a mystification of maternity emanating from the possibility of transcending biological (and socially defined) reproductive incapacity. It is as if the recognition of infertility is now a catalyst – among some groups of women – for a motherhood quest that has become more compulsive and more openly ideological than during the nineteenth century. Considering the antiabortion campaign, it is not difficult to envision this contemporary ideological mystification of motherhood as central to the efforts to deny all women the legal rights that would help shift the politics of reproduction toward a recognition of our autonomy with respect to the biological functions of our bodies.

In the United States, the nineteenth-century cult of motherhood was complicated by a number of class- and race-based contradictions. Women who had recently emigrated from Europe were cast, like their male counterparts, into the industrial proletariat, and were therefore compelled to play economic roles that contradicted the increasing representation of women as wives/mothers. Moreover, in conflating slave motherhood with the reproduction of its labor force, the moribund slave economy effectively denied motherhood to vast numbers of African women. My female ancestors were not led to believe that, as women, their primary vocation was motherhood. Yet slave women were imprisoned within their reproductive role as well. The same socio-historical reasons for the ideological location of European women in an increasingly obsolete domestic economy as the producers, nurturers, and rearers of children caused slave women to be valuated in accordance with their role as breeders. Of course, both motherhood, as it was ideologically constructed, and breederhood, as it historically unfolded, were contingent upon the biological birth process. However, the one presumed to capture the moral essence of womanness, while the other denied, on the basis of racist presumptions and economic necessity, the very possibility of morality and thus also participation in this motherhood cult.

During the first half of the nineteenth century, when the industrial demand for cotton led to the obsessive expansion of slavery at a time when the importation of Africans was no longer legal, the "slaveocracy" demanded of African women that they bear as many children as they were biologically capable of bearing. Thus, women bore as many as eighteen children. My own grandmother, whose parents were slaves, was one of thirteen children.

At the same time, therefore, that nineteenth-century white women were being ideologically incarcerated within their biological reproductive role, essentialized as mothers, African women were forced to bear children, not as evidence of their role as mothers, but for the purpose of expanding the human property held by slave owners. The reproductive role imposed upon African slave women bore no relationship to a subjective project of motherhood. In fact, as Toni Morrison's novel _Beloved_ indicates – inspired as it is by an actual historical case of a woman killing her daughter – some slave women committed infanticide as a means of resisting the enslavement of their progeny.

Slave women were _birth mothers_ or _genetic mothers_ – to employ terms rendered possible by the new reproductive technologies – but they possessed no legal rights as mothers, of any kind. Considering the commodification of their children – and indeed, of their own persons – their status was similar to that of the contemporary _surrogate mother_. I am suggesting that the term _surrogate mother_ might be invoked as a retroactive description of their status because the economic appropriation of their reproductive capacity reflected the inability of the slave economy to produce and reproduce its own laborers – a limitation with respect to the forces of economic production that is being transformed in this era of advanced capitalism by the increasing computerization and robotization of the economy.

The children of slave mothers could be sold away by their owners for business reasons or as a result of a strategy of repression. Slave women could also be forced to give birth to children fathered by their masters, knowing full well that the white fathers would never recognize their black children as offspring. As a consequence of the socially constructed invisibility of the white father – a pretended invisibility strangely respected by the white and black communities alike – black children would grow up in an intimate relation to their white half-brothers and sisters, except that their biological kinship, often revealed by a visible physical resemblance, would remain shrouded in silence. This feature of slave motherhood was something about which no one could speak. Slave women who had been compelled – or had, for their own reasons, agreed – to engage in sexual intercourse with their masters would be committing the equivalent of a crime if they publicly revealed the fathers of their children.[1] These women knew that it was quite likely that their children might also be sold or brutalized or beaten by their own fathers, brothers, uncles, or nephews.

If I have lingered over what I see as some of the salient reproductive issues in African-American women's history, it is because they seem to shed light on the ideological context of contemporary technological intervention in the realm of reproduction. Within the contemporary feminist discourse about the new reproductive technologies – in vitro fertilization, surrogacy, embryo transfer – concern has been expressed about what is sometimes described as the "deconstruction of motherhood"[2] as a unified biological process. While the new technological developments have rendered the fragmentation of maternity more obvious, the economic system of slavery fundamentally relied upon alienated and fragmented maternities, as women were forced to bear children, whom masters claimed as potentially profitable labor machines. Birth mothers could not therefore expect to be mothers in the legal sense. Legally these children were chattel and therefore motherless. Slave states passed laws to the effect that children of slave women no more belonged to their biological mothers than the young of animals belonged to the females that birthed them.[3]

At the same time, slave women and particularly those who were house slaves were expected to nurture and rear and mother the children of their owners. It was not uncommon for white children of the slave-owning class to have relationships of a far greater emotional intensity with the slave women who were their "mammies" than with their own white biological mothers. We might even question the meaning of this conception of "biological motherhood" in light of the fact that the black nurturers of these white children were frequently "wet nurses" as well. They nourished the babies in their care with the milk produced by their own hormones. It seems, therefore, that black women were not only treated as surrogates with respect to the reproduction of slave labor, they also served as surrogate mothers for the white children of the slave owners.

A well-known lullaby that probably originated during slavery has been recorded in versions that powerfully reflect the consciousness of slave women who were compelled to neglect their own children, while lavishing their affection on the children of their masters. "Hushaby, / Don't you cry / Go to sleep, little baby. / And when you wake, / You shall have a cake / And all the pretty little ponies."[4]

In all likelihood this version – or verse – was directed to the white babies, while the following one evoked the forced isolation of their own children: "Go to sleep, little baby, / When you wake / You shall have / All the mules in the stable. / Buzzards and flies / Picking out its eyes, / Pore little baby crying, / Mamma, mamma!"[5]

A similar verse was sung to a lullaby entitled "Ole Cow": "Ole cow, ole cow, / Where is your calf? / Way down yonder in the meadow / The buzzards and the flies / A-pickin' out its eyes, / The po' little thing cried, Mammy."[6]

The economic history of African-American women – from slavery to the present – like the economic history of immigrant women, both from Europe and from colonized or formerly colonized nations, reveals the persisting theme of work as household servants. Mexican women and Irish women, West Indian women and Chinese women have been compelled, by virtue of their economic standing, to function as servants for the wealthy. They have cleaned their houses and – our present concern – they have nurtured and reared their employers' babies. They have functioned as surrogate mothers. Considering this previous history, is it not possible to imagine the possibility that poor women – especially poor women of color – might be transformed into a special caste of hired pregnancy carriers? Certainly such fears are not simply the product of an itinerant imagination. In any event, whether or not such a caste of women baby-bearers eventually makes its way into history, these historical experiences constitute a socio-historical backdrop for the present debate around the new reproductive technologies. The very fact that the discussion over surrogacy tends to coincide, by virtue of corporate involvement and intervention in the new technologies, with the debate over surrogacy for profit, makes it necessary to acknowledge historical economic precedents for surrogate motherhood. Those patterns are more or less likely to persist under the impact of the technology in its market context. The commodification of reproductive technologies and, in particular, the labor services of pregnant surrogate mothers, means that money is being made and that, therefore, someone is being exploited.

Once upon a time – and this is still the case outside the technologically advanced capitalist societies – a woman who discovered that she was infertile would have to reconcile herself to the impossibility of giving birth to her own biological offspring. She would therefore either try to create a life for herself that did not absolutely require the presence of children, or she chose to enter into a mothering relationship in other ways. There was the possibility of foster motherhood, adoptive motherhood, or play motherhood.[7] This last possibility is deeply rooted in the black community tradition of extended families and relationships based both on biological kinship – though not necessarily biological motherhood – and on personal history which is often as binding as biological kinship. But even within the biological network itself, relationships between, for example, an aunt and niece or nephew, in the African-American and other family traditions, might be as strong or stronger than those between a mother and daughter or son.

My own mother grew up in a family of foster parents with no siblings. Her best friend had no sisters and brothers either, so they invented a sister relationship between them. Though many years passed before I became aware that they were not "really" sisters, this knowledge had no significant impact on me: I considered my Aunt Elizabeth no less my aunt later than during the earlier years of my childhood. Because she herself had no children, her relation to me, my sister and two brothers was one of a second mother.

If she were alive and in her child-bearing years today, I wonder whether she would bemoan the fact that she lacked the financial resources to employ all the various technological means available to women who wish to reverse their infertility. I wonder if she would feel a greater compulsion to fulfill a female vocation of motherhood. While working-class women are not often in the position to explore new technologies, infertile women – or the wives/partners of infertile men – who are financially able to do so are increasingly expected to try everything. They are expected to try in vitro fertilization, embryo transplants, surrogacy. The availability of the technology further mythologizes motherhood as the true vocation of women. In fact, the new reproductive medicine sends out a message to those who are capable of receiving it: motherhood lies just beyond the next technology. The consequence is an ideological compulsion toward a palpable goal: a child one creates either via one's own reproductive activity or via someone else's.

Those who opt to employ a surrogate mother will participate in the economic as well as ideological exploitation of her services. And the woman who becomes a surrogate mother earns relatively low wages. A few years ago, the going rate was twenty thousand dollars. Considering the fact that pregnancy is a 24-hour-day job, what might seem like a substantial sum of money is actually not even a minimum wage. This commodification of motherhood is quite frightening in the sense that it comes forth as permission to allow women and their partners to participate in a program that is generative of life. However, it seems that what is really generated is sexism and profits.

The economic model evoked by the relationship between the surrogate mother and the woman [or man] who makes use of her services is the feudalistic bond between a servant and her employer. Because domestic work has been primarily performed in the United States by women of color, native-born as well as recent immigrants (and immigrant women of European descent), elements of racism and class bias adhere to the concept of surrogate motherhood as potential historical features, even in the contemporary absence of large numbers of surrogate mothers of color.

If the emerging debate around the new reproductive technologies is presently anchored to the socio-economic conditions of relatively affluent families, the reproductive issues most frequently associated with poor and working-class women of color revolve around the apparent proliferation of young single parents, especially in African-American communities. For the last decade or so, teenage pregnancy has been ideologically represented as one of the greatest obstacles to social progress in the most impoverished sectors of black America. In actuality, the *rate* of pregnancy among black teens – like that among white teens – has been waning for quite a number of years. According to a National Research Council study, fertility rates in 1960 were 156 births per 1,000 black women aged 15 to 19, and 97 in 1985.[8] What distinguishes teenage pregnancy in black communities today from its historical counterpart is the decreasing likelihood of teenage marriage. There is a constellation of reasons for the failure of young teenagers to consolidate traditional two-parent families. The most obvious one is that it rarely makes economic sense for an unemployed young woman to marry an unemployed young man. As a consequence of shop closures in industries previously accessible to young black male workers – and the overarching deindustrialization of the economy – young men capable of contributing to the support of their children are becoming increasingly scarce. For a young woman whose pregnancy results from a relationship with an unemployed youth, it makes little sense to enter into a marriage that will probably bring in an extra adult as well as a child to be supported by her own mother/father/grandmother.

The rise of single motherhood cannot be construed, however, as synonymous with the "fall" of the nuclear family within black communities – if only because it is an extremely questionable proposition that there was such an uncontested structure as the nuclear family to begin with. Historically, family relationships within black communities have rarely coincided with the traditional nuclear model. The nuclear family, in fact, is a relatively recent configuration, integrally connected with the development of industrial capitalism. It is a family configuration that is rapidly losing its previous, if limited, historical viability: presently, the majority of US families, regardless of membership in a particular cultural or ethnic group, cannot be characterized as "nuclear" in the traditional sense. Considering the gender-based division of labor at the core of the nuclear model, even those families that consist of the mother–father–children nucleus – often popularly referred to as "nuclear families" – do not, rigorously speaking, conform to the nuclear model. The increasingly widespread phenomenon of the "working mother," as opposed to the wife/mother whose economic responsibilities are confined to the household and the children, thoroughly contradicts and renders anachronistic the nuclear family model. Not too many mothers stay at home by choice anymore; not too many mothers can afford to stay at home, unless of course, they benefit from the class privileges that accrue to the wealthy. In other words, even for those whose historical realities were the basis of the emergence of this nuclear family model, the model is rapidly losing its ability to contain and be responsive to contemporary social/economic/psychic realities.

It angers me that this simplistic notion of the material and spiritual impoverishment of the African-American community as largely rooted in teenage pregnancy is so widely accepted. This is not to imply that teenage pregnancy is unproblematic. It is extremely problematic; however, I cannot assent to representations of teenage pregnancy as "the problem." There are reasons young black women become pregnant and/or desire pregnancy. I do not think I am far off-target when I point out that few young women who choose pregnancy are offered an alternative range of opportunities for self-expression and development. Are those black teenage girls with the potential for higher education offered scholarships permitting them to study at colleges and universities like Le Moyne? Are teenagers who choose pregnancy offered even a vision of well-paying and creative jobs?

Is it really so hard to grasp why so many young women would choose motherhood? Isn't this path toward adulthood still thrust upon them by the old but persisting ideological constructions of femaleness? Doesn't motherhood still equal adult womanhood in the popular imagination? Don't the new reproductive technologies further develop this equation of womanhood and motherhood? I would venture to say that many young women make conscious decisions to bear children in order to convince themselves that they are alive and creative human beings. As a consequence of this choice, they are also characterized as immoral for not marrying the fathers of their children.

I have chosen to evoke the reproductive issue of single motherhood among teenagers in order to highlight the absurdity of locating motherhood in a transcendent space – as the anti-abortion theorists and activists do – in which involuntary motherhood is as sacred as voluntary motherhood. In this context, there is a glaring exception: motherhood among black and Latina teens is constructed as a moral and social evil – but even so, they are denied accessible and affordable abortions. Moreover, teen mothers are ideologically assaulted because of their premature and impoverished entrance into the realm of motherhood while older, whiter, and wealthier women are coaxed to buy the technology to assist them in achieving an utterly commodified motherhood.

Further contradictions in the contemporary social compulsion toward motherhood – contradictions rooted in race and class – can be found in the persisting problem of sterilization abuse. While poor women in many states effectively have lost access to abortion, they may be sterilized with the full financial support of the government. While the "right" to opt for surgical sterilization is an important feature of women's control over the reproductive functions of their bodies, the imbalance between the difficulty of access to abortions and the ease of access to sterilization reveals the continued and tenacious insinuation of racism into the politics of reproduction. The astoundingly high – and continually mounting – statistics regarding the sterilization of Puerto Rican women expose one of the most dramatic ways in which women's bodies bear the evidence of colonization. Likewise, the bodies of vast numbers of sterilized indigenous women within the presumed borders of the US bear the traces of a 500-year-old tradition of genocide. While there is as yet no evidence of large-scale sterilization of African-American and Latina teenage girls, there is documented evidence of the federal government's promotion and funding of sterilization operations for young black girls during the 1960s and 70s. This historical precedent convinces me that it is not inappropriate to speculate about such a future possibility of preventing teenage pregnancy. Or – to engage in further speculation – of recruiting healthy young poor women, a disproportionate number of whom would probably be black, Latina, Native American, Asian, or from the Pacific Islands, to serve as pregnancy carriers for women who can afford to purchase their services.

A majority of all women in jails and prisons are mothers and 7 to 10 percent are pregnant.[9] On the other hand, women's correctional institutions still incorporate and dramatically reveal their ideological links to the cult of motherhood. Even today, imprisoned women are labeled "deviant," not so much because of the crimes they may have committed, but rather because their attitudes and their behavior are seen as blatant contradictions of prevailing expectations – especially in the judicial and law enforcement systems – of women's place. They are mothers who have failed to find themselves in motherhood.

Since the onset of industrial capitalism, women's "deviance" has been constructed in psychological terms; the site of female incarceration has been less the prison and more the mental institution. For this reason, the population of jails and prisons is majority male and a minority female, while the reverse is the case in the mental institutions. The strategic role of domesticity in the structure and correctional goals of women's prisons revolves around the notion that to rehabilitate women, you must teach them how to be good wives and good mothers. Federal prisons such as Alderson Federal Reformatory for women in West Virginia and state institutions like the California Institute for Women and Bedford Hills in the state of New York attempt to architecturally – albeit mechanistically – evoke family life. Instead of cells there are cottages; here women have historically "learned" how to keep house, wash and iron clothes, do the dishes. What bearing does this have on the politics of reproduction? I would suggest that there is something to be learned from the egregious contradiction of this emphasis on training for motherhood within a prison system that intransigently refuses to allow incarcerated women to pursue any meaningful relationship with their own children.

In the San Francisco Bay Area, there are only three alternative institutions where women serving jail sentences may live with their children – the Elizabeth Fry Center, Mandela House, and Keller House. In all three places combined, there is space for about 20 to 25 women. In the meantime, thousands of women in the area suffer the threat – or reality – of having their children taken away and made wards of the court. Imprisoned women who admit that they have drug problems and seek to rehabilitate themselves often discover that their admissions are used as evidence of their incapacity to be good mothers. In the jails and prisons where they are incarcerated, they are presumably being taught to be good mothers, even as they are powerless to prevent the state from seizing their own children. Excepting a small minority of alternative "correctional" institutions, where social stereotypes are being questioned (although in most instances, the structure of incarceration itself is left unchallenged), the underlying agenda of this motherhood training is to turn aggressive women into submissive and dependent "mothers," whose children are destined to remain motherless.

The process through which a significant portion of the population of young black, Latina, Native American, Asian, and Pacific women are criminalized, along with the poor European women who, by their association with women of color, are deemed criminal, hinges on a manipulation of a certain ideological representation of motherhood. A poor teenage black or Latina girl who is a single mother is suspected of criminality simply by virtue of the fact that she is poor and has had a child "out of wedlock." This process of criminalization affects the young men in a different way – not as fathers, but rather by virtue of a more all-embracing racialization. Any young black man can be potentially labeled as criminal: a shabby appearance is equated with drug addiction, yet an elegant and expensive self-presentation is interpreted as drug dealing. While it may appear that this process of criminalization is unrelated to the construction of the politics of reproduction, there are significant implications here for the expansion of single motherhood in black and Latino communities. The 25 percent of African-American men in jails and prisons,[10] for example, naturally find it difficult, even in a vicarious sense, to engage in any significant parenting projects.

In pursuing a few of the ways in which racism – and class bias – inform the contemporary politics of reproduction, I am suggesting that there are numerous unexplored vantage points from which we can reconceptualize reproductive issues. It is no longer acceptable to ground an analysis of the politics of reproduction in a conceptual construction of "woman" as a sex. It is not enough to assume that female beings whose bodies are distinguished by vaginas, ovarian tubes, uteri, and other biological features related to reproduction should be able to claim such "rights" to exercise control over the processes of these organs as the right to abortion. The social/economic/political circumstances that oppress and marginalize women of various racial, ethnic, and class backgrounds, and thus alter the impact of ideological conceptions of motherhood, cannot be ignored without affirming the same structures of domination that have led to such different – but related – politics of reproduction in the first place.

In conclusion, I will point to some of the strategic constellations that should be taken into consideration in reconceiving an agenda of reproductive rights. I do not present the following points as an exhaustive list of such goals, but rather I am trying to allude to a few of the contemporary issues requiring further theoretical examination and practical/political action. While the multiple arenas in which women's legal abortion rights are presently being assaulted and eroded can account for the foregrounding of this struggle, the failure to ensure economic accessibility of birth control and abortion has equally important results in the inevitable marginalization of poor women's reproductive rights. With respect to a related issue, the "right" and access to sterilization is important, but again, it is equally important to look at those economic and ideological conditions that track some women toward sterilization, thus denying them the possibility of bearing and rearing children in numbers they themselves choose.

Although the new reproductive technologies cannot be construed as inherently affirmative or violative of women's reproductive rights, the anchoring of the technologies to the profit schemes of their producers and distributors results in a commodification of motherhood that complicates and deepens power relationships based on class and race. Yet, beneath this marriage of technology, profit, and the assertion of a historically obsolete bourgeois individualism lies the critical issue of the right to determine the character of one's family. The assault on this "right" – a term I have used throughout, which is not, however, unproblematic – is implicated in the ideological offensive against single motherhood as well as in the homophobic refusal to recognize lesbian and gay family configurations – and especially in the persisting denial of custody (even though some changes have occurred) to lesbians with children from previous heterosexual marriages. This is one of the many ways in which the present-day ideological compulsion toward motherhood that I have attempted to weave into all of my arguments further resonates. Moreover, this ideology of motherhood is wedded to an obdurate denial of the very social services women require in order to make meaningful choices to bear or not to bear children. Such services include health care – from the prenatal period to old age – childcare, housing, education, jobs, and all the basic services human beings require to lead decent lives. The privatization of family responsibilities – particularly during an era when so many new family configurations are being invented that the definition of family stretches beyond its own borders – takes on increasingly reactionary implications. This is why I close with a point of departure: the reconceptualization of family and of reproductive rights in terms that move from the private to the public, from the individual to the social.

NOTES

1   See Harriet A. Jacobs, *Incidents in the Life of a Slave Girl*, ed. Jean Fagan Yellin (Cambridge, MA: Harvard University Press), 1987.

2 See Michelle Stanworth (ed.), *Reproductive Technologies: Gender, Motherhood and Medicine* (Minneapolis: University of Minnesota Press, 1987).

3 See Paula Giddings, *When and Where I Enter: The Impact of Black Women on Race and Sex in America* (New York: William Morrow, 1984).

4 Dorothy Scarborough, *On the Trail of Negro Folksongs* (Hatboro, PA: Folklore Associates, Inc., 1963; original edition published by Harvard University Press, 1925), 145.

5 Ibid., 148.

6 Ibid.

7 The tradition of black women acting as "play mothers" is still a vital means of inventing kinship relations unrelated to biological origin.

8 Gerald David Jaynes and Robin M. Williams, Jr (eds), *A Common Destiny: Blacks and American Society* (Washington, DC: National Academy Press, 1989), 515.

9 See Ellen M. Barry, "Pregnant Prisoners," *Harvard Women's Law Journal*, vol. 12 (1989).

10 See Marc Mauer, *Young Black Americans and the Criminal Justice System: A Growing National Problem* (Wahsington, DC: The Sentencing Project, February 1990).

14

Black Women and the Academy

These are very complicated times – in a sense the very fact that so many of us are able to come together as black women academics, students, faculty, staff – is indicative of the vast strides that have occurred since 1862, when Mary Jane Patterson became the first African-American woman to be awarded a BA degree. After graduating from Oberlin College, she went on to teach at the Institute for Colored Youth in Philadelphia and later became principal of the Preparatory High School for Colored Youth in Washington, DC (which was the predecessor of Dunbar High School).[1] Thus, as so many black women have done, she prepared younger generations for higher education. As bell hooks, referring to black women teachers in the South, wrote, "They were active participants in black community, shaping our futures, mapping our intellectual terrains, sharing revolutionary fervor and vision."[2]

But, while courageous people have organized and fought to make the walls of academia less impenetrable, these very victories have spawned new problems and foreshadowed new struggles. So today we are talking about defending our name within the system of higher education – as students, teachers, and workers.

I include workers – because it would be a mark of our having reproduced the very elitism which excluded and continues to exclude so many of us if we assumed that there is only one group of black women whose names are worth defending in the academy. Why, in fact, is it considered more important to defend the name of the assistant professor who is refused tenure than the secretary who is kept in a dead-end job? – or the woman-of-color janitor who is not allowed to unionize?

Certainly the academy is an important site for political contestations

First published by Johns Hopkins University Press in *Callaloo* (vol. 17, no. 2, summer 1994), this is Angela Y. Davis's closing address at the "Black Women in the Academy: Defending Our Name 1894–1994" Conference, Massachusetts Institute of Technology, Cambridge MA, January 15, 1994. Copyright © 1994 by Angela Y. Davis. Reprinted by permission of the author and the Johns Hopkins University Press.

of racism, sexism, and homophobia. In relation to some issues we choose to address, the academy may be a strategic site, but it is not the *only* site, especially if we commit ourselves to defending the name of black women.

Since we have all assembled this weekend under the motto, "Defending Our Name," I suggest we look at the historical significance of the conference's organizing theme. As we know, this theme, which we associate with the turn-of-the-century black women's club movement, was first formulated by Fannie Barrier Williams in an address she gave at a worldwide gathering of women during the 1893 Columbian World Exposition. Her words bear repeating now:

> I regret the necessity of speaking to the question of the moral progress of our women because the morality of our home life has been commented on so disparagingly and meanly that we are placed in the unfortunate position of being defenders of our name. While I duly appreciate the offensiveness of all references to American slavery, it is unavoidable to charge to that system every moral imperfection that mars the character of the colored American. The whole life and power of slavery depended upon an enforced degradation of everything human in the slaves. The slave code recognized only animal distinctions between the sexes and ruthlessly ignored those ordinary separations of the sexes that belong to the social state. It is a great wonder that two centuries of such demoralization did not work a complete extinction of all the moral instincts.[3]

Williams continued to explain that black southern women needed "protection": "I do not wish to disturb the serenity of this conference by suggesting why this protection is needed and the kind of men against whom it is needed."[4]

Williams's 1893 statement was admirable and courageous, but at the same time deeply influenced by the ideological climate of that era, which constructed womanhood – "true womanhood" – in explicitly middle-class terms, which did not always distinguish between sexual victimization and female sexual desire.

When the National Association of Colored Women was founded in 1896, it chose for its motto, "Lifting as We Climb." This motto called upon the most educated, the most moral, and the most affluent African-American women to recognize the extent to which the dominant culture's racist perceptions linked them with the least educated, the "most immoral," and the most impoverished black women. Mary Church Terrell described this cross-class relationship as a determination "to come into the closest possible touch with the masses of our women, through whom the womanhood of our people is always judged."[5] In other words, "[s]elf-preservation demands that [educated black women] go among the lowly, illiterate and even the vicious, to whom they are bound by ties of race and sex, to reclaim them."[6] Such postures helped to produce a distinguished tradition of progressive activism among black middle-class women from the NACW to the National Council of Negro Women and similar organizations today, but what was and remains problematic is the premise that middle-class women necessarily embody a standard their poorer sisters should be encouraged to emulate.

The black women's club movement was especially concerned with "defending their name" against pervasive charges of immorality and sexual promiscuity. Given the extent to which representations of black inferiority emanating from the dominant culture were bound up with notions of racial hypersexualization – the deployment of the myth of the black rapist to justify lynching is the most obvious example – it is hard to imagine that women like Fannie Barrier Williams, Ida B. Wells, and Mary Church Terrell could have been as effective as they were without defending the sexual purity of their sisters. Yet, in the process of defending black women's moral integrity and sexual purity, sexual agency was almost entirely denied. We should remember that in the aftermath of slavery, sexuality was one of the very few realms in which masses of African-American women could exercise some kind of autonomy: they could, at least, choose their sexual partners – and thus they could distinguish their post-slavery status from their historical enslavement.

I want to suggest that this denial of sexual agency was in an important respect the denial of freedom for working-class black women. At the same time, I do not want to underestimate the historical importance of the campaigns organized by the black women's club movement, which attempted to affirm the morality of black women and to defend black women's names. Since the vast majority of black women workers – from the end of slavery up to the late 1950s – were domestic workers, sexual harassment and abuse were serious job hazards, particularly because white public opinion tended to place the blame for any sexual activity between black women and white men on the women rather than the men. But, in the process of conducting a much needed, righteous struggle against sexual abuse, focusing on the racist way in which black women were depicted as inferior sexual animals, these ideological contestations tended to deny black women's sexuality altogether.

I refer to this historical process because of its contemporary resonance. For example, most campaigns today against teenage pregnancy fail to acknowledge the possibility and desirability of sexual autonomy in young black women. An article featured on the cover of *Jet Magazine* (January 10, 1994) was titled "Athletes for Abstinence Promotes 'Sexual Purity' for Teens Until Marriage." Consider also the program to distribute Norplant in the Baltimore school clinics. Female sexuality – young black women's sexuality – is the hidden and unspoken factor in the debates around the distribution of Norplant in the public schools.

George Will wrote an Op/Ed article in *The Washington Post* (March 18, 1993), decrying sexual activity, while mobilizing statistics in an especially virulent and reifying way: "This year 10 million teenagers will engage in 126 million acts of sexual intercourse resulting in 1 million pregnancies, 406,000 abortions, 134,000 miscarriages and 490,000 births, about 64 percent (313,000) of them illegitimate. In 1988, 11,000 babies were born to females under 15. In 1990, 32 percent of ninth grade females (14 and 15) had sexual intercourse."[7] He goes on to make racial distinctions, so as to support the extension of the Norplant program largely to young black women:

> A white suburban teenager who becomes pregnant is apt to get an abortion and go on to college. A black inner-city teenager's pregnancy is not apt to disrupt similar expectations. Furthermore, the pregnant teenager is apt to have a supportive matriarchy to rely on if she decides to have the baby resulting from the unwanted pregnancy.

> But the prospects for such babies are at best problematic. Better the unwanted pregnancy had not occurred. And Norplant may be the most feasible preventative.[8]

In the debates around the distribution of Norplant in the schools, the specter of black community genocide is often evoked by the opponents of this program. But what is omitted is a discussion of the young women themselves as subjects who engage in sexual activity for reasons that are not necessarily limited to reproduction. What is further omitted is a discussion of the need for education to assist the young women to protect themselves from HIV and AIDS as well as from other sexually transmitted diseases. Former US Surgeon General Dr Joycelyn Elders's promotion of the use of condoms is entirely ignored in these debates.

I want to return to the historical analysis I initially proposed. In "The Struggle of Negro Women for Sex and Race Emancipation," an article for a 1925 issue of *Survey Graphic*, Elsie Johnson McDougall wrote:

> [The Negro woman's] emotional and sex life is a reflex of her economic station. The women of the working class will react, emotionally and sexually, similarly to the working-class women of other races. . . . Superficial critics who have had contact only with the lower grades of Negro women, claim that they are more immoral than other groups of women. This I deny. This is the sort of criticism which predicates of one race, to its detriment, that which is common to all races. Sex irregularities are not a matter of race, but of socio-economic conditions.[9]

McDougall's attempt to shift the burden of sexuality – which, in its very acknowledgment, is equated with morality – from race to class ironically resonates with Will's argument and with contemporary patterns of racialization in which the role of race itself is denied.

As we approach the close of the only century that people of African descent have spent on this soil which has been free of slavery, we need to find ways to connect with, and at the same time be critical of, the work of our foremothers. There is no contradiction here. The most powerful way to acknowledge and carry on in a tradition that will move us forward is simultaneously to affirm historical continuity and to effect some conscious historical ruptures. Therefore, I want to pose a question: How much of the ideological tradition of "defending our name" do we wish to affirm and preserve? And what about it do we wish to break with? I only want to make a few points, and leave the rest to you.

First, we can no longer assume that there is a single monolithic force against which we position ourselves in order to defend our name – i.e., the white establishment. We have to defend our names in those places we consider home as well. Moreover, the corporate and political establishments are becoming increasingly integrated, while the structures of domination have become even more consolidated. Because black people were so instrumental in the election of Clinton, we often find it difficult to explore the extent to which the erasure of race by the new Democrats mirrors previous arguments against affirmative action and the invocation of reverse discrimination by neo-conservatives. In a sense, neo-liberalism and neo-conservatism are moving toward a dangerous embrace.

Second, we can no longer ignore the ways in which we sometimes end up reproducing the very forms of domination which we like to attribute to something or somebody else. "She ain't black. She don't even look black." Or else, "She's too black. Listen to how she talks. She sounds more like a preacher than a scholar." Or, "Her work isn't really about black women. She's only interested in lesbians." Or, more generally, "She's not a real scholar." It used to be that any work done by a black person about black issues was not acknowledged as "real scholarship." Consider how long it has taken us to compel the academy to recognize the work of W. E. B. Du Bois – or Zora Neale Hurston.

Third, we have to rid ourselves of the habit of assuming that the masses of black women are to be defined in accordance with their status as victims. However, there are those of us who have made it into the academy – or into the corporate world or into the political establishment – who consider ourselves the examples, the exemplary black women. "Don't judge us on the basis of what the black woman drug addict does." Yet, when it is advantageous, we like to represent ourselves as victims. As when Clarence Thomas invoked the idea that he was the victim of a "hi-tech lynching."

Fourth, we cannot afford to commit ourselves so fervently to defending our names that we end up positioning ourselves against our Asian, Latina, Pacific Island, and Native American sisters. As Jacqui Alexander put it, why do we not feel the need to develop a measure of fluency in the available literature by and about women of color other than ourselves? We are not the exemplary women of color. Ethnic solipsism is something we have always attributed to whiteness, Eurocentrism. Do we want simply to push aside one system of hierarchies in order to institute another? Do we want to accept the notion that discourses about race are essentially about black/white relations? As if to suggest that if you are not either black or white, then you are dispensable?

I could continue with this list – but I think you get the drift. The point is, let's try to take critical thinking seriously – not just narrowly in relation to scholarly projects. Many of us can be very critical when we are doing our research – but not necessarily in relation to the ideologies that inform our ideas and our lives. And critical thinking, while revered in the academy, is not the academy's exclusive property. We thank Patricia Hill Collins for her brilliant work on the production of black feminist knowledges in multiple cultural sites.

Having said all of this, I want to discuss a number of issues which have political implications for our research strategies as well as our organizing strategies.

The last point I made had to do with our positionalities as women of color. As not the only women of color, I should say. When we think of ourselves as women of color, that means we are compelled to think about a range of issues and contradictions and differences. Audre Lorde's work continues to challenge us to think about difference and contradiction not as moments to be avoided or escaped – not as moments we should fear – but rather as generative and creative.

In this context, I want to raise the issue of immigration before this conference. Immigrant women cross many borders – not only territorial ones. They cross racial and cultural borders as well. As black women, how do we forge ties of political solidarity with Latina immigrant women, Asian immigrant women, Haitian immigrant women?

On the West Coast, we cannot claim, unfortunately, that African Americans have visibly and in significant numbers challenged support for the crackdown on undocumented immigrants from Mexico and Central America. Perhaps we need to remind our communities that the presently acceptable scapegoating of immigrants was preceded by overtly racist calls for increased vigilance of the California border by white supremacists like Tom Meztger. Perhaps we also need to remind our communities that black migrants from the South were historically rejected in very much the same way as undocumented Latinos are rejected today. The defense of immigrant rights is a black women's issue. We need to speak out loudly against the anti-immigrant backlash. Joblessness in the black community – and unemployment has reached crisis proportions – is not a result of immigrant workers taking black jobs. As LA black community organizer Joe Williams III has pointed out:

> Like the Negro migrant, the Latino migrant today has become the scapegoat for a faltering capitalist economy. Perhaps it is not surprising that blacks, who find themselves at the bottom of the economic downturn, have all too readily bought the message. . . . But African-Americans – both our leaders and our community – should condemn rather than support the anti-immigrant back-lash. We should not allow politicians to reinvent the lie that was used against our own people 30 years ago.[10]

Many of you know that I try to be an unreconstructed activist, especially when it comes to capitalism. Just because socialist states have fallen – with the exception of Cuba – for reasons that had much more to do with the lack of democracy than with socialism itself, this does not mean that socialism is an obsolete political project. And it certainly does not mean that solidarity with working-class people is an obsolete political project.

Earlier, I distributed postcards and flyers about a boycott of the Jessica McClintock Corporation spearheaded by Chinese immigrant women in Oakland. The workers were not paid for the manufacture of McClintock garments after their employer – a contractor with McClintock – folded his business. None of the garment corporations take responsibility for what happens to the workers who produce their profitable clothing. I suggest that we send a message of support to Asian Immigrant Women Advocates (AIWA) indicating that the 2,010 women – and men, thank you very much my brothers – who gathered here to discuss issues around black women in the academy vow not to patronize Jessica McClintock until she changes her policies regarding workers' rights.

Another issue I want to raise here is the seductive representation of crime as the nation's single most important social problem. The contemporary law and order discourse is legitimized by democrats and liberals as well as republicans and conservatives. (It reminds me of the late 1960s and 1970s, of Richard Nixon and Ronald Reagan.) Communities of color are increasingly criminalized. In Latino communities, especially on the West Coast, the INS is a major disciplinary force along with the police and prison guards, who are the pivotal repressive agents for black people. And, unfortunately, calls for more police and more prisons emanate not only from white circles. As a matter of fact, the first black woman senator in US history has sponsored a deleterious anti-crime bill. While it may be important to support her in various contexts, this does not mean we cannot also challenge her. Write Carol Moseley Braun and strongly urge her to rethink this issue.

In a sense, Braun's support of the Senate Anti-Crime Bill response echoes contemporary ideological developments within black communities. In a way that cuts across class, educational level, and party affiliation, African-Americans are increasingly calling for more police and more prisons. At the same time, ever greater numbers of black people are trapped within the criminal justice system. More than a million people are in jails and prisons and – as a further impetus for the participants in this conference to take up this issue – women constitute the fastest-growing sector of the imprisoned population.

Drugs play an important role in the ideological merging of racialization and criminalization. Black people, according to a study done by the National Institute on Drug Abuse, constitute about twelve percent of those who use drugs regularly, which exactly mirrors the black proportion of this country's population. However, more than thirty-six percent of those arrested for drug violations are black – and I am fairly sure that this is an underestimation. How, then, do national sentencing policies serve to criminalize black communities? More than ninety percent of defendants in crack cases are black, and black people are about twenty-five percent of defendants in cases involving powdered cocaine. But the Omnibus Anti-Drug Abuse Act of 1986 requires five years in prison for possession of more than five grams of crack. In order to receive the same sentence on charges of possessing powdered cocaine, one must be caught with one hundred times as much. Drug policies are racialized and they criminalize by virtue of race.

On a related note, we need to think about ideological representations of criminals that we all tend to accept and therefore perpetuate. When criminality is evoked, who are the people we are imagining? Whom do we fear? Who do we imagine as dangerous?

In the realm of material reality, prison construction is very big business. And we wonder why there is so little money for education, for scholarships, for research. In his State of the State Address, California Governor Pete Wilson devoted 20 out of 35–40 minutes to crime. He evoked the Polly Klaas case, positioning Richard Allen Davis, presently charged with the abduction and brutal murder of the little girl, Polly Klaas, as the quintessential criminal. Wilson used this case to call for a draconian crackdown on criminals. So, where do women – or, more specifically, black women – fit into this scheme? Wilson argued that the best way to prevent crime was "a safe home with a nurturing two-parent family." In the final analysis, who is represented as responsible for crime?

Wilson went on to boast about having opened five new prisons during his tenure, and he asked for $2 billion more to open another six prisons. Prison construction is big business.

Where do black women figure in here? In the era of the war against drugs, black women comprise the fastest growing imprisoned population. The war against drugs serves as the pretext for police and military campaigns and an obscene proliferation of prisons and jails. The only alternatives to imprisonment are those managed by correctional systems. In defending the name of Surgeon General Joycelyn Elders, we acknowledge the courage she displayed in attempting to place the issue of decriminalization of drugs on the political agenda. Because she suggested a national conversation on a reasonable alternative to the present expansion of police and penal institutions – which tend to reproduce crime more than they deter it – she has been harshly rebuked by the White House, as have Lani Guinier and Johnnetta Cole.

In response to Elders' call for conversation on decriminalization, I want to offer a further suggestion about potential research and organizing agendas. I want to ask you to consider the prospect of abolishing jails and prisons for a substantial percentage of the imprisoned population. We might begin with a strategy of decarceration for women prisoners, the vast majority of whom are black women convicted of non-violent crimes, such as drugs, prostitution and welfare fraud. I am suggesting that we theorize – and organize – a new abolitionism, an approach that would propose institutions other than prisons to address the social problems that lead to imprisonment. I use the term "abolitionism" because of its historical resonance with nineteenth-century struggles against slavery. Moreover, when slavery was constitutionally abolished by the Thirteenth Amendment, a clause permitting the continued enslavement of people convicted of crimes was retained. Thus, structures of domination associated with slavery have survived, hidden away, behind prison walls. The vast majority of states do not even allow inmates to vote. As a matter of fact, Massachusetts, the site of this conference, is one of the few states, along with Maine and Vermont, that do allow inmates to vote. At least four million current and former prisoners in this country do not have the right to vote. A disproportionate number of them are black and Latino.

Scholars working in various disciplines are already doing work on incarcerated women. But think about the consequences for research and organizing if we decide to reject the inevitability of an expanding prison system in our society. This is only one example of many possible ways to link research agendas with radical organizing practices. Finally, if the presence of increasing numbers of black women within the academy is to have a transformative impact both on the academy and on communities beyond the academy, we have to think seriously about linkages between research and activism, about cross-racial and transnational coalitional strategies, and about the importance of linking our work to radical social agendas.

NOTES

1 Elizabeth L. Ihle (ed.), *Black Women in Higher Education: An Anthology of Essays, Studies and Documents* (New York and London: Garland Publishing Inc., 1992), x.
2 bell hooks, *Talking Back: Thinking Feminist, Thinking Black* (Boston: South End Press, 1989), 50.
3 *The Present Status and Intellectual Progress of Colored Women* (Chicago: 1893); quoted in Eleanor Flexner, *Century of Struggle: The Woman's Rights Movement in the United States* (New York: Atheneum, 1974), 187–8.
4 Ibid., n. 12, 358.
5 Mary Church Terrell, "What Role is the Educated Negro Woman to Play in the Uplifting of Her Race?"; quoted in Paula Giddings, *When and Where I Enter: The Impact of Black Women on Race and Sex in America* (New York: William Morrow, 1984), 98.
6 Ibid.
7 Will cites the source of these statistics as Douglas Besharov and Karen Gardiner in *The American Enterprise Journal.*
8 George Will, *The Washington Post*, March 18, 1993.
9 *Survey Graphic*, vol. 6, no. 6 (March 1925), 691; quoted in Gerda Lerner (ed.), *Black Women in White America* (New York: Vintage, 1970).
10 *Racefile*, vol. 1, no. 5 (November 1993).

PART III

Aesthetics and Culture

15

Art on the Frontline: Mandate for a People's Culture

In 1951, Paul Robeson made the following declaration at a Conference in New York City organized around the theme of equal rights for Negroes in the arts, sciences and professions:

> There are despoilers abroad in our land, akin to those who attempted to throttle our Republic at its birth. Despoilers who would have kept my beloved people in unending serfdom, a powerful few who blessed Hitler as he destroyed a large segment of a great people . . .
>
> All [the] millions of the world stand aghast at the sight and the name of *America* – but they love *us*; they look to *us* to help create a world where we can all live in peace and friendship, where we can exchange the excellence of our various arts and crafts, the manifold wonders of our mutual scientific creations, a world where we can rejoice at the unleashed power of our innermost selves, of the potential of great masses of people. To them *we* are the real America. Let us remember that.
>
> And let us learn how to bring to the great masses of the American people *our* culture and *our* art. For in the end, what are we talking about when we talk about American culture today? We are talking about a culture that is restricted to the very, very few. How many workers ever get to the theatre? I was in concerts for 20 years, subscription concerts, the two thousand seats gone before any Negro in the community, any worker, could even hear about a seat. . . . Only by going into the trade unions and singing on the picket lines and in the struggles for the freedom of our people – only in this way could the workers of this land hear me.[1]

More than three decades later, this problem articulated by Paul Robeson still remains one of the main challenges facing progressive artists and political activists: How do we collectively acknowledge our popular cultural legacy and communicate it to the masses of our people, most of whom have been denied access to the social spaces reserved for art and culture? In the United States, a rich and vibrant tradition of people's art has emerged from the history of labor militancy and the struggles of Afro-Americans, women, and peace activists. It is essential that we explore that tradition, understand it, reclaim it, and glean from it the cultural nourishment that can assist us in preparing a political and cultural counteroffensive against the regressive institutions and ideas spawned by advanced monopoly capitalism.

As Marx and Engels long ago observed, art is a form of social consciousness – a special form of social consciousness that can potentially awaken an urge in those affected by it to creatively transform their oppressive environments. Art can function as a sensitizer and a catalyst, propelling people toward involvement in organized movements seeking to effect radical social change. Art is special because of its ability to influence feelings as well as knowledge. Christopher Caudwell, the British Communist who wrote extensively on aesthetics, once defined the function of art as the socializing of the human instincts and the educating of human emotions:

> Emotion, in all its vivid coloring, is the creation of ages of culture acting on the blind, unfeeling instincts. All art, all education, all day-to-day social experience, draw it out . . . and direct and shape its myriad phenomena.[2]

Progressive art can assist people to learn not only about the objective forces at work in the society in which they live, but also about the intensely social character of their interior lives. Ultimately, it can propel people toward social emancipation. While not all progressive art need be concerned with explicitly political problems – indeed, a love song can be progressive if it incorporates a sensitivity toward the lives of working-class women and men – I want to specifically explore overt sociopolitical meanings in art with the purpose of defining the role art can play in hastening social progress.

Because the history of Afro-American culture reveals strong bonds between art and the struggle for black liberation, it holds important lessons for those who are interested in strengthening the bridges between art and people's movements today. Of all the art forms historically associated with Afro-American culture, music has played the greatest catalytic role in awakening social consciousness in the community. During the era of slavery, Black people were victims of a conscious strategy of cultural genocide, which proscribed the practice of virtually all African customs with the exception of music. If slaves were permitted to sing as they toiled in the fields and to incorporate music into their religious services, it was because the slaveocracy failed to grasp the social function of music in general and particularly the central role music played in all aspects of life in West

African society. As a result, black people were able to create with their music an aesthetic community of resistance, which in turn encouraged and nurtured a political community of active struggle for freedom. This continuum of struggle, which is at once aesthetic and political, has extended from Harriet Tubman's and Nat Turner's spirituals through Bessie Smith's "Poor Man's Blues" and Billie Holiday's "Strange Fruit," through Max Roach's "Freedom Suite," and even to the progressive raps on the popular music scene of the 1980s.

With the Afro-American spiritual, a language of struggle was forged that was as easily understood by the slaves as it was misinterpreted by the slaveholders. While the slaveocracy attempted to establish absolute authority over the slaves' individual and communal lives, the spirituals were both cause and evidence of an autonomous political consciousness. These songs formed a complex language that both incorporated and called forth a deep yearning for freedom. When the slaves sang, "Didn't My Lord Deliver Daniel and Why Not Every Man?," they utilized religious themes to symbolize their own concrete predicament and their own worldly desire to be free. When they sang "Samson Tore the Building Down," they made symbolic reference to their desire to see the oppressive edifice of slavery come crashing down.

> If I had my way,
> O Lordy, Lordy,
> If I had my way;
> If I had my way,
> I would tear this building down.

Oftentimes the religious music of the slaves played real and instrumental roles in the operation of the underground railroad and in the organization of antislavery insurrections. The lyrics of "Follow the Drinking Gourd," for example, literally provided a map of one section of the underground railroad, and "Steal Away to Jesus" was a coded song rallying together those engaged in the organization of Nat Turner's rebellion. But even when the spirituals were not linked to specific actions in the freedom struggle, they always served, epistemologically and psychologically, to shape the consciousness of the masses of Black people, guaranteeing that the fires of freedom would burn within them. As Sidney Finkelstein pointed out:

The antislavery struggle was the core of the struggle for democracy, so spirituals embodied in their music and poetry the affirmation of an unbreakable demand for freedom.[3]

The spirituals have directly influenced the music associated with other people's movements at various moments in the history of the United States.

Many songs of the labor and peace movements have their origins in the religious music of the slaves, and the "freedom songs" of the Civil Rights Movement were spirituals whose lyrics were sometimes slightly altered in order to reflect more concretely the realities of that struggle.

Even the blues, frequently misrepresented as a music form focusing on trivial aspects of sexual love, are closely tied to Black people's strivings for freedom. In the words of James Cone:

> For many people, a blues song is about sex or a lonely woman longing for her rambling man. However, the blues are more than that. To be sure, the blues involve sex and what that means for human bodily expression, but on a much deeper level . . . the blues express a black perspective on the incongruity of life and the attempt to achieve meaning in a situation fraught with contradictions. As Aunt Molly Jackson of Kentucky put it: "The blues are made by working people . . . when they have a lot of problems to solve about their work, when their wages are low . . . and they don't know which way to turn and what to do."[4]

And, indeed, Bessie Smith, the Empress of the Blues, reached the apex of her career when she composed and recorded a song transmitting an unmistakable political message, entitled "Poor Man's Blues." This song evoked the exploitation and manipulation of working people by the wealthy and portrayed the rich as parasites accumulating their wealth and fighting their wars with the labor of the poor.

Another pinnacle in the evolution of Afro-American music was Billie Holiday's incorporation of the political antilynching song "Strange Fruit" into her regular repertoire. Throughout Lady Day's career, thousands of people were compelled to confront the brutal realities of southern racism, even as they sought to escape the problems of everyday life through music, alcohol, and the ambiance of smoke-filled nightclubs. Undoubtedly, some went on to actively participate in the antilynching movement of that era.

That Billie Holiday recorded "Strange Fruit" in 1939 was no accident. Neither was the fact that the lyrics of this song were composed by progressive poet Lewis Allan, who was associated with activist struggles of the 1930s. The thirties remain the most exciting and exuberant period in the evolution of American cultural history. The process of developing a mature people's art movement today can be facilitated by a serious examination of that era's achievements. As Phillip Bonosky points out in a 1959 *Political Affairs* article entitled "The Thirties in American Culture:"

> There is every reason in the world why official reaction should want the thirties to be forgotten as if they never existed. For that period remains a watershed in the American democratic tradition. It is a period which will continue to serve both the present and the future as a reminder and as an

example of how an aroused people, led and spurred on by the working class, can change the entire complexion of the culture of a nation.[5]

Bourgeois ideologists have consequently attempted to

misrepresent and burn out of the consciousness of the American people, and first of all the artists and intellectuals, the fact that the making of a people's culture once did exist in the United States and was inspired, to a large degree, by the working class, often led, and largely influenced, by the Communist Party.[6]

Answering the charges leveled against the Communist party that it "belittles and vulgarizes the rule of culture," Bonosky argues that no other political party in the entire history of this country had ever manifested such a serious concern for art. The Communist party was involved, for example, in the 1935 Call for an American Writers' Congress – which claimed Langston Hughes, Theodore Dreiser, Richard Wright, and Erskine Caldwell among its signers. As a result of the work of the Communist party and other progressive forces, artists won the right to work as artists in projects under the auspices of the Works Progress Administration. What the WPA artists accomplished was an unprecedented achievement in the history of the United States: Art was brought to the people on a truly massive scale. It could no longer be confined to the private domain, monopolized by those whose class background made galleries, museums, theaters and concert halls routinely accessible. For the first time, American art became public art. This meant, for example, that working-class people utilizing the services of the post office could simultaneously appreciate the public murals painted there. Sculpture, music, and theater were among the other arts directly taken to the people during that era. Moreover, to quote Bonosky once more, when these programs were threatened with dissolution,

it was the Communist Party that struggled so heroically to save the art projects and with them of course the theory that art was responsible to the people of which these projects were the living embodiment. For the first time in American history artists and writers walked picket lines in the name of and in the defense of the right of artists to *be* artists.[7]

The radical approach to art and culture inspired by the Communist Party and other Left forces during the Great Depression involved more than the forging of an art that was publicly accessible to the masses. Much of the art of that period was people's art in the sense that artists learned how to pay attention to the material and emotional lives of working people in America in the process of working out the content of their aesthetic creations. Meridel LeSeuer explored the lives of working people in her literature as Woody Guthrie composed songs about their lives and struggles. This emerging people's art was therefore a challenge to the dominant bourgeois culture. Artists not only felt compelled to defend their right to communicate the real pains, joys, and aspirations of the working class through their art, but many went on to become activists in the labor struggles and in the fight for the rights of the unemployed and especially of Black people. In the process, of course, new artists were summoned up from the ranks of these struggles.

Bourgeois aesthetics has always sought to situate art in a transcendant realm, beyond ideology, beyond socioeconomic realities, and certainly beyond the class struggle. In an infinite variety of ways, art has been represented as the pure subjective product of individual creativity. Lenin's 1905 article "Party Organization and Party Literature" challenged this vision of art and developed the principle of partisanship in art and literature – a principle with which many progressive artists of the 1930s were, at least implicitly, in agreement. Lenin made it absolutely clear that in insisting that aesthetic creations be partisan, he was not advocating the dictatorship of the party over art and literature.

> There is no question that literature is least of all subject to mechanical adjustment or leveling to the rule of the majority over the minority. There is no question either that in this field greater scope must undoubtedly be allowed for personal initiative, individual inclination, thought and fantasy, form and content.[8]

He pointed out, however, that the bourgeois demand for abstract subjective freedom in art was actually a stifling of the freedom of creativity. Literature and art, he said, must be free not only from police censorship,

> but from capital, from careerism, and . . . bourgeois anarchist individualism. Partisan literature and art will be truly free, because it will further the freedom of millions of people.[9]

What are the current prospects for the further expansion of an art that is not afraid to declare its partisan relationship to people's struggles for economic, racial, and sexual equality? Not only must we acknowledge and defend the cultural legacy that has been transmitted to us over the decades, but we must also be in a position to recognize the overt as well as subtle hints of progressive developments in popular art forms today. Over the last several years, for example, such partisan films as *Silkwood* and *Missing* have emerged as beacons amid the routinely mediocre, sexist, violent, and generally antihuman values characterizing most products of the Hollywood cinema industry.

To consider another art form, some of the superstars of popular-musical culture today are unquestionably musical geniuses, but they have distorted the black music tradition by brilliantly developing its form while ignoring its content of struggle and freedom. Nonetheless, there is illumination to be found in contemporary black music in the works of such artists as Stevie Wonder and Gil Scott-Heron, who have acknowledged the legacy of black music in form and content alike. Their individual creations have awakened in their audiences a true sense of the dignity of human freedom.

Stevie Wonder's tune "Happy Birthday" touched the hearts of hundreds of thousands of young people, mobilizing them in support of the movement to declare Dr. Martin Luther King, Jr.'s birthday a national holiday. That President Ronald Reagan was forced to sign the bill enacting that law, despite his openly articulated opposition, demonstrated that popular sentiment could prevail over the most intransigent official racism this country has known in many years.

Gil Scott-Heron's immensely popular song "B-Movie," released shortly after Reagan was elected to his first term, mobilized strong anti-Reagan sentiments in young black public opinion. The song-poem particularly exposed the efforts of the Reagan propagandists to declare that he had received a "mandate" from the people.

> The first thing I want to say is "mandate" my ass
> Because it seems as though we've been convinced
> That 26% of the registered voters
> Not even 26% of the American people
> Form a mandate or a landslide . . .
> But, oh yeah, I remember . . .
> I remember what I said about Reagan
> Acted like an actor/Hollyweird
> Acted like a liberal
> Acted like General Franco
> When he acted like governor of California
> Then he acted like a Republican
> Then he acted like somebody was going to vote for him for president
> And now he acts like 26% of the registered voters
> Is actually a mandate
> We're all actors in this, actually

Bruce Springsteen's album *Born in the USA* was lauded by Reagan, who praised "the message of hope in the songs . . . of New Jersey's own Bruce Springsteen" as he campaigned in that state for re-election to the presidency in 1984. However, Reagan's aides more than likely simply assumed that Springsteen's red, white, and blue album cover indicated acceptance of the fraudulent patriotism promoted by the Reagan administration. Two days after Reagan's remark, Springsteen introduced a song entitled "Johnny 99" by saying, "I don't think the president was listening to this one," going on to sing about a desperate, debt-ridden, unemployed autoworker who landed on death row after killing someone in the course of a robbery. Another one of his songs, "My Hometown," is about the devastation wrought by plant shutdowns:

> Now Mainstreet's whitewashed windows and vacant stores
> Seems like there ain't nobody wants to come down here no more
> They're closing down the textile mill across the railroad tracks
> Foreman says these jobs are going, boys, and they ain't coming back
> To your hometown . . .

A new genre of music with roots in the age-old tradition of storytelling has gained increasing popularity among the youth of today. Rap music clearly reflects the daily lives of working-class people, particularly urban Afro-American and Latino youth. Many rap songs incorporate a progressive consciousness of current political affairs as revealed, for example, by the following rap by Grand Master Flash and Melle Mel which calls upon youth to associate themselves with the Reverend Jesse Jackson's 1984 campaign for the presidency:

> Oh beautiful for spacious skies
> And your amber waves of untold lies
> Look at all the politicians trying to do a job
> But they can't help but look like the mob
> Get a big kickback, put it away
> Watch the FBI watch the CIA
> They want a bigger missile and a faster jet
> But yet they forgot to hire the vets
>
> Hypocrites and Uncle Toms are talking trash
>   Let's talk about Jesse
> Liberty and Justice are a thing of the past
>   Let's talk about Jesse
> They want a stronger nation at any cost
>   Let's talk about Jesse
> Even if it means that everything will soon be lost
>   Let's talk about Jesse
> He started on the bottom, now he's on the top
>   Let's talk about Jesse
> He proved that he can make it, so don't ever stop
>
> Now let's stand together and let the whole world see
> Our brother Jesse Jackson go down in history

So vote, vote, vote
Everybody get up and vote . . .

Young people are becoming more and more conscious of the need to oppose the nuclear-arms race. A rap tune popularized by Harry Belafonte's film *Beat Street* contains the following warning:

A newspaper burns in the sand
And the headlines say man the story's bad
Extra extra read all the bad news
On the war or peace
That everybody would lose
The rise and fall of the last great empire
The sound of the whole world caught on fire
The ruthless struggle the desperate gamble
The games that left the whole world in shambles
The cheats the lies the alibis
And the foolish attempt to conquer the skies
Lost in space and what is it worth
The president just forgot about earth
Spending all time billions and maybe even trillions
Because the weapons ran in the zillions . . .
A fight for power a nuclear shower
The people shout out in the darkest hour
It's sights unseen and voices unheard
And finally the bomb gets the last word . . .
. . . We've got to suffer when things get rougher
And that's the reason why we've got to get tougher
So learn from the past and work for the future
Don't be a slave to no computer
'Cause the children of man inherit the land
And the future of the world is in your hands

While numerous examples of progressive trends in contemporary popular music might be proposed, it would be a gross misconstruction of the music industry to argue that such songs are representative of what young people are hearing on the airwaves today. In general, the popular-musical culture that greets young people has been rigorously molded by the demands of the capitalist marketplace, which measures its products according to their profit-making potential. While progressive messages sometimes manage to slip through the net of capitalist production, by and large the musical culture it advances promotes reified sexuality, crass individualism, and often violent, sexist, antiworking-class values. Many talented musicians ultimately destroy their artistic potential as they attempt to create music that conforms to what is deemed salable by the market. As Marx pointed out long ago in *Theories of Surplus Value*, "capitalist production is hostile to certain branches of spiritual production, namely poetry and art."[10]

We cannot expect mass popular art to express stronger and more efficacious progressive themes without the further development of an art movement philosophically and organizationally allied with people's struggles. In recent years, conscious political art has become increasingly evident. The importance of the Chicago Peace Museum, for example, should not be underestimated. Nor should the development of the national movement Artists' Call Against Intervention in Central America. This mobilization, which spread to twenty-five cities across the country, came as a response to an appeal from the Sandinista Cultural Workers' Association:

> May it go down in the history of humanity that one day during the twentieth century, in the face of the gigantic aggression that one of the smallest countries of the world, Nicaragua, was about to suffer, artists and intellectuals of different nationalities and generations raised along with us the banner of fraternity, in order to prevent our total destruction.[11]

In San Francisco alone, over two hundred artists participated in three major exhibitions. Funds collected nationwide by this movement were donated to the Association of Cultural Workers in Nicaragua, the University of El Salvador, a labor union in El Salvador, and to Guatemalan refugees. Another artists' movement in solidarity with Central America that emerged in the San Francisco Bay Area chose the name of PLACA, which means to make a mark, to leave a sign. They dedicated an entire street of murals with the theme of opposition to US intervention in Central America. In their manifesto, the artists and muralists proclaim:

> PLACA members do not ally themselves with this Administration's policy that has created death and war and despair, and that threatens more lives daily. We aim to demonstrate in visual/environmental terms, our solidarity, our respect, for the people of Central America.[12]

Similar to Artists' Call, a cultural movement in opposition to US support for the racist and fascist policies of the South African government declared October 1984 Art Against Apartheid Month. Exhibitions and cultural events advocating involvement in the campaign to free Nelson Mandela and all political prisoners in South Africa and Namibia were held throughout the New York City area and in other cities across the country. At the San Francisco Art Institute, a group of artists associated with the Art Against Apartheid movement organized a month-long festival in the spring of 1985 in solidarity with the people of South Africa.

One of the most exciting progressive cultural developments is the song movement, which has built musical bridges between the labor movement, the Afro-American movement, the solidarity struggles with Central America and South Africa, and the peace movement. Such politically committed musicians as Sweet Honey in the Rock, Holly Near, and Casselberry-Dupreé, have brought a keen awareness of these struggles into the women's movement. Bernice Johnson Reagon of Sweet Honey in the Rock has published numerous articles and delivered speeches appealing to those who support women's music to associate themselves with working-class struggles, antiracist movements, peace struggles, and solidarity work. And anyone familiar with Sweet Honey's songs can attest to the fact that they effectively and poignantly promote these coalition politics. Occupational health hazards – asbestosis, silicosis, brown-lung and black-lung disease – are the themes of "More Than a Paycheck," for example. In other songs, Sweet Honey evokes the civil-rights leader Fannie Lou Hamer and the murdered South African activist Steve Biko, and Mexican immigrants who fall prey to the repressive immigration laws of the United States. A recurring theme in their music is the need for all people to join together to prevent the outbreak of a nuclear war.

Sisterfire, the annual women's music festival in which Sweet Honey in the Rock has played an instrumental role, attempts to actualize the concept of coalition politics through cultural vehicles. In one of its manifestos, Sisterfire was described as

> a salutation to all women, working people, minorities and the poor who stand fast against dehumanizing political and economic systems.[13]

Moreover,

> culture, in its most valid form, expresses a mass or popular character. It must not be defined and perpetuated by an elite few for the benefit of a few. Culture must, of necessity, reflect and chart humanity's attempt to live in harmony with itself and nature. . . . We are building bridges between the women's movement and other movements for progressive social change. We are playing with fire, and we want nothing less from this event than to set loose the creative, fierce and awesome energies in all of you.[14]

Holly Near, who has been associated for many years with the women's music movement as well as with many other people's struggles, continues to encourage musicians to move beyond narrow social and political concerns and to promote justice for women and men of all races and nationalities. In 1984, she and Ronnie Gilbert did a "Dump Reagan" tour, which took them to twenty-five cities where they sang to over twenty-five thousand people. Another exemplary action in the bridge-building effort undertaken by the women's music movement was the song written by Betsy Rose for the mayoral campaign of black activist Mel King in Boston, entitled

"We May Have Come Here on Different Ships, but We're in the Same Boat Now."

Within the development of this song movement, Communists have played important roles. The Ad Hoc Singers, for example, who first came together during the 1980 presidential campaign, have brought to the movement songs that deepen the class consciousness of those who experience them. Their "People Before Profits," introduced during the first anti-Reagan campaign, is a virtual anthem of people's struggles. What is perhaps most important about the Ad Hoc Singers is that they bring to the song movement a dimension of concrete, activist experience in these struggles.

And, indeed, if we can anticipate the further expansion of people's culture today, it will be a direct function of the deepening and growing influence of mass movements. Progressive and revolutionary art is inconceivable outside of the context of political movements for radical change. If bold new art forms emerged with the Russian Revolution, the Cuban Revolution, and more recently the Sandinista and Grenada Revolutions, then we can be certain that if we accomplish the task before us today of strengthening and uniting our mass movements, our cultural life will flourish. Cultural workers must thus be concerned not only with the creation of progressive art, but must be actively involved in the organization of people's political movements. An exemplary relationship between art and struggle has been at the very core of the journal *Freedomways* – not only does it serve as a vehicle for the dissemination of progressive black literature, but it actively participates in the political struggles of Afro-Americans and their allies.

If cultural workers utilize their talents on an ever-increasing scale to accomplish the task of awakening and sensitizing people to the need for a mass challenge to the ultraright, the prospects for strengthening and further uniting the antimonopoly movement, bringing together labor, Afro-Americans, women, and peace activists will greatly increase. As that movement wins victories, existing artists will draw inspiration from the creative energy of this process, and new artists will emerge as a result. If we are able to set this dynamic in motion, we will begin to move securely in the direction of economic, racial, and sexual emancipation – indeed, toward the ultimate goal of socialism – and we will be able to anticipate a peaceful future, free of the threat of nuclear war.

NOTES

1   Paul Robeson, *Paul Robeson Speaks* (New Jersey: Citadel Press, 1978), 303–4.
2   Christopher Caudwell, *Studies in a Dying Culture* (New York: Monthly Review Press, 1971), 183.

3   Sidney Finkelstein, *How Music Expresses Ideas* (New York: International Press, 1971), 118.

4   James Cone, *The Spirituals and the Blues* (New York: Seabury Press, 1972), 115–16.

5   Phillip Bonosky, "The Thirties," *Political Affairs*, January 1959.

6   Ibid.

7   Ibid.

8   V. I. Lenin, "Party Organization and Party Literature," in *Lenin on Literature and Art* (Moscow: Progress Publishers, 1970), 24.

9   Ibid.

10 *Marx and Engels on Literature and Art* (Moscow: Progress Publishers, 1976), 141.

11 "Artists Call Against Intervention in Central America" (brochure, San Francisco, 1984).

12 PLACA Mural Group: General Statement (in brochure issued by PLACA, San Francisco, 1985).

13 "Sisterfire: Statement of Purpose" (leaflet issued by Sisterfire, Washington, D.C., 1982).

14 Ibid.

16

I Used To Be Your Sweet Mama: Ideology, Sexuality, and Domesticity

You had your chance and proved unfaithful
So now I'm gonna be real mean and hateful
I used to be your sweet mama, sweet papa
But now I'm just as sour as can be.

"I Used To Be Your Sweet Mama"[1]

Like most forms of popular music, African-American blues lyrics talk about love. However, what is distinctive about the blues, particularly in relation to other American popular music forms of the 1920s and 1930s, is its intellectual independence and representational freedom. One of the most obvious ways in which blues lyrics deviated from that era's established popular music culture was their provocative and pervasive sexual – including homosexual – imagery.[2]

By contrast, the popular song formulas of the period demanded saccharine and idealized non-sexual depictions of heterosexual love relationships.[3] Those aspects of lived love relationships that were not compatible with the dominant, etherealized ideology of love – such as extramarital relationships, domestic violence, and the ephemerality of many sexual partnerships – were largely banished from the established popular musical culture. These themes pervade the blues. What is even more striking is the fact that initially the professional performers of this music – the most widely heard individual purveyors of the blues – were women. Bessie Smith earned the title "Empress of the Blues" not least through the sale of three-quarters of a million copies of her first record.[4]

The historical context within which the blues developed a tradition of openly addressing both female and male sexuality reveals an ideological framework that was specifically African American.[5] Emerging during the decades following the abolition of slavery, the blues gave musical expression to the new social and sexual realities encountered by African Americans as free women and men. The former slaves' economic status had not undergone a radical transformation – they were no less impoverished than they had been during slavery.[6] It was the status of their personal relationships that was revolutionized. For the first time in the history of the African presence in North America, masses of black women and men were in a position to make autonomous decisions regarding the sexual partnerships into which they entered.[7] Sexuality thus was one of the most tangible domains in which emancipation was acted upon, and through which its meanings were expressed. Sovereignty in sexual matters marked an important divide between life during slavery and life after emancipation.

Themes of individual sexual love rarely appear in the music forms produced during slavery. Whatever the reasons for this – and it may have been due to the slave system's economic management of procreation, which did not tolerate, and often severely punished, the public exhibition of self-initiated sexual relationships – I am interested here in the disparity between the individualistic, "private" nature of sexuality and the collective forms and nature of the music that was produced and performed during slavery. Sexuality after emancipation could not be adequately expressed or addressed through the musical forms existing under slavery. The spirituals and the work songs confirm that the individual concerns of black people given musical expression during slavery centered on a collective desire for an end to the system declaring them unconditional slaves to their white masters. This does not mean there was an absence of sexual meanings in the music produced by African-American slaves.[8] It means that slave music – both religious and secular – was quintessentially collective music. It was collectively performed and it gave expression to the community's yearning for freedom.[9]

The blues, on the other hand, the predominant post-slavery African-American musical form, articulated a new valuation of individual emotional needs and desires. The birth of the blues was aesthetic evidence of new psycho-social realities within the black population. This music was presented by individuals singing alone, accompanying themselves on such instruments as the banjo or guitar. The blues therefore marked the advent of a popular culture of performance, with the borders of performer and audience becoming increasingly differentiated.[10] Through the emergence of the professional blues singer – a predominantly female figure accompanied by small and large instrumental ensembles – as part of the rise of the black entertainment industry, this individualized mode of presenting popular music crystallized into a performance culture that has had an enduring influence on African-American music.

The spirituals, as they survived and were transformed during the post-slavery era, were both intensely religious and the aesthetic bearers of the slaves' collective aspirations for worldly freedom.[11] Under changed historical circumstances in which former slaves had closer contact with the religious practices and ideologies of the dominant culture, sacred music began to be increasingly enclosed within institutionalized religious spaces. Slave religious practices were inseparable from other aspects of everyday life – work, family, sabotage, escape. Post-slavery religion gradually lost some of this fluidity and came to be dependent on the church. As sacred music evolved from spirituals to gospel, it increasingly concentrated on the hereafter. Historian Lawrence Levine characterizes the nature of this development succinctly. "The overriding thrust of the gospel songs," he writes,

> was otherworldly. Emphasis was almost wholly upon God with whom Man's relationship was one of total dependence. . . . Jesus rather than the Hebrew children dominated the gospel songs. And it was not the warrior Jesus of the spirituals but a benevolent spirit who promised His children rest and peace and justice in the hereafter.[12]

The blues rose to become the most prominent secular genre in early twentieth-century black American music. As it came to displace sacred music in the everyday lives of black people, it both reflected and helped to construct a new black consciousness. This consciousness interpreted God as the opposite of the Devil, religion as the not secular, and the secular as largely sexual. With the blues came the designations "God's music" and the "Devil's music." The former was performed in church – although it could also accompany work[13] – while the latter was performed in jook joints, circuses, and traveling shows.[14]

Despite the new salience of this binary opposition in the everyday life of black people, it is important to underscore the close relationship between the old music and the new. The new music had old roots, and the old music reflected a new ideological grounding of black religion. Both were deeply rooted in the same history and culture.

God and the Devil had co-habited the same universe during slavery, not as polar opposites, but rather as complex characters who had different powers and who both entered into relationships with human beings. They also sometimes engaged with each other on fairly equal terms. As Henry Louis Gates and others have argued, the Devil was often associated with the trickster god Legba or Eleggua in Yoruba religions.[15] Some of the folk tales Zora Neale Hurston presents in *Mules and Men* portray the devil not as evil incarnate, but as a character with whom it was possible to identify in humorous situations.[16]

In describing the religious household in which she was reared, veteran blueswoman Ida Goodson emphasizes that the blues were banned from her childhood home. Nevertheless, she and her playmates often played and sang the blues when her parents were away. On those occasions when the parents showed up unexpectedly, they easily made the transition to gospel music without missing a beat:

> My mother and father were religious persons. And they liked music, but they like church music. They didn't like jazz like we do. And of course we could not even play jazz in our home while they were there. But just the moment they would turn their back, go to their society or church somewhere or another, we'd get our neighborhood children to come in there and we'd get to playing the blues and having a good time. But still we'd have one girl on the door watching to see when Mr. Goodson's coming back home or Mrs. Goodson. Because I knew if they came and caught us what we would get. . . . Whenever we'd see my father or my mother coming back home, the girl be saying, "There come Mr. Goodson 'nem." And they'd be so close up on us, we'd change the blues, singing "Jesus keep me near the cross." After that my mother and father would join us and we'd all get to singing church songs.[17]

As if reconciling the two positions – that of herself as a young musician and that of her religious parents – Goodson later explains that "The Devil got his work and God got his work."

During slavery, the sacred universe was virtually all-embracing. Spirituals helped to construct community among the slaves and infused this imagined community with hope for a better life. They retold Old Testament narratives about the Hebrew people's struggle against Pharaoh's oppression, and thereby established a community narrative of African people enslaved in North America that simultaneously transcended the slave system and encouraged its abolition. Under the conditions of US slavery, the sacred – and especially sacred music – was an important means of preserving African cultural memory. Karl Marx's comments on religion as the "opium of the people"[18] notwithstanding, the spirituals attest to the fact that religious consciousness can itself play a transformative role. As Sojourner Truth and other abolitionists demonstrated – as well as insurrectionary leaders Nat Turner and Denmark Vesey, and the Underground Railroad conductor Harriet Tubman – religion was far more than Marx's "illusory sun." Spirituals were embedded in and gave expression to a powerful yearning for freedom.[19] Religion was indeed, in Marx's words, the "soul" of "soulless conditions."[20]

The spirituals articulated the hopes of black slaves in religious terms. In the vast disappointment that accompanied emancipation – when economic and political liberation must have seemed more unattainable than ever – blues created a discourse[21] that represented freedom in more immediate and accessible terms. The material conditions for the freedom about which the slaves had sung in their spirituals seemed no closer after slavery than they had seemed before, but there were nevertheless distinct differences between the slaves' personal status under slavery and during the post-Civil War period. In three major respects, emancipation had radically transformed their personal lives: (1) there was no longer a proscription on free individual travel; (2) education was now a realizable goal for individual men and women; (3) sexuality could be explored freely by individuals who now could enter into autonomously chosen personal relationships. The new blues consciousness was shaped by and gave expression to at least two of these three transformations: travel and sexuality. In both male and female blues, travel and sexuality are ubiquitous themes, handled both separately and together. But what finally is most striking is the way the blues registered sexuality as a tangible expression of freedom; it was this dimension that most profoundly marked and defined the secularity of the blues.

James Cone offers the following definition of the blues, agreeing with C. Eric Lincoln's succinct characterization of them as "secular spirituals." Cone writes,

> They are secular in the same sense that they confine their attention solely to the immediate and affirm the bodily expression of black soul, including its sexual manifestations. They are spirituals because they are impelled by the same search for the truth of black experience.[22]

It is not necessary to accede to Cone's essentialist invocation of a single metaphysical "truth" of black experience to gain from it a key insight into why the blues were condemned as the Devil's music. It was because they drew upon and incorporated sacred consciousness and thereby posed a serious threat to religious attitudes.

Levine emphasizes the blurring of the sacred and the secular both in gospel music and in the blues. It may not have been the secularity of the blues that produced such castigation by the church, he argues, but rather, precisely their sacred nature. He writes,

> The blues was threatening not primarily because it was secular; other forms of secular music were objected to less strenuously and often not al all. Blues was threatening because its spokesmen and its ritual too frequently provided the expressive communal channels of relief that had been largely the province of religion in the past.[23]

Although both Cone and Levine make references to Mamie Smith, Ma Rainey, Bessie Smith, and other women who composed and performed blues songs, they, like most scholars, tend to view women as marginal to the production of the blues. Note that in the passage quoted above, Levine refers quite explicitly to the "spokesmen" of the blues. With the simple substitution of "spokeswomen," the argument he suggests would become more compelling and more deeply revealing of the new religious consciousness about which he writes.

Blues practices, as Levine asserts, did tend to appropriate previously religious channels of expression and this appropriation was associated with women's voices. Women summoned sacred responses to their messages about sexuality.[24] During this period, religious consciousness came increasingly under the control of institutionalized churches, and male dominance over the religious process came to be taken for granted. At the same time that male ministers were becoming a professional caste, women blues singers were performing as professional artists and attracting large audiences in revival-like gatherings. Gertrude "Ma" Rainey and Bessie Smith were the most widely known of these women. They preached about sexual love, and in doing so they articulated a collective experience of freedom, and gave voice to the most powerful evidence there was for many black people that slavery no longer existed.

The expression of socially unfulfilled dreams in the language and imagery of individual sexual love is, of course, not peculiar to the African-American experience. As part of the capitalist schism between the public and the private realms within European-derived American popular culture, however, themes of romantic love had quite different ideological implications from themes of sexuality within post-slavery African-American cultural expression. In the context of the consolidation of industrial capitalism, the sphere of personal love and domestic life in mainstream American culture came to be increasingly idealized as the arena in which happiness was to be sought.[25] This held a special significance for women, since love and domesticity were supposed to constitute the outermost limits of their lives. Full membership in the public community was the exclusive domain of men. Therefore, European-American popular songs have to be interpreted within this context and as contributing to patriarchal hegemony.

The blues did not entirely escape the influences that shaped the role of romantic love in the popular songs of the dominant culture. Nevertheless, the incorporation of personal relationships into the blues has its own historical meanings and social and political resonances. Love was not represented as an idealized realm to which unfulfilled dreams of happiness were relegated. The historical African-American vision of individual sexual love linked it inextricably with possibilities of social freedom in the economic and political realms. Unfreedom during slavery involved, among other things, a prohibition of freely chosen, enduring family relationships. Because slaves were legally defined as commodities, women of childbearing age were valued in accordance with their breeding potential and were often forced to copulate with men – viewed as "bucks" – chosen by their owners for the sole purpose of producing valuable progeny.[26] Moreover, direct sexual exploitation of African women by their white masters was a constant feature of slavery.[27] What tenuous permanence in familial relationships the slaves did manage to construct was always subject to the whim of their masters and the potential profits to be reaped from sale. The suffering caused by forced ruptures of slave families has been abundantly documented.[28]

Given this context, it is understandable that the personal and sexual dimensions of freedom acquired an expansive importance, especially since the economic and political ingredients of freedom were largely denied to black people in the aftermath of slavery. The focus on sexual love in blues music was thus quite different in meaning from the prevailing idealization of romantic love mainstream popular culture. For recently emancipated slaves, freely chosen sexual love became a mediator between historical disappointment and the new social realities of an evolving African-American community. Ralph Ellison alludes to this dimension of the blues, I think, when he notes that "their mysteriousness . . . their ability to imply far more than they state outright and their capacity to make the details of sex convey meanings which touch on the metaphysical."[29]

Sexuality was central in both men's and women's blues. During the earliest phases of their history, blues were essentially a male phenomenon. The archetypal blues singer was a solitary wandering man accompanied by his banjo or guitar, and, in the words of blues scholar Giles Oakley, his principal theme "is the sexual relationship. Almost all other themes, leaving town, train rides, work trouble, general dissatisfaction sooner or later reverts to the central concern."[30] In women's blues, which became a crucial element of the rising black entertainment industry, there was an even more pronounced emphasis on love and sexuality.

The representations of love and sexuality in women's blues often blatantly contradicted mainstream ideological assumptions regarding women and being in love. They also challenged the notion that women's "place" was in the domestic sphere. Such notions were based on the social realities of middle-class white women's lives, but were incongruously applied to all women, regardless of race or class.[31] This led to inevitable contradictions between prevailing social expectations and black women's social realities. Women of that era were expected to seek fulfillment within the confines of marriage, with their husbands functioning as provider and their children as evidence of their worth as human beings. The sparsity of allusions to marriage and domesticity in women's blues therefore becomes highly significant.

In Bessie Smith's rendition of "Sam Jones Blues" – which contains one of the few commentaries on the subject of marriage to be found in her body of work – the subject is acknowledged only in relation to its dissolution. Her performance of this song satirically accentuates the contrast between the dominant cultural construction of marriage and the stance of economic independence black women were compelled to assume for their sheer survival. Referring to a wandering husband, Bessie Smith sings,

> . . . I'm free and livin' all alone
> Say, hand me the key that unlocks my front door
> Because that bell don't read "Sam Jones" no more
> No, you ain't talkin' to Mrs Jones, you speaking to Miss Wilson now.[32]

Although the written lyrics reveal a conversation between "proper" English and black working-class English, only by listening to the song do we experience the full impact of Smith's manipulation of language in her recording. References to marriage as perceived by the dominant white culture are couched in irony. She mocks the notion of eternal matrimony – "I used to be your lofty mate" – singing genteel words with a teasing intonation to evoke white cultural conceptions. On the other hand, when she indicates the perspective of the black woman, Miss Wilson – who "used to be Mrs Jones" – she sings in a comfortable, bluesy black English. This song is remarkable for the way Smith translates into musical contrast and contention the clash between two cultures' perceptions of marriage – and particularly women's place within the institution. It is easy to imagine the testifying responses Smith no doubt evoked in her female audiences, responses that affirmed working-class black women's sense of themselves as relatively emancipated if not from marriage itself then at least from some of its most confining ideological constraints.

The protagonists in women's blues are seldom wives and almost never mothers. One explanation for the absence of direct allusions to marriage may be the different words mainstream and African-American cultures use to designate "male spouse." African-American working-class argot refers to both husbands and male lovers (and even in some cases female lovers) as "my man" or "my daddy." But these different linguistic practices cannot be considered in isolation from the social realities they represent, for they point to divergent perspectives regarding the institution of marriage.

During Bessie Smith's era most black heterosexual couples – married or not – had children. However, blues women rarely sang about mothers, fathers, and children. In the subject index to her book *Black Pearls*, black studies scholar Daphne Duval Harrison lists the following themes: advice to other women; alcohol; betrayal or abandonment; broken or failed love affairs; death; departure; dilemma of staying with man or returning to family; disease and afflictions; erotica; hell; homosexuality; infidelity; injustice; jail and serving time; loss of lover; love; men; mistreatment; murder;

other woman; poverty; promiscuity; sadness; sex; suicide; supernatural; trains; traveling; unfaithfulness; vengeance; weariness, depression and disillusionment; weight loss.[33] It is revealing that she does not include children, domestic life, husband, and marriage.

The absence of the mother figure in the blues does not imply a rejection of motherhood as such, but rather suggests that blues women found the cult of motherhood irrelevant to the realities of their lives.[34] The female figures evoked in women's blues are independent women free of the domestic orthodoxy of the prevailing representations of womanhood through which female subjects of the era were constructed. . . .

★   ★   ★   ★   ★

The woman in Ma Rainey's "Lawd Send Me a Man Blues" harbors no illusions about the relationship she desires with a man. She is lonely and is wondering "who gonna pay my board bill now." Appealing for any man she can get, she pleads, singing with a bluesy zeal,

> Send me a zulu, a voodoo, any old man
> I'm not particular, boys, I'll take what I can.[35]

Bessie Smith's "Baby Doll" conveys a similar message:

> I want to be somebody's baby doll
> So I can get my loving all the time
> I want to be somebody's baby doll
> To ease my mind.[36]

These blues women had no qualms about announcing female desire. Their songs express women's intention to "get their loving." Such affirmations of sexual autonomy and open expressions of female sexual desire give historical voice to possibilities of equality not articulated elsewhere. Women's blues and the cultural politics lived out in the careers of the blues queens put these new possibilities on the historical agenda. . . .

By focusing on the issue of misogynist violence, the first activist moments of the contemporary women's movement exposed the centrality of the ideological separation of the public and private spheres to the structure of male domination. In the early 1970s women began to speak publicly about their experiences of rape, battery, and about the violation of their reproductive rights. Obscured by a shroud of silence, these assaults against women traditionally had been regarded as a fact of private life to be shielded at all costs from scrutiny in the public sphere. That this cover-up would no longer be tolerated was the explosive meaning behind feminists' defiant notion that "the personal is political."[37]

The performances of the classic blues women – especially Bessie Smith – were one of the few cultural spaces in which a tradition of public discourse on male violence had been previously established. One explanation for the fact that the blues women of the 1920s – and the texts they present – fail to respect the taboo on speaking publicly about domestic violence is that the blues as a genre never acknowledges the discursive and ideological boundaries separating the private sphere from the public. Historically, there has been no body of literature on battering because white, well-to-do women who were in a position to write about their experiences in abusive relationships have only recently been convinced that such privately executed violence is a suitable subject for public discourse.

There is, however, a body of preserved oral culture – or "orature," to use a term employed by some scholars[38] – about domestic abuse in the songs of blues women like Gertrude Rainey and Bessie Smith. Violence against women was always an appropriate topic of women's blues. The contemporary urge to break the silence surrounding misogynist violence, and the organized political movement challenging violence against women has an aesthetic precursor in the work of the classic blues singers.

Women's blues have been accused of promoting acquiescent and therefore anti-feminist responses to misogynist abuse. It is true that some of the songs recorded by Rainey and Smith seem to exemplify acceptance of male violence – and sometimes even masochistic delight in being the target of lovers' beatings. Such claims do not take into account the extent to which blues meaning is manipulated and transformed – sometimes even into its opposite – in blues performance. Blues make abundant use of humor, satire, and irony, revealing their historic roots in slave music, wherein indirect methods of expression were the only means by which the oppression of slavery could be denounced. In this sense, the blues genre is a direct descendant of work songs, which often relied on indirection and irony to highlight the inhumanity of slave owners so that their targets were sure to misunderstand the intended meaning.[39]

Bessie Smith sings a number of songs whose lyrics may be interpreted as condoning emotional and physical abuse as attendant hazards for women involved in sexual partnerships. But close attention to her musical presentation of these songs persuades the listener that they contain implicit critiques of male abuse. In "Yes Indeed He Do," Bessie Smith's sarcastic presentation of the lyrics transforms their observations on an unfaithful, abusive and exploitative lover into a scathing critique of male violence:

> Is he true as stars above me? What kind of fool is you?
> He don't stay from home all night more than six times a week
> No, I known that I'm his Sheba and I know that he's my sheik
> And when I ask him where he's been he grabs a rocking chair
> Then he knocks me down and says it's just a love lick dear.[40]

Edward Brooks, in *The Bessie Smith Companion*, makes the following comment about this song:

> Bessie delivers the song with growling gusto, as if it were really a panegyric to an exemplary lover; she relates his wrongs with the approval of virtues and it comes as a jolt when the exultation in her voice is compared with her actual words.[41]

Brooks's analysis assumes that Smith was unselfconscious in her performance of this song. He therefore misses its intentional ambiguity and complexity. Smith was an accomplished performer, actor and comedian and was therefore well acquainted with the uses of humor and irony. It is much more plausible to characterize her decision to sing "Yes Indeed He Do" with mock praise and elation as a conscious effort to highlight, in the most effective way possible, the inhumanity and misogyny of male batterers. . . .

The female characters memorialized in women's blues songs, even in their most despairing moods, do not fit the mold of the typical victim of abuse. The independent women of blues lore are women who do not think twice about wielding weapons against men who they feel have mistreated them. They frequently brandish their razors and guns, and dare men to cross the lines they draw. While acknowledging the physical mistreatment they have received at the hands of their male lovers, they do not perceive or define themselves as powerless in face of such violence. Indeed, they fight back passionately. In many songs Ma Rainey and Bessie Smith pay tribute to fearless women who attempt to avenge themselves when their lovers have been unfaithful. In "Black Mountain Blues," Bessie Smith sings:

> He met a city gal and he throwed me down
> I'm bound for Black Mountain, me and my razor and my gun
> Lord I'm bound for Black Mountain, me and my razor and my gun
> I'm gonna shoot him if he stands still and cut him if he run.[42]

In Smith's "Sinful Blues," a woman's rage also turns into violence:

> Gonna get me a gun long as my right arm
> Shoot that man because he done me wrong.
> Lord, now I've got them sinful blues.[43]

In Ma Rainey's "See See Rider Blues," the protagonist, who has discovered that her man has another woman friend, announces her intention to buy herself a pistol and to "kill my man and catch the Cannonball."[44] Her concluding resolution is: "If he don't have me, he won't have no gal at all."

In Rainey's "Rough and Tumble Blues," the woman attacks not the man, but the women who have attempted to seduce him:

> I got rough and killed three women 'fore the police got the news
> 'Cause mama's on the warpath with these rough and tumble blues.[45]

The lives of many of the blues women of the twenties resembled those of the fearless women memorialized in their songs. We know that at times Bessie Smith was a victim of male violence and also that she would not hesitate to hurl violent threats – which she sometimes carried out – at the men who betrayed her. Nor was she afraid to confront the most feared embodiments of white racist terror. One evening in July of 1927, robed and hooded Ku Klux Klansmen attempted to disrupt her tent performance by pulling up the tent stakes and collapsing the entire structure. When Smith was informed of the trouble, she immediately left the tent and, according to her biographer:

> . . . ran toward the intruders, stopped within ten feet of them, placed one hand on her hip, and shook a clenched fist at the Klansmen. "What the fuck you think you're doin'," she shouted above the sound of the band. "I'll get the whole damn tent out here if I have to. You just pick up them sheets and run!"
>
> The Klansmen, apparently too surprised to move, just stood there and gawked. Bessie hurled obscenities at them until they finally turned and disappeared quietly into the darkness . . .
>
> Then she went back into the tent as if she had just settled a routine matter.[46]

Blues women were expected to deviate from the norms defining orthodox female behavior, which is why they were revered by both men and women in black working-class communities. Ida Cox's "Wild Women Don't Have the Blues" became the most famous portrait of the nonconforming, independent woman, and her "wild woman" has become virtually synonymous with the blues queen herself:

> Wild women don't worry, wild women don't have the blues
> You never get nothing by being an angel child
> You'd better change your ways and get real wild.[47]

"Prove It On Me Blues," composed by Gertrude Rainey, portrays just such a "wild woman," who affirms her independence from the orthodox norms of womanhood by boldly flaunting her lesbianism. Rainey's sexual involvement with women was no secret among her colleagues and her audiences. The advertisement for the release of "Prove It On Me Blues" showed the blues woman sporting a man's hat, jacket and tie and, while a policeman looked on, obviously attempting to seduce two women on a street corner. The song's lyrics include the following:

> Went out last night with a crowd of my friends
> They must've been women 'cause I don't like no men . . .
>
> Wear my clothes just like a fan
> Talk to the gals just like any old man.[48]

Sandra Lieb has described this song as a "powerful statement of lesbian defiance and self-worth.[49] "Prove It On Me Blues" is a cultural precursor to the lesbian cultural movement of the 1970s, which, it is interesting to note, began to crystallize around the performance and recording of lesbian-affirming songs. (In fact, in 1977, Teresa Trull recorded a cover of Ma Rainey's song for an album entitled *Lesbian Concentrate.*[50])

Hazel Carby has insightfully observed that "Prove It On Me Blues"

> vacillates between the subversive hidden activity of women loving women [and] a public declaration of lesbianism. The words express a contempt for a society that rejected lesbians. . . . But at the same time the song is a reclamation of lesbianism as long as the woman publicly names her sexual preference for herself. . . .

Carby argues that this song "engag[es] directly in defining issues of sexual preference as a contradictory struggle of social relations."[51]

"Prove It On Me Blues" suggests how the iconoclastic blueswomen of the twenties were pioneers for later historical developments. The response to this song also suggests that homophobia within the black community did not prevent blues women from challenging stereotypical conceptions of women's lives. They did not allow themselves to be enshrined by the silence imposed by mainstream society.

The blues songs recorded by Gertrude Rainey and Bessie Smith offer us a privileged glimpse of the prevailing perceptions of love and sexuality in post-slavery black communities in the United States. Both women were role models for untold thousands of their sisters to whom they delivered messages that defied the male dominance encouraged by mainstream culture. The blues women openly challenged the gender politics implicit in traditional cultural representations of marriage and heterosexual love relationships. Refusing, in the blues tradition of raw realism, to romanticize romantic relationships, they instead exposed the stereotypes and explored the contradictions of those relationships. By so doing, they redefined women's "place." They forged and memorialized images of tough, resilient and independent women who were afraid neither of their own vulnerability nor of defending their right to be respected as autonomous human beings.

NOTES

1   Bessie Smith, "I Used to Be Your Sweet Mama," Columbia 14292-D, Feb. 9, 1928. Reissued on *Empty Bed Blues*, Columbia CG 30450, 1972.
2   According to Hazel Carby, "[w]hat has been called the 'Classic Blues,' the women's blues of the twenties and early thirties, is a discourse that articulates a cultural and political struggle over sexual relations: a struggle that is directed against the objectification of female sexuality within a patriarchal order but which also tries to reclaim women's bodies as the sexual and sensuous objects of song." "It Just Be's Dat Way Sometime: The Sexual Politics of Women's Blues," *Radical America*, 20, no. 4 (June–July 1986), 12.
3   See Henry Pleasants, *The Great American Popular Singers* (New York: Simon & Schuster, 1974). According to Lawrence Levine, "the physical side of love which, aside from some tepid hand holding and lip pecking, was largely missing from popular music, was strongly felt in the blues." *Black Culture and Black Consciousness: Afro-American Thought from Slavery to Freedom* (New York: Oxford University Press, 1975), 279.
4   Bessie Smith's first recording, a cover of Alberta Hunter's "Down Hearted Blues," sold 780,000 copies in less than six months. Chris Albertson, *Bessie* (New York: Stein & Day, 1972), 46.
5   The central place of the blues in the elaboration of a post-slavery black cultural consciousness has been examined widely in works like LeRoi Jones's pioneering *Blues People* and Lawrence Levine's engaging study *Black Culture and Black Consciousness*. While both suggest important approaches to the understanding of racial dimensions of African-American culture, scant attention is accorded gender consciousness. Daphne Duval Harrison's trailblazing study *Black Pearls: Blues Queens of the 1920s* (New Brunswick: Rutgers University Press, 1988) reveals, in fact, how rich women's blues can be as a terrain for explorations of the place gender occupies in black cultural consciousness.
6   See W. E. B. Du Bois, *Black Reconstruction in America* (New York: Harcourt, Brace, 1935).
7   See Herbert Gutman, *The Black Family in Slavery and Freedom, 1750–1925* (New York: Pantheon, 1976), ch. 9.
8   Lawrence Levine cites a rowing song heard by Frances Kemble in the late 1830s and characterized by her as nonsensical, but interpreted by Chadwick Hansen as containing hidden sexual meanings.

> Jenny shake her toe at me,
>   Jenny gone away;
> Jenny shake her toe at me,
>   Jenny gone away.

Hurrah! Miss Susy, oh!
  Jenny gone away;
Hurrah! Miss Susy, oh!
  Jenny gone away.

Levine, *Black Culture and Black Consciousness*, p. 11. (Frances Anne Kemble, *Journal of a Residence on a Georgian Plantation in 1838–1839* [1863; reprint, New York: Knopf, 1961], 163–4.) "Chadwick Hansen [in "Jenny's Toe: Negro Shaking Dances in America," *American Quarterly*, 19 (1967), 554–63] has shown that in all probability what Miss Kemble heard was not the English word 'toe' but an African-derived word referring to the buttocks." The Jenny of whom the slaves were singing with such obvious pleasure was shaking something more interesting and provocative than her foot.

9   According to James Cone, "The spiritual . . . is the spirit of the people struggling to be free . . . [it] is the people's response to the societal contradictions. It is the people facing trouble and affirming, 'I ain't tired yet.' But the spiritual is more than dealing with trouble. It is a joyful experience, a vibrant affirmation of life and its possibilities in an appropriate esthetic form. The spiritual is the community in rhythm, swinging to the movement of life." *The Spirituals and the Blues: An Interpretation* (New York: Seabury, 1972), 32–3.

10   Popular musical culture in the African-American tradition continues to actively involve the audience in the performance of the music. The distinction, therefore, is not between the relatively active and relatively passive stances of the audience. Rather it is between a mode of musical presentation in which everyone involved is considered a "performer" – or perhaps in which no one, the song leader included, is considered a "performer" – and one in which the producer of the music plays a privileged role in calling forth the responses of the audience.

11   See James Cone's discussion of the liberation content of the spirituals. John Lovell, Jr (*Black Song: The Forge and the Flame*, New York: Macmillan, 1972) also emphasizes the relationship between the slave community's yearning for liberation and the music it produced in the religious tradition of Christianity.

12   Levine, *Black Culture and Black Consciousness*, 175.

13   Religious themes are to be found in some of the prison work songs recorded by folklorists such as Alan Lomax during the thirties, forties, and fifties.

14   See Giles Oakley, *The Devil's Music: A History of the Blues* (New York and London: Harcourt Brace Jovanovich, 1976), 97–9.

15   See Henry Louis Gates, Jr, *The Signifying Monkey: A Theory of African-American Literary Criticism* (New York: Oxford University Press, 1988), ch. 1.

16   See Zora Neale Hurston, *Mules and Men* (Bloomington: Indiana University Press, 1978), stories on Jack and the Devil, 164, and about "unh hunh" as a word the Devil made up, 169.

17   *Wild Women Don't Have the Blues*, dir. Christine Dall, Calliope Film Resources, 1989, videocassette.

18   When applied to the religious contours and content of slave-initiated cultural community, the infamous observation by the young Karl Marx that religion is the "opium of the people" elucidates the utopian potential of slave religion;

but, in this context, Marx's observation simultaneously goes too far and not far enough.

> *Religious* suffering is at the same time an *expression* of real suffering and a protest against real suffering. Religion is the sigh of the oppressed creature, the sentiment of a heartless world, and the soul of soulless conditions. It is the *opium* of the people. . . . Religion is only the illusory sun around which man revolves so long as he does not revolve around himself.

Karl Marx, "The Critique of Hegel's Philosophy of Right," in Karl Marx, *Early Writings*, ed. T. B. Bottomore (New York: McGraw-Hill, 1963), 43–4.

Marx goes too far in the sense that he assumes a necessarily and exclusively ideological relationship between religious consciousness and material conditions, i.e., that religion is fundamentally false consciousness and that the "self" or community it articulates is necessarily an illusion. Such an all-embracing conception of religion cannot account for its extra-religious dimensions. On the other hand, he does not go far enough when he dismisses the revolutionary potential of religious consciousness.

19 See Lovell, *Black Song*, chs 17 and 18.

20 Marx, "Critique of Hegel's Philosophy," 44.

21 See Houston A. Baker, Jr, *Blues, Ideology, and Afro-American Literature* (Chicago: University of Chicago Press, 1984).

22 Cone, *The Spirituals and the Blues*, 112. C. Eric Lincoln originated the term "secular spirituals."

23 Levine, *Black Culture and Black Consciousness*, 237.

24 Julio Finn argues that "the jook joint is to the blues what the church is to the spiritual, and the bluesman on stage is in his pulpit. Contrary to the 'holy' atmosphere which reigns in the church, the jook joint is characterized by its rowdiness – the noise and smoke and drinking are necessities without which its character would be fatally altered, for that would alter the music, which is in no small way shaped by it." Julio Finn, *The Bluesman* (London: Quartet, 1986), 202. Unfortunately, Finn confines his discussion to blues men and does not consider the role of women.

25 See Joan Landes, "The Public and the Private Sphere: A Feminist Reconsideration," in Johanna Meehan (ed.), *Feminists Read Habermas* (London: Routledge, 1995). According to Aida Hurtado in "Relating to Privilege: Seduction and Rejection in the Subordination of White Women and Women of Color" (*Signs: A Journal of Women and Culture in Society*, 14, no. 4 [Summer 1989]), "the public/private distinction is relevant only for the white middle and upper classes since historically the American state has intervened constantly in the private lives and domestic arrangements of the working class. Women of Color have not had the benefit of the economic conditions that underlie the public/private distinction. Instead the political consciousness of women of Color stems from an awareness that the public is *personally* political."

26 Du Bois points out that in many border states, slave-breeding became a main industry: "The deliberate breeding of a strong, big field-hand stock could be

carried out by selecting proper males, and giving them the run of the likeliest females. This in many Border States became a regular policy and fed the slave trade." *Black Reconstruction in America*, 44.

27 Gutman, *The Black Family*, 80, 388.

28 Slave narratives by Frederick Douglass, Solomon Northrup, and Harriet Jacobs contain poignant descriptions of family separations. See also Gutman, *The Black Family*, ch. 8.

29 Ralph Ellison, *Shadow and Act* (New York: Vintage, 1972), 245.

30 Oakley, *The Devil's Music*, 59.

31 Angela Y. Davis, *Women, Race, and Class* (New York: Random House, 1981).

32 Bessie Smith, "Sam Jones Blues," Columbia 13005-D, Sept. 24, 1923. Reissued on *Any Woman's Blues*, Columbia G 30126, 1972.

33 Harrison, *Black Pearls*, 287.

34 See Mary P. Ryan's discussion of the cult of motherhood in *Womanhood in America: From Colonial Times to the Present* (New York: Franklin Watts, 1975).

35 Gertrude "Ma" Rainey, "Lawd, Send Me a Man Blues," Paramount 12227, May 1924. Reissued on *Queen of the Blues*, Biograph BLP-12032, n.d.

36 Bessie Smith, "Baby Doll," Columbia 14147-D, May 4, 1926. Reissued on *Nobody's Blues but Mine*, Columbia CG 31093, 1972.

37 See Sara Evans's study, *Personal Politics: The Roots of Women's Liberation in the Civil Rights Movement and the New Left* (New York: Knopf, 1979).

38 See Michere Githae Mugo, *Orature and Human Rights* (Rome: Institute of South African Development Studies, NUL, Lesotho, 1991).

39 See Oakley's discussion of work and song, *The Devil's Music*, 36–46.

40 Bessie Smith, "Yes, Indeed He Do."

41 Edward Brooks, *The Bessie Smith Companion* (New York: Da Capo, 1982), 143.

42 Bessie Smith, "Black Mountain Blues," Columbia 14554-D, June 22, 1930. Reissued on *The World's Greatest Blues Singer*, Columbia CG 33, 1972.

43 Bessie Smith, "Sinful Blues," Columbia 114052-D, Dec. 11, 1924. Reissued on *The Empress*, Columbia CG 30818, 1972.

44 Gertrude "Ma" Rainey, "See See Rider Blues," Paramount 12252, Dec. 1925. Reissued on *Ma Rainey*, Milestone M-47021, 1974.

45 Gertrude "Ma" Rainey, "Rough and Tumble Blues," Paramount 12303, 1928. Reissued on *The Immortal Ma Rainey*, Milestone MLP 2001, 1966.

46 Albertson, *Bessie*, 132–3.

47 Ida Cox, "Wild Women Don't Have the Blues," Paramount 12228, 1924. Reissued on *Wild Women Don't Have the Blues*, Riverside RLP 9374, n.d.

48 Gertrude "Ma" Rainey, "Prove It On Me Blues," Paramount 12668, June 1928. Reissued on *Ma Rainey*, Milestone M-47021, 1974.

49 Sandra Lieb, 125.

50 *Lesbian Concentrate: A Lesbianthology of Songs and Poems*. Ouvia Records MU 29729, 1977.

51 Carby, "It Just Be's Dat Way Sometime," 18.

17

Underexposed: Photography and Afro-American History

In 1969, the Metropolitan Museum of Art presented an exhibition entitled "Harlem on My Mind: Cultural Capital of Black America, 1900–1968." According to its coordinator, Allon Schoener, the exhibition "could be one of the most important . . . to have been presented in an art museum in the twentieth century because it redefined the role and responsibility of museums, their audiences, and the types of exhibitions they could present."[1] Nonetheless black community activists organized a protest to mark the opening of the show. Among those who marched on the picket line was one of the most prominent contemporary Afro-American photographers of the time, Roy DeCarava, who strongly challenged the merits of "Harlem on My Mind":

> It is evident from the physical makeup of the show that Schoener and company have no respect for or understanding of photography, or, for that matter, any of the other media that they employed. I would also say that they have no great love for or understanding of Harlem, black people or history.[2]

The controversy unleashed by this exhibition – which was no doubt a sincere attempt to break the cycle of racism within the US art establishment – revealed deeper influences of racism even on apparently progressive cultural perceptions and definitions.

If it were possible to consider "Harlem on My Mind" – the exhibition and the subsequently published book – an unqualified success, even this would not have begun to reverse the conspicuous sparsity of images depicting Afro-American life within the recorded history of photography. There have indeed been a few important moments such as Frances Benjamin Johnston's photographic documentation of Hampton Institute around the turn of the century or W. Eugene Smith's 1951 photo-essay in *Life* entitled

This essay first appeared in *A Century of Black Photographers: 1840–1960*, ed. Valencia Hollins Coar (Providence RI: Museum of Art, Rhode Island School of Design, 1983), to accompany an exhibition of the same name at the School's Museum of Art, March 31 – May 8 1983. Reprinted with permission of the publishers. The essay also appeared in Angela Y. Davis, *Women, Culture, and Politics* (New York: Random House, 1988).

"Nurse-Midwife." Yet such glimpses of black life have incorporated the vision of white artists, necessarily outsiders to the culture from which their images were taken. From the era of photography's emergence up to the present period, black photographers have been forcibly and systematically rendered invisible. "One of the few positive effects of 'Harlem on My Mind'," according to photography critic A. D. Coleman, "was that it brought to the attention of critics and public alike the work of James Van Der Zee."[3] Van Der Zee, Gordon Parks, and Roy DeCarava (who refused to participate in the Harlem show) are among the very few whose names have recently begun to be recognizable. Not one of them, however – not a single Afro-American photographer, in fact – has been included in the most current authoritative history of the medium to be published in the US.[4] Thus the momentous character of the present assemblage of eleven decades of black photography.

Many will find it astonishing that black people became involved in photography shortly after the invention of the daguerreotype: Jules Lion, who became acquainted with this process in France, may well have introduced it to the city of New Orleans. But then, how many prominent scientists, scholars, and artists have been banished from historical records for no other reason than their racial heritage, only to be revealed, shamefully late, as outstanding contributors in their fields? Jules Lion, Robert Duncanson, and J. P. Ball ought not now to evoke new responses of surprise. Rather, they should be celebrated as evidence of what knowledgeable persons should have strongly suspected all along – yes, black photographers were active during the very earliest stages of their medium's history. Granted, there were but few, for slavery imposed an historical prohibition on virtually all forms of aesthetic creation. Only music, misunderstood as it was by the slaveocracy, was permitted to flourish. But what about the untapped artistic potential of those millions of slaves? Do we dare imagine how many pioneering black photographers there might have been, had more favorable socio-economic circumstances prevailed?

Perhaps a less speculative question should be considered: What was the posture of early black photographers toward the collective predicament of Afro-American people? W. E. B. Du Bois wrote:

> The innate love of harmony and beauty that set the ruder souls of his people a-dancing, a-singing raised but confusion and doubt in the souls of the black artist; for the beauty revealed to him was the soul-beauty of a race which his larger audience despised, and he could not articulate the message of another people.[5]

Could this be the reason why the works and careers of the few early photographers appear entirely removed from the situations and aspirations of the masses of Afro-Americans? Where, in the works of daguerreotypist James P. Ball, was the black population's powerful yearning for freedom to be found? Did the photographic images of his black contemporaries and immediate successors bear witness, in any discernible manner, to the common dreams of an enslaved people, whose songs and struggles focused on their collective liberation? If these questions cannot be answered unreservedly in the affirmative, it is due, no doubt, to the pressures exerted by that "larger audience" to which Du Bois refers. Black people, the vast majority of whom were slaves prior to 1863, were simply not considered appropriate subjects of serious visual art, except as stereotypes. Indeed, this was no less true for Afro-American painters, sculptors, and photographers than for their white contemporaries.

The paucity of distinctive black features in the works of early black photographers should not be misconstrued as permission to dismiss the issue of these artists' relationship to the collective experience of their race. However they subjectively chose to address – or ignore – the racial politics of their times, they could hardly avoid being influenced in some way by objective historical conditions. And there were turbulent stirrings in the black population and among their white allies during the decade that closed with the invention of the daguerreotype. There were Nat Turner's awesome slave rebellion of 1831 and the founding conference, two years later, of the American Anti-Slavery Society. By 1837, there were also white martyrs like the abolitionist newspaperman Elijah P. Lovejoy, viciously murdered by a racist mob in Illinois. The next year, a momentous escape occurred, effected by the slave soon to be known as Frederick Douglass, the eloquent orator and powerful abolitionist leader. This was the year when the black anti-slavery activist Robert Purvis formally organized the Underground Railroad.

If this was an era when the black pursuit of freedom emerged as one of the nation's dominant social concerns, it was also a period of vibrant and prolific artistic expression related to the anti-slavery cause. At the same time as George Mose Horton published his "Poems of a Slave," Longfellow's "Poems on Slavery" also appeared. Although this was apparently an exceptional case, there was an Afro-American visual artist, the engraver and lithographer Patrick Reason, who devoted much of his work to abolitionist themes. Reason "spoke out vehemently against slavery, devoting much of his time to illustrating abolitionist literature."[6] His portrait of Henry Bibb, author of one of the epoch's popular slave narratives, expressed a certain determination to link the work of black visual artists – like their people's literature and still unrecognized musical creations – to black people's historic social strivings for liberation.

It is a great misfortune that the racist requirements of "American" art excluded black slaves in a virtual *a priori* fashion as potential subjects of serious visual art, for an abundance of profoundly inspiring material could have been gleaned from their lives and deeds, material waiting to be shaped by the artist's hand into exciting new creations. Consider, for example, the fascinating case of Henry "Box" Brown, the slave who escaped inside a box, which was shipped to the North by the operators of the Underground Railroad. And the dramatic escape by William and Ellen Craft in 1849: Ellen, passing for white, donned male attire and posed as her husband's master. The couple successfully traveled from Georgia to the free city of Philadelphia. While Harriet Tubman's escape that same year was not itself distinctively dramatic, its consequences would be earthshaking and historic. Countless freedom treks would be made by this fearless woman, destined to become her people's "Moses."

The Afro-American photographer J. P. Ball was active during the 1850s. One is tempted to speculate about the extent to which he and others were touched by the feats of freedom fighters like Harriet Tubman. While concrete answers must await further specific historical research, it is clear that by the decade of the '50s, the issue of slavery had emphatically moved to the center of national attention. It had become a question no one, black or white – and especially not scholars and cultural workers – could be permitted to ignore. Indeed, one of the era's most popular pieces of literature was *Uncle Tom's Cabin*, the crusading, anti-slavery novel by Harriet Beecher Stowe. The very popularity of Stowe's work was irrefutable evidence of the novel's outstanding role in defending the abolitionist cause. Yet it was also responsible for popularizing social attitudes toward black people which seemingly contradicted its progressive, anti-slavery intent. For even as it encouraged black people's right to be free, it legitimized and gave definitive, popular form to stereotypical notions of racial inferiority. In fact, precisely the process through which Stowe's novel evoked a popular revulsion toward slavery also furnished the literary weapons for an ideological victory – however unintentional – of racism.

Uncle Tom's Cabin facilitated – not alone, but in a major sense – the increasingly deeper penetration of racist images and attitudes into the country's cultural life. Consider an 1883 painting entitled *Uncle Tom and Little Eva* and its depiction of a large, but obviously helpless black man who looks to an angelic little white girl for light and direction. This painting, which incorporates Stowe's stereotypes in their original forms, is not the work of a naive white artist, as might be suspected. Rather it was produced by an Afro-American, Robert Scott Duncanson. And Duncanson was not the only one to be inspired in this fashion to project unintentionally destructive images of his people. Yet Afro-Americans had also furnished the means with which to expose the racist distortions in Stowe's portrayal of black people, for by this time the slave narrative had become a well established literary genre. Solomon Northrup and Frederick Douglass, for example, had presented firsthand accounts of their lives, their sufferings, and their hopes under the "peculiar institution." Black people's burgeoning literary creations at mid-century included the works of William Wells

Brown, who went on, after authoring a slave narrative, to become Afro-America's first novelist and playwright. Among poets at mid-century, Frances E. W. Harper was destined to receive the widest acclaim for her work. While she herself was born "free," she wrote her most brilliant and celebrated verse on the righteous struggles of her enslaved people – poems, for example, like "The Slave Auction," and "Bury Me in a Free Land." Such was the flourishing and often militant literary context within which mid-century black photographers – whether consciously or not – pursued their potentially powerful craft. Like their colleagues who wielded the pen, they possessed the ability to utilize the camera to forge creative, affirmative images of their people.

> There came the slow looming of emancipation. Crowds and armies of the unknown, inscrutable, unfathomable Yankees; cruelty behind and before; rumors of a new slave trade; but slowly, continuously, the wild truth, the bitter truth, the magic truth, came surging through.
> There was to be a new freedom! . . . They prayed; they worked; they danced and sang; they studied to learn; they wanted to wander.[7]

Slavery was banned from history, but while black people certainly felt the falling of their chains, they also soon realized that they had by no means achieved their collective goal of liberation. If a new promise was later offered, during the years of Radical Reconstruction, it would be abruptly snatched away by the Hayes-Tilden Compromise of 1877, which ushered in a period of pervasive, destructive racism. Segregation was legalized in the South and the population of former slaves began to suffer systematic disfranchisement. Mob violence and lynchings claimed countless lives, while the use of racist terror and other tactics of intimidation became the routine approach to black peasants and workers adopted by white officials and employers in the South. In 1890, for example, there were 85 reported lynchings, 112 in 1891, and 160 in 1892 – and, as the last years of the century rolled by, this wave of racist violence would continue to swell.

This was the socio-historical background against which the lives and careers evolved of such photographic artists as Harry Shepherd and Hamilton S. Smith. As they worked with their cameras, selecting their subjects, composing their images, how were they affected by the raging violence of racist mobs, those massacres of black people euphemistically known as "race riots"? Were the images they recorded influenced at all by the knowledge that untold thousands of black bodies had hung from trees or gone up in flames at the stake? Their literary contemporary, Charles Chesnutt, published a novel in 1901 entitled *The Marrow of Tradition*, based directly on the 1898 massacre in Wilmington, North Carolina. Were any Afro-American photographers inspired by Chesnutt's example?

By the beginning of the twentieth century, photography in the United States and Europe had entered its historical state of maturity. Mathew Brady had photographed the Civil War, Timothy H. O'Sullivan had conducted expeditions to photograph remote areas of the West, and countless millions of human portraits had been recorded on film. According to the census of 1900, at least 247 Afro-Americans were professional photographers. Of course, it can be assumed that the vast majority concentrated their work on studio portraits, but if James Van Der Zee is at all typical, many, like him, photographed street scenes, parades, political rallies, and whatever might have been transpiring in their immediate world. A. D. Coleman reports that during most of his career, Van Der Zee "was entirely unaware of what was happening in the medium, even of what was going on with black photographers; such names as Steichen, Stieglitz, Hine and van Vechten rang no bells in his memory."[8]

Yet, was it really necessary to be familiar, for example, with Jacob Riis's images of the poor and their environment in order to move toward the photographic documentation of oppression? Was it necessary for black photographers to look toward white models in order to recognize that photography could be a profoundly social art form, capable of generating human urges toward progressive change?

To continue the line of questioning begun above, did any of the early twentieth-century black photographers attempt to record images reflecting the omnipresent and devastating racism of those years? How did black photography address the 1906 race riots in Springfield, Ohio, and Atlanta, Georgia – and the notorious assaults the same year on black soldiers in Brownsville, Texas? Were any visual challenges inspired by the 1916 lynching of Jesse Washington, who was burned to death in Waco, Texas, before a cheering crowd of 15,000 white people – men, women, and even children? Included in the "Harlem on My Mind" exhibition was a photograph of a march in Harlem protesting at the East Saint Louis race riots of 1917. How many more images remain to be discovered which evoke the presence of and resistance to the terrible violence of 1917 and the murderous Red Summer of 1919?

With the rise of the film industry during the first decades of the twentieth century, racist stereotypes began to acquire definitive perceptual forms, a process that was masterfully executed in D. W. Griffith's *Birth of a Nation*. What Afro-American photographers sought to forge images whose creative power could expose and condemn the evolving visual mythology of racism? Certainly, James Van Der Zee's impressive imagery provides affirmative, realistic evidence of the urbanized Afro-American, and specifically, the inhabitants of Harlem during the 1920s – from the socialite in repose to the protesting Garveyite. Although mainstream photography scholarship treats Van Der Zee as an exception – that is, if he is acknowledged at all – there must be more, many, many more.

The 1920s were very special years for black artists in the United States – particularly for the writers and painters who, unlike the musicians of that era, had not yet established themselves within a cultural continuum that was distinctly and affirmatively Afro-American. "We younger Negro artists who create now intend to express our individual dark-skinned selves without fear or shame."[9] This was Langston Hughes's proclamation in "The Negro Artist and the Racial Mountain." By the end of that decade, black literary and visual artists had laid the foundation for an explicitly Afro-American esthetic, one which reflected the socio-historical conditions of the black community's development and gave expression to the cultural traditions created and preserved in that process.

> Let the blare of Negro jazz bands and the bellowing voice of Bessie Smith singing the blues penetrate the closed ears of the colored near-intellectuals until they listen and perhaps understand. Let Paul Robeson singing "Water Boy" and Rudolph Fisher writing about the streets of Harlem and Jean Toomer holding the heart of Georgia in his hands and Aaron Douglas drawing strange fantasies. . . .[10]

And, we might add, James Van Der Zee capturing photographic images of Harlem, P. H. Polk preserving via the camera something of the historical import of Tuskegee Institute.

Then came the Great Crash of 1929 and the economic depression that brought misery to the entire population, but whose impact was most fatal for the Afro-American masses, especially the agricultural workers of the South. Poor black people appeared in the work of the Farm Security Administration photographers – Dorothea Lange, Ben Shahn, Carl Mydans, Walker Evans – whose documentation of rural life during the Depression years is of inestimable importance. Countless images of poverty in the United States have been preserved, yet black people, like their white counterparts, were not simply poor. Their lives expressed far more than the "dignity despite poverty" often intentionally captured in the photographs. Where are the other images? Those of black people organizing, struggling, fighting back as sharecroppers and tenant farmers in rural Alabama? As union militants in Detroit, for example, or as unemployed protesters in Chicago – and as people, real human beings? In short, as a maturing complex community of oppressed people in relentless pursuit of a humane collective existence, a pursuit that continued throughout the 1940s, 1950s and to the present time? If such images are to be unearthed, if new images of this sort are to be forged in substantial numbers, Afro-American photographers will have borne – and must continue to bear – the overwhelming burden of this responsibility.

The photography critic Gisele Freund has argued that the medium's importance is related not only to its capacity to develop as an art form, but also, and perhaps even more significantly, to "its ability to shape our ideas, to influence our behavior and to define our society."[11] If racism is to be conquered in the United States, both in its institutional and attitudinal manifestations, then certainly Afro-American photographers must play a special role in the process of redefining the ideologically tainted imagery of their people. This process involves not only their own technical expertise, not only their esthetic and social sensitivity, but also, in a very fundamental sense, the end of their socially imposed invisibility. Referring to a brilliant contemporary photographer, A. D. Coleman wrote:

> It is little short of tragic that our prejudices should have deprived Roy DeCarava of the wide audience he deserves, and deprived that audience of an artist with so much to reveal that they desperately need to know."[12]

Roy DeCarava and how many more?

NOTES

1 Allon Schoener (ed.), *Harlem on My Mind: Cultural Capital of Black America, 1900–1968* (New York: Dell, 1979), 11.
2 Ibid.
3 Ibid., 16.
4 Beaumont Newball, *The History of Photography* (New York, The Museum of Modern Art, 1982).
5 W. E. B. Du Bois, *The Souls of Black Folk* (New York: New American Library, 1969), 46–7.
6 David C. Driskell, *Two Centuries of Black American Art* (New York: Alfred A. Knopf; Los Angeles County Museum of Art, 1976), 36.
7 W. E. B. Du Bois, *Black Reconstruction in America* (New York: Meridian Books, 1964), 122.
8 A. D. Coleman, 17.
9 Langston Hughes, "The Negro Artist and the Racial Mountain" (first published in *The Nation*, June 23, 1926), in Williams and Harris (eds), *Amistad I* (New York: Vintage, 1970), 305.
10 Ibid., 304–5.
11 Gisele Freund, *Photography and Society* (Boston: David R. Godine, 1980), 5.
12 Coleman, 28.

18

Afro Images: Politics, Fashion, and Nostalgia

Not long ago I attended a performance in San Francisco by women presently or formerly incarcerated in the County Jail, in collaboration with Bay Area women performance artists. After the show, I went backstage to the "green room," where the women inmates, guarded by deputy sheriffs stationed outside the door, were celebrating with their families and friends. Having worked with some of the women at the jail, I wanted to congratulate them on the show. One woman introduced me to her brother, who at first responded to my name with a blank stare. The woman admonished him: "You don't know who Angela Davis is?! You should be ashamed." Suddenly a flicker of recognition flashed across his face. "Oh," he said, "Angela Davis – the Afro."

Such responses I find, are hardly exceptional, and it is both humiliating and humbling to discover that a single generation after the events that constructed me as a public personality, I am remembered as a hairdo. It is humiliating because it reduces a politics of liberation to a politics of fashion; it is humbling because such encounters with the younger generation demonstrate the fragility and mutability of historical images, particularly those associated with African-American history. This encounter with the young man who identified me as "the Afro" reminded me of a recent article in the *New York Times Magazine* that listed me as one of the fifty most influential fashion (read: hairstyle) trendsetters over the last century.[1] I continue to find it ironic that the popularity of the "Afro" is attributed to me, when, in actuality, I was emulating a whole host of women, both public figures and women I encountered in my daily life, when I began to wear my hair natural in the late sixties.

But it is not merely the reduction of historical politics to contemporary fashion that infuriates me. Especially disconcerting is the fact that the distinction of being known as "the Afro" is largely a result of a particular economy of journalistic images of black women in which mine is one of the relatively few that has survived the last two decades. Or perhaps the very segregation of those photographic images caused mine to enter into the then dominant journalistic culture precisely by virtue of my presumed "criminality." In any case, it has survived, disconnected from the historical context in which it arose, as fashion. Most young African Americans who are familiar with my name and twenty-five-year-old image have encountered photographs and film/video clips largely in music videos, and in black history montages in popular books and magazines. Within the interpretive context in which they learn to situate these photographs, the most salient element of the image is the hairstyle, understood less as a political statement than as fashion.

The unprecedented contemporary circulation of photographic and filmic images of African Americans has multiple and contradictory implications. On the one hand, it holds the promise of visual memory of older and departed generations, of both well-known figures and people who may not have achieved public prominence. However, there is also the danger that this historical memory may become ahistorical and apolitical. "Photographs are relics of the past," John Berger has written. They are "traces of what has happened. If the living take that past upon themselves, if the past becomes an integral part of the process of people making their own history, then all photographs would acquire a living context, they would continue to exist in time, instead of being arrested moments."[2]

In the past, I have been rather reluctant to reflect in more than a casual way on the power of the visual images by which I was represented during the period of my trial. Perhaps this is due to my unwillingness to confront those images as having to some extent structured my experiences during that era. The recent recycling of some of these images in contexts that privilege the "Afro" as fashion – revolutionary glamor – has led me to reconsider them both in the historical context in which they were first produced (and in which I first experienced them) and within the "historical" context in which they often are presented today as "arrested moments."

In September 1969, the University of California Regents fired me from my post in the philosophy department at UCLA because of my membership in the Communist Party. The following summer, charges of murder, kidnapping, and conspiracy were brought against me in connection with my activities on behalf of George Jackson and the Soledad Brothers. The circulation of various photographic images of me – taken by journalists, undercover policemen, and movement activists – played a major role in both the mobilization of public opinion against me and the development of the campaign that was ultimately responsible for my acquittal.

Twenty-five years later, many of these photographs are being recycled and recontextualized in ways that are at once exciting and disturbing. With the first public circulation of my photographs, I was intensely aware of the invasive and transformative power of the camera and of the ideological contextualization of my images, which left me with little or no agency. On the one hand I was portrayed as a conspiratorial and monstrous Communist (i.e., anti-American) whose unruly natural hairdo symbolized black militancy (i.e., anti-whiteness). Some of the first hate mail I received tended to collapse "Russia" and "Africa." I was told to "go back to Russia" and often in the same sentence (in connection with a reference to my hair) to "go back to Africa." On the other hand, sympathetic portrayals tended to interpret the image – almost inevitably one with my mouth wide open – as that of a charismatic and raucous revolutionary ready to lead the masses into battle. Since I considered myself neither monstrous nor charismatic, I felt fundamentally betrayed on both accounts: violated on the first account, and deficient on the second.

When I was fired by the UC Regents in 1969, an assortment of photographs appeared throughout that year in various newspapers and magazines and on television. However, it was not until felony charges were brought against me in connection with the Marin County shootout that the photographs became what Susan Sontag has called a part of "the general furniture of the environment."[3] As such, they truly began to frighten me. A cycle of terror was initiated by the decision of the FBI to declare me one of the country's ten most-wanted criminals. Although I had been underground for over a month before I actually saw the photographs the FBI had decided to use on the poster, I had to picture how they might portray me as I attempted to create for myself an appearance that would be markedly different from the one defined as armed and dangerous. The props I used consisted of a wig with straight black hair, long false lashes, and more eyeshadow, liner, and blush than I had ever before imagined wearing in public. Never having seriously attempted to present myself as glamorous, it seemed to me that glamor was the only look that might annul the likelihood of being perceived as a revolutionary. It never could have occurred to me that the same "revolutionary" image I then sought to camouflage with glamor would be turned, a generation later, into glamor and nostalgia.

After the FBI poster was put on display in post offices, other government buildings, and on the television program *The FBI*, *Life* magazine came out with a provocative issue featuring a cover story on me. Illustrated by photographs from my childhood years through the UCLA firing, the article probed the reasons for my supposedly abandoning a sure trajectory toward fulfillment of the middle-class American dream in order to lead the unpredictable life of a "black revolutionary." Considering the vast circulation of this pictorial magazine,[4] I experienced something akin to what Barthes was referring to when he wrote "I feel that the Photograph creates my body or mortifies it according to its caprice (apology of this mortiferous power certain Communards paid with their lives for their willingness or even their eagerness to pose on the barricades: defeated, they were recognized by Thiers's police and shot, almost every one)."[5] The life-size headshot on the cover of the magazine would be seen by as many people if not more, than the much smaller portraits on the FBI poster. Having confronted my own image in the store where I purchased the magazine I was convinced that FBI chief J. Edgar Hoover had conspired in the appearance of that cover story. More than anything else it seemed to me to be a magnification and elaboration of the WANTED poster. Moreover the text of the story gave a rather convincing explanation as to why the pictures should be associated with arms and danger.

The photograph on the cover of my autobiography,[6] published in 1974, was taken by the renowned photographer Phillipe Halsman. When I entered his studio with Toni Morrison, who was my editor, the first question he asked us was whether we had brought the black leather jacket. He assumed, it turned out, that he was to recreate with his camera a symbolic visual representation of black militancy: leather jacket (uniform of the Black Panther Party), Afro hairdo and raised first. We had to persuade him to photograph me in a less predictable posture. As recently as 1993, the persisting persuasiveness of these visual stereotypes was made clear to me when I had to insist that Anna Deavere Smith rethink her representation of me in her theater piece *Fires in the Mirror*, which initially relied upon a black leather jacket as her main prop.

The most obvious evidence of the power of those photographic images was the part they played in structuring people's opinions about me as a "fugitive" and a political prisoner; their broader and more subtle effect was the way they served as generic images of black women who wore their hair "natural." From the constant stream of stories I have heard over the last twenty-four years (and continue to hear), I infer that hundreds, perhaps even thousands, of Afro-wearing black women were accosted, harassed, and arrested by police, FBI, and immigration agents during the two months I spent underground. One woman who told me that she hoped she could serve as a "decoy" because of her light skin and big natural, was obviously conscious of the way the photographs – circulating within a highly charged racialized context – constructed generic representations of young black women. Consequently, the photographs identified vast numbers of my black female contemporaries who wore naturals (whether light- or dark-skinned) as targets of repression. This is the hidden historical content behind the continued association of my name with the Afro.

A young woman who is a former student of mine has been wearing an Afro during the last few months. Rarely a day passes, she has told me, when she is not greeted with cries of "Angela Davis" from total strangers. Moreover, during the months preceding the writing of this article, I have received an astounding number of requests for interviews from journalists doing stories on "the resurgence of the Afro." A number of the most recent requests were occasioned by a layout in the fashion section of the March 1994 issue of *Vibe* magazine entitled "Free Angela: Actress Cynda Williams as Angela Davis, a Fashion Revolutionary." The spread consists of eight full-page photos of Cynda Williams (known for her role as the singer in Spike Lee's film *Mo' Better Blues*) in poses that parody photographs taken of me during the early 1970s. The layout, by stylist Patty Wilson, is described as "'docufashion' because it uses modern clothing to mimic Angela Davis's look from the '70s."[7]

Some of the pictures are rather straightforward attempts to recreate press photos taken at my arrest, during the trial, and after my release. Others can be characterized as pastiche,[8] drawing elements like leather-jacketed black men from contemporary stereotypes of the sixties–seventies era of black militancy. They include an arrest scene with the model situated between two uniformed policemen and wearing an advertised black satin blouse (reminiscent of the top I was wearing on the date of my arrest). As with her hair, the advertised eyewear are remarkably similar to the glasses I wore. There are two courtroom scenes in which Williams wears an enormous Afro wig and advertised see-through minidresses and, in one of them, handcuffs. Yet another revolves around a cigar-smoking, bearded man dressed in fatigues with a gun holster around his waist, obviously meant to evoke Che Guevara. (Even the fatigues can be purchased – from Cheap Jack's!) There is no such thing as subtlety in these photos. Because the point of this fashion spread is to represent the clothing associated with revolutionary movements of the early seventies as revolutionary fashion in the nineties, the sixtieth-anniversary logo of the Communist Party has become altered in one of the photos to read 1919–1971 (instead of 1979). And the advertised dress in the photo for which this logo is a backdrop is adorned with pin-on buttons reading "Free All Political Prisoners."

The photographs I find most unsettling, however, are the two small headshots of Williams wearing a huge Afro wig on a reproduction of the FBI wanted poster that is otherwise unaltered except for the words "FREE ANGELA" in bold red print across the bottom of the document. Despite the fact that the inordinately small photos do not really permit much of a view of the clothing Williams wears, the tops and glasses (again quite similar to the ones I wore in the two imitated photographs) are listed as purchasable items. This is the most blatant example of the way the particular history of my legal case is emptied of all content so that it can serve as a commodified backdrop for advertising. The way in which this document provided a historical pretext for something akin to a reign of terror for countless young black women is effectively erased by its use as a prop for selling clothes and promoting a seventies fashion nostalgia. What is also lost in this nostalgic surrogate for historical memory – in these "arrested moments," to use John Berger's words – is the activist involvement of vast numbers of black women in movements that are now represented with even greater masculinist contours than they actually exhibited at the time.

Without engaging the numerous debates occasioned by Frederic Jameson's paper "Postmodernism and Consumer Society," I would like to suggest that his analysis of "nostalgia films" and their literary counterparts, which are "historical novels in appearance only," may provide a useful point of departure for an interpretation of this advertising genre called "docufashion," as "[W]e seem condemned to seek the historical past," Jameson writes, "through our own pop images and stereotypes about that past, which itself remains forever out of reach."[9] Perhaps by also taking up John Berger's call for an "alternative photography," we may develop strategies for engaging photographic images like the ones I have evoked, by actively seeking to transform their interpretive contexts in education, popular culture, the media, community organizing, and so on. Particularly in relation to African-American historical images, we need to find ways of incorporating them into "social and political memory, instead of using [them] as a substitute which encourages the atrophy of such memory."[10]

NOTES

1   *New York Times Magazine*, n.d.
2   John Berger, *About Looking* (New York: Pantheon Books, 1980), 57.
3   Susan Sontag, *On Photography* (New York: Farrar, Straus and Giroux, 1978), 27.
4   During the 1960s, *Life* magazine had a circulation of approximately forty million people. (Gisele Freund, *Photography and Society* [Boston: David R. Godine, 1980], 143.)
5   Roland Barthes, *Camera Lucida* (New York: Hill and Wang, 1981), 11.
6   Angela Y. Davis, *Angela Davis: An Autobiography* (New York: Random House, 1974).
7   *Vibe*, vol. 2, no. 2 (March 1994), 16.
8   I use the term *pastiche* both in the usual sense of a potpourri of disparate ingredients and in the sense in which Frederic Jameson uses it. "Pastiche is, like parody, the imitation of a peculiar or unique style, the wearing of a stylistic mask, speech in a dead language: but it is a neutral practice of such mimicry, without parody's ulterior motive, without the satirical impulse, without laughter. . . . Pastiche is black parody, parody that has lost its sense of humor." (Frederic Jameson, "Postmodernism and Consumer Society," in Hal Foster, ed., *The Anti-Aesthetic: Essays on Postmodern Culture* [Port Townsend, Washington: Bay Press, 1983], 114.) Jameson's essay has appeared in several versions. I thank Victoria Smith for suggesting that I reread this essay in connection with the *Vibe* story.
9   Jameson, "Postmodernism and Consumer Society," 118.
10 Berger, *About Looking*, 58.

19

Meditations on the Legacy
of Malcolm X

Malcolm had said to . . . black women earlier in December, 1964 that we
were the real educators. We were the setter of fires that would burn until our
people let themselves free.

                                                              Patricia Robinson

Patricia Robinson's engaging account of Malcolm X's political bequest to
and acknowledgment of African-American women has been all but eclipsed
by representations in contemporary black popular culture that tend to
portray Malcolm as the quintessential "black man," as that historical figure
whose style and rhetoric are the measure by which the revolutionary potential of African-American youth in the 1990s should be judged. "On Sunday
afternoon, February 21, 1965," Robinson mused, "all of us, who had
waited for centuries for that revolutionary son and brother to be reborn,
gratefully and humbly accepted the revolutionary responsibility as it passed
out of Malcolm's slowly descending body."[1] She contended that after
Malcolm's disillusionment with the Nation of Islam, he began to turn
toward and to listen to black women in a way that had not been possible as
long as he functioned under the ideological tutelage of a man – Elijah
Muhammad – whose political/religious vision and whose personal life were
thoroughly shaped by male supremacy. Relying on the paradigm of the
family, she interpreted his legacy as that of the "black revolutionary son"
driven by a new historical impulse to recognize and assist in a process of
empowering the "mother" and the "sister." As problematic as this model
might be, with its unavoidable masculinist implications, it seems to me that
Robinson was calling for a feminist appreciation of Malcolm's political
contributions.

   In 1992, within a context constructed by ubiquitous images of Malcolm
as the *essential black man*, the juxtaposition of the words "Malcolm" and

This essay first appeared in *Malcolm X: In Our Own Image*, ed. Joe Wood (New York: St.
Martin's Press, 1992), copyright © 1992 by Joe Wood. Reprinted by permission of the Faith
Childs Literary Agency, Inc. on behalf of the editor.

"feminist" rings strange and oxymoronic. Yet this is precisely why I feel compelled – using Robinson's analysis as a point of departure – to formulate a number of questions regarding some possible feminist implications of his legacy. I will not presume to answer all the questions I pose. Indeed, many of them are speculative in the Socratic sense, designed more to shift the focus of the popular discourse on Malcolm X rather than guide a substantive inquiry into his political history.

The first set of questions: Is it possible that if Malcolm had not been shot down on February 21, 1965, he might be identifying with the global feminist movement today? Would he have allowed his vision to be disrupted and revolutionized by the intervention of feminism? Or, in order to discuss the feminist implications of his legacy, is it even necessary to argue about the positions Malcolm X, the man, might have assumed?

Rather than directly address these questions, I want to parenthetically evoke my own recent experience with one of the persisting themes in Malcolm's political discourse – South African apartheid. When I visited South Africa in September 1991, political consciousness regarding the marginalization and oppression of women appeared to be transforming the character of the battle for democracy there. Not only were women in the various organizations of the Liberation Alliance, the African National Congress (ANC), the South African Communist Party (SACP), Congress of South African Trades Unions (COSATU), and so on developing creative strategies for involving masses of women in the revolutionary process, they also were challenging the entrenched male dominance in the leadership of their organizations. Although a proposed affirmative action plan for women within the ANC was not accepted at the last convention, it was clearly gaining support as a legitimate means of reversing the decades-old assumptions that men deserved the preponderance of leadership positions.

Women in South Africa also were redefining the pervasive political violence (perpetrated by black organizations such as Buthelezi's Inkatha, but supported by the white government) in terms that included the violence they suffered at the hands of their husbands at home. The women activists whom I encountered spoke of the futility of seeking to eradicate this epidemic public violence while their bodies continued to be battered by the violence defiling their private lives.

Feminist consciousness like this disrupts traditional modes of struggle, and many – men and women alike – in yearning for the simplicity of the "good old days" would wish it away, if such magical solutions were possible. In light of the misogynist attitudes often represented in the media (particularly in film and in the music videos and rap lyrics associated with hip-hop) as the consensus of contemporary young black men, for whom Malcolm is the ultimate hero, I am led to pose another set of speculative questions that preempts the first, since what matters is not the "good old days," or what Malcolm might have become – what matters is what Malcolm's legacy means today. And so, is it the legacy of Malcolm X to wish such a feminist consciousness away? Is it his legacy to long for simple formulations and simple answers? Is it the legacy of Malcolm X to ignore the radical reconceptualization of the struggle for democracy urged by South African women?

Making a case for the possibility of responding to these questions, I will develop an argument based on the critical connotations of Malcolm's own eventual interrogation of his philosophical adherence to black nationalism.

On January 23, 1963, Malcolm X delivered an address sponsored by the African Students Association and the campus NAACP at Michigan State University and later published under the title "Twenty Million Black People in a Political, Economic and Mental Prison." He prefaced his speech with words of thanks to the two sponsoring organizations "for displaying the unity necessary to bring a very controversial issue before the students here on campus. The unity of Africans abroad and the unity of Africans here in this country can bring about practically any kind of achievement or accomplishment that black people want today."[2] On the eve of his assassination two years later, Malcolm seemed to be deeply interrogating the nationalist philosophical grounds that had led him to use racialized metaphors of imprisonment at the core of his analysis of the African-American predicament and to advocate an exclusively black unity as the strategic basis for emancipatory practice. While the thematic content of his speeches retained previous invocations of black imprisonment – the dialectics of social and psychological incarceration – what was different about his approach two years later was a more flexible construction of the unity he proposed as a strategy for escape. At what was no doubt a tentative moment in the process of questioning his previous philosophy, a moment never fully developed because of his premature death, Malcolm appeared to be seeking an approach that would allow him to preserve the practice of black unity – his organization was called the Organization for Afro-American Unity – while simultaneously moving beyond the geopolitical borders of Africa and the African diaspora.

Because Malcolm was in the process of articulating the pitfalls and limitations of nationalism, I want to suggest that implied in that critical revisiting of his black nationalist philosophy might be a similar revisiting of the male supremacist ramifications of black nationalism. This is what he said about black nationalism:

> I used to define black nationalism as the idea that the black man should control the economy of his community, the politics of his community and so forth. But, when I was in Africa in May, in Ghana, I was speaking with the

Algerian ambassador who is ex-militant and is a revolutionary in the true
sense of the word. . . . When I told him that my political, social and economic
philosophy was black nationalism, he asked me very frankly, well, where
did that leave him. Because he was white. He was an African, but he was
Algerian, and to all appearances he was a white man. And he said if I defined
my objective as the victory of black nationalism, where does that leave
him? Where does that leave revolutionaries in Morocco, Egypt, Iraq,
Mauritania?[3]

While acknowledging the problematic racialization of the North African
man whose questioning caused Malcolm to interrogate his own position as
a black nationalist, I would point out that nonetheless, his internationalist
recontextualization of the liberation struggle as a "Third World" struggle
revealed and accentuated the narrowness and provincial character of the
nationalism Malcolm had espoused before that time.

So I had to do a lot of thinking and reappraising of my definition of black
nationalism. Can we sum up the solution to the problems confronting our
people as black nationalism? And if you notice, I haven't been using the
expression for several months. But I still would be hard pressed to give a
specific definition of the over-all philosophy which I think is necessary for the
liberation of black people in this country.[4]

These remarks, made in an interview published in the March–April 1965
issue of the *Young Socialist* shortly before his assassination, indicate that
even at a mature stage of the development of his philosophical position,
Malcolm did not hesitate to re-examine his ideas and consider the possibility of radical shifts in that position. He was not afraid to explore the
likelihood that his ideas could not stand the test of the complexities he
encountered in his political travels. During the same international travels,
he discovered that in a number of African countries and African liberation
movements, women were becoming visible in new and important ways.[5]
While I do not wish to appear to ignore the extremely complicated and
often contradictory position in which women find themselves within processes of dismantling colonial systems, I do want to suggest that it is
appropriate to speculate about a philosophical shift in Malcolm's thinking
with respect to the place, position, and empowerment of women – specifically but not exclusively about African women and women in the African
diaspora.

I am not certain about the political path Malcolm himself might have
taken had he not been assassinated at such an apparently critical juncture
in the evolution of his political philosophy and practice. My meditations on
Malcolm X are not necessarily about the ideas a dead man might have
arrived at if his life had been spared; what concerns me more is what I

would call the "progressive philosophical space" that can be discovered within the legacy of Malcolm X.

In 1992 Malcolm's legacy is being contested within the realm of popular culture. A number of major battles are currently unfolding, whose aim is to capture this legacy and fix it once and for all. There is the debate around the film on Malcolm directed by Spike Lee. Initially, Spike Lee's argument for replacing the original director, Norman Jewish, with himself, was based on the claim that a white director could never do justice to Malcolm's legacy. Once the film was in progress, Amiri Baraka claimed that Lee himself could not do justice to Malcolm's legacy. What is so striking about the debate is its anchoring point: the very conception of black nationalism – with its conservative racializing limitations and strong masculinist implications – that Malcolm problematized at the end of his life.

Popular representations of Malcolm's legacy abound in contemporary youth culture. As Nick Charles has pointed out, "In death the X has become ubiquitous, seen mainly on baseball and knit caps. The face, handsome and goateed, peers sternly from T-shirts, jackets and bags. His slogans, 'No Sellout' and 'By Any Means Necessary,' have taken on the dimensions of commandments."[6] This is Malcolm's commodified "legacy," as conjured and evoked in wearable images, flashed in music videos, and sampled in rap songs. Who or what is this commodified Malcolm, the seller of T-shirts and jackets and caps? What does the mark of the X mean to those who mark themselves with this sign that signifies everything and nothing? How is the legacy of Malcolm perceived by those who locate him as a movable image, a wandering voice traveling in and out of music videos and rap tunes such as Public Enemy's "Welcome to the Terrordome"? and Paris's "Brutal" and "Break the Grip of Shame"? What does it mean to the youth who catch a glimpse of Malcolm speaking and Malcolm dead lying in his coffin in Prince Akeem and Chuck D's "Time to Come Correct"? How is Malcolm's legacy constructed in Def Jef's "Black to the Future," in Public Enemy's "Shut Em Down"? What is the meaning of the words "By Any Means Necessary" as flashed in bold letters across the screen in the last video?

In assuming a critical attitude *vis-à-vis* this iconization and, because of its commodified character, this reification of Malcolm's legacy, I do not thereby dismiss my own emotional response of enthusiasm about the sense of closeness the younger generation has for this African-American historical figure. And I do not wish to belittle the sense of pride young people express in Malcolm as an ancestral champion of our rights as African-Americans. Young people feel connected to Malcolm in a way I could not have even begun to envision experiencing in my own youth, for example, in a sense of familiarity with Ida B. Wells. (In fact, when I was a teenager I didn't even know she had existed.) From this position of ambivalence, I express my anxiety in the face of the one-dimensional iconization of Malcolm X because the iconization tends to close out possibilities of exploring other implications of Malcolm's legacy that are not heroic, nationalist, and masculinist.

From the vantage point of an African-American feminist with revolutionary aspirations toward socialism that refuse to go away, I experience myself as, in part, a product of that historical moment informed, in part, by Malcolm's discourse, his oratory, and his organizing. Hearing him speak as an undergraduate at Brandeis University before an audience composed of the almost entirely white student population had a profound effect on my own political development. No one could have convinced me then that Malcolm had not come to Brandeis to give expression to my own inarticulate rage and awaken me to possibilities of militant practice. I therefore feel repelled by the strong resonances of unquestioned and dehistoricized notions of male dominance in this contemporary iconization of Malcolm X. This is not to imply that Malcolm was not as much a perpetrator of masculinist ideas as were others – men and women alike – of his era. What disturbs me today is the propensity to cloak Malcolm's politics with insinuations of intransigent and ahistorical male supremacy that bolster the contemporary equation of nationalism and male dominance as representative of progressive politics in black popular culture.

Such slogans associated with Malcolm X as "The Ballot or the Bullet" are accorded a significance that overlooks the fact that the rhetorical brandishing of guns served a very specific purpose with respect to the 1960s mass movement for black liberation. Not one to resort to circumvention and euphemism, Malcolm certainly meant what he said. Malcolm did not oratorically invoke the bullet for the primary purpose of shaping a romantic, masculinist image of "the black Man" – which is not to say that this notion of "the black Man" was not implied in his words – but rather to emphasize the black community's determined quest for political power. Likewise, "Revolution By Any Means Necessary," another slogan through which Malcolm is evoked within a contemporary context, is used by some black youth today to exalt abstract masculinist notions of political activism, with little or no reference to such indispensable aspects of revolutionary politics as strategies and tactics of organizing. In this sense, the slogans become anchoring points for surrogate "revolutionism" that denies access to new ways of organizing contemporary political movements.

I am not suggesting that we leave historical figures, phrases, and images in their original contextualization. What I am saying is that it becomes rather dangerous to project such one-dimensional appropriations on our past history and to establish them as standards for contemporary political consciousness. This kind of process flattens history to a video image that deflects rather than summons more complex efforts at comprehension. With respect to Malcolm X in particular, his pervasive presence in the lives of young black people today has begun to be reduced to the letter he chose to replace "Little," his last name. The "X" was a sign indicating refusal to accept names accorded to Africans by the white families (although there were a few black ones as well) who asserted ownership of our ancestors as slaves. Now it seems, the X etched on baseball caps, jackets and medallions strives to represent the essence of Malcolm X, the quintessential X. It is no longer necessary to include the "Malcolm" in Malcolm X for the sign is the X and that X is invested with an abstract affirmation of black identity, black dignity, black resistance, black rage. I wonder whether young people feel that by wearing the X, they are participating in the experience of something that cannot be defined and fixed once and for all: freedom – the freedom of African-Americans and thus human freedom.

A question often posed in connection with the exaltation of Malcolm: "Are you black enough?" Can this question be posed in relation to Latinos/ Latinas or Native Americans or Asians or Pacific Islanders or European Americans or indeed in relation to African-American women who wear the X? Another question: "Are you revolutionary enough?" Are you willing to fight, to die? Can this question be posed in relation to women who wear images of Malcolm?

Thus, my third set of questions: Does the passive reception of Malcolm – adorning one's body with his images and consuming movable video images and voice samples of the hero – fix male supremacy as it appears (and perhaps only appears) to challenge white supremacy? Does the contextualization of bits – infobytes – of Malcolm's body, voice, and political wit amid references to women as bitches, groupies, and whores invest our historical memory of Malcolm with a kind of vicious putdown of women that contradicts a possible turn toward feminism that some of us might associate with his legacy?

Again, instead of directly addressing the questions, I turn to Malcolm, the man – and more specifically Malcolm the husband and father as represented by his wife, Betty Shabazz. In the February 1992 issue of *Essence*, Betty Shabazz reflects on her life with Malcolm, on her love for him and on some of the conflicts in their marriage arising out of the prevailing acceptance of patterns of male dominance in heterosexual partnerships and marriage. "I shared Malcolm," she says, "but I don't know if he could have shared me to the same extent. He was possessive from the beginning to the end, though I think he learned to control it. . . . All my stress was over the fact that I wanted to work and he wouldn't even entertain the idea. He didn't want anybody to have any influence over me that would in any way compete with his. Each time I left him, that's why I left. . . ."[7] Shabazz says that she left Malcolm three times – after each of their first three children were born.

Like all of us from that generation, Shabazz has been affected by the changing economic roles of women as well as by the rise and circulation of feminist ideas. As she reflects upon her own personal transformation, she does not find it difficult to say:

> I think Malcolm probably needed me more than I needed him – to support his life's mission. But I don't think that what I would look for in a man today would be what I looked for in a man then. I was very accepting. I just wanted love. I found a sharing and mature man – and I was lucky.[8]

I want to engage for a moment in some speculative reflection, pausing on the question of whether Malcolm might have sufficiently transformed with respect to his personal relations in order to fulfill the contemporary hopes of his wife Betty Shabazz. My purpose is to try to begin to liberate his legacy from the rigid notions of male dominance that were a part of the ideological climate in which Malcolm grew to personal and political maturity. Considering the willingness of Malcolm to re-evaluate his political positions, I would like to think that under new ideological circumstances he might have also reconfigured his relationship with his family – and that if Betty Shabazz were hypothetically to re-encounter Malcolm during these contemporary times, she might find more of what she seeks today in the man than the historical Malcolm was capable of providing.

But again I am indulging in speculations about what a dead man – a man who has been dead for almost three decades – might be like today, if he were not dead, when I have repeatedly insisted that I do not intend to suggest that definitive statements may be made regarding what Malcolm X might or might not have been. So, once more I remind myself that I am really concerned with the continuing influence of both those who see themselves as the political descendants of Malcolm, and our historical memory of this man as shaped by social and technological forces that have frozen this memory, transforming it into a backward and imprisoning memory rather than a forward-looking impetus for creative political thinking and organizing. It is highly ironic that Malcolm's admonition regarding the mental prison in which black people were incarcerated can be evoked today with respect to the way his own legacy has been constructed.

How, then, *do* we contest the historical memory of Malcolm invoked by Clarence Thomas, who did not hesitate to name Malcolm as one of his role models and heroes? Is it not possible to argue that Anita Hill, in challenging the widespread presumption that male public figures – or any man, for that matter – can continue to harass women sexually with impunity, has situated herself within a complex tradition of resistance? Such a tradition would bring together the historical movements for black liberation and for women's liberation, drawing, for example, both on Malcolm's legacy and on the legacy of Ida B. Wells, whose anti-lynching efforts also challenged the sexual violence inflicted on black women's bodies. This tradition can be claimed and further developed not only by African-American women such as Anita Hill and those women among us who like myself identify with feminist political positions, but also by our brothers as well as by progressive women and men of other cultures and ethnicities.

My interrogation of Malcolm X's contemporary legacy means to encourage discussion of some of the urgent contemporary political issues that some who claim to be Malcolm's descendants are reluctant to recognize. Thus my final set of questions. How do we challenge the police violence inflicted on untold numbers of black men, such as Rodney King, and at the same time organize against the pervasive sexual violence that continues to be perpetrated by men who claim to be actual or potential revolutionaries? How do we challenge the increasingly intense assault on women's reproductive rights initiated by the Reagan and Bush administrations? How do we bring into our political consciousness feminist concerns – the corporate destruction of the environment, for example – that have been historically constructed as "white people's issues"?[9] How do we halt the growing tendency toward violence perpetrated by African-Americans against Asians? How do we reverse established attitudes within the African-American community – and especially in popular youth culture, as nourished by the iconization of Malcolm X – that encourage homophobia, sometimes even to the point of violence, associating such backward positions with the exaltation of the black man? How do we criticize Magic Johnson's compulsion to distinguish himself as a heterosexual who contracted HIV through heterosexual relations, thereby declaring his own innocence, which effectively condemns gay men with HIV? How can we speak out against racist hate crimes, while simultaneously breaking the silence about anti-gay hate crimes that occur within the black community, perpetrated by black homophobes against black or Latino/Latina or white gay men and lesbians?

More generally, how do we live and act at this juncture of history – in the five hundredth year since Columbus's invasion of the Americas? What are our responsibilities to the indigenous people of this land where we all now live? To Leonard Peltier, who remains a political prisoner, and to Assata Shakur, who remains in exile? How do we make it forever impossible for sports teams to bear such racist, derogatory names as the Washington "Redskins" and the Atlanta "Braves"?

If in 1992 we talk about the necessary means, as in "Revolution By Any Means Necessary," it might make more sense to figure out the means necessary to rethink and reshape the contours of our political activism. I have a fantasy; I sometimes daydream about masses of black men in front of the Supreme Court chanting "End sexual harassment by any means necessary; Protect women's reproductive rights, by any means necessary." And we women are there too, saying "Right on!"

NOTES

1 Patricia Robinson, "Malcolm X, Our Revolutionary Son and Brother," in John Henrik Clarke (ed.), *Malcolm X: The Man and His Times* (Trenton, NJ: Africa World Press, 1990), 63.

2 Bruce Perry (ed.), *Malcolm X: The Last Speeches* (New York: Pathfinder Press, 1989), 25.

3 Interview in *Young Socialist* (March–April 1965), excerpted in George Breitman (ed.), *Malcolm X Speaks* (New York: Grove Weidenfeld, 1990), 212.

4 Ibid., 212–13.

5 In an interview conducted by Bernice Bass on December 27, 1964, Malcolm made the following comment: "One thing I noticed in both the Middle East and Africa, in every country that was progressive the women were progressive. In every country that was underdeveloped and backward, it was to the same degree that the women were undeveloped or underdeveloped and backward" (Perry, ed., *Malcolm X: The Last Speeches*, 98). During the same interview, he spoke of his meeting with Shirley Graham Du Bois, who at that time was the national director of television in Ghana: "She's a woman, and she's an Afro-American, and I think that should make Afro-American women mighty proud" (p. 96).

6 Nick Charles, "Malcolm X, The Myth and the Man," *Cleveland Plain Dealer Magazine*, February 2, 1992.

7 Betty Shabazz (as told to Susan Taylor and Audrey Edwards), "Loving and Losing Malcolm," *Essence*, 22, no. 10 (February 1992), 50.

8 Ibid.

9 Three out of five African Americans live in communities with abandoned toxic waste sites. Three of the five largest commercial hazardous waste landfills (that is, 40 percent of the nation's landfill capacity) are located in predominantly African-American communities. In Los Angeles, 71 percent of African Americans and 50 percent of Latinos live in areas with the most polluted air – as compared with 34 percent of white people. See Robert D. Bullard, "Urban Infrastructure: Social, Environmental, and Health Risks to African Americans," in Billy Tidwell (ed.), *The State of Black America, 1992* (Washington, DC: National Urban League, 1992), 185, 190.

20

Black Nationalism: The Sixties and the Nineties

In this discussion of masculinist dimensions of black nationalism and cultural challenges to male supremacy, I reflect on the kindred character of black nationalism(s) and ideologies of male dominance during the sixties. Revisiting my own experiences with the nationalisms of the sixties, I suggest ways in which contemporary black popular culture may have been unduly influenced by some of the more unfortunate ideological convergences of that era.

I begin with some thoughts on the impact of Malcolm X's nationalist oratory on my own political awakening, which I would later think of in terms similar to Frantz Fanon's description of the coming to consciousness of the colonized in *The Wretched of the Earth*.

I remember the moment when I first felt the stirrings of "nationalism" in my – as I might have articulated it then – "Negro Soul." This *prise de conscience* occurred during a lecture delivered by Malcolm X at Brandeis University, where I was one of five or six black undergraduates enrolled. I might have said that I felt "empowered" by Malcolm's words – except that the notion of power had not yet been understood in a way that separated the exercise of power from subjective emotions occasioned by an awareness of the possibility of exercising it. But I recall that I felt extremely good – I could even say I experienced the joy that Cornel West talked about – momentarily surrounded by, feeling nurtured and caressed by black people who, as I recall, seemed to have no particular identity other than that they were black.

This invitation to join an empowering but abstract community of black people – this naive nationalist consciousness – was extended to me in a virtually all-white setting. It was a strange, but quite logical, reversal. Having grown up in one of the most segregated cities in the South, I had never personally known a white person in my hometown. The only one with whom I remember having any contact was the Jewish man who owned the grocery store in our neighborhood. White people lived across the street from my family's house, but we literally lived on the border separating black from white and could not cross the street on which our house was located. Because of the mandatory character of the black community in which I grew up I came to experience it as somewhat suffocating and desperately sought a way out.

Now finally, on the other side of this feeling evoked in me by the offensive nationalist rhetoric of Malcolm X – offensive, both because he offended the white people in attendance and because he was ideologically on the offensive – I was able to construct a psychological space within which I could "feel good about myself." I could celebrate my body (especially my nappy hair, which I always attacked with a hot comb in ritualistic seclusion), my musical proclivities, and my suppressed speech patterns, among other things. But I shared these feelings with no one. It was a secret thing – like a collective, fictive playmate. This thing distanced me from the white people around me while simultaneously rendering controllable the distance I had always felt from them. It also meant that I did not have to defer to the mandatoriness of my Negro community back home. As a matter of fact, as a result of this experience into which Malcolm's words launched me, I felt a strengthening of the ties with the community of my birth.

This nationalist appeal of the early Malcolm X, however, did not move me to activism – although I had been something of an activist since the age of thirteen. I didn't particularly feel the need to *do* anything. It ended for me where it began in changing the structure of my feeling. Don't get me wrong. I really needed that. I needed it at least as much as I would later need the appeal of the image of the leather-jacketed, black-bereted warriors standing with guns at the entrance to the California legislature. (I saw that image in a German newspaper while studying with Theodor Adorno in Frankfurt.) That image, which would eventually become so problematic for me, called me home. And it directed me into an organizing frenzy in the streets of South Central Los Angeles.

In a sense, the feeling that Malcolm had conjured in me could finally acquire a mode of expression – collective, activist, and, I hoped, transformative. Except that once I arrived in Southern California – with contacts I had gotten from Stokely Carmichael, whom I met, along with Michael X, in London at a "Dialectics of Liberation" conference – my inquiries and enthusiasm were interpreted as a desire to infiltrate local Black organizations. After all, I had just gotten off the boat from Europe. I had to be CIA or something. But, eventually, I did embark upon an exploration of some of the nationalisms of the era. I found out, during my initial contacts, that Ron Karenga's group was too misogynist (although I would not have used that word then). Another organization I found too middle class and elitist. Yet another fell apart because we, women, refused to be pushed to the back of the bus. And even though we may have considered the feminism of that period white, middle class, and utterly irrelevant, we also found compulsory male leadership utterly unacceptable.

Today, I realize that there is no simple or unitary way to look at expressions of black nationalism or essentialism in contemporary cultural forms. As my own political consciousness evolved in the sixties, I found myself in a politically oppositional stance to what some of us then called "narrow nationalism." As a Marxist, I found issues of class and internationalism as necessary to my philosophical orientation as inclusion in a community of historically oppressed people of African descent. But, at the same time, I needed to say "black is beautiful" as much as any of the intransigent anti-white nationalists. I needed to explore my African ancestry, to don African garb, and to wear my hair natural as much as the blinder-wearing male supremacist cultural nationalists. (And, by the way, I had no idea my own "natural" would achieve its somewhat legendary status; I was simply emulating other sisters.)

My relationship to the particular nationalism I embraced was rooted in political practice. The vortex of my practice was always the progressive, politicized black community – though I frequently questioned my place as a black woman in that community, even in the absence of a vocabulary with which to pose the relevant questions. Within the Communist Party, "black" was my point of reference – which did not prevent me from identifying with the multiracial working class and its historical agency. I am not suggesting that the negotiation of that relationship was not fraught with many difficulties, but I do know that I probably would not have joined the Communist Party at that time if I had not been able to enter the Party through an all-black collective in Los Angeles called the Che-Lumumba Club.

The sisters who were my closest comrades, in SNCC, in the Black Panther Party, in the Communist Party, fought tenaciously – and we sometimes fought tenaciously among ourselves – for our right to fight. And we were sometimes assisted in this by sympathetic men in these organizations. We may not have been able to talk about gendered racism; "sexuality" may have still meant sexiness; homophobia, as a word, may not yet have existed; but our practice, I can say in retrospect, was located on a continuum that groped and zigzagged its way toward this moment of deliberation on the pitfalls of nationalism and essentialism. I revisit my own history here to situate myself, in this current exploration of postnationalism, as a revolutionary activist during an era when nationalist and essentialist ideas about black people and the black struggle in the United States crystallized in such a way as to render them capable of surviving in the historical consciousness of people of African descent throughout the diaspora, but especially in the collective imagination of large numbers of

African-American youth today. Perhaps we might make a similar observation about the Garveyism of the 1920s, but, among other things, the undeveloped state of – and forced exclusion from – both media technology and popular historical consciousness prevented us from later being inspired in the same way as by those slogans and images of the late sixties.

Today, of course, young people are explicitly inspired by what they know about Malcolm X and the Black Panther Party. And I find myself in a somewhat problematic position because my own image appears now and then in visual evocations of this nationalist impulse that fuel the advocacy of revolutionary change in contemporary hip-hop culture. These days, young people who were not even born when I was arrested often approach me with expressions of awe and disbelief. On the one hand, it is inspiring to discover a measure of historical awareness that, in our youth, my generation often lacked. But it is also unsettling, because I know that almost inevitably my image is associated with a certain representation of black nationalism that privileges those particular nationalisms with which some of us were locked in constant battle.

Contemporary representations of nationalism in African-American and diasporic popular culture are far too frequently reifications of a very complex and contradictory project that had emancipatory moments leading beyond itself. For example, my own first major activist effort as a budding "nationalist" was the construction of an alliance with Chicano students and progressive white students in San Diego for the purpose of demanding the creation of a college we called Lumumba-Zapata. It is the only college in the University of California, San Diego system, that is identified today by its number – Third College – rather than by a name.

A further example: Look at the issue of the Black Panther Party newspaper in the spring of 1970 in which Huey Newton wrote an article urging an end to verbal gay bashing, urging an examination of black male sexuality, and calling for an alliance with the developing gay liberation movement. This article was written in the aftermath of Jean Genet's sojourn with the Black Panther Party, and Genet's *Un Captif Amoureux* reveals suppressed moments of the history of sixties nationalism.[1]

Such moments as these have been all but eradicated in popular representations today of the black movement of the late sixties and early seventies. And I resent that the legacy I consider my own – one I also helped to construct – has been rendered invisible. Young people with "nationalist" proclivities ought, at least, to have the opportunity to choose which tradition of nationalism they will embrace. How will they position themselves en masse in defense of women's rights and in defense of gay rights if they are not aware of the historical precedents for such positionings?

With respect to the exclusion of such progressive moments in the sixties' history of black nationalism, the mass media is not the sole culprit. We also

have to look at the institutions that package this history before it is disseminated by the media – including some of the academic sites occupied by
obsolete and inveterate nationalists. Furthermore, we need to look at who
packages the practice. The only existing mass black organization that can
claim the so-called authority of having been there during the formative
period of contemporary black nationalism, and therefore, of carrying forth
Malcolm X's legacy, is the Nation of Islam. Who is working with gang
members in South Central Los Angeles today? Who is trying, on an
ongoing basis, to end the violence and to bring warring gangs together in
dialogue? Why is the rap artist Paris, who calls himself the Black Panther of
Rap, a member of the Nation of Islam? Why is Ice Cube studying with the
Nation? Impulses toward collective political practice are being absorbed, in
this instance, by a movement that accords nationalism the status of a
religion.

As enthusiastic as we might be about the capacity of hip-hop culture to
encourage oppositional consciousness among today's young people, it
sometimes advocates a nationalism with such strong misogynist overtones
that it militates against the very revolutionary practice it appears to promote. Where is the door – or even the window – opening onto a conception
of political practice?

Where cultural representations do not reach out beyond themselves,
there is the danger that they will function as surrogates for activism, that
they will constitute both the beginning and end of political practice. I
always go back to Marx's eleventh Feuerbach. This is because, as Cornel
would say, it brings me joy: "Philosophers have interpreted the world in
various ways. The point, however, is to change it."

NOTE

1   Jean Genet, *Un Captif Amoureux* (Paris: Gallimard, 1986); translated as *Prisoner
of Love* (London: Pan Books, 1989).

PART IV

Interviews

21

Coalition Building Among People of Color: A Discussion with Angela Y. Davis and Elizabeth Martinez

Elizabeth "Betita" Martinez, author and longtime activist, writes on Latino issues and works with the Women of Color Resource Center in Berkeley, as well as with youth groups. On May 12, 1993, Ms Davis and Ms Martinez spoke at the University of California, San Diego, on "Building Coalitions of People of Color" with students, staff, and community members. Edited comments from the transcript and questions from audience members are presented here.

How can different people of color come together to build a coalition when their communities have different needs?

Martinez: First of all, we have to reject any hierarchy of needs of different communities. The whole idea of making a hierarchy of demands is sure death from the beginning. I don't mean that some communities or some groups on a campus or in any other community will not want to emphasize certain needs. That's inevitable and there's nothing wrong with it. But we cannot be trapped in arguing about "My need is greater than yours," or "A women's center is more important than a Latino cultural center," or whatever. We have to fight together because there is a common enemy. Especially if you are up against an administration being divisive, I think everybody has to come together and form an alliance or a set of goals

together. There are various forms of working together. A coalition is one, a
network is another, an alliance is yet another. And they are not the same;
some of them are short-term, and some are long-term. A network is not the
same as a coalition. A network is a more permanent, ongoing thing. I think
you have to look at what the demands are, and ask: What kind of coming
together do we need to win these demands? And if you know the administration will pick your groups off one by one, then the largest umbrella you
can possibly get is probably the best one. *Some* of the answers to your
question are tactical and depend upon the circumstances. But the general
idea is no competition of hierarchies should prevail. No "Oppression
Olympics"!

Davis: As Betita has pointed out, we need to be more flexible in our
thinking about various ways of working together across differences. Some
formations may be more permanent and some may be short-term. However, we often assume that the disbanding of a coalition or alliance marks
a moment of failure, which we would rather forget. As a consequence, we
often fail to incorporate a sense of the accomplishments, as well as of the
weaknesses, of that formation into our collective and organizational memories. Without this memory, we are often condemned to start from scratch
each time we set out to build new coalitional forms.

   This is not the first period during which we have confronted the difficult
problem of using difference as a way of bringing people together, rather
than as incontrovertible evidence of separation. There are more options
than sameness, opposition, or hierarchical relations. One of the basic challenges confronting women of color today, as Audre Lorde has pointed out,
is to think about and act upon notions of equality across difference. There
are so many ways in which we can conceptualize coalitions, alliances, and
networks that we would be doing ourselves a disservice to argue that there
is only one way to construct relations across racial and ethnic boundaries.
We cannot assume that if it does not unfold in one particular way, then it
is not an authentic coalition.

*There do seem to be a lot of problems with that idea of coming together across
differences. For example, some people want to spend more time just on African-
American issues, which might not be the priority of a multicultural coalition.*

Davis: Some people may want to do work specifically around African-
American issues. But this approach does not have to exclude working
across and beyond racial boundaries as, for example, the National Black
Women's Health Project focuses on black women's health issues and, at the
same time, is involved in the Women of Color Coalition for Reproductive
Rights. At the same time, this idea of "spending more time with one's own
group" needs to be interrogated. How would you define "one's own

group"? For African-Americans, would that include every person who meets the requirements of physical appearance or every person who identifies as African-American, regardless of their phenotype? Would it include Republican African-Americans who are opposed to affirmative action?

I think we need to be more reflective, more critical and more explicit about our concepts of community. There is often as much heterogeneity within a black community, or more heterogeneity, than in cross-racial communities. An African-American woman might find it much easier to work together with a Chicana than with another black woman whose politics of race, class, gender, and sexuality would place her in an entirely different community. What is problematic is the degree to which nationalism has become a paradigm for our community-building processes. We need to move away from such arguments as "Well, she's not really black." "She comes from such-and-such a place." "Her hair is . . ." "She doesn't listen to 'our' music," and so forth. What counts as black is not so important as our political commitment to engage in anti-racist, anti-sexist, and anti-homophobic work.

Martinez: There is also a tendency to say "That's a Latino issue," or "That's an African-American issue," or whatever, and to see those issues as separate. Or there are people concerned with gender issues, people concerned with gay and lesbian rights, etc. As if those matters all separate, as if there's no connection. Cornel West, the African-American philosopher and writer, spoke recently in San Francisco, talking about the importance of linkages. For example, he said gay and lesbian rights are an issue in the African-American community. They aren't separate, outside of the community. Just because the issue is not welfare, or racism, or gangs, that doesn't mean it's not a black community issue. I think that's a very useful and important way to look at things. I know a lot of Latinos wouldn't agree that gay and lesbian rights are a Latino issue. But we need to work for this understanding and make it clear that the issue is not a problem for a bunch of people outside the Latino community who happen to be gay or lesbian. It's *inside* our community. Taking that kind of position is the only way that in fact makes sense.

Did you ever have any tensions with other people who ask, "Well, are you a person of color first and a woman next? Or are you with women's issues first and people of color come second to that?" Did you have any trouble saying, "Well, I'm a person of color and a woman at the same time . . ."?

Davis: Last fall at UC Santa Cruz, we established a Women of Color Research Cluster within which faculty, graduate students, and staff discuss their individual work, engage in collaborative projects, sponsor talks by women of color scholars and activists. We are presently working on a journal, edited by Maria Ochoa and Teresia Teaiwa. Another member of the cluster, Margaret Daniel, organizes an annual Women of Color Film and Video Festival on campus. The term "women of color" is often used in a nominalistic way, without substantive meaning. However, within this research cluster, women of color can really wrestle with the hard questions about working together, building collaborative forms, exploring cross-racial/cultural/ethnic relations among women, whether they be conflictual and antagonistic or collaborative and coalitional. As Chela Sandoval has argued, this is an era during which "women of color" are being constructed as a new social/political subject.

In thinking about women of color as a political subject, it may be helpful for those of us who are African American to recall that the "black" subject is a subject that was historically created. I grew up thinking of myself as a "Negro," largely unable to articulate the extent to which social inferiority was constructed as an essential dimension of the "Negro." It is important to recognize the various forms of agency with which identities can be and are constructed, in order not to get stuck in them, in order not to assume that racialized identities have always been there. A "black" subject was created. We can also create a "women of color" subject. That is what much of this forum is about: How can we construct political projects that rethink identities in dynamic ways and lead to transformative strategies and radical social change?

Martinez: There is a tremendous tendency in this culture to establish rigid categories, and not to have any kind of a dialectical understanding of the society or its forces; this tendency makes us incapable of seeing that something both is and isn't at the same time. There's pressure to say you're a woman or you're a person of color. It's a dead-end discussion, and one to be resisted. There's no way to separate what you experience as a person in the Raza community from what you experience as a result of being a woman. You might concentrate on certain issues and give them more attention than others at a given moment. But separation as self-definition? No. Don't box me in.

Do you think it's necessary to have ideological unity to build a coalition? And if we do not use ideology as a basis to build coalitions, what is the basis that we use?

Davis: First of all, people who subscribe to similar ideologies can and do come together. Historically, the particular formations within which they work have been called political parties. Until a few years ago, I was a member of the Communist Party, for example. However, ideological affinity is not essential to coalition work, and that is what we presently are concerned with. For twenty years I was co-chairperson of the National

Alliance Against Racist and Political Repression (I am presently Chair Emeritus). Our work initially was framed by a project to free political prisoners. This work raises questions: How do you develop campaigns to free political prisoners? Does one have to identify, for example, with the philosophical nationalism of a black nationalist political prisoner in order to join the effort to free her? Or can one articulate a position of opposition to political repression, while disagreeing with the prisoner's particular politics?

Take the movement that developed around my case. My Communist politics did not deter the vast numbers of people and the over 250 separate committees, in this country and abroad, many of whom may have absolutely disagreed with my politics, from becoming active in the "Free Angela Davis" Campaign. There are many ways of configuring networks, alliances, and coalitions, departing from people's commitment to social change. Again, I want to emphasize the importance of historical memory in our contemporary efforts to work together across differences. I raise the importance of historical memory not for the purpose of presenting immutable paradigms for coalition-building, but rather in order to understand historical trajectories and precisely to move beyond older conceptions of cross-racial organizing.

It would seem to me that once you establish the issue that a group or a coalition is going to work on, that would be the ideology. Maybe I'm confusing "issue" and "ideology," and if I am, what's the distinction between the two?

Martinez: One handy distinction is to think of coalitions being built around issues, and ideology being a worldview. An ideology is a set of ideas that explains what makes society tick and what its values are. You don't have to agree on that with other people in order to fight for health care, housing, affirmative action, or whatever. You do have to agree with somebody's ideology, I think, if you're going to join certain kinds of organizations that demand ideological unity, from the Boy Scouts to the Communist Party. But coalitions, networks, and alliances should never make the mistake of demanding ideological unity. They can expect unity around an issue.

Davis: Let me offer a rather simple example. Suppose I am a revolutionary who announces the ultimate intention of overturning the system of capitalism. I am therefore interested in establishing a socialized health-care system. It would be absurd to argue – although, during the course of my career as an activist, I have heard this many times – that first we have to overthrow the government, then we can consider reconfiguring the health-care system. Consequently, I pursue a political relationship with women who are effective church organizers, who might be utterly unwilling to talk about revolutionary change. We can decide to put forth ideas about health care that are much stronger than Clinton's, and decide about principles around which we will organize a mass campaign. At the same time, we may be very different ideologically.

We often expect individuals to be theoretically informed activists from the outset, in possession of a full-blown political consciousness, as well as having the capacity to organize for social change. As a matter of fact, most people get involved as a result of being hailed by a visible political movement. Drawing from my own personal history, I felt summoned by the students' entrance into the Civil Rights Movement. Although I felt that I was missing out on a powerful movement, because I had left the South and was in high school in New York at the time, I discovered a way to feel connected with Civil Rights activism.

At age fifteen, I participated in a youth project of picketing the Woolworth's near the 42nd Street library every Saturday morning. I was therefore also summoned by those who organized this particular way of expressing solidarity with the Southern movement. If there had been no movements to hail me, I have no idea what I would have done or would be doing today. If you are one of those organizers capable of pioneering initiatives, and we need such organizers in women of color movements today, and you want to activate youth, make sure you combine the political content with forms and styles of presentation that can dramatically hail young women and men.

How can the successful coalition of gay and lesbian communities be extended to a broader coalition of the entire human race, where all of us can be included in one broad coalition, fighting for the day when none of us will be recognized as African-American, or as Anglo-American, or as Spanish-American, but as a human being, and as one race, one person, one body?

Davis: Your moves are a little too fast for me. I am not sure that I would want to end up at a place where everybody is the same. I do not take a common future to mean a homogeneous future. While I absolutely agree with the importance you place on challenging compulsory heterosexuality, homophobia, hate crimes against lesbians, gay men and bisexuals, I don't know whether we can assume that multiracial coalitions have already been successfully constructed within gay communities. Racism is still a factor both within the gay movement and in the way the gay movement is publicly perceived. The ideological question of gay and white is still very much a problem. This is not, however, to underestimate the significant anti-racist work in predominantly white gay circles, nor is it to ignore the important work on multiple fronts by gay women and men of color.

In building alliances and coalitions, we have to consider carefully how to articulate issues so as to encourage racial boundary crossing. I personally am concerned about the way this question of lifting the ban on gays and lesbians in the military seemingly has moved to the top of the political agenda in a relatively uncomplicated articulation. Homophobia in the military should be opposed, unquestionably. The ban should be lifted. But to base this demand on formalistic arguments equating the soldierly abilities of gays and lesbians with those of straight people is extremely problematic.

In this context, the question would be: How is it possible to vigorously oppose the ban on gays and lesbians in the military, and at the same time to principly oppose the military? This is especially important within the context of coalitions involving African-Americans, since for young black men, the military, with its authoritarian structure and imperialistic projects, has become one of the only escape routes from joblessness, drugs, and prison. In the course of organizing against homophobia in the military, it should also be possible to raise demands for jobs, education, etc.

Martinez: The question asked just now also concerns the idea of seeing all human beings in one broad coalition. People ask: "Why can't we all see each other as human beings? Why do we have to emphasize these differences?" *or* "Why do we need feminism? Why can't we just have humanism? Doesn't talking about racism and the different races just perpetuate the problem?" This negates the structures of power that determine human relationships in this society in a way that is deadening for a great number of people, mostly, but by no means exclusively, people of color. You can't just say "let's all get along" until we get rid of those structures.

(Please comment on the fact that) UC Berkeley is planning to cut first year Spanish, and that move may have a domino effect (for Spanish programs on other UC campuses).

Martinez: I think students should be mobilizing against this move; both students who speak Spanish and those who really should learn to speak Spanish.

Davis: Perhaps we might develop a campaign to expand the general education requirements so that some knowledge of Spanish would be required of every student attending any campus of the UC system. As we approach the millennium, we need to demystify the notion that this country is monolingual.

Martinez: We're also probably going to have to think in terms of languages other than Spanish as the second language in a number of communities, according to the population there. This is something we really need to be working on.

Angela Davis, I'd like to know your definition of a feminist.

Davis: I don't think I would propose a single definition of the term "feminist." It is one of those categories/commitments that can have a range of definitions and I don't think that it is helpful to insist on prescriptions for feminism. But I do think we can agree that feminism in its many versions acknowledges the social impact of gender and involves opposition to misogyny. In my opinion, the most effective versions of feminism acknowledge the various ways gender, class, race, and sexual orientation inform each other.

Some women, especially women of color, see feminism as anchored to a particular historical experience of white middle-class women and they consequently are reluctant to use "feminist" as a self-referential term. Among these women, some have opted, along with Alice Walker, to call themselves "womanists." That's fine. This does not mean they are unwilling to work with "feminists."

Coalitional efforts among women of color should not require the self-reference of womanism any more than they should require the self-reference of feminism. And it should not be a question of who is "more feminist," because of sexual orientation, location in the academy or the factory, and so forth. We should seek a point of junction constructed by the political projects we choose to embrace. Even though feminism may mean different things for different women (and men), this should not prevent us from creating movements that will put us in motion together, across all our various differences.

Personally, it was only after many years of political involvement that I decided to embrace the term feminism. I now feel very comfortable calling myself a feminist. But the way I am a feminist tomorrow may be different from the way I am a feminist today. My own conception of myself as a feminist constantly evolves as I learn more about the issues that women's movements need to address. It is more productive, I think, not to adhere to rigid categories, to the idea that there is something called "African-American woman-ness," some essence we can discover. A vast range of identities can be encompassed by "African-American woman." What is important, I think, is to fight on and not about political terms, such as: agendas for jobs, student funding, health care, childcare, housing, reproductive rights, etc. Ways of feeling are very important, but we have to focus on substantive, radical institutional transformation as well. Empowerment will remain powerless if we do not change power relations.

This is a question for both of you. As student leaders here on the campus, a lot of times it's hard to motivate students, and as student leaders, of course, sooner or later we are going to graduate. Do you have any suggestions as to how to motivate students to become involved in our internal organization, so that we as students of color as well as student leaders can all unite and then maybe go off and form other coalitions? Because internally, if our business isn't really taken care of, how can we be effective in moving on to deal with other issues of multiculturalism?

Davis: There is a way in which the movements of the sixties and early seventies are set up as models of activism for young people today. Incredibly dramatic movements from that era remain etched in our national memory, whether we experienced them or not: the student movement, the Black Power Movement, movements of Chicanos, Native Americans, Asian Americans. Many young people are led to romanticize the participants and the strategies and styles of those movements. You don't necessarily consider how hard it was to organize. You don't necessarily realize that we had to grapple with many of the same questions that confront you in far more complicated forms today.

We often leapt into action even when we had no idea whether our strategies would work. I think you need to give yourselves permission to think and act in different ways, to take risks as you try to encourage political action, even when you may not be sure of the outcome. I can tell you many success stories from the sixties and seventies, but I can also tell you as many stories that did not end so triumphantly.

When I first came to UC San Diego, I had been studying in Europe. I returned in order to continue my studies with Herbert Marcuse, but within a context that would also allow me to participate in the black movement of that era. However, on this campus, it was weeks before I even saw another black person. Finally, two African-American undergraduates, a Caribbean professor, and I made plans to comb the campus in order to identify the black students who would be potential members of a Black Student Alliance. Since there were so few students, we reconceptualized the alliance to include staff and workers. It required a great deal of work to find the people, and then to convince them to participate in our joint effort. Soon it became clear that we could increase our chances of success if we entered into a coalition with the Chicanos on campus, who were simultaneously organizing a Mexican American Youth Association.

This was a period in which nationalist forms of organizing had become extremely popular, but we decided that as separate organizations, we would be relatively ineffective. But as a coalition, which eventually invited a white radical student group to join, we could effectively mount a campaign for control over the Third College, which we named Lumumba-Zapata College.

Martinez: I want to emphasize the point about risk. There's not a climate of taking risks today. There are reasons for that, such as the twelve years of Reagan–Bush, with all the "me first-ism" and cynicism they bred. That's part of what you're up against when you talk about how to motivate students today. The seven African-American students who sat down at that Woolworth's lunch counter at the first sit-in, April 1, 1960, had no idea they were going to start a huge movement, a nationwide movement. No idea. They just did it. They got ketchup thrown on them and were beaten, arrested. But they took a chance. There has to be some of that spirit today: let's experiment, we don't have to have all the answers, we certainly don't have to have the ideology down, you know, the whole package. But let's see some things that are wrong and try to change them, and take risks.

22

Reflections on Race, Class, and Gender in the USA

Lisa Lowe: Please begin by considering the social, political, and economic shifts that have taken place in the United States during the period of the 1960s to the 1990s. I would like to invite you to characterize what, in your opinion, has shifted and what has not. In other words, we no longer have the FBI and police assaults on Black Panther chapters all over the country; but we do have Mumia Abu-Jamal on death row in Pennsylvania. We no longer have Jim Crow segregation, but we have another kind of segregation: we have a Supreme Court ruling that it is unconstitutional to have racial preferences for affirmative action. I wonder if you could put this current moment in the 1990s into a dialectical relation with the 1960s.

Angela Davis: There are many ways to talk about the relationship between the '60s and the '90s. The social movements of the '60s – the civil rights movement, various movements of Native Americans, Chicanos/Latinos, Asian Americans, the women's movement, the student movement – did bring about significant, if not radical, transformations. Much of what we can call progressive change, particularly in the area of race, can be attributed to struggles waged by those movements. At the same time, a new terrain was established, which at times appears to contradict the meaning of the movements of the '60s. Did we work so hard in order to guarantee entrance of a conservative black man, who opposes affirmative action and women's reproductive rights, into the Supreme Court? Rather than simply despair that things are taking a reactionary turn, I think it is important to acknowledge the extent to which the black movement allowed for the emergence of a much more powerful black middle class and the breakup of an apparent political consensus. There are similar middle-class formations among other racial ethnic groups. So the question today is not so much how

This interview with Angela Y. Davis was conducted by Lisa Lowe in Oakland, California, July 1, 1995. It first appeared under the title "Angela Davis: Reflections of Race, Class, and Gender in the USA," in *The Politics of Culture in the Shadow of Capital*, eds Lisa Lowe and David Lloyd (Durham NC: Duke University Press, 1997), copyright © 1997 Duke University Press. Reprinted with permission of the publishers.

to reverse these developments to re-find ourselves, based on a kind of nostalgic longing for what used to be, but rather, to think about the extent to which movements for racial and gender equality can no longer be *simply* based on questions of desegregation. A different kind of "political," a different kind of politics, really, has to inform this movement. I don't know. Does that make any sense?

LL: It makes a great deal of sense. When Stuart Hall talks about the convergence of the different contradictions of race, class, and gender, he suggests that the material conditions of a given historical moment make a certain contradiction rise to the surface. Could you speak about the conditions of our current moment in relation to these contradictions, addressing the ways that capitalism utilizes racism and sexism? Has the conjunction of race, class, and gender shifted in our contemporary period?

AD: Well, one of the strongest factors that has brought about the current set of transformations is deindustrialization. And the increased mobility of capital. And what I would say initially is that the collapse of an international socialist community – for good reasons, one can point out – which has led to the assumption that capitalism is the only future alternative makes it increasingly difficult to draw connections between the deteriorating conditions in communities of color and the restructuring of global capitalism, for example, the focus on crime as the most serious social problem, and the rise of the punishment industry. Another example is the related criminalization of single mothers of color through the ideological representation of the "welfare queen" as the reproducer of poverty. So the connection between the globalization of capital and these developments – which began with the Reagan–Bush administration, but have reached their peak recently – aren't generally made.

LL: Are you saying that because of global restructuring, the proletarianization of women of color in the United States is simultaneous with the exploitation of women in the so-called third world? In other words, that both exploitations are specific to the global restructuring of capitalism?

AD: Absolutely. But at the same time, what I'm trying to get at is the way in which these developments are actually represented within social movements, for example, within the black community, the increased focus on young black males, which is important, but dangerous at the same time. Important because of the fact that black youth, young black men, certainly are very much at risk since a quarter of them are under the direct jurisdiction of the criminal justice system, either in prison, on parole, or on probation. But at the same time, the demonization and criminalization of young black women is often totally neglected. What is also neglected is the fact that the rate of increase in the incarcerated population of women is about twice the rate of increase in the rate of incarceration of men.

Consider the recent movement spearheaded by Reverend Ben Chavis and Minister Farrakhan of the Nation of Islam, which calls upon black men to reassert their primacy within black families and communities. A Washington demonstration of "a million black men" in the fall of 1995 is predicated on the fact that women will stay at home in support of "their men." Certainly, in this period of increased mobility of capital, there is a gendered assault on young black men – jobs that used to be available have migrated to other parts of the world. However, to assume that saving black communities is equivalent to saving black men harks back to a dangerous, unreflected masculinist nationalism that informed black movements earlier on. There are productive ways in which a gender analysis can specifically identify ways in which men are disproportionately affected by deindustrialization. Moreover, during this period, if black men choose to organize as men, questions such as male support of women's reproductive rights and of lesbians' right to adopt and male opposition to violence against women should be emphasized. Rather than male primacy in families and communities, gender equality in private as well as public spheres needs to be foregrounded.

LL: From your vantage point now, when you think about the breakup and the transformations of black liberation struggles in the '60s, what is your understanding of the relationship between the external assault from the FBI, the police, and the state and the internal difference and conflict about priorities, about methods?

AD: In a sense, the external assaults worked hand in hand with the internal contradictions. We know that J. Edgar Hoover identified the Black Panther Party as the greatest threat to the internal security of the country, and that the FBI orchestrated assaults from one end of the country to the other, in collaboration with local police departments. This has been documented. What has not been taken as seriously is the internal struggles within radical black and Latino organizations. It was the inability to address questions of gender and sexuality that also led inevitably to the demise of many organizations. Many elder activists, as well as people who had not yet been born during the era, mourn the passing of the Black Panther Party, and nostalgically look back to that period as one in which questions of who and what constituted the enemy were crystal clear. The recent film by Melvyn Van Peebles represents the Black Panther Party in that kind of nostalgic and romantic way. If you look at Elaine Brown's book, which has been abundantly criticized – for good reasons, in part – she does reveal the extent to which the BPP and many of its fraternal organizations were very much informed by masculinist notions of what it meant to engage in struggle. These notions of struggle depended on the subordination of women, both ideologically and in practice. The women were responsible for a vastly disproportionate amount of work in a struggle constructed as one for the freedom of "the black man." This kind of critique has to continue. A number of recent Ph.D. dissertations look at women's roles in organizations like the Young Lords, the Black Panther Party, the Brown

Berets, and the American Indian Movement. Tracy Matthews, who was in the history department at the University of Michigan, has written her dissertation on women in the Black Panther Party. Hopefully there will be a nice collection of books coming out in the next few years, which will begin to demystify the images of radical organizations of people of color in the late '60s and early '70s, for the sake of young people who desire to do activist work in the contemporary period.

LL: Can I ask a little more about a different kind of contradiction? In *Racial Formation in the United States,* Michael Omi and Howard Winant argue that during the period of civil rights struggles, civil rights legislation was in a way the state's attempt to appropriate and co-opt certain parts of the broader, wider variety of social movements pressuring for more change on race.[1] Would you agree with this analysis?

AD: During the civil rights era, the primary struggles were for legal transformation. It was important at the time to break down the legal barriers, to change the laws, to challenge the juridical status of people of color. Parenthetically, one of the real weaknesses of the civil rights movement was its paradigmatic black–white focus on race. But Omi and Winant point out correctly that social movements addressed issues that went beyond the legal construction of race. Beyond voting rights and desegregation, issues of education, health care, police repression, issues of jobs, etc. were raised. Organizations like SNCC [Student Nonviolent Coordinating Committee] that were rooted in voter registration and desegregation struggles initially focused on those issues, but then went on to address questions that emerged from the urban northern black communities as well.

LL: They don't argue, of course, that there was total co-optation. But rather that civil rights legislation was the response of the state to activist social movements, some of which could have called for much more radical change.

AD: Absolutely.

LL: In a way, it goes along with what you were pointing out earlier, that Clarence Thomas is where he is because of affirmative action and the contradictions of liberalism. Yet, despite such contradictions, we must still insist on the concept of rights, and humanity, and fight to keep in place the legislation that is now under attack.

AD: Yes, but the assumption that the state is the primary guardian of the victories that were won by the Civil Rights Movement has led to a great deal of chaos, and an inability to conceptualize where social movements can go from here. At the same time, many of the leaders of the Civil Rights Movement now occupy putative positions of power within the state structure. Look, for example, at Ron Dellums, who was initially associated with the Black Panther Party in Oakland, California. As a matter of fact, he was elected to Congress on the basis of his militant and radical positions. For the past twenty-five years, he's had to negotiate very different kinds of positions. His work within Congress has been very important. But the constituencies which were activist constituencies became electoral constituencies. With the election of Clinton, which ended the Republican Reagan–Bush era, there was the assumption that now, yes, the state will fulfill the goal that was set for it during the transformative period of the civil rights struggle. And that, as a matter of fact, the reliance on the new administration led to the absorption of oppositional organizations – and sometimes almost entire movements – into state structures.

LL: With the priority, would you say, on enfranchisement and assimilation into the state, as opposed to working for a larger transformation?

AD: That is true, and it is a rather complicated process. In many instances people truly believe that they will be able to bring about radical transformations from and within new positions of state power. The work that I am doing on prisons is a case in point. Many people whose connection with prison issues comes from their earlier involvement in oppositional struggles – who were involved in and in some instances were initiators of the prisoner rights movement – are now working within correctional bureaucracies. Here in San Francisco, the current sheriff and assistant sheriff have a long history of involvement in progressive movements. The assistant sheriff spent many years in prison during the '60s and early '70s and was associated with George Jackson and the internal prisoner movement. He was one of the founders of the California Prisoners Union. Now he inhabits the very positions which were once occupied by his adversaries. Under his leadership people have been hired to work within the jail structures who are former prisoners (such as myself and Johnny Spain, once of the San Quentin Six) and who were once visible as militant activists (such as Harry Edwards, who organized the protests at the 1968 Mexico City Olympics). The assumption, of course, is that these individuals will press for transformation. However, under such conditions transformation is conceptualized very differently. The formulation of radical prison work as leading toward the reduction of prison populations and the abolition of jails and prisons as the primary means of addressing social problems such as crime, unemployment, under-education, etc. recedes and is replaced with the goal of creating better, more progressive jails and prisons. I am not suggesting that we should not use whatever political arenas are available to us. However, once one becomes integrated into state structures, it becomes increasingly difficult to think about ways of developing radical oppositional practices.

LL: You have always been a voice for feminist concerns within black liberation struggles, yet it has been difficult for Marxist antiracist work to find a "home" in feminism as it has existed in the US women's movement. In *Women, Race, and Class*, but also in your lectures "Facing Our Common

Foe" and "We Do Not Consent," you argue that racism and classism affect the construction of political agendas even and especially in the white women's movement regarding race and reproductive rights.[2] I wonder if you could discuss the struggles within US feminism in the last decade. You argue eloquently that historically rape has been defined as rape of the white woman's body, who is the property of elite white men, which obscures the possibility of thinking of black women's bodies as victims of rape, or victims of assault, and subordinates the issue of black women's health. Has the antiracist critique successfully changed white feminism?

AD: From one vantage point, those critiques have been very successful. Which isn't to say that hegemonic white feminism, in the sense in which Chela Sandoval uses the term, has really substantively changed. But it is no longer possible to ignore issues of race. Even those who only pay lip service to race analysis understand this. Twenty-five years ago, dominant feminism began to evolve as if women of color did not exist. As a result, vast numbers of women of color who were interested in women's issues did not associate themselves with early feminist approaches. Toni Morrison, who is very much associated with black feminists today, wrote an article in the early 1970s in the *New York Times Magazine* in which she argued that feminism belonged to white women and had no relevance for black women. The most interesting developments in feminism, I think, over the past couple of decades have occurred within the theories and practices of women of color. US feminism would not be what it is today, US feminisms would not be what they are today, if it hadn't been for the interventions by women of color. So I think that's a very positive sign. At the same time, within communities of color, feminism has become a much more powerful force and has had an impact on all kinds of issues, on the way issues are constructed, the way campaigns are developed. The critique has to continue, though; I'm not suggesting that the work has been done. It's a lot more complicated today. Women of color who refer to themselves as feminists still find that it is not easy to identify as a feminist. For one, feminism is often considered obsolete. There are a number of new works that have been published by young feminists, both feminists of color and white feminists, that, in order to dissociate themselves from traditional feminism, tend to revert to prefeminist ideas.

LL: I would like to ask you to situate yourself in women of color discourse. Many people would locate women of color critique in the antiracist critique of white feminism: Cherrie Moraga, Gloria Anzaldua, or Audre Lorde would be key figures in this nexus. Or alternatively, others would locate it in the black feminist critique of male-dominated cultural nationalism. But I understand the genealogy of your work and practice as articulating a feminist antiracist critique within the Marxist critique of capitalism. Yours is a most important synthesis that really advances women of color critique. Please share your thoughts about women of color as a political project and as a research project.

AD: Well, I don't know if we can talk about women of color politics in a monolithic way.

LL: It's perhaps even difficult to understand it as a social movement. In a way it's a critique that has various locations.

AD: There've been really interesting developments over the past fifteen years or so, since most people date the development of women of color as a new political subject from 1981, when *This Bridge Called My Back* was published.[3] Women of color conceptualized as a political project, to borrow Chandra Mohanty's notion, is extremely important. You might also use Omi and Winant's notion and argue that it is possible to think about women of color as a different kind of racial formation. And the work that you, Lisa, have done on women of color emphasizes the fact that it is a provisional identity that allows the move beyond identity politics articulated in the traditional way. The fact that race is placed at the forefront of women of color politics is important, because it also challenges the influence of nationalism on identity politics. Women of color formations are compelled to address intersectionality and the mutual and complex interactions of race, class, gender, and sexuality. That is what is so exciting about the possibilities of women of color research and organizing strategies. For the last four years or so I have been working with the Research Cluster for the Study of Women of Color in Collaboration and Conflict. Many students and faculty involved locate their work within a progressive scholarly and activist tradition that seeks to bring about structural and ideological change. The Women of Color Resource Center here in the San Francisco Bay Area attempts to forge stronger ties between researchers and grassroots organizers. Asian Immigrant Women's Advocates (AIWA) is one of the groups associated with the Women of Color Resource Center. This organization traces its genealogy back to the Third World Women's Alliance founded in 1970. This means that what we call women of color work predates 1981, the year in which *This Bridge Called My Back* was published, which is usually evoked as the originating moment of women of color consciousness. During the earlier era, the anti-imperialist character of third world women's work inflected it with a strong anticapitalist kind of critique. The influence of Marxism is still very much visible in, for example, the Combahee River Collective manifesto. While it is important to affirm the momentous cultural work initiated with the publication of *This Bridge*, the earlier, more explicitly anticapitalist traditions should not be erased.

LL: And those connections are like a history that needs still to be written.

AD: Yes. What we call women of color work or US third world women's work can be traced back to the civil rights era. During the 1964 campaign spearheaded by SNCC in Mississippi, Georgia, and Alabama, there was an emergent antimasculinist critique, directed against the obstinately male leadership. This critique crystallized in an internal organization of black women, which later established itself as an autonomous organization, the Black Women's Alliance. While cross-racial coalitions were not as self-conscious as they tend to be today, the political projects to which Puerto Rican women (antisterilization work, for example) and Asian American women (Vietnam solidarity work, for example) were drawn, were also embraced by the Black Women's Alliance, which later reconceptualized itself as a Third World Women's Alliance. Some of the same women associated with those efforts in the late '60s – like Elizabeth Martinez, Linda Burnham, Fran Beal – continue to be active through organizations like the Women of Color Resource Center. Around the same time, numerous lesbians of color organizations emerged. In fact, the term *lesbian of color* acquired currency before *women of color* entered into our political vocabulary. In other words, although we refer to "women of color" as a new political subject, there is a rich, unexplored history of women of color political projects. We shouldn't assume that women of color work has been going on for only a decade or so.

LL: Or that it's a reaction against . . .

AD: . . . what we used to call white middle-class feminism. NOW was founded in 1964. We can also trace the emergence of a radical women of color feminism back to the same year.

LL: Would you speak a bit about your recent book project on women and the blues? I'm wondering if you could comment on the question of cultural forms as alternative spaces, or popular culture as an informal site for the transmission of oppositional strategies and popular wisdom about survival.

AD: The fact that historical modes of transmitting culture are not mechanically determined by economic relations does not mean that all modes are equally possible regardless of a group's class position. I have been interested in the history of gender consciousness in black communities since the research I did around *Women, Race, and Class*. Much of the material I utilized in that work – even that which specifically addressed issues of working-class women's consciousness – was produced by women and men who can be defined as members of the black intelligentsia. My own interest in popular culture is related to an attempt to expand that original project on gender consciousness in black communities, focusing on the blues as a site for reflecting on black working-class feminist consciousness and on the transmission of that consciousness. In this book, which is called *Blues Legacies and Black Feminisms*, I try to present blues performances as an alternative site for recovering historical forms of working-class women's consciousness.

LL: In your autobiography you wrote, "the forces that have made my life what it is are the very same forces that have shaped and misshaped the lives of millions of my people. I'm convinced that my response to these forces has been unexceptional as well, that my political involvement, ultimately as a member of the Communist Party, has been a natural logical way to defend our embattled humanity."[4] I wonder if you could talk about your formation in Marxism and what Marxism has meant to you.

AD: From where I stood – which was a very different location from that of the vast numbers of people who followed my trial – I did not feel that my life experiences were exceptional enough to merit inscription in an autobiography. Besides, I was very young. So I had to think about that project as a "political" autobiography. At the time I didn't realize that I had conceptualized it in the tradition of the black autobiographical genre that could be said to go back to the slave narrative. That didn't occur to me until long after I had written it. It's difficult to identify a single development that led me to Marxism. I grew up in a family which had numerous ties to individuals in the Communist Party. Although my mother never joined the Communist Party, she worked in organizations with black communists who were organizing in Birmingham, which, because of the steel mills, had become an industrial center in the '30s. She was an officer in the NAACP and in the Southern Negro Youth Congress, which had been established by communists. Because of my mother's connection with communists, we were often followed by the FBI during the McCarthy era. By the age of six, I was already aware of the extent to which the government would pursue people who had different ideas of what kind of social order should prevail in this country. While I was attending a progressive high school in New York, I read the *Communist Manifesto* for the first time. I was fortunate enough to have a history teacher who openly espoused Marxism and encouraged us to think critically about the class interests represented by dominant historiography. At the same time I was active in a communist youth organization and for many months picketed Woolworth's every Saturday because of their policies of segregation in the South. I guess you might say that I learned very early to take for granted the insightfulness of Marxist literature and also to draw connections between theory and practice.

As an undergraduate, my interest in Marxism was further stimulated by professors like Herbert Marcuse. As a French major, I became very interested in the way Marxism was integrated into existentialist philosophy – and by Sartre's political activism. Working with Marcuse, I began to study the philosophical history of Marxism and read Kant, Hegel, as well as Marx. As a young activist in high school, I already considered myself a Marxist. By the time I finished college, I was even more convinced that Marxist analyses could help me make sense of a world which seemed to be so saturated with racism and class exploitation. I guess I had the good fortune to sort of grow into Marxism or grow up with Marxism, rather than having to later work to replace dominant modes of thought with a critical Marxist approach. I should probably point out that the high school I attended, Elizabeth Irwin High School, was rather exceptional. It was actually cooperatively owned by teachers, many of whom had been blacklisted as a result of their political involvements during the McCarthy era.

LL: How important is it, do you think, for young students and people who want to be activists to read Marx and to have a rich education in Marxist theory?

AD: I think it's extremely important. However, many students today encounter Marx's ideas not so much by reading the original works, but rather through their reception in contemporary theoretical literature and in popular culture. Many students might be familiar with Marx the political economist, but are entirely unfamiliar with the early philosophical writings. While I would not make the kind of argument that conservatives present regarding the need to return to the basic – to the "classical" texts in the Western intellectual tradition – I do think that a closer familiarity with Marx's writings might help students to assess critically our contemporary conditions.

LL: Moving into a discussion of the university, pedagogy, and the role of intellectuals of color, I wonder if I could ask you about how you think of your role as an educator and your role in the formation of intellectuals of color.

AD: I grew up in a household of teachers. Both my mother and father were teachers. Although my own decision to go into education came much later, I learned very early to value education and its liberatory potential. In the black community in which I was reared, teachers were among the most respected members of the community and were expected to provide leadership – perhaps in even more fundamental ways than ministers, who are often considered the community's natural leaders. Education and liberation were always bound together. I was persuaded very early in my life that liberation was not possible without education. This is one of the reasons I always felt drawn to the radical potential of education and why I am particularly interested in working not only with students of color, but with white students as well who make this connection.

LL: Who and what were your influences in this regard?

AD: Studying with both Adorno and Marcuse allowed me to think early on about the relationship between theory and practice, between intellectual work and activist work. Adorno tended to dismiss intellectual work that was connected with political activism. He argued that the revolution had failed, not so much because of problems presenting themselves in the practical implementation of revolutionary theory, but rather because the theory itself was flawed, perhaps even fundamentally flawed. He therefore insisted that the only sure way to move along a revolutionary continuum was to effect, for the present, a retreat into theory. No revolutionary transformation was possible, he said, until we could figure out what went wrong in the theory. At the time, student activism was on the rise in Germany. I studied in Frankfurt from 1965 to 1967, which was a period during which the German Socialist Student Organization gained in membership and influence. Because many of the student leaders were directly inspired by the history of the Frankfurt School – and some young professors affiliated with the Frankfurt School like Oscar Negt were actively involved in the SDS (Sozialitische Deutsche Studentenverbund) – we were able to critically engage with Adorno's ideas. Interestingly enough, many of Horkheimer's and Adorno's ideas were mobilized in challenging this advocacy of theory as the only possible mode of practice. I was involved, in fact, in the production of a pirate edition of *Dialectic of Enlightenment*, which Adorno and Horkheimer were not yet willing to republish. We typed the text on stencils, mimeographed it, and sold it for the cost of its production. A similar edition of Lukács's *History and Class Consciousness* was also produced.

Marcuse, of course, called for a very different relationship between intellectual work and political practice. There is a story I like to tell about Marcuse's involvement in UCSD [University of California–San Diego] campus politics, which certainly informed my ideas on the role of the teacher and on the need to maintain always a creative tension between theory and praxis. Back in the late '60s, the emergent black student organization, in alliance with the Chicano student organization, decided to campaign to create a new college at UCSD, which we wanted to name the Lumumba-Zapata College. We envisioned it as a college which would admit one-third Chicano students, one-third black students, and one-third working-class white students. We had it all worked out! Or at least we thought we did. At one point in a rather protracted campaign, we decided to occupy the registrar's office. I said I would ask Herbert about his possible participation in the takeover. I explained to him that we would have to break a window in order to gain entrance. In other words, we risked being charged with breaking and entering and trespassing. If he were the first person to enter the building, we were less likely to be arrested and/or expelled from the university. Without a moment's hesitation, Herbert agreed: "Of course I'll do it." There was no question in his mind. At that time he was about seventy-five years old. He was the first person to walk into the registrar's office. Our work acquired a legitimacy that would have been impossible without his participation. In the classroom and through his writings and lectures, Marcuse defended the radical activism of the late '60s. The emergence of an international student movement, the social movements of people of color, the rise of feminist activism brought a new, more optimistic dimension to Marcuse's ideas. The seduction of the "one-dimensional society" could be resisted. He not only theorized these developments, but actively participated in mobilizations both in the United States and Europe. Working so closely with him during that period, I learned that while teaching and agitation were very different practices, students need to be assured that politics and intellectual life are not two entirely separate modes of existence. I learned that I did not have to leave political activism behind in order to be an effective teacher. Of course, this insight got me fired from my first job at UCLA and during my first year there spies recorded every comment I made in class which might have political undertones. I was first fired for my membership in the Communist Party. The second time I was fired it was because of my off-campus activities in support of political prisoners.

LL: Please speak about your teaching, how you encourage students to do projects that are both activist and intellectual. What sort of role do you take in shaping these projects? Perhaps you could describe the Women of Color Research Cluster at UC–Santa Cruz.

AD: Many of the students who work with me are involved in very interesting projects on social movement history, cultures of resistance, applying new historiographical approaches. One student is attempting to rethink black women's involvement in the labor movement. Another is attempting to develop new ways of theorizing Puerto Rican migration, foregrounding questions of gender and sexuality. My students are doing very interesting work, work that can potentially make a difference.

The Women of Color Research Cluster at UC–Santa Cruz was formed four years ago. It was the brainchild of Margaret Daniels, a History of Consciousness graduate student who is doing her dissertation on women of color film festivals. She examines these film and video festivals as an important site for the construction of women of color as a political subject. Maria Ochoa, also a History of Consciousness student, worked closely with her. Thanks to their leadership, an impressive number of graduate students, faculty, staff, and some undergraduates came together under the auspices of the Cluster, funded by the Center for Cultural Studies. A major project undertaken by the Cluster was the editing of a special issue of *Inscriptions*, the journal of the Center for Cultural Studies.[5] I should point out that the full name of the group is the Research Cluster for the Study of Women of Color in Collaboration and Conflict. Its emergence represented a desire not only to explore the possibilities of cross-racial coalition and alliance, but also to think about the inevitable tensions and conflicts among women of color. We took note of the important role black and Korean women were playing in the effort to negotiate a relationship between these communities that had become especially difficult in the aftermath of the 1992 Los Angeles uprising.

Other projects we have developed include writing groups for students, a lecture series involving cross-racial conversations, colloquia, meetings with the Women of Color Resource Center in Oakland. When I was chosen to hold the UC Presidential Chair, it meant that the Women of Color Cluster would receive more substantial funding. A significant aspect of my proposal – which was the basis for my selection – was a curriculum development project that would be directed by the Cluster. Over the next period we will develop a number of courses to satisfy the Ethnic Studies requirement at UC-Santa Cruz. These courses will be collaboratively taught by graduate students and tenured faculty. The Cluster will not only collaboratively develop these courses, but there will also be focused deliberations on pedagogical questions.

LL: You mention the focus on women of color "in collaboration and conflict." Moving outside of the university in order to think more broadly about the forging of the alliances across groups, what are the difficulties and the opportunities for black, Chicana-Latina, and Native and Asian American women working together? What are the specific issues for each group that need to be addressed in order for coalition to take place? What sorts of things keep coming up?

AD: This work is very difficult. Coalition building has never been easy. But I think it might be more productive to move away from constructions of women of color as a coalition. The assumption behind coalition building is that disparate groups or individuals come together with their own separate – and often racially based – agendas, which have to be negotiated and compromised in order for the group to come together. Coalitions also have an ephemeral and ad hoc character. I am not suggesting that the concept *women of color* is not here to stay, but I do think that it might be a very difficult political project. First of all, not all "women of color" choose to embrace this identity. In fact, an Asian-American woman who might prefer to call herself Chinese American might be equally reluctant to identify as a woman of color. But that's all right. There is no hard and fast requirement in the sense that a woman of African descent has little choice but to identify as black. However, those who do involve themselves in women of color projects need to make strong commitments – to borrow Jacqui Alexander's formulation – "to become fluent in each other's stories."

This is not to say that significant women of color work has not taken place within coalitional formations. There is, for example, the Women of Color Coalition on Reproductive Health that has brought together representatives from four different health organizations: the Asian Women's Health Organization, the Latina Women's Health Project, the National

Black Women's Health Project, and the Native American Women's Health Organization. This coalition played an important role at the UN Conference on Reproductive Rights which took place in Cairo the year before the women's conference and NGO forum in Beijing. However, it has been beset with serious problems that afflict many coalitional forms, which emanate from the difficulties of compromise and agenda negotiation. Women of color work also takes place within caucus and task-force formations that often develop within predominantly white organizations such as the National Women's Studies Association and the National Coalition Against Domestic Violence. It is interesting that women of color formations emerged within both of these organizations in 1981 – a pivotal year for women of color. Early on, women of color groups also organized within a number of lesbian groups.

The groups I find most interesting, however, are those that consider "women of color" a point of departure rather than a level of organizing which rises out of and breaks down into a series of racially specific agendas: in other words, those organizations that challenge the census-category approach to "women of color." Which means that women of color work can foreground race at a time when dominant discourse attempts to erase it, yet at the same time avoid the pitfalls of essentialism. I referred earlier to the Women of Color Resource Center. This organization develops projects which bring grassroots organizers and scholars together. It also sponsors projects like AIWA – Asian Immigrant Women's Advocates – which in turn appeals to all women of color (and white women as well) to support campaigns like the Jessica McClintock boycott. I have also referred to the Women of Color Research Cluster, which does not establish its agenda by considering so-called priority issues.

A woman of color formation might decide to work around immigration issues. This political commitment is not based on the specific histories of racialized communities or its constituent members, but rather constructs an agenda agreed upon by all who are a part of it. In my opinion, the most exciting potential of women of color formations resides in the possibility of politicizing this identity – basing the identity on politics rather than the politics on identity.

LL: You have written about visiting Egypt, and the complications of being both a black woman activist and yet also a "representative" from the United States, a dominant first world power.[6] Taking up these complications, I wonder if you could comment about the importance, the possibilities, and the difficulties of work between radical US women and women in the third world.

AD: Women's organizations have been engaged in international solidarity work at least since the previous century, since the beginning of this century. I think it's important to acknowledge this internationalism. Some of this work was supported by the former socialist countries: the former Soviet Union, the German Democratic Republic, where the NGO Women's International Democratic Federation was located. Women for Racial and Economic Equality, a US-based organization, has ties with women's organizations all over the third world. I am suggesting that there are precedents for the kind of organizing across borders that women are presently attempting to do. However, during the earlier period, women's organizations tended to be rather confined to specific agendas: peace, for example, which was certainly important. But now the possibilities are vaster, considering the globalization of capital and the circuits that have been opened up by migrating corporations. In other words, it is even more important today to do transnational organizing – around labor issues, sexual trafficking, and violence against women. While there is not enough time to make specific reference to all the current international struggles US women are and need to be connected with, I would like to mention the need to strengthen women of color work in opposition to the economic embargo of Cuba. Cuban women are hurt most by the blockade and are on the front lines of opposition. Alice Walker and I are presently helping to organize a campaign to "Boycott the Blockade." In general, considering the impact of NAFTA, the need for networking and international organizing among women trade unionists in Canada, the United States, and Mexico is especially great. Considering the global assembly line – and the extent to which immigrant women working within the United States may work for the same corporations that are exploiting women in Asia, in Canada, in Mexico – organizing possibilities are vast.

LL: Yes. Can I ask you about immigration, since we touched on that? How do you think the influx of Asians and Latin Americans into the United States, particularly since 1965, has changed communities of color and race relations in the United States? Is the current policing of immigration and immigrant communities an index of similar, yet different, contradictions than those that operated in the 1960s?

AD: Well, it's no longer possible to talk about issues of race in exclusively black and white terms. While large communities of color that are not black – Native American, Asian, Latina/o – have parallel histories of racism, oppression, and militant resistance, civil rights discourse established terms that were largely based on a certain construction of black history that excluded women, gays and lesbians, and other marginalized groups. Especially since questions of immigration are moving to the fore, it is no longer possible to confine race discourse and antiracist activism to a simple black–white binary. New issues, new problems, new contradictions have emerged and old ones have been uncovered. Many veteran activists bemoan the fact that there are so many tensions and contradictions within and among communities of color and that it can no longer be assumed that a person who is not white will necessarily assume progressive positions on racial issues – on affirmative action, for example. They bemoan the fact that you cannot expect a person of color by virtue of her/his racial location to speak out against racism, regardless of the group targeted. This has become especially apparent in the failure of significant numbers of black organizations to actively mobilize against Proposition 187 in California and similar measures in other states. I am afraid that the impact of anti-immigrant rhetoric on black communities is inhibiting the development of a political awareness of the radical potential of Latin American and Asian immigrant workers. It used to be the case that within the more progressive sectors of the trade union movement, black workers were acknowledged as a radical and militant force. Today, if there is any hope for the labor movement, it will come, in my opinion, from the new forms of organizing that immigrant workers are developing.

LL: Asian women and Latinas in the garment industry.

AD: Yes. Absolutely. What is really exciting are the new forms of organizing that aren't contained within single trade unions, nor are they focused on narrow trade union issues. It's been virtually impossible within the labor movement over the decades to address issues that aren't traditional union issues. Like wages, benefits, workplace – these are extremely important. But there are also issues that go beyond the workplace that affect workers as well.

LL: Childcare, language.

AD: Yes. Environmental issues, as well. I'm thinking about the work that's being done in Los Angeles immigrant communities, a project that is a multi-union effort with a community base. Considering these new forms of resistance, there are ways to think about these changes in an optimistic way.

LL: Yes. I really agree. We could say that even though there's been an intensification of the exploitation of women of color and third world women, it has also generated new methods and strategies for addressing that exploitation.

Regarding different organizing strategies for the new kinds of populations of workers and the specificities of labor exploitation under new capitalist modes like "mixed production" and "flexible accumulation," perhaps we can get back to the initial discussion of the shifts over the past thirty years. We know that conditions have worsened particularly for the women in communities of color. What kinds of activist projects are possible now? In these times, how do we measure what significant change means?

The Southwest Network for Environmental and Economic Justice is really interesting to me, the group under which AIWA along with La Fuerza

Unida organized the Levi Strauss boycott. It seems that the issues of the environment, health, and toxic waste dumping are places where labor concerns and racialized community concerns come together.

AD: Exactly. The environmental justice movement is a relatively new and very promising organizing strategy in communities of color. New strategies are also suggested by the workers' centers in Chinatown that link work against exploitative sweatshop conditions with campaigns against domestic violence and simultaneously make appeals for multiracial solidarity. We will have come a long way if we succeed in convincing a significant number of black women's organizations, for example, to support Asian immigrant women's labor and community struggles. This would be yet another form of women of color consciousness that is politically rather than racially grounded and at the same time anchored in a more complex antiracist consciousness.

LL: There's a project in San Diego called Beyond Borders that has a support committee for *maquiladora* workers in Baja California, Mexico, and Central America. They document working conditions and occupational health and safety violations in the *maquilas*, publicize the attacks on workers' rights to organize, and promote cross-border worker organizing by connecting US trade unionists with their counterparts in Mexico. Interestingly enough, a number of the women who work in this group are Asian American.

AD: This kind of cross-racial, cross-border organizing needs to be encouraged in many different contexts.

LL: You've done considerable work with women in prisons, political prisoners, and prisoners' rights. Could you say a bit about your different projects with prisoners?

AD: My work with prisoners – both research and organizing work – has been one of the most consistent themes of my political life. It seems that the struggle to free political prisoners is unending. The campaign to free Mumia Abu-Jamal is a case in point. With respect to women prisoners, I am presently working on a project with Kum-Kum Bhavnani, who teaches sociology at UC-Santa Barbara and has a similar political history. We have interviewed women prisoners in an attempt to add new voices to the debate around prisons and to suggest that abolitionist strategies need to be taken seriously. In general, we need more activist projects against the proliferation of prisons, against what Mike Davis calls the "prison-industrial complex."[7] Our earlier discussion of labor is relevant here, too. There is a dangerous privatization trend within the correctional industry, which involves not only the privatization of entire state correctional systems and some sectors of the federal system, but the increasing reliance on prison labor by private corporations as well. The state of California can boast of the largest prison systems in the country – and one of the largest in the world. The Department of Corrections in California has established a joint venture system, which invites corporations to establish their shops on prison grounds. The advertising scheme represents prisoners as a cheap labor force that does not require employers to respect minimum wage provisions or provide health benefits. One advertisement points out that prison workers never ask for paid vacations or have transportation or babysitting problems. This means that prisoners are considered cheap labor in the same sense that immigrants within the United States and third world workers abroad are treated as the most profitable labor pools. Rather than crossing national borders, corporations simply go behind prison walls.

LL: Perhaps that's the "Made in the USA" label.

AD: Yes, that's the "Made in the USA" label at 50 cents an hour with no benefits. Prisoners have been unsuccessfully trying to organize labor unions for decades. Perhaps we need to think about organizing that will bring together prisoners, prisoners' rights groups, immigrant worker organizations, and some of the traditional labor unions. In other words, there *is* a place for coalitions. While I find identity-based coalitions problematic, I do concur with Bernice Reagon when she says that coalition work must be central in late twentieth-century political organizing. However, I think that we should focus on the creation of unpredictable or unlikely coalitions grounded in political projects. Not only prisoners, immigrant workers, and labor unions, but also prisoners and students, for example. This might be the most effective way to contest the shifting of the funding base for education into prison construction and maintenance. One of the other coalitions that should be encouraged is between welfare rights and gay and lesbian organizations. Both welfare mothers and gays and lesbians are directly targeted by conservative emphasis on "family values."

LL: Such a coalition could include legal and undocumented immigrants, too, if it were organized around the proposed Personal Responsibility Act, which bars not only undocumented immigrants but legal permanent residents from receiving federal benefits.

AD: That's right. We might also think about coalition work that would bring together legal and undocumented immigrant youth, on the one hand, and young African-American and Latino-American youth, on the other, who are all targeted by a devious criminalization process that replaces a legitimate need for jobs, education, and health care with a very effective demonization of these groups. And it is certainly time to revive the demand for a reconsideration of the eight-hour workday. A shorter workday could help provide jobs for undocumented immigrants as well as the vast unemployed sectors among youth in communities of color. If the new cultural arenas that have developed over the past decade are utilized, young activists might be able to create powerful campaigns.

NOTES

1 Michael Omi and Howard Winant, *Racial Formation in the United States, from the 1960s to the 1990s* (New York: Routledge, 1994).
2 Angela Y. Davis, *Women, Race, and Class* (New York: Random House, 1981), chapters 11 and 12. "Facing Our Common Foe: Women and the Struggle against Racism" and "We Do Not Consent: Violence against Women in a Racist Society," in Angela Y. Davis, *Women, Culture, and Politics* (New York: Random House, 1988).
3 Cherrie Moraga and Gloria Anzaldua (eds), *This Bridge Called My Back: Writings by Radical Women of Color* (New York: Kitchen Table Press, 1981).
4 Angela Y. Davis, *Angela Davis: An Autobiography* (New York: Random House, 1974).
5 Maria Ochoa and Teresia Teaiwa (eds), "Enunciating Our Terms: Women of Color in Collaboration and Conflict," *Inscriptions*, 7 (1994).
6 Angela Y. Davis, "Women in Egypt: A Personal View," in *Women, Culture, and Politics*.
7 Mike Davis, "A Prison-Industrial Complex: Hell-Factories in the Field," *The Nation*, 260, no. 7 (1995), 229–34.

PART V

Appendix

Opening Defense Statement Presented by Angela Y. Davis in Santa Clara County Superior Court, March 29, 1972

Members of the Jury:

You have heard a rather lengthy outline of what the prosecutor expects to prove in this case. I do not expect that our opening statement will be as long. I am sure you will not find this unusual, for throughout the voir dire you have heard that insofar as the trial is concerned, it is the prosecutor's case to prove beyond a reasonable doubt – not ours to disprove.

The prosecutor has the burden of proof upon him. I, the defendant, need not say anything, if I so desire.

As you have already been informed, none of what the prosecutor has said may be considered as evidence in this case. All the evidence must be presented to you in the form of sworn testimony and other matters which the judge will permit you to consider. At this stage in the proceedings, the prosecutor has done no more than explain to you what *he* contends his evidence will prove. You are the ones who, in the final instance, must judge whether his contentions have any validity or whether his case is unsupported by his own evidence.

Similarly, what I am about to say to you must not be considered as evidence. At this moment I am speaking to you in the stance of my own counsel. And of course you will distinguish between what I am about to say and the evidence you will hear.

The prosecutor has introduced you to the long and complicated path down which he hopes his evidence will lead you during the course of this

This statement was originally published in *Frame Up*, a pamphlet issued in 1972 by the National United Committee to Free Angela Davis. Copyright © 1972 by NUCFAD.

trial. He says that this path will point squarely in the direction of my guilt. He says that his evidence is so conclusive that it will leave you with no choice but to convict me of these very serious crimes of murder, kidnapping, and conspiracy. He says that his evidence will wipe away every single reasonable doubt you might entertain with respect to my guilt.

We say to you that the prosecutor's evidence itself will demonstrate to you that his case is no case at all. The evidence will show that I am totally innocent of the charges of murder, kidnapping, and conspiracy. It will reveal that the prosecutor's contentions are entirely without substance. They are based on guesswork, speculation, and conjecture – to use the words Mr Moore used during the voir dire.

By now you have heard a great deal about the events of August 7, 1970. The evidence will confirm the fact that four human beings lost their lives in the vicinity of the Marin County Courthouse on that day. Judge Harold Haley was killed, as were Jonathan Jackson and two prisoners from San Quentin, James McClain and William Christmas. Human beings were wounded. An assistant district attorney from Marin County – Gary Thomas – and a juror – Mrs Maria Graham – were wounded, as was Ruchell Magee, a prisoner at San Quentin.

We do not dispute the truth of these facts – that lives were lost and persons were wounded on that day, facts which, as the evidence will show, have now become a matter of public knowledge. But, we remind you of something which was said during the voir dire, namely, that there are two separate issues involved here. There is the issue of whether deaths occurred on August 7. There is the issue of whether I had anything to do with the occurrence of those deaths.

As you listen to the testimony in this case – and I am confident that you will all listen with the greatest degree of attentiveness – you will undoubtedly reach the conclusion in your own minds that the prosecution is creating its case out of a labyrinthine network of false assumptions.

Now, members of the jury, what must the prosecutor show you about me in order to prove his case. If Mr Harris desires to prove that I am guilty of the crimes as charged – murder, kidnapping, and conspiracy – here are basically three things he must prove beyond a reasonable doubt. First of all, he must prove beyond a reasonable doubt that there was a plan which pre-dated the events of August 7, 1970. Secondly, he must prove beyond a reasonable doubt that I had foreknowledge of a plan which was to be executed on that day. Thirdly, he must prove beyond a reasonable doubt that I took certain steps with the deliberate intent to further that plan. But he will not prove these things. He will be unable to prove them, members of the jury, because they simply are not true.

A brief review of the case will show you conclusively why the prosecutor cannot prove these three essential facts. Before I go into this, however, you should be aware that we will not now present to you the totality of our defense. In this opening statement, members of the jury, you will be given a skeletal outline of the evidence with which we intend to contest the prosecution's contentions. This will be the skeleton, so to speak – flesh will be added to the bones as the trial progresses. Basically, the purpose of this opening statement is to give you some material and some categories in the form of evidence with which you can place the prosecutor's evidence in its proper perspective. In this way, you will have a more comprehensive view of the case as it unfolds before you.

It is important to understand the nature of this case. The evidence will reveal that I was not present at the Marin County Civic Center when the events themselves transpired. The prosecutor of course, has at no time indicated that he will attempt to place me there. He has indicated, however, that I participated in a preconceived plan, a conspiracy, to commit the crimes of murder, kidnapping, escape and rescue.

But I did nothing of the sort and he will not be able to prove this. He will certainly not be able to prove his claims beyond a reasonable doubt as he must in order to demand a conviction. As the various phases of this trial unfold before you, as the evidence accumulates, you will see that we are right and the prosecutor is wrong.

It is your duty as jurors to objectively judge all the evidence which the judge permits to become part of this case. We ask you to keep your eyes focused on the evidence which goes to the two essential issues in this case. If indeed there was a plan there are only two issues which can have some bearing on my guilt or innocence. They are knowledge and intent – whether I had knowledge of what was to transpire on August 7, 1970, and whether I did anything with the deliberate intent to further those events.

I repeat, the only two elements of this case which have a direct bearing on me are knowledge and intent. You must continually seek out, through the huge maze of evidence which will confront you, that testimony which relates directly to whether I had foreknowledge of what occurred on August 7 and whether I did anything to intentionally further the commission of the crimes of murder, kidnapping, and conspiracy. As you sift through the evidence, this is what you must look for. And you may be sure that no testimony which comes to you from this witness stand will prove the prosecutor's claims that I had foreknowledge of the events and that I had an intent to participate in them.

The prosecutor has already indicated that a great deal of time will be consumed in re-creating in the courtroom here the events of August 7. He has told you that you will hear much testimony from people who were present that day, people who allegedly witnessed the events which transpired that day. But, as you know, the evidence will show that I was not there. Therefore, what bearing do the events have on the critical issues of the case against me? What bearing can these events have on the question of my foreknowledge and my intent with respect to them?

When all the testimony surrounding the events of August 7 is complete, the prosecutor will certainly have demonstrated that in some way lives were lost and individuals were wounded on August 7, 1970. But, members of the jury, this is all he will have proven. He will not have proven that I participated in the formulation of the plans which led to these events – if indeed there were any plans at all. He will have proven nothing – absolutely nothing – with respect to my guilt.

We dispute the accuracy of the prosecutor's version of what actually happened in the Marin County Civic Center on August 7. But many of these differences are of no real moment in the case at hand. They are not so important because basically, if the prosecutor is to prove anything at all, he must prove that I had knowledge of the events beforehand and that I deliberately promoted them. Basically, we say again, this case boils down to the questions of knowledge and intent. For this reason, we may often refrain from engaging the prosecutor in controversy where our differences do not relate to these two questions – to the only real issues in the case, to knowledge and intent. The prosecutor claims that he is in possession of certain evidence – evidence through which he attempts to draw me into a plan to commit the crimes of murder, kidnapping, and conspiracy. What, then, are those elements of the prosecutor's case whereby he attempts to explicitly link me to the occurrence of the events of August 7?

First of all, he contends that the overriding or primary purpose of what happened on August 7 was to achieve the freedom of George Jackson. He claims that I was in love with George Jackson and that my feelings would have forced me to employ any means to free him from prison. In this way the prosecutor would have you believe, members of the jury, that I had a motive to participate in a plan relating to the events of August 7.

He then points to my association and friendship with Jonathan Jackson, George's brother, as evidence that I participated with Jonathan in the events at the Marin County Civic Center.

Let us deal with the evidence the prosecutor intends to present to you in support of his contention that I had a motive to participate in the events of August 7. He began by telling you Monday that he is building his case against me as a crime of passion. He said that my passion for George Jackson was so great that it knew no bounds – that it had no respect for human life. He went on to say later in his statement that I was not concerned with the struggle to free all political prisoners – that I was not concerned with the movement to improve the character of prisons in the United States. The prosecutor told you that he intends to prove that I was exclusively interested in the freedom of one man – George Jackson – and that this interest was motivated by pure passion.

Members of the jury, the prosecutor is aware, himself, that his case is the product of guesswork, speculation, and conjecture. The evidence will show that when I was indicted, the Grand Jury of Marin County considered evidence of my participation in the movement to free the Soledad Brothers – not only George Jackson, but also Fleeta Drumgo and John Clutchette. The evidence will show that the "First Overt Act" of the conspiracy count consists of a description of a rally around the Soledad Brothers, other political prisoners, and prison conditions in general. On June 19, 1970, I was exercising constitutional rights guaranteed me by the First Amendment when I participated in this rally. Yet, this was the first overt act of the conspiracy count – evidence that I had participated in a conspiracy to free the Soledad Brothers through the events of August 7.

Recently, the prosecutor moved the court to strike the first overt act from the indictment. Monday, he told you that he will present no evidence with respect to speeches I made around the Soledad Brothers' case. He says that he will present no evidence which entails constitutionally protected activities.

The evidence will show, members of the jury, that this indictment provoked widespread concern – throughout the world – that I was a victim of political repression. Is it not reasonable to infer that the prosecutor is aware that no fair-minded juror would convict me on the basis of such evidence?

Therefore, the prosecutor has attempted to change the character of his case. Now, he would have you believe that I am a person who would have committed the crimes of murder, kidnapping, and conspiracy, having been motivated by pure passion. He would have you believe that lurking behind my external appearance are sinister and selfish emotions and passions, which, in his words, know no bounds.

Members of the jury, this is utterly fantastic, this is utterly absurd. Yet it is understandable that Mr Harris would like to take advantage of the fact that I am a woman – and women in this society are supposed to act only in accordance with the dictates of their emotions and passions. This is a symptom of the male chauvinism which prevails in this society.

The evidence will show that my involvement in the movement to free the Soledad Brothers began long before I had any contact with George Jackson as a person. You will learn that shortly after Fleeta Drumgo, John Clutchette, and George Jackson were indicted before a Monterey County Grand Jury, I began to attend meetings which were called to establish the basis for a movement to publicly defend them from the unfounded charges that they had killed a guard behind the walls of Soledad Prison.

But before we introduce you to the evidence you will hear regarding my activities in the struggle to free the Soledad Brothers and other political prisoners, let us retrace our steps for a moment. Let us consider a fundamental aspect of the prosecutor's case, namely the existence or non-existence of a pre-formulated plan which was to be executed on August 7, 1970.

Was there really a plan? There is absolutely no consistent, credible proof of what the precise purpose of August 7 was.

The prosecutor will try to establish that the freedom of George Jackson and along with him, the freedom of John Clutchette and Fleeta Drumgo was the primary purpose of the events which unfolded that day. He will try to prove that a mere statement was made by someone during the course of the events demanding the freedom of the Soledad Brothers. But there will also be contradictory evidence as to the accuracy of that statement.

And even if he can establish to your satisfaction that such a statement was made – a simple statement – will there be anything else to support the position that the freedom of the Soledad Brothers was, in fact, the purpose of the events? We say that the evidence will not support the prosecutor's contentions.

There will be absolutely no evidence to indicate that those who participated in the events of August 7 made concrete arrangements for the release of the Soledad Brothers. There will be no evidence that they specified a procedure to make an exchange; nor will there be evidence that they specified a place for the exchange to occur.

Would a mere statement, uttered in passing, be sufficient to convince you, members of the jury, that the release of the Soledad Brothers was a purpose of August 7?

There will be no evidence to prove that the release of the Soledad Brothers was what motivated those who acted on August 7.

The evidence will show that my own efforts to free George Jackson always expressed themselves within the context of the movement to free all the Soledad Brothers and all men and women who are unjustly imprisoned.

Precisely what will the evidence show about my association with the struggle to free the Soledad Brothers? You will see that because of my own commitment to the struggle to achieve freedom for all oppressed people, upon learning of the plight of these three men, I along with others took steps to build whatever support we could for the movement around them, around other political prisoners and prison conditions in general.

What about the activities of this movement? It will be confirmed on the witness stand that all the activities of the Soledad Brothers Defense Committee, of which I was the Los Angeles co-chairwoman, were open and legal. The evidence will show that our meetings were open to anyone who wanted to participate. You will learn that we organized demonstrations, rallies, leafleting campaigns, and various other informational and educational activities.

You will learn that before any of us had any personal contact with any of the Soledad Brothers, we on the defense committee felt that these three black men, charged with killing a white prison guard, were being persecuted, not because they had committed this crime behind the walls of Soledad Prison, but rather because of their militant political stance and because of their efforts to improve the character of prison life from within.

Because this is the way we viewed the Soledad Brothers' case, our most effective approach had to be that of informing and educating the public about their case, other cases, and about prison conditions in general. We attempted to show people everywhere that they were victims of political repression. We attempted to show why they had been singled out as defendants in that very serious case.

Members of the jury, you will see – when testimony is adduced to this effect – that we sought out those kinds of activities which permitted us to involve ever greater numbers of people in the public defense of the Soledad Brothers. Testimony will make it clear that we felt that the influence of large numbers of people would help win them an acquittal – and that they would be freed, in this way, from an unjust prosecution.

Members of the jury, we were correct in our understanding of the case of the Soledad Brothers. Monday morning as you sat here listening to the prosecution's opening statement, and as you heard that I was not interested in furthering the movement to free all the Soledad Brothers, the ultimate fruits of our labors were attained. The twelve men and women who for a period of many months had listened to all the evidence which the prosecution could muster against the Brothers, entered a courtroom in San Francisco and pronounced the Soledad Brothers NOT GUILTY. If George Jackson had not been struck down by San Quentin guards in August of last year he too would have been freed from that unjust prosecution.

The evidence will show that as I worked with the Committee, I and others spoke to college students, high school students, and various community organizations about the things people could do to promote a defense of the Soledad Brothers. The evidence will show that each time we spoke we made concrete proposals to them regarding ways in which they could participate in the movement to free the Soledad Brothers.

The evidence will establish that we spoke at churches about the things that church members could do to further the cause of justice and freedom in the Soledad Brothers' case.

We always suggested, the evidence will show, that people make contributions – financial contributions – to the legal defense fund set up to cover the lawyers' expenses and other expenses related to the litigation in court. We organized benefits – film showings, art auctions, cocktail parties, etc. – in order to raise money for these legal costs.

The evidence will show that we attempted to influence public opinion about the need to transfer the site of the trial from Monterey County to a county where the Brothers might have a better chance of receiving a fair trial.

The evidence will show that every single activity organized by the Soledad Brothers Defense Committee was totally within the realm of legality. What relevance do the crimes of murder, kidnapping, and conspiracy have to these, my efforts to free the Soledad Brothers?

The evidence will clearly establish my participation in exclusively lawful, open, political activity in defense of the Soledad Brothers and other political prisoners. The evidence will clearly establish the principled opposition of the Soledad Brothers Defense Committee, of which I was co-chairwoman in Los Angeles, to any illegal form of activity. You will therefore see that my activities towards the freedom of the Soledad Brothers and the freedom of George Jackson, in particular, far from being evidence of my guilt, are on the contrary evidence of my innocence.

The evidence will show that when I became involved in the Soledad Brothers Defense Committee, this was by no means my first experience in the struggle for black and brown liberation – and the struggle of oppressed people everywhere. All my political activity, covering a span of many years, had been similar in thrust and content to what I have described as the activities of the Soledad Brothers Defense Committee. The evidence will show that I had been associated with the Black Student Council at the University of California in San Diego, the Southern California Black Student Alliance, the Black Congress in Los Angeles, the Student Nonviolent Coordinating Committee, the California Federation of Teachers, the Black Panther Party, and, of course, the Che-Lumumba Club of the Communist Party – of which, the evidence will show, I am now a member.

I have been associated with the struggle to protect and extend the rights of working people whether they be black, Chicano, Latino, Native American, Asian or white. I have done much work in the movement to end the war in Indochina. I have been involved in the fight to achieve equality for women who are oppressed in this society. I have also fought to preserve the basic principles of academic freedom from unconstitutional political assaults. In all of my activities my goal has been to aid in the creation of a movement encompassing millions of people, indeed the majority of the people in the United States today, a movement which will ultimately usher in a more humane, socialist society.

When I became involved in the struggle to free George Jackson, John Clutchette, and Fleeta Drumgo this was not the first time I had assisted in the building of movements around political prisoners. Over a period of a few years the Black Panther Party found many of its members incarcerated on criminal charges. I contributed to the movement to free the 18 members of the Black Panther Party who were arrested in January 1970 in Los Angeles.

I participated in the struggle to free other Soledad Brothers – the Soledad 7, seven black prisoners charged with a crime similar to the one involving the Soledad 3. The evidence will show that I corresponded with them concerning my deep love and compassion for them. (Parenthetically, all the cases I have just named have resulted either in acquittals or in dismissal of charges.)

Indeed you will hear much evidence about my participation in other defense movements. The evidence will show that my political experiences include many different illustrations of my concern, compassion, and solidarity with the plight of men and women in prison. The nature of my efforts to free George Jackson, that is to say my activities in the Soledad Brothers Defense Committee, is bound up with and is an extension of all my other political experiences. When you have heard all this evidence, when you are able to see in detail that my commitment to free George Jackson was fully and exhaustively expressed in this defense movement I have described, it will become abundantly clear to you that the prosecution's contention that I participated in the commission of crimes on August 7th is utterly lacking in foundation.

The prosecutor has said that this trial has nothing to do with a political frame up. But, members of the jury, during the period of my active involvement with the Soledad Brothers, I was the object of an extensive spy campaign. The prosecutor is in possession of numerous reports to various police agencies about my activities in the movement to free the Soledad Brothers. He has police reports on rallies where I spoke, police tapes of speeches I made throughout the state of California, films of demonstrations and rallies where I and others proclaimed our support of the Soledad Brothers.

Members of the jury, the prosecutor contends that I was not interested in bringing about prison reform. But he has in his possession police reports made for the administration of Soledad Prison concerning my activities in this field.

The prosecutor contends that during the period prior to August 7, I was a mere creature of passion, and not one who was genuinely striving towards the elimination of political repression in the prisons.

Members of the jury, the prosecutor has evidence that will refute his own contentions – evidence gathered by a whole network of police spies and spies from the Department of Corrections on the content of my efforts to free George Jackson, Fleeta Drumgo, and John Clutchette. But this is the evidence he will not present to you. He will not present this evidence to you, members of the jury, because it will show you the process whereby an innocent person can be set up and accused of outrageous crimes.

No, he will not bring this evidence before you; he will continue to tell you that I am not the person you see standing before you, but rather an evil, sinister creature pushed to the brink of disaster by ungovernable emotions and passions.

But let us now move on to another area.

What may you expect to hear with respect to my friendship and association with Jonathan Jackson? As the evidence is presented, you will learn about the source and context of my friendship with Jonathan. You will learn that as the Soledad Brothers Defense Committee was consolidated, the families of all the brothers participated in the discussions and projects.

The evidence will show that I became friends with members of Fleeta Drumgo's family, John Clutchette's family, and George Jackson's family. As time progressed, I came to know Inez Williams, the mother of Fleeta Drumgo, Mrs Doris Maxwell, the mother of John Clutchette, and Mrs Georgia Jackson, the mother of George Jackson. At this moment, however, I will confine my remarks to the relationships which developed between me and the Jackson family.

The evidence will show that I became close friends with Mr and Mrs Jackson, their daughters, Penny and Frances, and their son Jonathan. You will learn that on many occasions, we attended rallies and demonstrations together. While sometimes we would appear all together, at other times I traveled with Mr or Mrs Jackson alone – or with Penny, Frances, or Jonathan alone. The evidence will show that I spent much time visiting in the home of the Jackson family – and that members of the Jackson family visited in my home. You will see that we traveled together not only within the area surrounding Los Angeles, but on some occasions, we traveled by car to the Bay Area in order to share our experiences with members of the Soledad Brothers Defense Committee which had been organized in this part of the state.

The evidence will show that because of the controversy surrounding my teaching post at UCLA – because there were constant threats on my life issuing from extremist elements in the community – it was not safe for me to travel any distance in Los Angeles outside the company of others. You will learn that wherever possible, I tried not to move from place to place alone. You will see that for this reason – and also because we became close friends – Jonathan Jackson and I were often together.

As time progressed, I became closer, not only to Jonathan, but to the entire Jackson family. My love and affection for George grew. However, it was not until I had been arrested and had become like him a political prisoner that my relationship with him grew stronger and my affection deeper.

Jonathan, as well as other members of George Jackson's family, played a vital role in the activities of the Soledad Brothers Defense Committees. Jonathan was a unique part of our group, for he brought with him the angry frustrations and concerns of a young man who had no memories of his older brother except those which were obscured by prison bars. Young Jonathan was a child of seven when his brother was first taken to jail. For ten long years, he had accompanied various members of his family to prisons across the state to visit his brother. These visits must have left an indelible impression on him of what a prisoner's life was like. Even though he was only seventeen years old, Jonathan must have been extremely and intimately sensitive to the plight, the frustrations, the feelings of desperation and futility that men like James McClain, Ruchell Magee, and William Christmas must have felt.

In retrospect, I now understand the very deep frustrations, the very deep desperation that Jonathan must have been experiencing.

My friendship with Jonathan is absolutely no basis whatever for contending that I played some role in the events of August 7, 1970. And members of the jury, we expect that the evidence of my association with Jonathan will make it readily apparent how he might have come to acquire weapons which were registered in my name, books allegedly bearing my name, as well as other personal property of mine.

Aside from the matters of which we have already spoken, there are yet other aspects of the prosecutor's non-case against me – aspects with which he attempts to draw me into the events of August 7. The prosecutor also plans to offer what in legal terminology is called "eye-witness testimony" of a circumstantial nature. He contends that sometime prior to August 7, I was present in the vicinity of certain areas involved in the case. He contends that I was present on three occasions at San Quentin Prison and on one occasion near the Marin County Civic Center.

He also contends that the purchase of weapons by me is some evidence of my guilt and that further evidence of my guilt lies in my departure from the Bay Area and my subsequent unavailability to the authorities. What about this so-called proof of my guilt?

Let us first consider the purchase of the guns. The prosecutor has informed you that he will present evidence to prove that I purchased a number of weapons over a certain period of time. Testimony and exhibits will purport that some of the guns claimed to have been found on the scene at the Marin County Civic Center are the same guns that I purchased. Out of this network of facts, he says, evidence will emerge to support his contention that I am guilty of the crimes as charged.

We say to you that quite to the contrary, the evidence will prove that while I did purchase guns, I did nothing to furnish Jonathan Jackson or anyone with the weapons which were utilized during the action of August 7.

There are very good reasons why I saw fit to purchase guns – reasons wholly unrelated to any criminal activities. You will become aware, as the trial progresses, that my experience with guns dates far back into my childhood. You will learn why the neighborhood in which we lived – where my parents still live – came to be called Dynamite Hill (our house being built on the very top of the hill).

Because of the constant threats and actual incidents of violence, my father had to keep guns in the house. We will tell you in testimony about our fears and apprehensions that we might be the next victims of a racist assault. We will tell you about our close friends, including the four young girls killed in church bombings – who were struck down at the hands of racist bombers. You will understand that for a black person who had grown up in the South – and particularly during that period – guns had to be a normal fact of life.

As you will see, when I left Birmingham, it was impossible to leave behind fears which had accumulated over all the early years of my life. When I came to California, my fears and apprehensions were, in fact, confirmed. As I became involved in radical movements calling for social change, I learned that some of the people who disagreed with the goals we were seeking to achieve might express their disagreements in violent ways. The evidence will show that we who were working towards radical social transformations felt that it would he necessary for us to obtain means to protect ourselves.

The evidence will show that this was true when I worked in the liberation movement in San Diego, California. It was true when I worked with the Student Nonviolent Coordinating Committee in Los Angeles. And it was true as I worked with the Black Panther Party. During all the time I have been a member of the Communist Party – and have worked with the Che-Lumumba Club in Los Angeles – it has been necessary for us to be in possession of means to defend ourselves from potential attacks by extremists in the community.

The evidence will demonstrate that the situation in this regard became particularly tense after my position in the Department of Philosophy at the University of California at Los Angeles was threatened by the Regents of the university system. Their attempts to fire me because of my membership in the Communist Party made me a public figure, subject to myriad forms of harassment – both by those who merely misunderstood the nature of the Communist Party and by those who were consciously determined to attack communism and communists in whatever way they could.

There will be testimony regarding the hundreds and thousands of threats on my life during the period of my contract with UCLA. During some periods, hardly a day would pass when I would not receive a threat of some sort.

When you have heard all this, there will be no doubt in your mind that I was convinced with good reason that I needed some sort of protection if I intended to live out my years. There will be no doubt in your mind that my reason for purchasing those weapons was related to my fears for my own life and for the lives of those around me.

The evidence will demonstrate to you that I purchased weapons not only for my own personal protection – but also for the protection of others with whom I worked and lived. As you can probably surmise, few individuals who have devoted their lives to the struggle against oppression – their entire lives – are financially well-off. During the time I taught at the University of California, I was receiving far more in terms of my salary than most of my friends in the movement. As we all shared whatever we had, it was often I who paid for weapons used by others – as I often paid rent, medical costs, and other necessary expenses for my comrades.

The evidence will show that my purchase of weapons was totally unrelated to any illegal activities. Further, each time I purchased a weapon, I did it in my own name and provided evidence as to my identity – my name, address, and place of my birth. Does this sound like the kind of evidence which could be invoked in order to prove my guilt?

It was no secret that I was the owner of the weapons. And because my feelings about weapons reflect what one of you said during the voir dire, I felt that I should learn how to handle them. Indeed the evidence will show that as soon as I bought my first gun, I immediately proceeded to go target practicing at various ranges in Southern California. You will learn that, aside from using weapons as a potential means of self-protection, I developed an interest in shooting as a sport. Consequently, I spent some of my spare time engaging in target practicing at ranges and in areas of the county where shooting was legally permitted.

Contrary to the speculations and conjectures of the prosecution, my purchase of ammunition is attributable to the fact that I engaged in this target practice. In fact, the evidence will show that for a few years prior to August 7, 1970, I frequently bought large quantities of ammunition – that is, whenever I was target practicing on a frequent basis. The prosecutor made a considerable point of the fact that I purchased a banana clip. As evidence can show, contrary to Mr Harris's contrivances, if you are target practicing it is much more convenient to use a clip which holds thirty rounds than one which holds five. Furthermore, Mr Harris made repeated references to a carbine. Although he insists that he can find no words to describe this gun, it may easily be described as a carbine with a collapsible stock. It is a common type of gun, it is easily accessible in gun shops all over the country, and it is used for a wide variety of sports and hunting activities.

This is not evidence of participation in a crime.

The prosecutor has placed heavy emphasis on the fact that the shotgun registered in my name, allegedly used during the August 7 events, was purchased on the very eve of the incident. During the course of the trial, the purchase of the shotgun by me on August 5 will be fully accounted for by the evidence. You may be sure, however, that there will be no evidence that this gun was bought in connection with any criminal intent or purpose.

Judicial history is replete with instances where innocent people like me have been convicted on the basis of mistaken identifications. This is particularly true when it is a question of white people identifying black people. We ask you to examine this testimony cautiously and critically.

The evidence will further show that the procedures used in connection with these identifications were tainted. The identifications were made through unduly suggestive procedures.

The evidence will show that these identifications stand completely alone and isolated and are uncorroborated by any other evidence.

What about the so-called flight from the Bay Area? The evidence will show conclusively that I did not flee from the Bay Area August 7, 1970. I did make PSA flight 422 from San Francisco to Los Angeles. It will become abundantly clear that I bought a ticket with my own check and conducted myself at that time in the same manner as any other person who would have been catching that flight at that time.

Members of the jury, this evidence reveals the absurdity of the prosecution's entire case. By this evidence, Mr Harris attempts to transmute normal, every-day human conduct – namely, being rushed to catch a plane – into evidence of guilt. I repeat, there will be no evidence that my trip from San Francisco to Los Angeles on August 7, 1970 constituted flight from the Bay Area. Indeed, you will hear no evidence whatever which can establish the fact that at that time I was even aware of the events which had taken place. The prosecutor will attempt to show that I dropped out of sight immediately following the events of August 7. But there is no evidence to this effect.

The evidence will, however, show that I eventually became the target of a state-wide search and investigation in connection with the events at the Marin Civic Center. It was only after my safety was thereby placed in danger that I departed from the state of California.

The evidence will show that there was good reason for me to make myself unavailable at that time. The evidence will show that I had good reason to fear police violence should I voluntarily submit to the authorities at that time. The evidence will show that on many occasions in the past, black and Chicano people – particularly political activists – have been victims of police violence. The evidence will show that I had ample reason to fear unjust treatment by the courts of California, that I had reason to fear the prospect of many months of incarceration without bail, an eventual trial before an all-white jury, therefore a jury not composed of my peers, and many other obstacles to my efforts to protect my innocence.

You will hear testimony that many other people, when faced with similar situations, also reacted in similar ways. The evidence will demonstrate that particularly in the black and Chicano communities, there are great fears that once one is accused of a crime, one may find it extremely difficult to overcome the many obstacles which stand in the way of protecting one's innocence.

Members of the jury, the evidence will conclusively show that my un-availability to the authorities in Marin County cannot be interpreted as a basis for contending that I am guilty. On the contrary, the evidence will show that it was my innocence that motivated me to leave the state of California at that time.

It is a sick kind of game which the prosecutor is playing; he has invented a scheme, a diagram, a conspiracy. Now he must fit his conspirator, his criminal into the picture. He has a crime scheme, a plan; how can he pull me into it so that it still appears plausible? Since I committed no crimes, since all my activity was open and above board, the prosecutor is left with only one alternative; he must shape his circumstantial case by transforming ordinary activity into criminal activity. Guess and speculation will help you find that link; you don't find it in Mr Harris's evidence. And he makes no bones about asking you to draw the inferences.

Take for example the simple fact that I moved from one apartment to another around the beginning of July. Can you fathom what this has to do with any conspiracy? The prosecutor never did tell you on Monday; you are left to wonder, to guess, to speculate. She moved – it must have been in connection with some conspiracy, he asks you to think. He tells you that Jonathan Jackson lived for some three weeks in my apartment. The evidence will demonstrate that he did not live in my apartment. Clearly the prosecutor has said this because he wants you to speculate that we were living together in that apartment in order to participate together in a conspiracy.

And what about the $100 check that he says I cashed on August 4. He tells you about the $100 then in the very next breath, he says: Jonathan Jackson rented a van on August 6 and paid the rental fee with two $20 bills. You are to put these two facts together – facts totally unrelated to each other – and then guess that I had something to do with the rental of a van. I cashed a check in Oakland for $100; two days later someone rented a van in San Francisco for $40; ergo, I rented the van. Is there any way you can hook up these two facts – the cashing of a check by me and the rental of a van by another two days later – and find criminal intent without making a wild guess? There will be no evidence that I gave Jonathan Jackson $40 to rent the van.

And that is not the wildest of the guesses that prosecutor is asking you to make. Again, what about the inference that I supplied weapons to Jonathan Jackson to use on August 7? What is there to help one to arrive at that inference? Is there a single piece of evidence to show that Jonathan Jackson took my guns with my knowledge and consent? Only guess, speculation, and conjecture can lead one to that unnatural inference. Indeed all the evidence points one only to the contrary inference for I did not knowingly supply Jonathan with any guns for use on August 7.

Mr Harris not only asks you to guess in order to get you to the inference that weapons used on August 7 were knowingly supplied to Jonathan Jackson by me, but he carries it even a step further. He asks you to draw, out of thin air, the conclusion that the shotgun purchase of August 5 and the carbine purchase of July 25 were made specifically for use on August 7. Not a shred of evidence supports this inference; you must reach it by the same road you traveled to conclude that I was the supplier of the guns. You must guess, you must speculate, you must surmise, that I had crime and conspiracy in my mind when I bought those guns. You must guess that I bought them intending their use in a conspiracy despite the fact that I identified myself upon making the purchases and am the registered owner of the guns. You are asked to draw the conclusion that I purchased the shotgun for a crime even though Mr Harris's own witness will tell you that I signed my name at the time of the purchase. Only guess, speculation, and conjecture will take you down the path on which the prosecutor seeks to lead you.

What else are you left to guess about? On Monday the prosecutor told you he will prove Jonathan Jackson registered in a hotel in San Francisco on the night of August 6. He said Jonathan Jackson was with another person. If, indeed, he was with a second person, is there any evidence as to who the mystery man or woman was? Was it I? I don't know whether the prosecutor knows who the person was who accompanied Jonathan. I know and he knows that it was not I. He doesn't even suggest that it was I. But he leaves an inference hanging. You are to guess who was with Jonathan Jackson on that evening. You are to guess, based on no evidence, just Mr Harris's statement that another person accompanied Jonathan Jackson.

When we get to August 7, you must make another guess about my purposes. I wasn't at the Marin County Civic Center, the scene of the crime. But I was at the San Francisco Airport at some time during that day. With his prosecutorial legerdemain, Mr Harris widens the scene of the crime to include me where I was that afternoon – trying to catch a plane at the airport. Is there any evidence that my purpose for being at the airport was to participate in a conspiracy? Not a shred. You must guess that I was at the airport not to buy a ticket with my own check and to take a plane to Los Angeles, but to participate in a conspiracy – a conspiracy to do what, to fly where? My presence at the airport for a few moments before I took the plane to Los Angeles had absolutely nothing to do with a conspiracy.

And what of the oblique suggestion that I had some connection with a Volkswagen allegedly borrowed by Jonathan Jackson – which apparently turned up at the San Francisco Airport some two weeks after the August 7 events?

And before I conclude this section, let me mention another guess the prosecutor is asking you to make without saying it straight forward. He says Jonathan Jackson had a slip of paper with the number of a telephone booth at the airport. Then he says dramatically, "You don't call a public telephone booth unless you expect someone to be there!" Well, who is Mr Harris referring to? When was Jonathan to call that booth? Was he to stop the van on Route 101 and place a call to the airport? Was someone supposed to be waiting in the booth to receive the call? Who? Again, members of the jury, you must resort to guess and surmise. Only by highly imaginative speculation can a meaningless phone number become evidence of a criminal conspiracy.

Only your own guesses, members of the jury, can fill the gigantic gaps in the prosecution case.

Members of the jury, the charges against me are the logical extension of the unlawful attacks which began with the actions of the governor of this state and of the Regents of the University of California when they unlawfully dismissed me from my post at UCLA. Like the Regents, the prosecution has contended that I didn't live solely in the world of ideas, but that I was committed to action. Specifically, he referred to me as a "student of violence" and stated that behind my "cool academic veneer" was a woman capable of the crimes of murder, kidnapping, and conspiracy. To give credence to this contention, Mr Harris cites two books allegedly found in the possession of Jonathan Jackson, allegedly bearing my signature, entitled *Violence and Social Change*, and *The Politics of Violence: Revolution in the Modern World*.

The evidence will show that in the summer of 1970, I was engaged in research for my doctoral dissertation. The object of my study is the theory of force in Kant's political philosophy of history and in German idealism in general. Contrary to the conjectures of the prosecution – which seeks to transform an academic endeavor into a commitment to violence – the two books in question, and several others not mentioned, were objective studies of conditions of violence in Vietnam, Latin America, Africa, and in the black and brown and white communities in the US. I read these sociological studies in connection with my work in philosophy. To study the theory of force in philosophy can hardly be construed as evidence that I am a practitioner of violence.

Further, as the evidence will show, my political commitment, my political experience, including in the Communist Party, has manifested itself in terms of what I am capable of doing – writing, teaching, speaking and organizing around the plight of all oppressed people, political prisoners in general, the Soledad Brothers specifically, and thereby helping to organize an effective political movement for progressive social change. The prosecution's own evidence will show that I was not committed to individual acts of escape, but that I was committed to the building of a movement capable of creating a climate of public opinion in which the death penalty could be declared unconstitutional, and in which juries could acquit prisoners of politically-inspired charges – an event we witnessed the day before yesterday with the acquittal of the two surviving Soledad Brothers.

Members of the jury, we reach the conclusion of our opening statement, and we ask you to think towards the conclusion of this trial. When you will have sat patiently, almost to the point of exhaustion and will have heard all sides of the heated contest which will unfold in this courtroom – when you will have sat in calm reflection and deliberation – we know – we have the utmost confidence – that your verdict will be the only verdict that the evidence and justice demand in this case. We are confident that this case will terminate with your pronouncement of two words – **NOT GUILTY!!!**

Selected Bibliography

Books

Davis, Angela Y. *Blues Legacies and Black Feminism: Gertrude "Ma" Rainey, Bessie Smith, and Billie Holiday* (New York: Pantheon, 1998).
—— *Women, Culture, and Politics* (New York: Random House, 1988).
—— *Women, Race, and Class* (New York: Random House, 1981).
——*Angela Davis: An Autobiography* (New York: Random House, 1974).
——*If They Come in the Morning: Voices of Resistance*, ed. (New York: Third Press, 1971).

Articles and Chapters in Books

Davis, Angela Y. "Race and Criminalization: Black Americans and the Punishment Industry," *The House that Race Built*. Wahneema Lubiano, ed. (New York: Pantheon, 1997).
Davis, Angela Y., and Kum-Kum Bhavnani. "'Fighting For Her Future': Human Rights and Women's Prisons in the Netherlands," *Social Identities*, vol. 3, no. 1 (February 1997).
Angela Y. Davis. "Gender, Class and Multiculturalism: Rethinking 'Race' Politics," *Mapping Multiculturalism*. Avery Gordon and Christopher Newfield, eds (Minneapolis: University of Minnesota Press, 1996).
——"Incarcerated Women: Transformative Strategies" (with Kum-Kum Bhavnani), *Psychology and Society: Radical Theory and Practice*. Ian Parker and Russell Spears, eds (London: Pluto Press, 1996).
——"'I Used To Be Your Sweet Mama': Ideology, Sexuality, and Domesticity in the Blues of Gertrude 'Ma' Rainey and Bessie Smith," *Sexy Bodies: The Strange Carnalities of Feminism*. Elizabeth Grosz and Elspeth Probyn, eds (London and New York: Routledge, 1995).
——"Surrogates and Outcast Mothers: Racism and Reproductive Rights," *It Just Ain't Fair: The Ethics of Health Care for African Americans*. Annette Dula and Sara Goering, eds (Westport, CT: Praeger, 1994).
——"Afro Images: Fashion, Politics and Nostalgia," *Picturing Us: African American Identity in Photography*. Deborah Willis, ed. (New York: The New Press, 1994).
——"Billie Holiday's 'Strange Fruit': Music and Social Consciousness," *Speech and Power: The African American Essay and its Cultural Content from Polemics to Pulpit* (vol. 2). Gerald Early, ed. (New Jersey: Ecco Press, 1993).
——"Clarence Thomas as 'Lynching Victim': Reflections on Anita Hill's Role in the Thomas Confirmation Hearings," *African American Women Speak Out on*

Anita Hill–Clarence Thomas. Geneva Smitherman, ed. (Detroit, MI: Wayne State University Press, 1993).

——"Remembering Carole, Cynthia, Addie Mae and Denise," *Essence Magazine,* September 1993.

——"Meditations on the Legacy of Malcolm X," *Malcolm X: In Our Own Image.* Joe Wood, ed. (New York: St. Martin's Press, 1992).

——"Nappy Happy: A Conversation with Ice Cube," *Transition,* no. 58 (1992).

——"Women of Color and the Law," Keynote Address at Third National Conference on Women of Color and the Law, *Stanford Law Review,* 43.6 (July 1991).

——"Sick and Tired of Being Sick and Tired: The Politics of Black Women's Health," *The Black Women's Health Book: Speaking For Ourselves.* Evelyn C. White, ed. (Seattle, WA: Seal Press, 1990).

——"Black Women and Music," *Wild Women in the Whirlwind: Afra-American Culture and the Contemporary Literary Renaissance.* Joanne M. Braxton and Andree McLaughlin, eds (New Brunswick, NJ: Rutgers University Press, 1990).

——"Childcare or Workfare," *New Perspectives Quarterly,* 7.1 (Winter 1990).

——"Lifting as We Climb: Radical Perspectives on the Empowerment of Afro-American Women," *Harvard Educational Review,* Summer 1988.

——"Violence Against Women and the Ongoing Challenge to Racism," pamphlet in the Freedom Organizing Series, published by Kitchen Table: Women of Color Press, 1985.

——"For a People's Culture," *Political Affairs,* March 1985.

——"Photography and Afro-American History," in *A Century of Black Photographers:* 1840–1960. Valencia Hollins Coar, ed. (Providence RI: Museum of Art, Rhode Island School of Design, 1983).

——"Michelle Wallace: A Critical Evaluation," *Freedomways,* 19.3 (1979), 7.

——"Viol et racisme dans le contexte capitaliste" and "La Désuétude prochaine du travail ménager," *La Condition Féminine, Centre d'études et de recherches marxistes* (Paris, Editions Sociales, 1978).

——"Racism and Male Supremacy," *Political Affairs,* vol. 56 (1977).

——"Women and Capitalism: Dialectics of Oppression and Liberation," *Marxism, Revolution, and Peace.* Howard Parsons and John Sommerville, eds (Amsterdam: B. R. Grüner, 1977).

——"Racism and Contemporary Literature on Rape," *Freedomways,* 16.1 (1976).

——"JoAnne Little: The Dialectics of Rape," *Ms. Magazine,* June 1975.

——"Reflections on the Black Woman's Role in the Community of Slaves," *The Black Scholar,* vol. 3, no. 4 (December 1971).

Index